AUTHORS AND AUTHORITIES IN ANCIENT PHILOSOPHY

Ancient Greek and Roman philosophy is often characterised in terms of competitive individuals debating orally with one another in public arenas. But it also developed over its long history a sense in which philosophers might acknowledge some other particular philosopher or group of philosophers as an authority and offer to that authority explicit intellectual allegiance. This is most obvious in the development after the classical period of the philosophical 'schools' with agreed founders and, most importantly, canonical founding texts. They also developed a tradition of commentary, interpretation, and discussion of texts which itself became a mode of philosophical debate. As time went on, the weight of a growing tradition of reading and appealing to a certain corpus of foundational texts began to shape how later antiquity viewed its philosophical past and also how philosophical debate and inquiry was conducted. In this book, leading scholars explore aspects of these important developments.

JENNY BRYAN is Lecturer in Classical Philosophy in the Department of Classics and Ancient History at the University of Manchester. She is the author of *Likeness and Likelihood in the Presocratics and Plato* (Cambridge, 2012).

ROBERT WARDY is Reader in Ancient Philosophy at the University of Cambridge and a Fellow of St Catharine's College. He is the author of *The Chain of Change: A Study of Aristotle's Physics VII* (Cambridge, 1990), *The Birth of Rhetoric: Gorgias, Plato and their Successors* (1996), *Aristotle in China: Language, Categories and Translation* (Cambridge, 2000), and *Doing Greek Philosophy* (2005).

JAMES WARREN is Professor of Ancient Philosophy at the University of Cambridge and a Fellow of Corpus Christi College. He is the author of *Epicurus and Democritean Ethics: An Archaeology of Ataraxia* (Cambridge, 2002), *Facing Death: Epicurus and His Critics* (2004), *Presocratics* (2007), and *The Pleasures of Reason in Plato, Aristotle, and the Hellenistic Hedonists* (Cambridge, 2014) alongside articles on a range of topics in ancient philosophy, including on various topics in Epicureanism and ancient scepticism. He is the editor of *The Cambridge Companion to Epicureanism* (Cambridge, 2009), and, with Frisbee Sheffield, *The Routledge Companion to Ancient Philosophy* (2013).

CAMBRIDGE CLASSICAL STUDIES

General editors
R. G. OSBORNE, W. M. BEARD, G. BETEGH,
J. P. T. CLACKSON, R. L. HUNTER, M. J. MILLETT,
S. P. OAKLEY, T. J. G. WHITMARSH

FRONTISPIECE

Photo: Wei Liu, courtesy of Bev Sedley

AUTHORS AND AUTHORITIES IN ANCIENT PHILOSOPHY

Edited by

JENNY BRYAN
University of Manchester

ROBERT WARDY
University of Cambridge

JAMES WARREN
University of Cambridge

CAMBRIDGE
UNIVERSITY PRESS

University Printing House, Cambridge CB2 8BS, United Kingdom

One Liberty Plaza, 20th Floor, New York, NY 10006, USA

477 Williamstown Road, Port Melbourne, VIC 3207, Australia

314–321, 3rd Floor, Plot 3, Splendor Forum, Jasola District Centre,
New Delhi – 110025, India

79 Anson Road, #06-04/06, Singapore 079906

Cambridge University Press is part of the University of Cambridge.

It furthers the University's mission by disseminating knowledge in the pursuit of
education, learning, and research at the highest international levels of excellence.

www.cambridge.org
Information on this title: www.cambridge.org/9781316510049
DOI: 10.1017/9781108186650

© Faculty of Classics, University of Cambridge 2018

This publication is in copyright. Subject to statutory exception
and to the provisions of relevant collective licensing agreements,
no reproduction of any part may take place without the written
permission of Cambridge University Press.

First published 2018

Printed and bound in Great Britain by Clays Ltd, Elcograf S.p.A.

A catalogue record for this publication is available from the British Library.

Library of Congress Cataloging-in-Publication Data
Names: Bryan, Jenny, 1979– editor. | Wardy, Robert, editor. |
Warren, James, 1974– editor.
Title: Authors and authorities in ancient philosophy / edited by
Jenny Bryan, Robert Wardy, James Warren.
Other titles: Cambridge classical studies.
Description: Cambridge: Cambridge University Press, 2018. |
Series: Cambridge classical studies |
Includes bibliographical references and index.
Identifiers: LCCN 2018015096 | ISBN 9781316510049 (hardback)
Subjects: LCSH: Authority. | Philosophy, Ancient. | Plato. | Aristotle. | Socrates.
Classification: LCC B171.A98 2018 | DDC 180–dc23
LC record available at https://lccn.loc.gov/2018015096

ISBN 978-1-316-51004-9 Hardback

Cambridge University Press has no responsibility for the persistence or accuracy
of URLs for external or third-party internet websites referred to in this publication
and does not guarantee that any content on such websites is, or will remain,
accurate or appropriate.

For David

CONTENTS

List of Contributors	*page* xi
List of Abbreviations	xiii

Introduction: Authorship and Authority
in Ancient Philosophy   I
JENNY BRYAN, ROBERT WARDY, AND
JAMES WARREN

1. Reconsidering the Authority of Parmenides' *Doxa*   20
JENNY BRYAN

2. Authority and the Dialectic of Socrates   41
NICHOLAS DENYER

3. Socratic Discussions of Death and Immortality
in Plato   58
ALEX LONG

4. A Superannuated Student: Aristotle and
Authority in the Academy   78
DOROTHEA FREDE

5. Words, Deeds, and Lovers of Truth in Aristotle   102
SARAH BROADIE

6. Aristotle's *Categories* 7 Adopts Plato's View
of Relativity   120
MATTHEW DUNCOMBE

7. Theophrastus and the Authority of the *de Sensibus*   139
KELLI RUDOLPH

Contents

8. Pseudo-Archytas and the *Categories*   162
   MYRTO HATZIMICHALI

9. Numenius on Intellect, Soul, and the Authority of Plato   184
   GEORGE BOYS-STONES

10. Demetrius of Laconia on Epicurus *On the Telos* (Us. 68)   202
    JAMES WARREN

11. Lucretius the Madman on the Gods   222
    DAVID BUTTERFIELD

12. In and Out of the Stoa: Diogenes Laertius on Zeno   242
    A. A. LONG

13. The Emergence of Platonic and Aristotelian Authority in the First Century BCE   263
    GEORGIA TSOUNI

14. Cicero on *Auctoritas*   278
    MALCOLM SCHOFIELD

15. Authors and Authorities in Ancient China: Some Comparative Observations   296
    G. E. R. LLOYD

16. Antique Authority?   313
    ROBERT WARDY

References   331
Index Locorum   349
General Index   367

CONTRIBUTORS

GEORGE BOYS-STONES is Professor of Ancient Philosophy at Durham University.

JENNY BRYAN is a Lecturer in Classical Philosophy at the University of Manchester.

SARAH BROADIE is Professor of Philosophy and Wardlaw Professor at the University of St Andrews.

DAVID BUTTERFIELD is a Lecturer in Classics at the University of Cambridge and a Fellow of Queens' College.

NICHOLAS DENYER is a Senior Lecturer in Classics at the University of Cambridge and a Fellow of Trinity College.

MATTHEW DUNCOMBE is an Assistant Professor in Philosophy at the University of Nottingham.

DOROTHEA FREDE is Professor Emerita on the History of Philosophy at the University of Hamburg.

MYRTO HATZIMICHALI is a Lecturer in Classics at the University of Cambridge and a Fellow of Homerton College.

G. E. R. LLOYD is Emeritus Professor of Ancient Philosophy and Science at the University of Cambridge.

A. A. LONG is Professor of the Graduate School and Chancellor's Professor Emeritus of Classics and Irving G. Stone Professor Emeritus of Literature; Affiliated Professor of Philosophy and Rhetoric at the University of California, Berkeley.

ALEX LONG is a Senior Lecturer in Classics at the University of St Andrews.

KELLI RUDOLPH is a Lecturer in Classics and Philosophy at the University of Kent, Canterbury.

Contributors

MALCOLM SCHOFIELD is Emeritus Professor of Ancient Philosophy at the University of Cambridge and a Fellow of St John's College.

GEORGIA TSOUNI is Postdoctoral Assistant to the Chair of History of Philosophy at the University of Bern.

ROBERT WARDY is Reader in Ancient Philosophy at the University of Cambridge and a Fellow of St Catharine's College.

JAMES WARREN is Professor of Ancient Philosophy at the University of Cambridge and a Fellow of Corpus Christi College.

ABBREVIATIONS

For abbreviations for ancient authors and works see the *Index Locorum*

DK	H. Diels and W. Kranz (1952) *Die Fragmente der Vorsokratiker*, 6th edn, Berlin
FHSG	William W. Fortenbaugh, Pamela M. Huby, Robert W. Sharples, and Dimitri Gutas (1993) *Theophrastus of Eresus. Sources for His Life, Writings, Thought and Influence* (2 vols.), Leiden
IG	*Inscriptiones graecae*
IK	*Inschriften griechischer Städte Kleinasiens*
LSJ	H. G. Liddell, R. Scott, and H. S. Jones (1925) *A Greek-English Lexicon*, 9th edn, Oxford
PHerc.	Herculaneum Papyrus
SSR	G. Giannantoni (1990) *Socratis et socraticorum reliquiae*, Naples
SVF	H. von Arnim (1903–5) *Stoicorum ueterum fragmenta*, Stuttgart
Us.	H. Usener (1887) *Epicurea*, Leipzig

INTRODUCTION: AUTHORSHIP AND AUTHORITY IN ANCIENT PHILOSOPHY

JENNY BRYAN, ROBERT WARDY, AND JAMES WARREN

Ancient Greek and Roman philosophy is often characterised in terms of competitive individuals debating orally with one another in public arenas. In this respect it is perhaps surprising to think about any notion of philosophical authority besides what is generated by the force of a simple argument, conclusion or piece of persuasion. But it also developed over its long history a sense in which philosophers might acknowledge some other particular philosopher or group of philosophers as an authority and offer to that authority explicit intellectual allegiance. This is most obvious in the development after the classical period of the philosophical 'schools' with agreed founders and, most importantly, canonical founding texts.[1] And there also developed a tradition of commentary, interpretation, and discussion of texts – written by such 'authorities' – which often became the focus of disagreement between members of the same school or movement and also useful targets for critics interested in attacking a whole tradition. Discussions of the meaning, force, precise wording, and even the very authorship of these texts – for example: attempts to undermine the authority of a work by arguing that it is spurious or excluding it from an agreed corpus – became modes of philosophical debate. As time went on, the weight of a growing tradition of reading and appealing to a certain corpus of foundational texts began to shape how later antiquity viewed its philosophical past and also how philosophical debate and inquiry was conducted.

---

[1] For an account of the varieties of allegiance in the Hellenistic period, see Sedley (1989).

I

Jenny Bryan, Robert Wardy, and James Warren

The essays in this collection consider aspects of the relationship between authorship and authority across a wide chronological and doctrinal range of ancient philosophical texts and schools. They also consider a wide range of relationships between ancient readers or pupils and the various philosophical authorities concerned. Certainly by the first century BC, there came to be explicit appeals in discussions of ancient philosophical works to *auctoritas* – a Latin term with a broad meaning connoting an individual's prestige, political weight, and power, and even the warrant for a particular action or decision – in philosophical writings. That same term also connoted the sense of originating an action or decision – being its *auctor* – and therefore combined the notions of founding a particular idea or argument and lending weight to that idea such that it deserves serious consideration.[2] Consider, for example, this brief comment from Cicero's *Academica*:

Platonis autem auctoritate, qui uarius et multiplex et copiosus fuit, una et consentiens duobus uocabulis philosophiae forma instituta est Academicorum et Peripateticorum, qui rebus congruentes nominibus differebant.

Following Plato's complex and eloquent lead, a single and concordant system of philosophy developed under two names: the philosophy of the Academics and Peripatetics. Despite their difference in name, they agreed in their doctrine. (Cicero, *Academica* 1.17, trans. C. Brittain)

Charles Brittain's translation here emphasises the notion that Plato's *auctoritas* marks him out as the originator of a general philosophical outlook that later became the shared Academic and Peripatetic tradition. But Cicero also remarks here that Plato was complex, varied, and eloquent, terms most easily associated with the variety and complexity of his written output and therefore descriptions of his standing as an author. That variety of the Platonic *corpus* is precisely what is at the root of what the speaker here, Varro, takes to be the merely apparent or verbal differences between the Academic and Peripatetic schools. His philosophical output is such that it lends not

---

[2] Sedley (1997) 111: 'Just because the Greek language could not express the notion of *auctoritas*, it does not follow that the phenomenon which it describes was absent from Greek philosophical schools.'

Aristotle and Authority in Ancient Philosophy

only an authoritative weight to his views but also allows for the various interpretative squabbles between its readers and followers.[3] In that case, Plato's *auctoritas* does indeed refer both to his particular mode of philosophical writing – 'authorship' – and the way in which he stands as an acknowledge source of philosophical insight and truth – 'authority' – while also neatly showing how these two are closely related to one another. It is in part because of Plato's authorial choices that he is a philosophical authority, and, more specifically, Cicero notes that the varied forms of his textual output are why Plato has been able to become a philosophical authority for both his own sceptical Academy and also the dogmatic Peripatos.[4]

Nearly 600 years later, the Neoplatonic commentator Simplicius offers the following advice for anyone interested in writing about Aristotle:

τὸν δὲ ἄξιον τῶν Ἀριστοτελικῶν συγγραμμάτων ἐξηγητὴν δεῖ μὴ πάντῃ τῆς ἐκείνου μεγαλονοίας ἀπολείπεσθαι. δεῖ δὲ καὶ τῶν πανταχοῦ τῷ φιλοσόφῳ γεγραμμένων ἔμπειρον εἶναι καὶ τῆς Ἀριστοτελικῆς συνηθείας ἐπιστήμονα. δεῖ δὲ καὶ κρίσιν ἀδέκαστον ἔχειν, ὡς μηδὲ τὰ καλῶς λεγόμενα κακοσχόλως ἐκδεχόμενον ἀδόκιμα δεικνύναι μηδὲ εἴ τι δέοιτο ἐπιστάσεως, πάντῃ πάντως ἄπταιστον φιλονεικεῖν ἀποδεῖξαι, ὡς εἰς τὴν αἵρεσιν ἑαυτὸν ἐγγράψαντα τοῦ φιλοσόφου. δεῖ δὲ οἶμαι καὶ τῶν πρὸς Πλάτωνα λεγομένων αὐτῷ μὴ πρὸς τὴν λέξιν ἀποβλέποντα μόνον διαφωνίαν τῶν φιλοσόφων καταψηφίζεσθαι, ἀλλ' εἰς τὸν νοῦν ἀφορῶντα τὴν ἐν τοῖς πλείστοις συμφωνίαν αὐτῶν ἀνιχνεύειν.

The worthy exegete of Aristotle's writings must not fall wholly short of the latter's (i) greatness of intellect (*megalanoia*). He must also have (ii) experience of everything the Philosopher has written and must be (iii) a connoisseur of Aristotle's stylistic habits. (iv) His judgement must be impartial so that he may

---

[3] Tsouni also discusses this passage in her contribution to this volume on p.268. See also Schofield's contribution. Compare Cicero *Acad.* 1.34: 'Speusippus and Xenocrates, however, were the first people to take over Plato's theory and authority (*Platonis rationem auctoritatemque susceperant*), and after them Polemo and Crates, along with Crantor – all fellow Academics – diligently preserved the doctrines they had received from their predecessors (*ea quae a superioribus acceperant*)' (trans. C. Brittain).

[4] Compare the advice for readers of Platonic dialogues offered in Diogenes Laertius 3.65, which may derive from Thrasyllus. See Tarrant (1993), esp. 1–30. The simple matter of the availability of texts and the way in which a corpus is presented and organised will also affect the manner in which later readers can engage with them. For the history of the texts of Plato and Aristotle through to the first century BC, see Hatzimichali (2013b).

3

neither, out of misplaced zeal, seek to prove something well said to be unsatisfactory nor ... should he obstinately persist in trying to demonstrate that [Aristotle] is always and everywhere infallible, as if he had enrolled himself in the Philosopher's school (*hairesis*). [The good exegete] must, I believe (v) *not* convict the philosophers of discordance by looking only at the letter (*lexis*) of what [Aristotle] says against Plato; but he must look towards the spirit (*nous*), and track down the harmony which reigns between them on the majority of points. (Simplicius *In Arist. Cat.* 7.23–32, trans. M. Chase)

Here again we see the idea, present also in Cicero, that there is an underlying harmony to be found between Plato and Aristotle. And, although that particular assumption may not win over the majority of modern readers, Simplicius' other points of advice still sound worthwhile.[5] They are based upon an intellectual encounter with Aristotle that is textual rather than personal. That text is to be accorded an appropriate level of care and attention: it is worth taking seriously and taking it seriously involves reading widely and carefully. Aristotle deserves serious thought because Aristotle has *megalonoia*: he is a great and serious thinker, something reflected in Simplicius' reference to him simply as 'the philosopher'.[6] He is not an unassailable and infallible authority, however, and a good interpreter should be ready to point out where errors are made. Simplicius does not want to encourage any of us to become slavish disciples of Aristotle and that attitude must be reflected in our engagement with Aristotle as an author.[7]

A good example of Simplicius putting this advice into practice is the well-known opening to the so-called *Corollary on Place*, a digression within his commentary on the *Physics*. There, Simplicius notes that Aristotle's account of place contains a number of difficulties that exercised his successors

---

[5] See Baltussen (2008) 33–8.

[6] Aristotle could be invoked as a moral authority too: Aulus Gellius *Noctes Atticae* 19.2.5.

[7] Compare Ammonius *In Cat.* 8.11–19, who similarly instructs us to read Aristotle carefully and closely but also critically. He concludes: 'One must examine each point closely and, if it should turn out that way, prefer the truth to Aristotle' (trans. Cohen and Matthews), presumably recalling Aristotle's own preference for the truth over his friends who posit Forms: *NE* 1096a16–17.

4

Aristotle and Authority in Ancient Philosophy

to such a degree that Simplicius feels moved to set out these objections and 'bring to light the cause of [Aristotle's] faulty argument about place' (καὶ τὴν αἰτίαν τοῦ παραλογισμοῦ τοῦ περὶ τὸν τόπον ὑποδεῖξαι: *In Phys.* 601.1–4, trans. J. O. Urmson). This will also allow Simplicius to discuss and examine the views on place that emerged after Aristotle: something he is sure that Aristotle himself would appreciate and welcome, since it is doubtless what Aristotle would have done had he encountered these ideas (*In Phys.* 601.6). So Simplicius takes very seriously the task of critically examining and explaining Aristotle's views but not to the extent that he feels it necessary to overlook their difficulties or failings; rather his job is to show how and why Aristotle's reasoning went astray. Moreover, he takes Aristotle's own practice itself to be licensing this endeavour and attitude to Aristotle's own work; here Aristotle's method as revealed in the source text is taken to be an authoritative guide to the proper attitude to take to Aristotle's own views.[8]

That same part of Simplicius' text also sheds some light on the way in which Aristotle's text was treated by the very earliest Peripatetics. Simplicius notes at *In Phys.* 604.5–7 (FHSG 146) that Theophrastus too (or perhaps 'even Theophrastus') raised various *aporiai* about Aristotle's account of place.[9] So Aristotle was certainly not beyond criticism and correction even from someone who knew him personally and was engaging closely with his works. Theophrastus' own *On the soul*, for example, which appears to be a close commentary on Aristotle's work of the same title, raises various concerns and questions about Aristotle's account of the intellect (see FHSG 307–27). As he discussed these areas of Aristotle's philosophical output, Theophrastus evidently felt free to raise problems, point out weaknesses or discrepancies between passages, and exercise his own independent judgement. Aristotle and Aristotle's texts are to be taken very seriously but once again

---

[8] See Hoffman and Golitsis (2016).

[9] ἱστέον δὲ ὅτι καὶ ὁ Θεόφραστος ἐν τοῖς Φυσικοῖς ἀπορεῖ πρὸς τὸν ἀποδοθέντα τοῦ τόπου λόγον ὑπὸ τοῦ Ἀριστοτέλους τοιαῦτα. See Sorabji (1988a) 186–201.

the method of philosophical engagement they promote licences a critical attitude to their own contents.[10]

The appropriate balance between charitable and careful interpretation and critical engagement is difficult to strike and that balancing act is familiar to all of us who think and write about ancient philosophy even now. There are examples also in ancient engagements with earlier philosophical texts of both deliberately uncharitable interpretations and also of the slavish insistence on the infallibility of a particular author, although most examples will fall somewhere between these two extremes. Much will depend, of course, on the reader's own prior relationship to the target text. If, for example, the reader is someone Simplicius might have in mind as already 'enrolled in the school', the interest and goal of engaging with an authoritative school text is going to be very different from that even of Simplicius' charitable and careful exegete, let alone that of someone from an opposing philosophical school or with perhaps no prior philosophical allegiance at all. And even members of the same school can sometimes find reason to question or correct their foundational texts, albeit in perhaps more deferent tones. All of these different stances nevertheless point to the important sense in which ancient Greek and Roman philosophy was, almost from the very outset, aware of constructing for itself a tradition of repeated engagement with previous generations, thinking of them either as sources of great wisdom and insight which later readers need to study and appreciate or else as adversaries to be pulled apart, criticised, and undermined.

This story of the gradual textualisation of ancient philosophical practice and the accompanying changes in later authors' attitudes to their predecessors is certainly an important theme that has received significant recent scholarly attention and is the place where the two aspects of *auctoritas* – authority and authorship – most obviously intersect. To offer some context for the various contributions in this volume, we can

---

[10] For more discussion of Theophrastus' engagement with Aristotle, see Sharples (1998) and Gottschalk (1998) 284–8.

begin by outlining three broad changes discernible between the very earliest periods of Greek philosophical activity and later antiquity. First, there is certainly some truth in the general picture of a gradual shift from early philosophers and poets making bold claims for their personal originality and – sometimes even divinely granted – authority to a later picture of more or less stable philosophical schools and movements with their own preferred foundational and authoritative texts; claims to originality give way to clear accounts of one's place within an intellectual tradition. Second, this change is accompanied by a gradual dispersal of philosophical activity from the central focus on Athens in the classical and earlier Hellenistic period to a more scattered picture in later antiquity.[11] Third, it is doubtless true that the way in which engagement with predecessors and teaching came to be dominated by studying and commenting on certain corpora of texts rather than face-to-face discussion is a significant contributor to the nature of ancient philosophical practice as it developed over time.[12]

These three broad changes are of course related to one another. For example, in very simple terms, geographical distance makes personal contact harder and philosophers separated by physical and chronological distance are more likely to be encountered as authors than in any direct personal encounter. Moreover, the gradual accumulation of a set of philosophical texts and ideas and the gradual construction of an acknowledged history of philosophy encourage each new generation to set their own views explicitly in relation to what has gone before and, as time goes by, much of that tradition becomes accessible solely through a corpus of texts. The passage of time generates a weight of tradition, exerted principally through texts, for this emerging intellectual practice to acknowledge and work with in various ways.

However, there are important qualifications that should be added to that simple general picture. In particular, it seems

[11] See Sedley (2003).

[12] Hatzimichali (2013b) 1: 'One of the main developments that characterise first-century BC philosophy is that the detailed study of texts became an autonomous and often central philosophical activity in its own right.'

wrong to conclude that there is a clear and smooth movement from an earlier period in which philosophical authority was in the main acquired and wielded in face-to-face oral encounters to a later period in which texts were the principle means by which philosophical authority was won and demonstrated. Certainly, by later antiquity the great classical philosophers – Plato and Aristotle above all – had acquired a central role in philosophical education and the interpretation of their texts had become central to philosophical practice most generally. Nevertheless, the overall picture of authority in ancient philosophy is still best tackled on a case-by-case basis bearing in mind the particular historical and institutional context. For example, although the vibrant philosophical culture of classical and early Hellenistic Athens no doubt did encourage close-quarter face-to-face encounters both between philosophical mentors and pupils and also between adherents of opposing schools, it is not obvious that this personal acquaintance had previously been the principal model for philosophical engagement. Throughout this history of ancient philosophy, it is likely that intellectual authority was won as much by the circulation of texts as by personal connections and influence. In other words, it is possible that the knowledge that Parmenides had of Heraclitus, for example, was primarily through indirect engagement with the text – in whatever form – of Heraclitus' book and not through personal interaction. Similarly, it is likely that the atomist philosophy of Leucippus and Democritus was developed in part as a reaction to Eleatic arguments. The most likely way in which these philosophers in Abdera were acquainted with the works of Parmenides, Zeno, and Melissus is through their writings. And Melissus' engagement with Parmenides and Zeno was itself probably via their written works.[13] Socrates himself, we might note, is depicted in Plato's *Phaedo* as having encountered Anaxagoras' philosophy through purchasing his book after hearing it trailed by public performance in the agora; there was no face-to-face

---

[13] Zeno complains about the circulation of unauthorised copies of his book at Plato *Parmenides* 128d6–e1.

Aristotle and Authority in Ancient Philosophy

engagement there either.[14] And it is perhaps worth mentioning that in general the world of ancient philosophy prior to the impact of Socrates and his followers on the scene was geographically rather dispersed. Of course, ties of guest-friendship and visits to and performances at Panhellenic festivals may have led some of these thinkers to come to know each other. And the early Ionian natural philosophers presumably enjoyed some kind of personal acquaintance. But we should imagine that in this earlier period too a great deal of philosophical interaction took place via the reception of written works, whether performed or read. The distinction between oral philosophical interaction and encountering philosophical ideas through the transmission of texts is not in itself, therefore, likely to be the most important factor for understanding how issues of authority developed through the long history of ancient philosophy.

Next, we should distinguish between doctrinal and methodological authority. Some philosophers acquired an authoritative status based on their adoption of a certain manner of doing philosophy rather than the articulation of a certain set of dogmatic views, and a number of the essays in this collection are interested in ways in which ancient philosophers were interested in challenging as much as generating or accepting forms of doctrinal authority. This methodological authority may in fact point to a fracture between authorship and doctrinal authority because it is a useful tool for understanding how certain philosophers who wrote nothing (or whose works were inaccessible) nevertheless acquired and continue to enjoy a certain authority in the absence of being authors and, sometimes, in the absence of offering any dogmatic philosophical position at all. Socrates, most notably, but also Pyrrho, for example, came to stand for and recommend certain ways of doing philosophy rather than particular philosophical views and therefore were able to attract detractors and supporters in a fashion analogous to but distinct from their more textually

---

[14] Plato *Phaedo* 97b8–c6.

Jenny Bryan, Robert Wardy, and James Warren

productive colleagues.[15] The lesson to draw from examples such as Socrates and Pyrrho is surely that the phenomenon of philosophical authority in antiquity does not line up in any straightforward fashion with dogmatic versus sceptical or written versus unwritten philosophy.

Third, there is also a strong anti-authoritarian tradition in philosophy as a whole and in ancient philosophy in particular. There is, after all, something curious about an intellectual practice devoted to the clear-eyed scrutiny of every argument and conclusion and the acceptance of no authority other than the truth which finds itself dealing with certain authoritative individuals and texts as accepted sources of insight. That tradition too is well exemplified by Socrates and by those who followed in his wake as independent arbiters of others' claims. The Academic tradition, for example, was sometimes keen to stress how the *auctoritas* of the proponents of various views should be granted no weight when exercising one's independent intellectual judgement.[16]

Here, Plato's authorial choice of a dialogue form might also be invoked as a sign that it is important to dissociate one's admiration for a particular individual's intellectual standing from the question of what the most plausible and convincing argument might be.[17] Plato is therefore a particularly interesting case for exploring notions of ancient philosophical *auctoritas* in so far as he is himself responding to and depicting an unusual and charismatic philosopher – Socrates – who showed no deference to any philosophical authority besides whatever argument seemed to him at the time to be the most convincing. And, whatever his own personal approach to his pupils, through his writings Plato himself became an inspiration and an authority both to philosophers minded to take the dialogue form as an invitation to liberate themselves too from any particular personal philosophical authority and also

---

[15] Diogenes Laertius 1.16 gives a list distinguishing between those philosophers who left behind their writings and those who wrote nothing at all: καὶ οἱ μὲν αὐτῶν κατέλιπον ὑπομνήματα, οἱ δ' ὅλως οὐ συνέγραψαν.

[16] See e.g. Cicero *Tusc.* 1.55; Sedley (1997) 118–20.

[17] See also Frede's contribution in this volume.

10

to those who found in the same writings a systematic and dogmatic philosophical system – Platonism – to be uncovered, appreciated, and defended.[18]

The papers collected in this volume serve to illuminate the various models of and attitudes towards authorship and authority outlined above and are testament to the variety of approaches such a topic demands. Several reflect on the distinction between doctrinal and methodological authority, pointing out the role of one type of authority where we might more readily expect the other. So, for example, Jenny Bryan offers a reconsideration of the doctrinal authority of Parmenides' *Doxa*. For all that his philosophy takes the form of a revelation, Parmenides has generally been read as a philosopher primarily committed to the authority of argument. This has led to attempts to deny the doctrinal authority of the less argumentative parts of his poem, notably the cosmology of the *Doxa*. In fact, however, ancient readers of Parmenides were happy to read the *Doxa* as representing Parmenides' own cosmology and this approach has been enjoying something of a renaissance in recent years. Bryan offers a reading of the *Doxa* which attempts to harmonise the argumentative authority of the *Aletheia* with the cosmological commitments of the *Doxa*. She concludes that Parmenides' methodological authority as a critic of mortal thinking need not be incompatible with the doctrinal authority of his cosmology.

In some cases, the gap between doctrinal and methodological authority is nuanced by the further influence of *personal* authority, as attributed to certain significant, often enigmatic, individuals. This is particularly the case where those individuals, most notably Pythagoras and Socrates, leave a 'doctrinal space' through their lack of writing, to be filled by those who come after. Of course, the act of not writing can itself be read as an anti-authoritarian move. Socrates is undoubtedly one of the most prominently anti-authoritarian figures in ancient philosophy, yet he is also an individual who exerts significant authority as the figurehead of the Socratic tradition. Nicholas

---

[18] See Sedley (1997), Boys-Stones (2001) 110ff., Baltzly (2014).

Denyer considers the explicitly anti-authoritarian Socrates' commitment to the authority of argument within dialectic and his parallel critique of the empty authority of rhetoric. Denyer scrutinises the nature of Socrates' particular commitment to question-and-answer within his philosophical conversations and argues that this is not simply a result of a blanket disapproval of rhetoric. Rather, Socrates uses question-and-answer as a means of establishing 'common knowledge' to facilitate collaborative reasoning or, indeed, as a coercive tool. Socrates' chosen method acts as a form of dialectical compulsion, forcing interlocutors to examine their own belief set. In this way, Socrates also forces his interlocutors to acknowledge the authority of their own beliefs and their consequences, thereby avoiding any claim to philosophical authority for himself.

A. G. Long is similarly concerned with the appropriateness of Plato's decision to attribute eschatological authority to the notoriously anti-authoritarian Socrates. Focusing on the *Apology* and *Phaedo*, Long argues that Plato is careful to connect Socrates' potentially surprising discussions of death to recognisably Socratic elements, thereby extending the scope of what is suitably or recognisably Socratic, rather than outright inventing his authority. Just as Denyer argues that Socrates' dialectic relies in part on the authority of the interlocutor's own beliefs, so Long argues that Socrates' method of dialectic is what enables him to speak with authority on topics beyond the explicitly ethical. Both Denyer and Long recognise Socrates' resistance to authority whilst attributing to him an authority that is primarily and importantly methodological.

In considering Plato's representation of Socrates' authority, Long also touches on the issue of Plato's own self-representation as a Socratic authority. Other aspects of Platonic authority and, particularly, its interaction with Aristotelian authority within antiquity provide the focus for several of the contributions to the volume. Here again, we see the influence of different kinds of methodological, personal, and doctrinal authority, sometimes in surprising ways. Dorothea Frede addresses the question of what kind of Platonic authority lurks behind the uncertainty of the dialogues. Frede considers the role of Plato within the Academy and builds a picture of an institution encouraging research and freedom from Platonic doctrinal commitments. Aristotle provides a revealing test case for this situation, since, as Frede makes clear, the influence of Plato on Aristotle's work is presented in the form of a robust critical engagement. Aristotle undoubtedly treats Plato and his dialogues as a source of authority, but this is, as Frede neatly puts it 'an authority one could haggle with'. Frede points to the disagreement over the interpretation of Plato's dialogues within the Academy, which seems to have been a phenomenon even during his lifetime, as evidence that Plato was not treated, or did not set himself up, as a doctrinal authority. Returning to the question of Plato's attitude towards the authority of Socrates as 'the best, the wisest and the most upright' (*Phaedo* 118a) (a passage also treated by Long), Frede suggests that Plato's treatment of Socrates offers a complex set of models of the critical scrutiny of philosophical authorities for his followers. In this way, then, Frede presents Plato as following in the anti-authoritarian footsteps of his teacher.

The question of Aristotle's attitude towards Platonic authority recurs in Sarah Broadie's discussion of Aristotle's interest in the 'authorial authenticity' of ethical doctrine. To what degree should we expect a philosopher to live in a way that is consistent with their teachings and how should such concerns affect our assessment of the authority of their arguments? Broadie suggests that Aristotle is not above citing his own example in support of his arguments, but notes that it is always the arguments themselves that ultimately carry the weight of authority. Looking to Aristotle's treatment of Eudoxus' hedonism, Broadie notes that he may have considered some arguments simply unworthy of support in authorial authenticity. In his treatment of Plato, Broadie suggests, Aristotle demonstrates his respect for Plato as a friend in the pursuit of truth, even if Platonist arguments are deserving of robust criticism and rejection. In fact, it is precisely this shared concern with truth that justifies and encourages Aristotle's intellectual independence.

Offering some resistance to the anti-authoritarian spirit of previous chapters, Matthew Duncombe presents a close engagement with a piece of apparent Aristotelian haggling with Platonic authority. Duncombe asserts that Aristotle's *Categories* are rather more receptive to Plato's thought than has generally been believed. Focusing on *Categories* 7, Duncombe argues that Aristotle is directly influenced by and in general agreement with Plato in developing his account of relativity. Duncombe presents the evidence for reading a shared commitment to an intensional view of relatives as the result of direct influence, arguing that there is good reason to think that Aristotle draws his examples directly from Plato. Duncombe's characterisation of Aristotle's response to Plato is thus rather more irenic in emphasis than that of Frede. Nevertheless, there is good reason to think that, where Aristotle accepts Plato's views, it is because he had reasoned his way to agreement in a manner compatible with Frede's account of intellectual life in the Academy, as opposed to a matter of simple deference.

The reception of Platonic authority within the Peripatos also provides the focus of K. C. Rudolph's chapter on Theophrastus' *de Sensibus*. This is one of several chapters in the volume which deal explicitly with the question of what sort of authority should be attributed to the ancient commentators. Rudolph offers a defence of Theophrastus against those who have accused him of failing in his attempt to represent the philosophical positions of his predecessors. She rejects the notion that Theophrastus' own authority as a commentator is dependent on the accuracy of his account, arguing via a detailed analysis of the *de Sensibus*' treatment of the *Timaeus* that Theophrastus should be considered a success on his own terms. Rudolph thereby rejects the suggestion that Theophrastus' role as a commentator is in tension with his adherence to Aristotelian authority. Adopting an approach more sympathetic to Theophrastus' authorial intentions and habits grants a much more nuanced appreciation of his status as a particular kind of authority, both on Plato and, potentially, on pre-Aristotelian philosophy in general.

Myrto Hatzimichali uses the afterlife of Aristotle's *Categories* as the focus for a discussion of the complex web of authoritative influences at work in the Hellenistic period. Noting the coincidence between a revival of interest in Pythagoreanism towards the end of the Hellenistic period and a boom in the authorship of pseudo-Pythagorean writings, Hatzimichali considers the potentially puzzling nature of these texts as primarily engaged with Platonic and Aristotelian doctrines. Is the aim of such works to bolster the authority of the later thinkers by establishing roots in the earlier tradition, or rather to enhance the status of Pythagoreanism as possessing such significant influence? Hatzimichali considers the negotiations of authority that lie behind pseudo-Archytas' *On the Universal Logos* and gives an intriguing account of the manner in which its own authority as a commentary on the *Categories* was established. Like Rudolph, Hatzimichali makes a case for scrutinising the authority of the ancient philosophical commentaries on their own terms, as part of a complex nexus of retrospective interpretative influence and the construction of a tradition of authorship and authority.

Frede argues that Platonic authority within the Academy was more a matter of critical example than of doctrine. George Boys-Stones demonstrates that a similar attitude to Platonic authority can be identified in the later Platonist tradition. Boys-Stones argues that Platonists such as Numenius reasoned their way to Platonism on the basis of a certain characterisation of his epistemic success, which served as the foundation of his authority. Just as in the case of Duncombe's Aristotle, this is an active engagement with authority, rather than a matter of simple deference. Numenius offers a subtle and philosophically informed approach to the history of philosophy, establishing Plato's authority as the ideal philosopher whose truth we seek to replicate in our own efforts. Here then, we see a difference between the early Academic reception of Plato's authority as set out by Frede and that of the later Platonist tradition described by Boys-Stones. Both are interested primarily in methodology, but they differ in that the latter seeks to use a methodology to recreate Plato's thought (as represented in the dialogues) whereas, on Frede's account, the early Academy deliberately eschewed such reconstructive efforts. It is telling that, as Boys-Stones notes, the Academy itself seems to be an irrelevance to Platonists such as Numenius. His interest in the authority of truth over doctrine is what allows Numenius to identify himself as a Pythagorean. Once knowledge is our criterion of authority, then anyone who possesses that knowledge is thereby authoritative.

Boys-Stones suggests that Numenius provides a telling counterexample to (or at least refiguring of) the Hellenistic model of 'school' allegiance and quasi-religious authority. Three of the chapters in this volume consider the way in which the personal authority of the founders of the Hellenistic schools was constructed and negotiated. The idealisation and divinisation of Epicurus as an authority is well known. James Warren scrutinises the notion of a so-called 'proof text', a citation from Epicurus' *On the Telos* (Us. 68) for the interpretation of Epicurean hedonism. Warren draws our attention to the authority of context and the ancient reception in considering such truncated citations and in shaping our understanding of their original intended meaning. In this way he echoes many of the concerns raised by Rudolph and Hatzimichali in their discussions of the ancient commentary tradition. Pointing out that the ambiguity of Us. 68 was acknowledged as early as Demetrius of Laconia, Warren sets out a case against reading this citation as carrying the authority of an official definition of the Epicurean *telos*.

Warren argues that we have reason to doubt the particular sort of authority attributed to this citation of Epicurus. David Butterfield, meanwhile, questions the nature of Epicurus' authority for Lucretius. It has long been a commonplace that Lucretius exhibits a 'fundamentalist' adherence to Epicurus in a manner that sets him apart from the developments of the Epicurean school. Butterfield argues that this adherence is evident even in his account of the nature of the gods, an area in which Lucretius has often been thought to depart from the possible idealism of Epicurus. Butterfield's Lucretius thus possesses his own authority as offering a sincere and accurate representation of Epicurus' theological doctrine, even if following Epicurus in this direction seems to have led him (in the eyes of some, at least) beyond the realms of sense.

In a broad-brush account, it is perhaps easier to establish the personal authority of Epicurus for Epicureans than of Zeno within the Stoic school. A. A. Long sets out the evidence for Zeno's enduring dominance and influence as founder of the school, the disagreement between individual Stoics notwithstanding. Long uses Diogenes Laertius' biography of Zeno to consider the gap between the perception of Zeno presented by contemporary authors and his later representation. Long reads Diogenes' life of Zeno as indicative of uncertainties over the appropriate representation of Zeno after his death, with the result that the variant versions compiled by Diogenes can be read as relatively accurate in their representation of his influences and, to some extent, his own way of life. Other aspects of the account, particularly its anecdotes, may result from a combination of the reminiscences of his contemporaries with the sort of stories that were generally attributed to philosophical authorities.

The apparent tension between personal or doctrinal authority and methodological authority becomes embedded in the jargon of Roman philosophical writing, as a conflict between *auctoritas* and *ratio*. Two of our contributors draw our attention to the nuances of philosophical *auctoritas* as formulated and developed in the first century BCE. Malcolm Schofield considers the use to which Cicero puts appeals to *auctoritas* within the political and philosophical arenas. As Schofield notes, one might expect Cicero's allegiance to Academic Scepticism to be an obstacle to appeals to *auctoritas* such as are found in his political writings. Schofield investigates the degree to which the dominance of *ratio* in philosophy stands at odds with an appeal to authority. Via a consideration of Cicero's *De Natura Deorum*, Schofield argues that, in the sphere of religion at least, *ratio* and *auctoritas* were treated as incommensurable, or at least as governing different questions, and thus free from even apparent tensions. Further, not only does Cicero treat philosophical *ratio* as, in some circumstances, applicable to politics, there is also good reason to respect the presence of *auctoritas* within his philosophical writings. This is clear from the explicit interest Cicero has in the *dignitas* of his chosen interlocutors, which aids Cicero's aim of encouraging the application of appropriate *ratio* to the relative positions. Thus *ratio* and *auctoritas* are complementary in philosophical writings, particularly when focused on ethical questions in which experience speaks of good judgement.

Georgia Tsouni also takes *auctoritas* as her theme, sharing both Schofield's concern with Cicero's account of *auctoritas* (as representative of the agenda of Antiochus) and the interest of several earlier chapters in the later reception and reconstruction of the authority of Aristotle and Plato. Tsouni sets out to examine the nature of *auctoritas* as attributed by Antiochus to his predecessors. Once again the question of doctrinal allegiance to an individual as opposed to some particular method (*auctoritas* vs *ratio*) comes to the fore and Tsouni echoes the nuanced reading of Cicero put forward by Schofield. Tsouni emphasises the Antiochean commitment to the texts as conveying a body of doctrines and draws out the particular nature of Antiochean authority as harmonising, since it is transferable from master to pupil, and dynamic, insofar as it admits of progress. Both of these aspects allow Antiochus to read those after Plato as offering authoritative elaboration on his thought.

The collection concludes with two chapters seeking to provoke us to look beyond our own assumptions about the role and scope of authority within ancient philosophy. Geoffrey Lloyd sets out some salient and provocative points of comparison between the tradition of philosophical authority in Greece and Rome and patterns of intellectual influence in ancient China. Lloyd highlights shared efforts to attribute important texts to authoritative figures and divergent attitudes towards foundation texts. He points to an interesting difference in terms of the practical and political authority commonly claimed by Chinese authors. In the final chapter of the volume, Robert Wardy offers a staunch rejection of the notion that successful philosophical activity can tolerate 'authority' in any but the most circumscribed sense. He thereby highlights a key question addressed by many of the chapters, namely that of how a tradition committed to critical reasoning can rely on reverence for predecessors. As we see, in fact, it is rarely the case (at least in those examples treated in the chapters in this volume) that philosophical authority equates to simple deference. Rather, the methodological or even doctrinal authority of any philosopher often seems to be hard won and open to interpretation if not outright challenge.

This collection thus presents a variety of perspectives on the relationship between authority and authorship in antiquity, with a broad thematic and chronological scope. In this respect, it is a testament to the impressive and wide-ranging body of work of its inspiration, David Sedley. Most of the essays in the collection derive from papers delivered at a conference held in Cambridge in September 2014 to mark David's retirement as Laurence Professor of Ancient Philosophy. That conference was generously supported by the Faculty of Classics, St Catharine's College, Cambridge, University College, London, the Institute of Classical Studies, the Mind Association, the British Society for the History of Philosophy, and Cambridge and Oxford University Presses.

The nature of David's own authority in the field reflects many of the aspects discussed in the collection. He has served as an authoritative commentator and even, one might argue (though he might disagree), a source of doctrinal authority. He has certainly exercised the authority of a prolific author and a generous critical paradigm.

CHAPTER I

RECONSIDERING THE AUTHORITY
OF PARMENIDES' *DOXA*

JENNY BRYAN

This chapter considers the possibility of reading Parmenides' *Doxa* both as significant to his poem, and thus to his philosophy, as a whole, and as representative of Parmenides' own cosmological doctrine (in keeping with the overwhelming ancient tradition). It is, I think, possible to draw a useful distinction between 'argumentative authority' and 'doctrinal authority' within Parmenides' poem. The former can be attributed to the conclusions to which the goddess leads us in the *Aletheia*. The latter has a broader scope, in that it identifies the content of the revelation, including its description of the cosmos (and presumably the fact of the revelation itself), as teachings to which Parmenides is committed as their author.[1] The *Doxa*'s doctrinal authority lies primarily in what it demonstrates about the way that mortals think about and explain the world and what this indicates about their own implicit attitudes towards plurality. This is compatible with its having a role to play in supporting the authority of the *Aletheia*'s arguments. It is also compatible with the possibility that Parmenides offered the *Doxa* as a genuine attempt at an explanation of sense experience. In fact, the *Doxa*'s cosmology can be seen to be more authoritative in its analysis of mortal thinking and in its support of the *Aletheia* precisely because Parmenides, as a mortal, strives to provide a plausible account of the physical world.

---

[1] The goddess herself indicates an authority beyond that of reasoning as endorsed in B7.

Reconsidering the Authority of Parmenides' *Doxa*

The Doctrinal Authority of the *Doxa*

At one time, it was not uncommon to deny the doctrinal authority of the cosmological section of Parmenides' poem.[2] It was suggested that, whatever kind of cosmology the *Doxa* described, it was certainly not that of Parmenides. Thus G. E. L. Owen, in setting out his influential reading of the *Doxa* as a 'dialectical exercise', asserts that, for all that he wrote the cosmology, 'Parmenides did not write *as* a cosmologist.'[3] On this interpretation, Parmenides presents a critique of the thinking of others (either of mortals in general or of specific individuals) rather than a natural philosophy of his own. The *Doxa* is thus Parmenidean only insofar as he composed it to represent other people's thinking, without committing himself (indeed explicitly withholding commitment) to the details of the system it describes. Whatever authority the *Doxa* possesses lies in its status as a paradigm of the inherent speciousness of such endeavours.[4]

The motivation for denying Parmenides' commitment to the content of the cosmology is not simply the significant fact that its pluralist system is incompatible with the truths about what-is established in the *Aletheia*. The goddess herself appears to undermine the authority of the *Doxa* with her description of its content as a 'deceitful ordering' (κόσμος ἀπατηλός, B8.53) lacking in 'true conviction' (πίστις ἀληθής, B1.30). For some, this is sufficient evidence both of the *Doxa*'s falsehood and of Parmenides' disavowal of its content.[5]

Whilst such explanations of the *Doxa* offer an attempt to account for the cosmology's presence within the poem as a whole, they do little to explain its extensive and detailed nature, which is hinted at by the surviving fragments and made clear in the *testimonia*.[6] For even if we accept that the *Doxa* represents

---

[2] Curd (1998) 98–100 provides a useful summary of interpretations of the *Doxa*.

[3] Owen (1960b) 101, my emphasis.

[4] On this reading, the *Doxa*'s 'doctrinal authority' would be in representing Parmenides' commitment to the failings of natural philosophy.

[5] Thus Barnes (1982) 156 reads Parmenides as stating 'unequivocally' that the *Doxa* is false.

[6] Plutarch *Adv. Col.* 1114B–C suggests that the *Doxa* was comprehensive in scope. See Granger (2002) 101 n. 2 on the *Doxa*'s estimated length.

Jenny Bryan

the faults of mortal thinking, it is difficult to account for the need to systematize, as opposed to simply diagnose, those faults in such an original and detailed way. In fact, scholars have increasingly argued that the *Doxa* should be read as representative of Parmenides' own natural philosophy.[7] It is now perhaps more commonly read as seriously intended and original cosmology to which Parmenides himself is committed *as* a cosmologist. In this way, the *Doxa* is taken to be just as representative of Parmenides' views as the *Aletheia*, for all that the two parts appear incompatible.

In accepting the *Doxa* as offering genuine Parmenidean doctrine, scholars are rehabilitating the view of the vast majority of ancient readers of the poem. For it is clear that, whilst figures such as Aristotle or Plutarch certainly show an awareness of the tension between the *Aletheia* and the *Doxa*, they also regard both parts as carrying doctrinal authority.[8] Parmenides' ancient readers, even in possession of the poem in its complete form and aware of the arguments of the *Aletheia*, had no qualms about attributing the content of the *Doxa* to Parmenides or treating Parmenides as a natural philosopher.[9] In fact, Plutarch goes so far as to describe him as 'a man who stands at the origins of natural philosophy (ἀρχαῖος ἐν φυσιολογίᾳ) and who composed his own book rather than plundering another's'.[10]

Nevertheless, anyone seeking to rehabilitate the authority of the *Doxa* is faced with precisely the problem that motivated the previous tendency to deny it. How can Parmenides the

---

[7] Tor (2015) 6 n. 13 surveys interpretations of the *Doxa* as representing Parmenides' own views, a line which he too pursues.

[8] Aristotle *Metaphysics* 986b27–34 suggests that Parmenides is committed to the claim that 'being is one' and that his explanation in terms of two principles is a result of 'being forced to follow the phenomena, and supposing that being is one in definition but many according to sensation'. See Palmer (2009) 32–45 for a detailed assessment of views on the relation between the *Aletheia* and *Doxa* in antiquity.

[9] The denial of the *Doxa*'s authority was not entirely unknown in antiquity. Plutarch's assertion at *Adv. Col.* 1114D that 'Parmenides, however, does away with neither nature, but gives each its due' is presented as a direct response to the Epicurean Colotes' claim that Parmenides 'does away with everything by hypothesizing that being is one'. See Palmer (2009) 38–9.

[10] *Adv. Col.* 1114C.

Reconsidering the Authority of Parmenides' *Doxa*

metaphysician and author of the *Aletheia* be reconciled with Parmenides the natural scientist? Further, why, if Parmenides is committed to its content as his own natural philosophy, is it so disparaged by the goddess? The most popular answer, which echoes those of Aristotle and Plutarch, is to suggest that the resolution lies in recognizing the significant difference between the two endeavours. So, for example, it is suggested that Parmenides is describing two different aspects of the same thing (e.g. necessary and non-necessary being) or two essentially different modes of thinking (divine and mortal).[11] The thought seems to be that, once we have acknowledged and understood what it is that differentiates the two accounts, we can and should allow both to stand as Parmenidean doctrine. There is no fundamental conflict between the two parts if they are viewed in their proper context and with an understanding of their specific aims.

As we have seen, such interpretations have the authority of the ancient reception of Parmenides on their side. However, they still have to explain the goddess' own negative characterization of the *Doxa*. How can we regard as Parmenidean doctrine an account that is explicitly undermined by the poem's own internal source of authority? In fact, of course, the goddess makes it clear that mortal beliefs are something that should be learned alongside the truth (B1.28–32).[12] Even when making the transition from her 'trustworthy account' (πιστὸς λόγος) about truth to her description of mortal beliefs at the end of B8, she characterizes the account that follows as 'deceitful' rather than false.[13] Indeed, no matter how one understands the description of the 'arrangement' (διάκοσμος) to follow as 'likely' (ἐοικώς) at B8.60, there can be no doubt that line 61's 'so that no opinion of mortals shall ever outstrip you'

---

[11] Palmer (2009) 159–75 provides the former sort of explanation. Tor (2015) suggests the latter.

[12] Further, B10's promise that 'you shall know' (εἴσηι) suggests that it is possible to have knowledge of the cosmos.

[13] Similarly, B1.30 can be read as denying the presence of genuine convincingness rather than truth *per se* in mortal beliefs. As Johansen (2015) 3 notes, this denial is compatible with the *Doxa* 'being true, or credible or persuasive in a weaker sense [than the *Aletheia*]'.

is intended as *some* sort of endorsement of what follows in the cosmology.[14] The goddess' description of the *Doxa* not only fails to justify a complete dismissal of its authority, it actually gives us good reason to think that it has an important and positive role to play within the poem (and Parmenides' philosophy) as a whole. Of course, once we have accepted this, the problem returns of explaining why she *also* seems to undermine its status. Interpretations seeking to rehabilitate the doctrinal authority of the *Doxa* have to explain why Parmenides would question the trustworthiness of his own cosmological doctrine. The standard explanation is that the root of the deception lies in the failure to recognize the significant difference between the nature and purpose of the *Aletheia* and *Doxa*, so that mortals are deceived insofar as they regard the *Doxa* as having the same status and purpose as the *Aletheia*, erroneously taking the *Doxa* to be a description of what-is.[15] Once we recognize the difference and understand what attitude to take towards each account, we, like Parmenides, will escape such confusion and avoid the deception. We can then engage with and learn from the cosmology that follows on its own terms.

The problem with this sort of explanation of the goddess' denigration is that it fails to account for the fact that the error in mortal thinking diagnosed at B8.53–9 is presented as systemic in nature.[16] However, we understand the controversial assertion that mortals 'decided to name two forms/of which it is not right to name one' (B8.53–4), it is clear that the mistake informs and, one could say, infects the conceptual framework on which the cosmology is based. The goddess tells us that it is 'in this that they have gone astray' (B8.54).[17] Whatever the precise nature of the error, it is one fundamental to the dualism of Light and Night around which the cosmology is constructed.

---

[14] Palmer (2009) 162 reads B8.60–61, along with B6.3–4, as signalling that the cosmology carries the goddess' authority.

[15] See, for example, Nehamas (2002) 58 n. 49, Palmer (2009) 163 and Tor (2015) 19–20.

[16] This is emphasized by the fact that it is the κόσμος ἐμῶν ἐπέων that is labelled deceptive. The goddess thereby suggests that there is something deceptive about a) the world order as it is described and b) the way the description is constructed, rather than simply about the attitude taken towards that order.

[17] Cf. B6.

Once we accept that there is a fundamental problem (whatever that may be) with the terms in which the cosmology is set out, it is hard to see how we can straightforwardly accept that system as genuine Parmenidean cosmological doctrine.[18] It is one thing to suggest that one's account will deceive those who fail to engage with it on its own terms. It is quite another to assert that the entire account is built upon a faulty distinction, the failings of which are demonstrated throughout the *Doxa*. In fact, I will suggest below that the *Doxa* emphasizes not only the problematic nature of the distinction on which the cosmology is based but also the inconsistent fashion in which mortals employ that distinction within their explanations. If I am justified in reading the *Doxa* as representing a deliberately inconsistent explanatory system, it seems that we will need to think harder about its purpose and status. It will not be enough to say that the *Doxa* is successful as long as it is read as fulfilling a particular purpose. Instead, we will need to find a reason for its fulfilling this purpose in this particular, apparently problematic, way.

There is, however, further reason to entertain the plausibility of the *Doxa*'s doctrinal authority. Parmenides is characterized in antiquity not simply as a cosmologist, but as an *innovative* and successful astronomer.[19] In particular, Parmenides is credited with the observations that the moon gets its light from the sun and that the morning star and evening star are one and the same.[20] These views are taken to be evidence that, if not

---

[18] Palmer (2009) 174–5 suggests that mortals are not wrong to hypothesize Light and Night as material principles of non-necessary being. Rather, their error lies in the assumption that such an account can offer the kind of understanding that is only possible for necessary being. I will suggest that the *Doxa*'s account fails not only as an account of being but also on its own terms as a pluralistic explanation.

[19] See, for example, Cerri (2011) and Mourelatos (2011). Even Barnes (1982) 156 n. 3, who thinks the *Doxa* entirely false, admits that it contains 'some interesting astronomy'. See Graham (2013) 85–108 for a detailed argument in favour of understanding Parmenides as a successful and innovative empirical scientist.

[20] The former view is attributed to Parmenides by Aëtius 2.26.2 and 2.28.5. Parmenides' commitment to the identity of the morning and evening stars is found at Aëtius 2.15. 7 and Diogenes Laertius 8.14. Parmenides is the earliest thinker for whom this view is attested. None of these texts suggest that these are Parmenidean discoveries as such. However, as Mourelatos (2011) 174 notes, B14 and B15, if read as identifying moonlight as reflected sunlight, would offer the first 'secure attestation' of this view.

actually responsible for these discoveries himself, Parmenides was 'grappling with quite recent discoveries made by others'.[21] This suggestion of an engaged interest in natural science is taken as further evidence for Parmenides' commitment to the content and subject matter of the *Doxa*.

It seems, then, that we are at something of an *impasse*. On the one hand, both the goddess' own authority and the evidence of the *Doxa* itself, as fragments of what seems to have been an extensive and detailed system, give reason to think that it should be read as Parmenides' own original cosmology. This view is further supported by the *testimonia* on Parmenides, which imply an active engagement with contemporary astronomical discoveries and repeatedly demonstrate a straightforward assumption of the *Doxa*'s doctrinal authority. On the other hand, the goddess' denigration of the *Doxa* seems to weigh against Parmenides' commitment to its content, as do her diagnosis of its fundamental error at B8.53–4 and, of course, its incompatibility with the arguments of the *Aletheia* itself. In fact, as I intend to show in what follows, the fragments of the *Doxa* also provide internal evidence of the cosmology's problematic status.[22] The inconsistency of its dualism, flagged up at the end of B8, is demonstrated in a variety of ways throughout the extant fragments. Perhaps surprisingly, however, this systemic inconsistency need not be taken as a blow to Parmenides' status as a natural philosopher. The philosophical significance of these failures is enhanced by the fact that they aim at an exhaustive and accurate account of the physical world. Parmenides seeks to demonstrate the inconsistency of mortal thinking about the change that we perceive in the world by doing the best he can to provide an accurate and comprehensive explanation of it.[23] In fact, I will suggest that

[21] Mourelatos (2011) 70.

[22] My account is thus in sympathy with that of Mourelatos (2008) 222–63. I differ in my analysis of the extent and nature of the *krasis* present in the *Doxa* and in claiming that such inconsistency is not incompatible with Parmenides' own commitment to the *Doxa*'s content.

[23] My claim then is not that the *Doxa* is deceptive because it correctly describes the world of change but is erroneously taken to be an account of what-is. Rather, it fails even in giving a consistent account of the world of change. But an inconsistent explanation can possess some degree of apparent accuracy in describing what it

Reconsidering the Authority of Parmenides' *Doxa*

Parmenides is attempting to demonstrate that the superiority of what-is as described in the *Aletheia* (and of its account of what-is) is felt even in our mortal observations about the world. In attempting and failing to explain the natural world, mortals reveal their implicit awareness of the nature of what-is. By doing cosmology, then, Parmenides demonstrates the possibility and perhaps the necessity of moving beyond it. Bearing all this in mind, it is high time to turn to the *Doxa* itself.

Krisis and *Krasis* in the *Doxa*

It has been noted that the cosmology of the *Doxa* is founded on a distinction (*krisis*) which explicitly echoes that established as fundamental to the arguments of the *Aletheia*.[24] But whereas the *krisis* of the *Aletheia* was the essential and necessary distinction between what-is and what-is-not (since the latter is excluded as an illegitimate object of inquiry), the *krisis* on which mortals are said to base their cosmology is presented as arbitrary and illegitimate, in addition to being introduced as the foundation of a 'deceitful ordering'.[25] Mortals are said to have 'decided to name two forms' and to have 'distinguished opposites in body' (ἄντια δ᾽ἐκρίναντο δέμας), namely Light (Fire) and Night. The interpretation of B8.54's qualification 'of which it is not right to name one' is particularly controversial.[26] For my purposes, however, what matters is that the mortal distinction is clearly informed by and depends upon the (re)introduction of what-is-not.[27] The goddess tells us that

---

seeks to explain. Parmenides attempts to offer a plausible and accurate description in order to demonstrate the inevitable failings of explanations of plurality.

[24] At B7.5–6, the goddess exhorts the *kouros* to make a decision (κρῖναι). At B8.15–18 she states that the decision (κρίσις) between what-is and what-is-not has been made (κέκριται). See Tor (2015) 14–19.

[25] As is only to be expected from mortals described at B6.7 as ἄκριτα. The arbitrary nature of the distinction is made clear by the use of κατέθεντο (B8.53) and ἔθεντο (55) to describe the process by which mortals establish the basic dualism around which their system is built.

[26] See Tor (2015) 16–17 for a recent assessment.

[27] If, as Aristotle suggests, Light is to be aligned or identified with what-is (*Metaphysics* 986b35–6; *On Generation and Corruption* 318b2–7) and Night with what-is-not, the problem with the mortal system is that they have introduced what-is-not in the form of the principle of Night. On an alternative (and more plausible) reading

Light is conceived of as 'everywhere the same as itself,/not the same as the other' (8.57–8). Night in turn is said to be 'by itself/ in contrast' (58–9).[28] The significance of this characterization is clear from its echo of the earlier description of what-is: 'the same and in the same, [it] lies by itself' (B8.29). Whereas what-is is stable, self-identical, and self-sufficient, Light and Night are introduced as conceptually co-dependent. They are defined in terms of what they are ('the same as itself' and 'by itself'), but also in terms of what they are not ('but not the same as the other' and 'in contrast'). Insofar as Light and Night are introduced as a pair of enantiomorphic opposites, it is impossible to conceive of one except in opposition to the other.[29]

Recognizing this, we can see that the mortal *krisis* is illegitimate in more than one way. First, its fundamental opposition is dependent on the notion of what-is-not. In fact, the mortal *krisis* can also be considered a *krasis*, insofar as it represents the conceptual combination of precisely those things (what-is and what-is-not) that the genuine *krisis* of the *Aletheia* set out to distinguish. Second, it is illegitimate in that it is an incomplete *krisis*, insofar as the enantiomorphic nature of the opposites means that they are conceptually combined and thus not truly distinct.[30] Neither can be understood in isolation from the other. From the very outset of his cosmology, Parmenides signals the difficulty, or perhaps even the impossibility, of establishing satisfactory terms in which to describe a world of plurality.[31]

---

of B8.53–9, the issue is that each of the two principles incorporates both what-is or what-is-not, in that they are opposites. As noted below, the plausibility of this reading is enhanced by B9's assertion that the principles are equal. It is conceivable that Aristotle's analysis of Light as what-is and Night as what-is-not represents an attempt to resolve the inconsistency that I want to suggest Parmenides is presenting as inherent in mortal accounts. Their system breaks down partly because they insist on the equality and interdependence of their principles. Aristotle solves this problem by making the *krisis* between them far more radical.

[28] As Tor (2015) 15 n. 42 notes, it seems clear that the two principles are each characterized symmetrically as self-identical but opposed to the other.

[29] See Curd (1998) 104–10 on Light and Night as enantiomorphic opposites.

[30] Mourelatos (2008) 221.

[31] Curd (1998) 111–6 suggests that a system based on two principles which were not interdefined would avoid the failings of the *Doxa*. I take it that Parmenides is claiming that any attempt to explain change will necessarily involve this sort of

Reconsidering the Authority of Parmenides' *Doxa*

In fact, this passage flags up a further, related problem with the manner in which mortals establish their cosmological terminology. We see that, in the first instance, they 'decided to name two forms' before going on to 'distinguish opposites in body' which, as we have seen, turn out to be conceptually dependent on one another. There is an interesting progression here that is, I think, significant for our understanding of the cosmology as a whole. Mortals begin with a mental distinction of two forms (μορφαί) to which they apply names. They then turn to the physical world, wherein they distinguish opposites *in body* (δέμας), i.e. they seek to explain the objects of perception in terms of their original distinction. Light and Night are then described in terms of their perceptual qualities (with Light as gentle and light in weight and Night as dark, dense and heavy). At this point, however, mortals' lack of commitment to the distinction becomes clear as it dissolves into the conceptual unity of the opposites. Here we have another flaw in the mortal *krisis*: for all that it begins as a conceptual distinction between two forms, its application to the physical world leads to the breakdown of that distinction, so that the applied dualism looks more like a unity (of opposites).[32] From the very outset, then, mortals are represented as failing to commit to the reality of the dualism established at B8.54. As we will see, this sort of ambivalence towards the dualism of the principles is a recurrent feature of the *Doxa*.

B8 represents Light and Night as enantiomorphic opposites, and thus as not only conceptually connected but in some sense equal. The equality of the principles is confirmed by B9's assertion that 'all is full of Light and obscure Night together, of both equally (ἴσων ἀμφοτέρων), since neither has no share'. It is far from clear how we should interpret this emphatic claim of equality between the principles. It looks like a claim of mutual ubiquity, i.e. a claim that both principles are physically present in equal amounts in any object in the physical world. However,

---

opposition (as a result of the role of what-is-not in change, see B8.35–41), and thus necessarily fail in this way.

[32] See Graham (2002) and Nehamas (2002) for discussion of Parmenides' possible interaction with Heraclitus.

Jenny Bryan

such a reading looks incompatible with B12's reference to a part of the cosmos containing 'unmingled fire'. In fact, this apparent inconsistency is not in itself a reason to reject a reading of B9 as implying mutual physical ubiquity. For B9 seems to echo the processes of (erroneous) reasoning I suggested were diagnosed as problematic in B8.53–9. It is notable that B9 presents the co-presence of the principles as a consequence of the fact that 'all things have been named Light and Night'.[33] Above, I suggested that B8.53–9 described the problematic consequences of attempting to apply a conceptual dualism to the physical world, insofar as that application leads to the dualism coming into focus as a unity of opposites. Looking at B9.2, we see a suggestion that it is precisely the decision to apply the labels Light and Night 'according to their powers' (κατὰ σφετέρας δυνάμεις) which results in the combined and equal physical presence of these principles in everything. It might seem odd to suggest that the naming process itself can bring about physical ubiquity, but I take it that the point is actually that the mortal decision to describe the world in terms of these enantiomorphic opposites (and the other related sets of opposites that follow along in their wake) is what necessitates that they adopt a further commitment to their physical equality and combination. Parmenides appears to be suggesting that the essential conceptual connection between these opposites determines how they can be identified and thought to function within the cosmological scheme of mortals. B8 tells us that the identity of each principle is determined in relation to its opposite. B9 indicates one of the consequences of this, which is that they must be regarded as a physical as well as a conceptual unity. Once again, in application, the conceptual dualism is presented as essentially unified, this time in an explicitly physical fashion.

What then are we to make of B12's reference to unmingled fire, which suggests that, even if Light and Night are always in proximity, they are not always co-present everywhere

---

[33] B9: 'For since (ἐπειδή) all things have been named Light and Night,/and these according to their powers to these things and those,/all is full of Light and obscure Night together,/of both equally, since neither has no share.'

Reconsidering the Authority of Parmenides' *Doxa*

throughout the cosmos? It is striking that the description of the cosmic order and processes in B12 recalls the explanatory development sketched out at the end of B8. B12 identifies the separation of physical fire and night, apparently in consecutive heavenly rings. What follows is a description of how things come to be via the union (μίξις) and mingling (μιγῆν) of male and female which, as a further set of enantiomorphic opposites, can be regarded as corresponding to the basic opposition of Light and Night (as did heavy/light, bright/dark and, perhaps, mild/dense in B8).[34] The fragment thus moves from a distinction between the two fundamental principles to a universalizing account of genesis in terms of mixture and union. In this way, it echoes B8's original move from a distinction in thought to a unity in opposition. B9 indicated that the equality of the principles is one consequence of their conceptual unity. B12, in turn, demonstrates that any system dependent upon explaining the cosmos in terms of the interaction between two principles ought to be able to hypothesize the physical separation of those principles.[35] It goes further, however, in indicating that generation itself will necessarily be a matter of the physical interaction, the union or mingling, of those principles. Once again, we see the *Doxa*'s *krisis* dissolving into *krasis*.[36]

B12 introduces a further indication of the incoherence of the dualist system it describes, particularly one in which the principles are posited as equal. Insofar as Light and Night are presented as equals in status and perhaps even in quantity, it is hard to see how they can provide a satisfactory explanation of the generative impulse. For Parmenides, equality seems to suggest stability rather than dynamism, so that an equally balanced opposition seems no more obviously compatible with generation than the homogeneous unity of the *Aletheia*.[37] In

[34] Note that B12 seems to represent male and female as equal and reciprocal partners in the process of combination.
[35] And presumably Parmenides thinks that two is the minimum number for such a process to be possible, since one is not sufficient to explain generation, as the arguments of the *Aletheia* make clear. See Sedley (1999a) 124.
[36] B13's claim that 'she devised Eros first of all the gods' suggests the chronological and explanatory priority of processes of mixture.
[37] B8.45–9 makes the connection between the equality of what-is and its stability.

Jenny Bryan

fact, B12 signals the explanatory insufficiency of the principles by positioning a goddess 'in the midst' (ἐν δὲ μέσωι) of the separate portions of Light and Night. It is this goddess who 'steers all things' by ruling over the 'birth and union of all things' and mingling male and female. On the surface, this failure of the dualist system is different from those described above: it is a matter of the introduction of something extra, rather than the collapse of the dualism into a unity. The problem here seems to be that mortals think that their system is dualist, in that the world is explained in terms of the interaction between Light and Night. In fact, however, that interaction is actually explained in terms of some further (divine) principle. This is not a case of analysing an apparent dualism as a unity, but it is a matter of the dualism being supplemented by a single, superior explanatory principle.[38]

Turning to the one word fragment B15a, 'water-rooted' (ὑδατόριζον), we see another way in which this tendency towards unification makes itself felt in the *Doxa*. The scholion in which the fragment is preserved tells us that Parmenides applies this term to the earth.[39] As Mourelatos has shown, comparison with *Theogony* 727–8, to which Parmenides is possibly alluding, demonstrates the unifying emphasis of B15a:[40]

αὐτὰρ ὕπερθεν
γῆς ῥίζαι πεφύασι καὶ ἀτρυγέτοιο θαλάσσης.

and above it
the roots of the earth and the barren sea.

---

[38] See Coxon (2009) 362–72 for a discussion of the doxographical tradition on the *Doxa*'s goddess. Simplicius *In Phys.* 9.31–9 cites B12 to argue that the goddess is an active agent separate from the material principles, a reading which is sympathetic to the interpretation offered above. Aëtius 2.7.1 and Cicero *On the Nature of the Gods* 1.28 both suggest that Parmenides identifies (some part of) the material of the heavens described in B12 as itself divine. Cicero's account, which identifies a 'circle of lights' as 'god', would import an inequality between the principles. Aëtius' suggestion that the goddess is to be identified with the 'most central of the mixed bands' would maintain equality between (some portion) of the principles, but would make some parts of the physical cosmos superior to others.

[39] *Scholion* XXV on St Basil *Humiliae IX in Hexameron*: 'Parmenides in his verse called the earth (ἡ γῆ) "water-rooted".'

[40] Mourelatos (2008) 236–7.

32

Where Hesiod has the roots of both earth and water, Parmenides has the roots of earth *in* water. Whereas Hesiod presents earth and water as a pair, Parmenides presents them as some kind of physical unity. Even Parmenides' most scientifically respectable fragments, B14 and 15, in which he appears to recognize that the moon takes its light from the sun, can be read as part of this unifying trend.[41]

I have been suggesting that the fragments of the *Doxa* give multiple indications that the initial distinction of B8, on which the cosmology is based, is inconsistent and unstable. We have seen several instances where the physical or conceptual unity of the principles as enantiomorphic opposites has been emphasized. In some cases, this is a matter of the dualist distinction breaking down in application to the physical world; in others, it is a matter of the physical unification of opposites in a process or state of mixture. Certainly, *krasis* is a recurrent feature of the *Doxa*, and not simply in the sense that it is founded on the illegitimate unification of what-is and what-is-not.[42]

One might object that the combination of two elements is not so much a problem of a dualist system as simply the process by which it functions.[43] However, the suggestion that Parmenides is emphasizing what is problematic about the dualism is supported by a closer look at his embryological fragments. B17 has a place in a notorious interpretative puzzle. In associating male with the right side (presumably of the womb) and female with the left, Parmenides aligns two sets of opposites in a fairly standard manner. The

---

[41] This is true both of the general claim that the moon shares its light with the sun and, as Mourelatos (2008) 224–5 notes, of the specific description of the moon as νυκτιφαές, an adjective which 'combines the predicates of darkness and light'.

[42] Kirk, Raven, and Schofield (1983) 260 emphasize the significance of Parmenides' choice of an explanation in terms of 'interaction and harmony of opposite powers' over the processes of 'separation from an original unity' preferred by the Milesians. Presumably Parmenides felt that the arguments of the *Aletheia* successfully disproved the possibility of genesis out of a unity. The *Doxa* offers an account with the minimal number of principles necessary to describe change and plurality. It goes on to demonstrate that any explanation of plurality will necessarily fail both by opening the door to what-is-not and by continually undermining the distinctions on which it must be based.

[43] Thus Plutarch *Adv. Col.* 1114B describes Parmenides as explaining appearances as the result of 'blending (μιγνύς) as elements the bright and the dark'.

testimonia, however, suggest a more problematic set of further associations. Aristotle tells us that 'Parmenides and some others say that women are hotter than men'.[44] In addition, Aëtius tells us that Parmenides associated males with greater density (and perhaps with cold, if north represents cold) and females with greater rarity.[45] If these accounts are correct, we appear to have a system on which the traditional alignments of opposites are, if not overturned, then certainly confused.[46] The association of male and right (generally viewed as positive qualities) with cold and dense (negative qualities) has worried scholars.[47] As a result, attempts have been made to explain away these problematic associations.[48] It is, however, possible to follow Gérard Journée in reading these complexities as a deliberate attempt to highlight the arbitrary nature of the polarities and their associations, as they are established in mortal thinking.[49] The *Doxa* begins with B8's indication of the arbitrary fashion in which mortals establish the fundamental cosmological opposition. Presumably the way in which other oppositions are lined up under the original pair is just as arbitrary. We have also seen that the distinction between different oppositions (Light and Night, male and female, wet and dry) is repeatedly shown to be less than strict, as they are mingled together and physically united. The thought that Parmenides might have further sought to undermine the traditional, presumably arbitrary,

---

[44] *PA* 648a25–31.

[45] Aëtius 5.7.2.

[46] The associations between male and dense on the one hand and female and rare on the other has led some to suggest a further association between male and Parmenides' Night, and female and Light (since Night and Light are described as dense and rare, respectively, in B8.56–9 and B12 suggests that the sexes are opposites which map onto Night and Light). See Journée (2012) 290–3.

[47] The worry is exacerbated by the suggestion in the doxography (e.g. Cicero *Academica* 2.118) that Night is the passive element, since this would, by association, render male passive. See Guthrie (1965) 77–80. As we have seen, there is good reason to think that Parmenides represented his two principles as equals.

[48] Guthrie (1965) 79 suggests that, whilst we can expect Parmenides to maintain a broadly traditional scheme of oppositions at the level of cosmology, the influence of empirical science in embryology may have resulted in more variety of opinion about the role of opposites.

[49] Journée (2012) argues, by emphasizing the connections between the *Doxa* and the *Proem*, that the female-Light/male-Night association is correct.

connections between different sets of opposites seems entirely in keeping with this general approach. Once again we find that the application of the conceptual framework of opposites to the physical world results in its destabilization.

B18, which survives only in a Latin translation, provides a particularly interesting example of the ways in which the *Doxa* problematizes the relation between equal and distinct opposites in a process of combination:

> When a woman and a man both mingle (*miscent*) the seeds of love, the formative power (*uirtus*) from the diverse blood in the veins, maintaining proper proportions, forms well-constituted bodies. For if, when the seed is mingled (*permixto*), the powers should clash, and not produce a unity in the mingled body, Furies will plague with double seed (*gemino uexabunt semine*) the sex of the offspring.[50]

There is good reason to think that B18 describes the interaction of equals. B12 has already indicated that both male and female are subject to the goddess' creative direction in a reciprocal fashion. B18 now suggests that *both* sexes make a contribution of *'formative power'* to the development of the embryo. If this mingling process is a success, the resulting offspring is well formed (*bene condita corpora*). If, however, the two generative contributions do not unify successfully (*nec faciant unam permixto in corpore*) the 'twin seed' will continue to negatively affect the child. The context of the fragment in Caelius Aurelianus presents it as a discussion of the causes of homosexuality, which Parmenides explains as a result of a problematic interaction between male and female. It is striking that the explanation is as a failure of the process of mixture. Here we see another potential problem for the explanatory success of dualism. The process of conception is described as a combination of opposites. If the process succeeds, the result is an appropriate and well-formed unity; a failure of combination equates to maintaining the original separation (and conflict) between the opposites. B18 implies that unity is actually preferable to dualism, at least in so far as the generative process is concerned.

---

[50] Caelius Aurelianus *On Chronic Diseases* 4.9.

Jenny Bryan

Authoritative Confusion?

We have seen that it is possible to identify a variety of ways in which the explanatory and causal role of the *Doxa*'s fundamental dualism is rendered problematic within the details of the cosmology. That the illegitimacy of the dualism is dependent on the introduction of what-is-not is commonly acknowledged. But we have also seen signs of the difficulty of consistently applying this pair (or any related pair) as a sufficient explanation of generation. In describing and explaining the physical world and its generative processes, mortals apply a distinction to which they seem not to be fully committed, as is suggested by the fact that they resort time and again to explanation in terms of unification. The cosmos of the *Doxa* is repeatedly shown to be one in which the *krisis* of Light and Night is inconsistent, unstable and incomplete. The problem is thus not simply that mortals draw up an illegitimate distinction, but also that they repeatedly undermine this distinction in applying it to the cosmos. By blending, unifying and confusing their opposites, mortals demonstrate their ambivalence towards their own arbitrary explanatory distinction.[51]

This line of interpretation provides an explanation for the detailed and extensive nature of Parmenides' cosmology. The comprehensive nature of the account both demonstrates that mortals attempt to apply their explanation generally and makes room for that account to fail in a variety of related ways. B8 indicates that there are problems with the explanatory (and logical and ontological) status of the dualism, but also points to the difficulties that mortals have in applying it to the physical world. The *Doxa* goes on to show how these problems are manifested repeatedly within the cosmological account and, in doing so, makes clear mortals' own general failure to commit to and maintain their original distinction.

We have, in fact, a further explanation as to why Parmenides would want to develop such an account, even once aware

---

[51] In this way, it is the *Doxa*'s κόσμος that is deceptive, in that its dualism masks a preference for unity.

36

Reconsidering the Authority of Parmenides' *Doxa*

of its problems. It is significant that, in failing to maintain their dualism, mortals tend towards explanation in terms of processes of unification. We have seen this in the *Doxa*'s embryology, cosmology, physics, astronomy, and even in the explanatory principles themselves.[52] My suggestion is that, in this way, mortals (including Parmenides) reveal what Mourelatos calls the 'felt attractiveness' of what-is.[53] Mortals establish a dualism and attempt to apply it systematically to the world, but in doing so they reveal their implicit awareness of, or even preference for, the unity, homogeneity, and balance of what-is.[54] For all that their explanation of change and plurality is erroneously dependent on what-is-not, it is also somehow influenced by an awareness of the genuine and superior nature of what-is. Mortals describe change and genesis in a way that is inconsistent, but which hints at the necessary nature of what truly exists. By emphasizing the preference for unity even in a system ostensibly predicated on a dualism, and particularly by demonstrating that unity is fundamental to opposition, Parmenides develops his cosmology to reinforce the nature of what-is as described in the *Aletheia*. Even when mortals appear to be ignorant of the nature of what-is, even when they are committed to plurality, they feel the pull of what-is.

At this point, my analysis of the *Doxa* may seem to have most in common with those that seek to dismiss it as entirely specious, or at least as primarily a critique of mortal thought. Can it make sense to claim that Parmenides is committed to the details of an explicitly inconsistent account? Perhaps it can, if Parmenides believes that there is *no* way to describe change and plurality except in these terms, so that it will be impossible to produce a cosmology free from such inconsistency.[55] Note that the problem is not simply that it is not

---

[52] Note that B16 offers an account of perception in terms of union (κρᾶσις). See Johansen (2015) 22–3 and Tor (2015) 9–14.

[53] Mourelatos (2008) 260.

[54] Johansen (2015) 15–6 interprets the presence of mixture in the *Doxa* as evidence of the cosmos' status as a likeness of what-is.

[55] See Tor (2015) 19. We may worry that a scrupulous philosopher such as Parmenides should avoid admitting to inconsistent beliefs. Perhaps it is not so objectionable

possible to produce a cosmology that avoids talk of what-is-not. For the *Doxa* also suggests that any distinction based on the introduction of what-is-not will be so weak as to be of little or no explanatory value. Parmenides is a mortal who perceives the world around him as one of change and plurality. There is no way for him to give an account of that world except by making room for what-is-not, i.e. by setting up multiple principles identified in distinction from one another. Nor is it possible to give such an account in a way that maintains the distinction in a strict fashion, once it is applied to physical entities and, particularly, to processes of generation. Nevertheless, the account is worth developing precisely to show how it must necessarily fail, and so its failure is not a bar to, but rather a justification for Parmenides' own development of a cosmology.

In addition, we have seen that Parmenides' cosmology has a positive purpose. In attempting an explanation of the world, he draws out the implicit awareness of what-is which seems both to underpin and to undermine its pluralism. Parmenides develops a cosmology not simply to show where it errs, but also to show where it tends towards truth.[56] A legitimate account of change, which excludes what-is-not, is impossible for Parmenides, as for all mortals. The illegitimate account is nonetheless worth giving for the sake of emphasizing both the superiority of the *Aletheia*'s account and mortals' implicit awareness of this superiority. Such a reading of the *Doxa* gives it a significant purpose within the poem. In hearing the cosmology we are encouraged to reflect on what sort of attitude we really take towards plurality within the world. There is perhaps even an optimistic hint that, if even erroneous attempts to explain change show some consistent awareness of what-is, we may not be so far behind the *kouros* in coming to understand

---

to admit to possessing inconsistent beliefs in the context of a suggestion that the perceptible world encourages such inconsistencies. One might acknowledge the apparent impossibility of rendering them consistent without necessarily taking the further step of denying that any are true or worthy of expression.

[56] This is consistent with the way that B8.60's ἐοικώς combines negative and positive implications. See Bryan (2012) 58–113.

Reconsidering the Authority of Parmenides' *Doxa*

it and progressing towards an understanding of its true nature. Parmenides' cosmology can thus be read as a kind of retrospective protreptic towards the route of what-is.

It is worth emphasizing that both of these purposes are better served by a cosmology that provides as comprehensive and plausible account of the world as is possible. Parmenides will persuade no one of either the failings or, perhaps more importantly, positive value of cosmology if his own attempt is unattractive or partial. If Parmenides' purpose with the *Doxa* is to help us to see that the way we think about the world of change actually points towards the truths of the *Aletheia*, then it makes sense for his cosmology to aim at the very least to provide an attempt to get to grips with the phenomena of that world. In fact, one could read the *Doxa*'s failings as lying in its attempts to explain, as opposed to describe. It can pick out plural phenomena and point to instances of change, but what it cannot do is provide a consistent and universal explanation of such things. It is also worth noting that Parmenides' worries about the difficulty or impossibility of talking consistently about generation need not be assumed to map onto an absolute denial of the world of change. Indeed, the fact that an awareness of what-is reveals itself even in our talk of plurality may suggest that the visible cosmos itself is not entirely disconnected from what-is.[57] Here, I think it is worth noting that both the astronomical novelties attributed to Parmenides by the doxographical tradition are observations that two things (the morning and evening star, the light of the sun and the light of the moon) are identical. Even as an astronomer, Parmenides seems to be interested in unification. Discussions of Parmenides' scientific endeavours are necessarily speculative, but it is interesting to consider the possibility that he saw evidence of the unified nature of what-is not only in the way

---

[57] The reintroduction of what-is-not is the source of the *Doxa*'s problems, but we must not lose sight of the fact that the cosmos is characterized as a combination of what-is-not *and what-is*. Perhaps the latter gives some value to mortal thought. This may also be suggested by the verbal echoes of the *Aletheia* within the *Doxa*. See Johansen's (2015) suggestion that the cosmos of the *Doxa* possesses some value as a likeness of what-is.

that mortals explain the natural world but even in the natural world itself.[58]

Conclusion

I have suggested that the *Doxa* possesses doctrinal authority in various ways. Parmenides is committed to its content as a critique of the necessary failings of explanations of change. He is also committed to it as revealing the implicit awareness of being that is revealed even in such unsuccessful accounts. Neither purpose is incompatible with Parmenides' own commitment to the details of the cosmological system as it is described. Indeed, once we understand its purpose, we can see the value in his providing a persuasive and comprehensive attempt to explain the world around us. The conclusions of the *Aletheia* are novel and challenging. Parmenides offers the *Doxa* as an attempt to show that, even in thinking about change, we have one foot on the Way of Truth.

---

[58] Similarly, Popper (1998) 96 suggests that Parmenides' rejection of sense perception is linked to his realization that the moon's observed changes are at odds with its reality.

CHAPTER 2

AUTHORITY AND THE DIALECTIC OF SOCRATES

NICHOLAS DENYER*

Socrates was the author of a hymn to Apollo and versifications of Aesopic fables. He was not the author of anything philosophical.[1] Socrates acknowledged the authority of gods, of Athenian law, and of his commanding officers.[2] He did not acknowledge any philosophical authority. Nor indeed did he claim any philosophical authority for himself. If Socrates belongs in a volume on Authors and Authorities, that is because, in line with the old slogan that 'For any one pair of opposites, there is a single branch of knowledge', he can illuminate philosophical authorship and philosophical authority by being so distant from them both.

If I want you to accept something, but do not have the authority that entitles you to take my word for it, then I must show you the thing in such a way that you can see it for yourself. For instance, I might turn out my pockets to show you that they are empty. But not all showing is as straightforward as that. Showing you something philosophical is more like showing you something in mathematics: I have to do it by presenting you with argumentation and reasoning.

Reasoning sometimes comes as an uninterrupted monologue, and sometimes as a dialectical sequence of questions and answers. Of course, not all reasoning is equally happy in either format. Imagine an argument for solipsism which concludes with: 'So you agree then that nothing exists apart from me?'

---

* In honour of David Sedley, who asks good questions and answers them.
[1] The evidence, such as it is, for Socrates' own writings, such as they were, is gathered in West (1972) vol. 2, 118–19.
[2] Gods: e.g. Plato *Apology* 21b, *Phaedo* 60d–61a. Athenian law: e.g. Plato *Crito* 50a–54e, Xenophon *Memorabilia* 4.4.1–4. Commanding officers: Plato *Apology* 28e.

41

'Indeed, I do agree; for you alone exist.' Or imagine an uninterrupted monologue which argues that the only arguments worth considering are dialectical. Sometimes Socrates' arguments verge on such incongruity; for example, in a speech addressed to Callicles at Plato *Gorgias* 486e–488a, he hymns dialectic monologically. More often, however, what Socrates argues does not by its content demand exposition in only one format. As Demetrius *On style* 296–7 points out:

In general, just as the same wax can be moulded into a dog by one person, into an ox by another, and into a horse by a third, so too the same material can be presented by one person in declarations and assertions ('People bequeath property to their children, but they do not bequeath with it the knowledge of handling their bequest' – this kind of expression is called Aristippean), while another will put forward the same material by way of insinuation, as often in Xenophon (such as 'For people should bequeath to their children, not only property, but also the knowledge of handling it'), while what is called the distinctively Socratic kind (of which Aeschines and Plato are thought to be the greatest aficionados) would transform the material we have described into questioning along some such lines as this: '"My boy, how much property did your father bequeath you? Quite a lot, I presume, and not easily totted up." "Yes Socrates, a lot." "So did he also then leave you the knowledge of handling it?"'

Since Socrates' reasoning could so often be presented in other modes, it is consequently all the more striking that, as Demetrius also points out, Socrates' favourite way of reasoning with people should be by getting them to answer his questions. But what is so good about question and answer?

In Plato *Protagoras* 334c–d, Socrates asks Protagoras to confine himself to brisk question and answer, on the grounds that Socrates' memory is too poor to cope with a long speech. But Socrates' poor memory, and his consequent inability to cope with a long speech, are manifest fictions. The last 52 Stephanus pages of the *Protagoras* are a single long speech by Socrates, as are the 20 pages of the *Lysis*, the 23 of the *Charmides*, and the 294 of the *Republic*. If you think that a long speech like this is a swizz, since it narrates a conversation consisting of shorter speeches, then recollect that Socrates often delivers long speeches that are not themselves narrated conversation: some examples are the Myth of Er in Plato *Republic* 614b–621d, the

Authority and the Dialectic of Socrates

exposition of Simonides in Plato *Protagoras* 342a–347a, and the Palinode about love in Plato *Phaedrus* 243e–257b. In any case 'long speech' (μακρὸς λόγος) is just an idiomatic term for the sort of rambling speech thought characteristic of slaves (Aristotle *Metaphysics* 1091a8–9, Euripides *Iphigeneia in Aulis* 313): it expresses disdain for a kind of speech contrasted with brisk question and answer, but it does not really give the grounds of that disdain.

We get closer to Socrates' grounds for preferring question and answer, when we reflect that a long speech is rhetoric, apt for bamboozling a mass audience, while an exchange of shorter speeches by contrast allows for pedantic focus on detail after detail. This contrast is explicit at the start of the Melian Dialogue (Thucydides 5.84–5), which I quote in the translation of Thomas Hobbes:

These ambassadors the Melians refused to bring before the multitude; but commanded them to deliver their message before the magistrates and the few; and they accordingly said as followeth: Athenians. 'Since we may not speak to the multitude, for fear lest when they hear our persuasive and unanswerable arguments all at once in a continued oration, they should chance to be seduced (for we know that this is the scope of your bringing us to audience before the few), make surer yet that point, you that sit here: answer you also to every particular, not in a set speech, but presently interrupting us, whensoever anything shall be said by us which shall seem unto you to be otherwise. And first answer us whether you like this motion or not?'

Here the Athenians take it to be a sign of the strength of their argument that it does not need continuous exposition before a mass audience to make it seem plausible. Plato's Hippias (*Hippias Minor* 369b–c) draws the same contrast between rhetoric and dialectic, only to suggest that it is a weakness of Socrates' argument that it could not win a vote when presented as a single long speech:

You, Socrates, are always weaving arguments like this: you pull out the most tricky bit of an argument, and keep hold of it, fixing on it detail by detail, and you don't engage with the general theme of the argument. For here is a case in point: I will, if you like, demonstrate to you by powerful argument, based on a lot of evidence, that Homer made Achilles better than Odysseus, and no liar, and made Odysseus deceitful and full of lies and worse than Achilles; and

43

> you, if you like, take your turn and contend with my argument by setting forth
> your own argument that Odysseus was better. Then these people here will know
> more fully which of us speaks better.

Yet even though Socrates does prefer dialectic to rhetoric, he does not uniformly disdain all rhetoric.[3] He has different attitudes to each of the three kinds into which rhetoric has been divided since Aristotle *Rhetoric* 1358a36–b29 drew his distinctions between epideictic, dicanic, and sumbouleutic.

The speaker of a sumbouleutic speech attempts to persuade an assembly of the wisdom of some proposal for future action. The speaker of a dicanic speech attempts to persuade a jury of the justice of his case, and the injustice of his opponent's. Not so the speaker of an epideictic speech, or display orator. 'Some [speeches] should be persuasive, others apt for display' (Demosthenes 61.2). 'Someone who is not just giving a display, but actually means to achieve something, must search out those arguments that will persuade this pair of cities' (Isocrates 4.17). The speaker of an epideictic speech does not attempt to persuade us of anything, except perhaps of his own virtuosity as a speaker. When he praises Athens in a funerary oration, like those in Thucydides 2.35–46, Demosthenes 60, and Lysias 2, the Athenian audience are already convinced anyway that theirs is a very splendid city. When, like Gorgias (B 11), he argues that Helen of Troy was an innocent victim of *force majeure*, the audience will be delighted at the audacity with which he defends the indefensible, but this will no more shift their beliefs about Helen than our beliefs about rabbits and hats are shifted by a conjuror. Or again, an epideictic orator might successfully praise pots and pebbles (Alexander *On starting points for rhetoric* 3.11–12), even though the audience remain as indifferent as ever on the entire issue of pots and pebbles.

---

[3] Much of what follows was sparked by Jamie Dow's 'Socrates' challenge: why dialogue is better than speechmaking', his contribution to the Keeling Colloquium 2013 at University College, London.

Authority and the Dialectic of Socrates

When your speech will not persuade, and is not even intended to persuade, then you need not fear that it will persuade people of anything wrong. Even the austerely and scrupulously honest can therefore indulge in epideictic oratory: hence, for instance, the speech at Plato *Protagoras* 342a–343c, in which Socrates praises the intellectual attainments of the Spartans. In Plato *Symposium* 198d–e, Socrates proposes a standard for proper praise that his speech about the Spartans does not meet:

> In my simplicity, I supposed that one should in every case tell the truth about the subject of the encomium, and, with this as basis, we should select from the truths about it those that are the most beautiful, and present them in the most becoming manner. And I was priding myself on how well I would speak, given my knowledge of the truth about praising a thing. But this turns out, apparently, not to be what it is to praise a thing well. On the contrary, to praise a thing well means offering it the biggest and most beautiful compliments, true or untrue; and if false, never mind.

But not even this more stringent standard prevents Socrates giving, in praise of Love, a speech that is, by the most conventional standard, a marvellous piece of epideictic.

Socrates is much more reluctant to give dicanic and sumbouleutic speeches, speeches of the kind that are meant to persuade. He gives dicanic speeches only at his own trial (Plato *Apology* 17d), and he never gives sumbouleutic speeches at all (Plato *Apology* 31c). In a conversation with Gorgias (Plato *Gorgias* 454e–455a) he gives some rationale for his reluctance:

SOC: So shall we posit two kinds of persuasion, one that gives belief without knowledge, and another that gives knowledge?

GORG: Certainly.

SOC: So which of these is produced by rhetorical persuasion in lawcourts and other mass gatherings about matters of justice and injustice? The one which gives belief without knowledge, or the one which gives knowledge?

GORG: Obviously, Socrates, the one which gives belief.

SOC: Rhetoric, it therefore seems, produces persuasion that gives belief, rather than instruction, about what is or isn't just.

GORG: Yes.

SOC: So the rhetorician has no capacity to instruct lawcourts and other mass gatherings about justice and injustice; his capacity is only to

45

persuade. For one could hardly instruct so big a mass gathering on such large matters in a little time.

GORG: Certainly not.

It is no accident that an orator in democratic Athens cannot hope to instruct a jury, but at best to persuade it without imparting knowledge. The jury was to be representative of the entire citizen body; there was no appeal from it to any higher authority, and it was addressed as 'O men of Athens', the term also used to address the entire Assembly. The entire citizen body of Athens was thought to amount to 'more than thirty thousand' (Plato *Symposium* 175e, Aristophanes *Ecclesiazousai* 1132). Quite how big a sample it takes to be representative of such a body depends of course on how closely we want the sample to match the body as a whole, and on how confident we want to be of that match. For example, statisticians often want to be at least 95 per cent confident that the sample diverges from the population as a whole by less than 5 per cent. If that is what we want – and for decisions with grave consequences we may well want more – then, as a matter of mathematical fact, our juries will have to contain at least 379 jurors. In Athens, they standardly contained at least 500; and for particularly important cases they might contain a multiple of 500. These large juries had to decide many cases (e.g. Aristophanes *Clouds* 206–8, *Peace* 503–5, and *Wasps passim*); and this too can hardly be avoided in a city with a large population of equals, subject to the rule of law, and not divided into the retinues of a handful of competing magnates. Many cases, each of which must be tried by a large jury, means that, if the citizens are to have enough time for other activities, there must be severe limitations on the time that a trial can take. And it is this fact – one might call it the transcendental deduction of the water clock – which ensures that dicanic oratory cannot reasonably hope to achieve the good kind of persuasion, the kind that imparts knowledge.

Here then is a reason for Socrates to shun dicanic oratory so far as lies in his power. And that will mean never bringing prosecutions against others. But it was not in his power to guarantee that others would never bring prosecutions against him. And, as a citizen law-abiding to the point of pedantry, he would have felt obliged, when prosecuted, to attend court and offer a defence. So Socrates eventually had to produce dicanic oratory. But while Socratic principles allowed his epideictic to meet the common standards for good epideictic, they required of him an unusual form of dicanic. He was reluctant to aim at the persuasion that results in mere belief without knowledge, even when the mere belief in which it results is a true belief. For there are things that speakers do in law courts that impart no knowledge but that might get people to form beliefs. In Plato's *Apology* Socrates mentions two, and declares that the court cannot expect either from him: stylish speech (17b–c), and a parade of sorrowing dependants (34c). If I am defending myself against criminal charges, then stylish speech or weeping children are simply not evidence that I am innocent – except of course in the unlikely circumstance that the crime with which I am charged is that of never speaking stylishly, or having uniformly dry-eyed children. So there is no need of such things. In fact, there is every need not to have such things: for a juror who sees my children weep, and on that basis concludes that I am innocent of corrupting the young men, has had his judgement corrupted. A good juror must instead 'focus simply and solely on the one question: is what I am saying just or not? For that is the virtue of a judge, as it is the virtue of a speaker to tell the truth' (18a). So whereas Socrates' epideictic oratory might look pretty much like other people's epideictic oratory, his dicanic oratory is going to look much more austere.

What about sumbouleutic oratory? Well, we can dream, as Socrates does in Plato *Gorgias* 504c–e, of an austere oratory that addresses the Assembly, making them just and sensible. But we can do no more than dream. Austere oratory before the Assembly is no more likely to be effective than austere oratory before a jury. And even if an orator deploys all manner of embellishments he is as liable to antagonise the Assembly as to mollify it. According to Ronald A. Knox's study of 41 of those who were most active in Athenian politics, 'only 19, less than half, avoid some kind of political catastrophe at the hands of (or, in the case of voluntary exile, because of fear of) their fellow citizens.'[4] Now these 41 were all more eager to please the demos than Socrates would have been. If those eager to please had a greater than even chance of coming to a sticky end, how much more likely is it that Socrates would have done so too? Socrates is not exaggerating when he says in Plato *Apology* 31d: 'if I had tried to take part in politics, I would have been killed long ago'. So a Socrates will avoid sumbouleutic oratory as far as possible. And that means completely. For while he might be prosecuted and so have to speak in a court, there is no way that he can be forced to speak in the Assembly.

Socrates therefore does not uniformly disdain all rhetoric. And even if he did, that would not explain his preference for question-and-answer dialectic. For question-and-answer dialectic is not the only alternative to addressing a large audience continuously for a time limited by the water clock. Another alternative would be addressing a small audience continuously for an unlimited time. We might call this Mr Gladstone's alternative, in memory of Queen Victoria's complaint that, even in a private audience, 'Mr Gladstone addresses me as if I were a public meeting.' We still need to explain why Socrates does not take Mr Gladstone's alternative. Why insist on question-and-answer? And if question-and-answer is the best way to expound thoughts, why must the person who gives the answers be different from the person who asks the questions? As Callicles asks Socrates in Plato *Gorgias* 505d: 'Couldn't you go through the argument yourself, whether asserting it all by yourself or giving answers to yourself?' Why is it that when, at Plato *Gorgias* 506c–507c, Socrates presents his argument by putting questions to himself, and answering them himself, he would much rather have Callicles do the answering? Or, to put the same question another way round, what do Callicles and others hope to avoid by not answering? Note how Callicles remains silent while in Plato *Gorgias* 515c Socrates says to him:

---

[4] Knox (1985) 143. Knox's figures exclude both assassinations by oligarchs, like those mentioned in Thucydides 8.65.2, and executions by the demos of more obscure politicians, like the six generals mentioned in Xenophon *History of Greece* 1.7.34 and the nine treasury officials mentioned in Antiphon 5.69.

Authority and the Dialectic of Socrates

By this stage, haven't we often agreed that this is how a statesman must act? Have we agreed it, or haven't we? Answer. 'We have agreed.' I will answer on your behalf.

Note again how Protagoras moves from saying yes, to nodding, to just about nodding, to complete lack of response, during the concluding exchange from Plato *Protagoras* 360c–d:

'But manliness,' I [Socrates] said, 'is opposite to cowardice.'
He [Protagoras] said it was.
'And wisdom about what is and isn't scary is opposite to ignorance about these things?'
At this point too, he still nodded his assent.
'And ignorance about these things is cowardice?'
At this point, he just about managed to nod his assent.
'So wisdom about what is and isn't scary is manliness, being opposite to ignorance about these things?'
At this point, he refused to nod his assent any longer; he just kept silent.
And I said 'What's up, Protagoras? You are not saying yes in answer to my questions, and not saying no either?'
'Finish it off yourself,' said he.

Note finally how at Plato *Gorgias* 506c Callicles tells Socrates:

Do the talking yourself, there's a good chap, and finish things off.

Why should it so matter to Socrates and his interlocutors which of them, Socrates or interlocutor, answers his questions? In the first place, when people explicitly state things for themselves, that can turn our – and their – beliefs or suspicions into certain knowledge. There is a neat example in *Much Ado About Nothing*. Beatrice and Benedick have met only to exchange insults. But Benedick is starting to suspect that he loves Beatrice, and, because of what his friends say, to suspect that Beatrice loves him. And her position is of course a mirror of his: Beatrice is starting to suspect that she loves Benedick, and, because of what her friends say, to suspect that Benedick loves her. Then they tell one another that they love one another. Before, they just suspected; now, they know. Likewise, when in Plato *Gorgias* 453b–c Socrates interrogates Gorgias:

As for what this rhetorical persuasion is that you're talking of, and what the subjects are on which it is persuasion, I have no clear knowledge, as you should

49

> be well aware, though I do have my suspicions about what you're talking of, and its subjects. All the same, I will nevertheless ask you what you say this persuasion is that depends on rhetoric, and what you say its subjects are. Now, given that I have my own suspicions, what will be the point of my asking you, rather than speaking myself? It won't be for your sake, but for the sake of the argument, for it to progress in such a way as to make it as plain as possible to us what it is an argument about.

Here it is evident that nothing other than Gorgias' own answer to this question will do.

In the second place, even when both parties already know a fact, an explicit declaration can turn their separate knowledge into what is called common knowledge[5] of that fact. To see this, let's change the example. Suppose I have treated you badly; you know it; and I know it. So what then is the point in my saying to you 'I have treated you badly', when I am only saying something that we both already know? Well, we now not only each know it; we both know that we both know it; and we both know that we both know that we both know it; and so on, *ad infinitum*. Once something is in this way common knowledge between two people, instead of simply being known separately by each of the two, all sorts of new things can happen. For example, you know that my flies are undone; I know that my flies are undone; and, to begin with, we each pretend not to have noticed. I might even realise that you have noticed, but pretend not to have realised this; and you might notice my realisation, and connive at my pretence. But when you tell me that my flies are undone, I decide there is no point in trying to act natural any more, and instead do them up. In short, when something is known by each of several people, but is not common knowledge between them, it is possible to keep up appearances, as in the tea-parties given by the less than opulent gentlefolk in Chapter I of *Cranford* (Gaskell (1853)):

> Everyone ... talked on about household forms and ceremonies as if we all believed that our hostess had a regular servants' hall, second table, with housekeeper and steward, instead of the one little charity-school maiden,

---

[5] There is a classic definition of common knowledge in Lewis (1969) 56.

Authority and the Dialectic of Socrates

whose short ruddy arms could never have been strong enough to carry the tray upstairs, if she had not been assisted in private by her mistress, who now sat in state, pretending not to know what cakes were sent up, though she knew, and we knew, and she knew that we knew, and we knew that she knew that we knew, she had been busy all the morning making tea-bread and sponge-cakes.

When one is not merely the audience of an argument presented monologically, but an interlocutor giving explicit assent to the steps of an argument presented dialectically, then it is common knowledge between all parties to the argument what they all agree on. Thus Xenophon *Symposium* 4.56:

> 'Let us start by agreeing on what it is that a pimp does. And whatever questions I ask, don't you lot hesitate to answer. The idea is that we will know what we are jointly agreed on. Do you accept that?' he [Socrates] said.
> 'Absolutely,' said they; and once they had said 'Absolutely,' they all kept saying this in unison thereafter.

And once it is common knowledge that we have agreed on something, I can hardly avoid agreeing – and indeed giving my explicit assent – when you put to me some evident consequence of what we have agreed on. If I refuse to assent, I simply look sulky or stupid.

This makes dialectical argument peculiarly coercive. It can leave us, as Callicles says in Plato *Gorgias* 482e 'trussed up and gagged'. Xenophon *Memorabilia* 4.6.15 puts essentially the same point in a more long-winded way:

> Whenever he went through something in an argument himself, he would proceed by steps that had the most assent, deeming this to be what makes an argument secure. And that is why, of all those known to me, he got much the most assent from those listening. He said that Homer accorded Odysseus the honour of being 'a secure speaker' [*Odyssey* 8.171] because he was good at taking arguments through steps with which people agreed.

Here 'by steps that had the most assent' translates διὰ τῶν μάλιστα ὁμολογουμένων. Gregory Vlastos translated this phrase originally as 'from the most generally accepted opinions' and later as 'from the most strongly held opinions'. Both earlier and later, he took this phrase to comment on the premises from which Socrates reasoned, and took the entire passage

51

to mean that the premises and conclusions of Socrates' arguments were particularly uncontroversial.[6] As Vlastos himself acknowledged, this interpretation makes Xenophon look silly: for how could Xenophon have thought that Socrates' conclusions were uncontroversial, or that reasoning from uncontroversial premises cannot lead to controversial conclusions? We can be kinder to Xenophon if we interpret him as talking instead of how, at each step of the argument, Socrates compels the interlocutor to signal his assent.

There is one way to answer Socrates' questions without getting trussed and gagged. It is to answer the questions, while making it clear that one does not mean one's answers seriously, that one gives them only to please – or to humour – the questioner. Callicles often does this in Plato's *Gorgias*:

CAL: For quite some time now, Socrates, I have been signalling agreement as I listen to you. I am conscious that, if anyone ever grants you anything, even in play, you delight in seizing on it, as if you were a youngster. (499b)
...

CAL: Let's grant you that, so that you can finish the argument. (510a)
...

SOC: Are we to lay it down that this is so?

CAL: Indeed we are, if that is what you find more pleasant. (514a)
...

SOC: Do you think this, or don't you?

CAL: Indeed I do – that's to gratify you. (516b)

It is in the same spirit that Thrasymachus says this to Socrates in Plato *Republic* 350e:

So either you let me have my say; or, if you want to ask questions, ask away – and I will say 'Right ho!' and nod and shake my head, as one does to old biddies when they are telling their tales.

The idea is to spoil Socrates' victory by making it look easy.

There is a comparison and a contrast to be drawn with an incident in Chapter 33 of *Catch 22* (Heller (1961)), when

---

[6] Vlastos (1983), reprinted in Fine (1999) 36–63 (which translates 'most generally accepted' on p. 49), and much revised as Chapter 1 of Vlastos (1994) (which translates 'most strongly held' on p. 14).

52

some Americans try to force an Italian to say uncle, that is, to acknowledge that they have her beat:

'Say uncle,' they said to her.
'Uncle,' she said.
'No, no. Say uncle.'
'Uncle,' she said.
'She still doesn't understand.'
'You still don't understand, do you? We can't really make you say uncle unless you don't want to say uncle. Don't you see? Don't say uncle when I tell you to say uncle. Okay? Say uncle.'
'Uncle,' she said.
'No, don't say uncle. Say uncle.'
She didn't say uncle.
'That's good!'
'That's very good.'
'It's a start. Now say uncle.'
'Uncle,' she said.
'It's no good.'

The Americans are not satisfied when the Italian promptly says uncle. So too Socrates is not satisfied when Thrasymachus and Callicles promptly agree with him. That is the comparison. The contrast is that because the Italian has absolutely no concern for or even awareness of the kind of victory that the Americans seek, she effortlessly makes the Americans' victory worthless, whereas Thrasymachus and Callicles, in striving to engineer the effect that the Italian accomplished so effortlessly, betray their fear that they will otherwise suffer an overtly humiliating defeat. In consequence, when Socrates reduces people to saying 'I will answer this way, but only to humour you', he has a victory of sorts. But his victory is not as comprehensive as it would be if the interlocutors engaged more seriously in the contest.

How then can Socrates get people, not merely to offer answers to his questions, but to offer them in a suitably serious spirit? Seriousness can have no simple warrant. If it did, Socrates could not so easily be suspected of teasing and dissimulation. But there are verbal devices that come as close as any verbal device can to ensuring seriousness, and Socrates makes ready use of such devices. Thus Socrates invokes the

Nicholas Denyer

name of Zeus, God of Friendship, to ask Euthyphro and Callicles to be serious (Plato *Euthyphro* 6b, *Gorgias* 500b, 519e), just as he invokes the same name to assure Alcibiades of his own seriousness (Plato *Alcibiades Major* 109d), and just as Phaedrus invokes the same name to ask him to be serious (Plato *Phaedrus* 234e). Another such device is switching from first or second person pronouns to using someone's name and title in a third person statement, as if solemnly minuting a declaration of his. Thus there is this exchange between Socrates and Callicles in Plato *Gorgias* 495d–e:

SOC: Come now, let us make a mental note of this: Callicles, from the deme of Acharnae, said that pleasant and good are the same thing, and that knowledge and manliness are different both from one another and from the good.

CAL: But does Socrates from the deme of Alopeke agree or not agree with us on these points?

SOC: He does not agree. And I think that Callicles will not agree either, once he has a proper view of himself.

Socrates uses the same device in two remarks from Plato's *Alcibiades Major*, both addressed to Alcibiades:

So it was stated that, on questions of justice and injustice. Alcibiades the Handsome, the son of Cleinias, has no knowledge, though he thinks he does, and is going to go to the Assembly to advise the Athenians about something about which he knows nothing? Wasn't that it? (113b)

...

Alcibiades the son of Cleinias, has not had, so it seems, and does not have now, any lover apart from one alone, and that, one with whom he has to be content, Socrates the son of Sophroniscus and Phaenarete. (131e)

In Plato *Theaetetus* 160d–e, Socrates uses a modest form of this device to Theaetetus, whose proposal that knowledge is perception he enters into the record using only the name 'Theaetetus'. It is those more slippery than Theaetetus who need also demotics and patronymics to ensure their seriousness.

Suppose that by these or other means Socrates does extract serious answers, and that his interlocutor does get trussed and gagged, that is, does get rendered incapable of denying the point for which Socrates is arguing. This does not yet mean

Authority and the Dialectic of Socrates

that Socrates has proved that point to the interlocutor. For assent can be extorted by dialectical argument, without persuasion of any kind, let alone the kind that imparts knowledge. In Plato *Republic* 487b–c, Adeimantus points this out, making a beautiful comparison between losing in dialectic and losing in a board game like chess or draughts:

> Socrates, nobody could contradict you on these points. But the fact is that whenever people hear you say what you're saying now, it has the following effect on them: they suppose that because they have no experience of question and answer, they get led astray by the argument, a little bit astray at each question; and when the little bits are put together at the end of the argument, their error turns out massive, quite the opposite of what they said at first. Just as, at the end of a game, people who are skilled at *petteia* leave those who are unskilled blocked in and unable to move, so too, at the end of a discussion, people feel blocked in and unable to speak, because of this other, as it were, *petteia*, played not with counters but with words. This is because they think that the truth is, for all that they have been defeated, not any more as you say.

The beauty of this comparison is how it demonstrates that reluctance to believe in your heart what you have been forced to accept with your lips need not be a sign of perversity. For if you lack skill in the board game, then you might lose a position from which you could have forced a win, had you but known how. And if you are wise enough to be aware of your lack of skill, then you will rightly allow that perhaps it, rather than any objective deficiency in the position you had to start with, explains your defeat.

However, even if the argument does not prove to the interlocutor its ostensible conclusion, it still proves something. For it proves that, whether or not the interlocutor is perverse in refusing to believe the ostensible conclusion, there is something wrong with the interlocutor somewhere. For if you are now right in refusing to believe what you are forced to say at the final stage of the argument, then you were wrong at earlier stages, either in the premises you accepted, or in the inferences you made from them, or both. And this you can hardly deny, however complacently you may insist that you could easily have done better. For example, in Plato's *Hippias Major*, even Hippias has to acknowledge that he has been shown up, although he tries to minimise

Nicholas Denyer

this by suggesting that he could easily do better if given a bit more time to think, unharassed by Socrates' questions:

> SOC: But, comrade, let's not give up just yet. For I still have some hope of making it clear just what the beautiful is.
>
> HIP: Of course, Socrates; that's not hard to discover. For I know well that if I had a short while in private to look at it by myself, I could tell you it more exactly than exactness in its entirety. (295a)
> ...
> SOC: As for me, I've no idea any longer where to turn; I'm at a dead end. But what about you? Can you say anything?
>
> HIP: Not just at the moment; but, as I was saying just now, once I have had a look, I know I will discover it. (297d–e)

Hippias has his pride, and that stops him acknowledging quite how deep are the roots of his failure to understand the beautiful. But that he suffers from some such failure is guaranteed by the fact that he has been dialectically compelled to admit to some such failure. For if it is dialectical compulsion, and not merely, for example, a wish to be agreeable, that leads to the admission, then he thinks, and does not merely say, that there is something wrong with his thoughts about the beautiful. And if he thinks that there is something wrong with them, then there is something wrong with them. The logic here is akin to the Epimenides paradox: once a Cretan tells us that we cannot always believe everything that a Cretan tells us, then it is bound to be true that we cannot always believe everything that a Cretan tells us.

There are undoubtedly many other ways to demonstrate that Hippias has only a faulty understanding of the beautiful. When Socrates demonstrates it by dialectically compelling him to admit it, the demonstration has a special merit that not all others share. For the demonstration is a demonstration, not just to the wise, or to ideal pupils, but to Hippias himself. For Hippias himself now comes to know what he has been forced to admit. And only his own admission can give him this knowledge. The united assurances of others could not. In Plato *Gorgias* 474a, Socrates says to Polus:

Authority and the Dialectic of Socrates

Whatever I am saying, I know to produce one witness for it, the very person to whom I am saying it, and I ignore the masses; and I know to put the issue to a vote of one person, but with the masses I do not so much as exchange a word.

This is simple truth, when what Socrates is saying is that Hippias has not got things straight. Hippias' own authority is the only sufficient authority that he can have for such a thing.

There is a further merit to such a demonstration. It not only makes the fact that Hippias has not got things straight known to him, it also makes that fact common knowledge to every participant in the conversation. They all know it, they all know that they all know it, they all know that they all know that they all know it, and so on indefinitely. Any pretence to the contrary is now no longer possible. This is why having your ignorance demonstrated in this way humiliates so painfully that it can be compared to snakebite, birthpangs and electric shock (Plato *Symposium* 218a, *Theaetetus* 151a, *Meno* 80a), so painfully that Callicles and Protagoras fall silent when such a humiliation looms up, so painfully that you might even be motivated to abandon complacent fantasies about how wise you already are, and set about becoming wise for real. And all this, without anyone having to take Socrates' word for anything. We can revere him for his philosophical expertise in bringing about such demonstration. But if this is his sole philosophical expertise, we cannot revere him as a philosophical authority.

CHAPTER 3

SOCRATIC DISCUSSIONS OF DEATH AND IMMORTALITY IN PLATO

ALEX LONG*

Socrates did not put his philosophy into writing, and he is not straightforwardly an authority, at least if authorities are thought to possess knowledge or expertise. All the same, for many later philosophers the voice that most urgently needed to be heard, on a range of moral, social, and educational questions, was that of Socrates. Sometimes that meant consulting and quoting earlier Socratic writing, but it could also mean – not only in the fourth century BC but even centuries after Socrates' death – composing new Socratic discussions.[1] From the fourth century a revived Socrates contributed to new debates and spoke once again about Athens and some of its most famous fifth-century citizens and visitors. To which debates could Socrates, or rather a fourth-century (or later) Socratic voice, make a contribution? Like other Socratic authors, Plato made Socrates address topics such as love, the virtues, and education, including in particular the intensely problematic education of Alcibiades. But Plato wished to make Socrates speak in further debates, and among them was the question of the human soul's immortality and its future after death, even though it is not at all obvious that a philosopher like Socrates is equipped to answer such a question. The subject of my chapter is how Plato makes Socratic discussions of death and immortality look plausible, especially in the *Phaedo* but also in the *Apology*.

---

* David Sedley guided my doctoral thesis to completion in its final year, and I had the good fortune to continue learning from him when we prepared a new translation of Plato's *Meno* and *Phaedo*. It is a pleasure to join others in paying tribute to his teaching and scholarship. My thanks to the editors, especially Jenny Bryan, for their comments on a previous draft of the paper, and to the Leverhulme Trust.

[1] See for example the voice of Socrates in Seneca's *De uita beata* (25, 26, 27).

Socratic Discussions of Death and Immortality

What could give *Socrates* access to such difficult subjects? Socrates' philosophical range is not static in Plato, but Plato expands it in a dialectical, not an authoritarian, spirit: he finds a way to connect the new topic – in this case death and immortality – with less controversially Socratic topics.

Death in the *Apology*

We can begin by considering why Plato makes Socrates speak about death and immortality. The most obvious stimulus is Plato's decision to write about Socrates' trial and execution. Plato explores in the *Apology* and *Crito* the decisions and actions that led to Socrates' death: his conduct in life, his speech in his trial and then his remaining in prison despite an opportunity to escape. As we will see shortly, Plato does not suggest that Socrates took those decisions with a view to gaining a superior kind of existence after death: instead, the explanations are that Socrates' obligations to the gods required him to continue pursuing philosophy,[2] and, in the *Crito*, that political obligations required him to remain in prison. All the same, Plato tries to show that these theologically and politically motivated decisions did not, despite appearances, harm Socrates, and in the *Apology*, as in the *Phaedo*, that requires some discussion of what death will involve for Socrates and his soul. And Socrates himself must deliver or at least participate in the discussion, if readers are to see that he went to his death fully aware that he had not brought harm on himself by refusing to yield to his jurors – or to friends, such as Crito, who tried to rescue him from death. Somehow, then, Socrates himself must become a guide, if not exactly an authority, on the subjects of death and immortality.

In the *Apology* Socrates discusses death more than once. He treats the subject at some length both before the jurors find him guilty (29a–d) and then again after he has been condemned to death (40a–42a). Only in the second passage does Socrates argue that death is a good (40c). In the first passage, by contrast,

---

[2] *Apology* 21e, 28e, 29d, 30a, 37e.

59

he says that he does not know whether it is good or bad. This does not show confusion on Plato's part.[3] In the earlier parts of the speech Socrates must take *some* attitude to death if he is to explain why the threat of death will not make him abandon his usual mode of philosophizing. Nevertheless, it is better to avoid suggesting that during his trial, and previously in his life, Socrates regarded death as something *good*. Plato has already had Socrates argue that he questioned others and, if released, intended to carry on questioning them, even if that put his life in danger, out of obedience to a divine command. To have Socrates now make the claim that death is good or beneficial might suggest a different explanation: he was actively seeking death, and so was trying to provoke the Athenians to put him on trial and then execute him. Arguments that death is good, however tentative they may be, must wait until after the jurors have not only found Socrates guilty but chosen death as his penalty;[4] at that point the question of what has been motivating him in his life and trial recedes, and the condemned Socrates can argue, without unwelcome implications, that there is something good or better awaiting him.

How does Socrates arrive at his two different positions about death? Plato uses Socrates' recognition of his own ignorance to explain his attitude towards death when he still had a chance of avoiding it. Socrates has already said that he is distinguished from others by being aware – finding the suitable cognitive term is difficult[5] – of his lack of knowledge or wisdom (21b, 23b). His attitude to death is then presented as an example of this recognition or awareness of the lack of knowledge. Other people show by their fear of death that they suppose themselves to have knowledge or wisdom about it (29a),[6] whereas Socrates

---

[3] Compare Rudebusch (1999) 72.

[4] Notice that when Socrates has been found guilty, but the death penalty has not yet been chosen, he still professes ignorance about whether death is good or evil (37b).

[5] See Fine (2008).

[6] Must a fearful person believe himself to have knowledge about the object of his fear? We might say out of charity that Socrates means that the particular way in which people fear death (e.g. they would suffer anything else rather than die) shows that kind of false belief, and we could cite in support of that 29a9–b1 ('they fear it as if they knew for sure that it is the greatest of evils'). But before that Socrates says more generally that 'fearing death' is to think oneself wise (29a5–6).

Socratic Discussions of Death and Immortality

both lacks 'sufficient' knowledge about Hades and *recognizes* this lack in himself (29b). Socrates does not say what 'sufficient' knowledge would amount to, but it must at least include knowledge of whether or not death is a good, and Socrates himself lacks that knowledge (29b).[7] But he does know that injustice and disobedience to a divine or human superior are evils (29b), and whenever the choice is between known evils and death, he will avoid the former (29b–c).[8] Even though, as I have suggested, Plato cannot yet make Socrates suggest that death is a good, he also needs to give Socrates some way to compare death with the alternatives, and he makes recognized ignorance about death, together with knowledge of the evil of injustice, the basis of the comparison.

After Socrates has been condemned to death, the goodness of his death can safely be defended, if tentatively: he says that being condemned to death was 'probably' good for him (40b).[9] In Plato's literary fiction it is Socrates' divine sign that prompts him to consider death again: its non-intervention, despite the outcome of the trial, gives him some reason for considering his death a good (40a–c). The timing is dramatically plausible: he now knows that he faces the penalty of death, rather than an acquittal, or some other penalty, and so now it is natural to consider why the divine sign has not tried to avert death. Strictly speaking, the non-intervention of his sign may show merely that death is not an evil: perhaps all the available

---

[7] Previously he has said that nobody knows whether or not death is the *greatest* good (29a). One could fail to know this but still know that death is a good. But in that earlier passage he is criticizing the fear of death as the greatest of evils, and the criticism is made rhetorically more effective by mentioning the possibility that, on the contrary, death may be the greatest of goods.

[8] Lesher (1987) 280 discusses Socrates' claim to knowledge here.

[9] At the end of the dialogue he says that it is clear only to god whether death will be better for him than life will be for his jurors, or at least the jurors who found him innocent (42a). He may still be confident that death will be better for him than continued life would be *for him*, given the 'troubles' that he faces (41d). The involvement of his jurors, and their interests, throughout this section is a complication that I cannot consider thoroughly here. Socrates is trying to extract from his experience something useful for the jurors who found him innocent (39e), and that encourages him to consider not only the goodness of his own death, as compared with continued life for him, but the goodness or badness of death for them too. For example, he reminds them how *they* would value talking with the very greatest poets (41a).

61

alternatives to death (life in Athens, life in exile) in some way involve harm, and so, if death is neither good nor evil, there would be no reason to protect Socrates from it. But Socrates tries all the same to show that, whether death is annihilation or translocation, it provides positive benefits, at least on the assumption that translocation involves what is 'said' about it (40c, 40e, 41c), particularly the company of heroes and poets.[10]

In both passages Plato connects the discussion of death to something recognizably Socratic – first the recognition of epistemic lacks or limitations, and then Socrates' divine sign – although the precise nature of the connection differs in the two passages. The non-intervention of the divine sign is, given the circumstances, sufficient evidence in itself that Socrates' death is no less in his interests than further life would be, although Socrates then argues, independently of the sign, that his death must be a good, given that the only two outcomes to which death could lead are both good. By contrast, the comparison between death and injustice never depends solely on Socrates' recognition of his ignorance about the former; it further requires Socrates to know that being unjust and disobeying a superior are evils, and to base his acts of avoidance on knowledge of evil. But both passages suggest that when Plato takes Socrates into the difficult subject of death and the afterlife, he does not ignore the fact that Socrates is the speaker. He tries to find Socratic points of entry into the subject.

Socrates, the Socratic, and the *Phaedo*

No Platonic dialogue is as preoccupied with death and immortality as the *Phaedo*, the dialogue that actually describes Socrates' death. At first sight it is hard to say to what extent the *Phaedo* is really about Socrates and his own philosophy. On the one hand, it would seem odd to deny it, particularly given the passages in the dialogue that praise Socrates. We must of course remember that the praise of Socrates is delivered by the narrator Phaedo, not by Plato directly, and Phaedo is

[10] For the argument, see Rudebusch (1999) 65–79.

Socratic Discussions of Death and Immortality

represented as a loyal and even devoted follower of Socrates.[11] But even at the most emotionally charged moment of the dialogue – the ending – Phaedo's praise is precise and not a careless outburst.[12] Phaedo declares Socrates to have been the best, wisest and most just of the men known by them at that time (118a16–17). The qualification ('of those whom we came to know in those days') leaves room for the possibility that Socrates had an equal or even superior contemporary somewhere else in the world, or that his followers might yet meet such a person.[13] Phaedo is not made to say more than he could possibly know, such as that Socrates was wiser or more just than anyone who had ever lived. Similarly, when Phaedo describes how Socrates rescued them from their doubts he is not made to exaggerate:

> Well, Echecrates, I'd often admired Socrates, but I never respected him more than when I was with him then. Now perhaps there is nothing surprising in his having something to say. But I particularly admired in him first how pleasantly, genially and respectfully he took in the young men's argument, then how discerningly he noticed the effect the arguments had had on us, and next how well he cured us and rallied us when we'd taken to our heels in defeat, so to speak, and spurred us on to follow at his side and consider the argument with him. (88e5–89a8)

Simmias retains some doubt at the end of the discussion (107a8–b3), so it would be an exaggeration to say that Socrates showed conclusively, and to everyone's satisfaction, that the soul is immortal. But that is not what Phaedo says. He says rather that Socrates cured the effect that they were feeling[14]

---

[11] See Long (2013) 74–86. For the character of Phaedo, see also Sedley (1995) and Boys-Stones (2004).

[12] My thanks to Sarah Broadie for drawing this to my attention.

[13] Not Plato, whom Phaedo already knows (59b10).

[14] This must be the paralysing effect of their suspicions that (1) they are worthless at judging arguments, and (2) the subject of discussion, namely the soul's immortality, does not allow for conviction (88c1–7). These concerns are then addressed in the discussion of hating arguments (89d1–91c6). It is true that Simmias' doubts at 107a8–b3 are reminiscent of (1) and (2): he draws a contrast between human weakness and the vast size of the subject. But there is still a cure for him: he is encouraged, and agrees (107b10), to join the group in considering the hypotheses of the argument. Whether or not Socrates agrees with Simmias about human weakness, he resists any suggestion that Simmias and the others should not rely on their own judgement about arguments.

63

and directed their attention to the shared examination of an argument. That is exactly where the discussion of the Last Argument leads: the group must carry on considering it and the hypotheses on which it relies (107b4–9). No doubt Phaedo's praise is meant to indicate the character's attitude to Socrates, but it is also written in such a way as to match, with some precision, Socrates' achievements in the dialogue. That suggests that it would be wrong to distance Phaedo's praise of Socrates from the author Plato.[15]

On the other hand, if the *Phaedo* really is a tribute to Socrates, then, we might think, at least some of the philosophical resources used in the defence of immortality should be his. That is, we would expect to see how *Socrates* could lead an inquiry into immortality. But instead it looks as if Plato is showing how his own theories, particularly concerning recollection and Forms, offer insights into that subject. David Sedley has argued that by making Socrates' interlocutors Simmias and Cebes, who have spent time with the Pythagorean Philolaus (61d), Plato intends to show that his own philosophy is a surer guide than Pythagoreanism: 'while Pythagoreanism merely confuses them (that is, Simmias and Cebes), Platonism enlightens them'.[16] Where then does that leave Socrates, who is, on the face of it, the dialogue's honorand?

It must be acknowledged that the theories we call 'Platonic' – Forms and recollection – are strongly associated with Socrates in the *Phaedo*. According to Cebes, Socrates has the habit of 'often' propounding the doctrine of recollection (70e). Socrates himself suggests that Forms, such as Goodness and Justice, have been the subject of their previous question-and-answer conversations (75c–d, 76d), and Simmias and Cebes do not respond to this with any surprise. We might take this to show that there should be no distinction between 'Socratic' and 'Platonic' theories,[17] or between the contributions to

[15] It is true that Phaedo also narrates Socrates' achievements. But as author Plato remains in control, and it was up to him to decide whether or not to introduce some discrepancy between the narrative and Phaedo's praise.

[16] Sedley (1995) 13.

[17] See in particular Rowe's study of Plato as a lifelong Socratic (2007). Compare Gill (2013) 116; Notomi (2013) 52.

Socratic Discussions of Death and Immortality

philosophy belonging to Socrates and to Plato. And it might be thought that any such distinction must depend on questionable assumptions about the historical Socrates.

It would, however, be wrong to assume that the only senses that can be given to 'Socratic' are (1) belonging to the historical Socrates, or (2) belonging to Socrates as represented by Plato, or some other *individual* author.[18] Even though Plato attributed to Socrates theories about Forms and recollection, he was evidently aware of other Socratic authors, such as Antisthenes and Phaedo, who did not attribute such theories to Socrates, for although he tends to keep very quiet about contemporary authors, some of them – Antisthenes, Aeschines, Euclides and Phaedo – are actually present in the *Phaedo*. Another, Aristippus, is mentioned but said to have been absent (59b–c). No matter how much Simmias and Cebes concede in the fiction of the dialogue, Plato could not have been unaware that these contemporary Socratic authors were offering their own accounts of Socrates and even, on occasion, writing against Plato himself.[19] Looking to fourth-century literature, not to the historical philosopher, we can distinguish between *more and less controversial* attributions to Socrates. If it was controversial, in this fourth-century context, to say that Socrates took the objects of definition to be Forms, it was less controversial to say that Socrates was interested in education, or that he had a special interest or expertise in erotic matters, or that he was a champion of consistency (between the various things one says, and between what one says and what one does), given that other Socratic authors attributed these interests or commitments to him.[20] This comment on fourth-century writing relies on no assumptions at all about the historical Socrates, even though we may suspect that there

---

[18] Contrast the second chapter of Vlastos (1991) ('Socrates *contra* Socrates in Plato').

[19] For the attack on Plato in Antisthenes' dialogue *Sathon*, see Athenaeus 220d–e, 507a and Diogenes Laertius 3.35. According to Diogenes Laertius 6.16 the dialogue was also called *On Contradiction*.

[20] Aeschines' Socrates advises Callias about the education of his son (SSR [= Giannantoni (1990)] VI A 62); Xenophon's Socrates gives advice to the courtesan Theodote (*Memorabilia* 3.11). For consistency, see Xenophon *Apology* 27 and p.70.

must have been *some* connection between that man and these subjects. So we can remain appropriately neutral about the historical Socrates by framing the question as follows: if the *Phaedo* is, among other things, a tribute to Socrates, we would expect Plato, when apportioning credit for the philosophical achievements of the dialogue, to give a share to what would be recognized as 'Socratic' by other authors of Socratic dialogues. Otherwise the Socrates who is honoured will be recognized as Socrates only by Plato himself and perhaps Plato's followers.

As we saw above, in the *Apology* Plato makes Socrates' claims about death depend, at least in part, on something that is less controversially Socratic: the disavowal of knowledge or wisdom, and then the divine sign, both of which are attributed to Socrates elsewhere in fourth-century writing.[21] It seems unlikely that Plato would not try also in the *Phaedo* to find some connection between the Socratic – again in the sense of less controversially Socratic – and the subjects of death and immortality, given that those subjects are far more central in the *Phaedo* and that there, more than in any other dialogue, he shows his awareness of contemporary Socratic authors.

Socrates' Autobiography and Second Voyage

In what follows I will focus my attention on the part of the *Phaedo* where Socrates, to quote Phaedo's words at 89a, 'rallies' the group. In this long passage (89a–107b) Socrates counters the objections of Simmias and Cebes with arguments against the theory of soul as an 'attunement', his own philosophical autobiography and the so-called 'Last Argument' for the immortality of the soul. Given that this is the part of the dialogue introduced by Phaedo's praise of Socrates (88e–89a, quoted on p.63), it seems the most promising place to look for Socratic achievements. So it is all the more noteworthy

---

[21] The divine sign recurs in Xenophon's portraits of Socrates (*Memorabilia* 1.1.2, 1.1.4, 4.8.5; *Apology* 4, 13; *Symposium* 8.5). Aeschines' Socrates (*SSR* VI A 53) says that he has no expertise or study that he can offer Alcibiades, but thought that his love would enable him to improve Alcibiades.

Socratic Discussions of Death and Immortality

that the discussion is not exclusively about ethics.[22] It is as a dialectician, not a narrowly ethical philosopher, that Socrates can be made to shed light on death and immortality. This is not to say that the passage has no bearing on ethics: Socrates' first step (89a–91c) is to restore their confidence in arguments, and one of the dialogue's major ethical themes concerns the proper use of arguments, the right attitude to them, and their effects on one's life. But in the sections that follow Socrates is somehow able to contribute to debates that, in the later tripartition of philosophy, would belong to physics rather than ethics: he shows that the soul is not an 'attunement' of the qualities present in the body and then that, at least on his own theory of causes, the soul is necessarily immortal. Socrates earns special respect from his friends by discussing the soul's immortality and a competing theory about its nature. How is this possible for him?

The passage that confronts that question is Socrates' autobiography (96a–100b), where he explains his previous inquiry into causes and his current philosophical practice. Perhaps the most striking part of the autobiography is the critique of previous philosophy,[23] especially the cosmology of Anaxagoras, and the call for a more sustained attempt to explain the world as the product of intelligent design (97b–99d). But that critique, despite its high importance for Plato's self-positioning in relation to previous science, occupies only part of the passage. Plato is also facing a different challenge: explaining Socrates' ability to establish the soul's immortality without bestowing on him unwarranted expertise. Plato's awareness of that constraint becomes obvious when Socrates describes himself as not having the right 'nature' (ἀφυής) for inquiry into nature (96c1–3).[24] By the end of the autobiography readers need to see how Socrates can address the question of immortality, but

---

[22] Notomi (2013), a study of Socrates in the *Phaedo*, explores the dialogue's ethical claims and challenges, and its commitment to a 'Socratic ethical ideal' (54, 68).

[23] For a recent analysis, see Menn (2010).

[24] There is probably a pun here (Socrates is ἀφυής for inquiry περὶ φύσεως), as Gábor Betegh has suggested to me.

he cannot simply be transformed, as it were by Platonic *fiat*, into an expert in natural philosophy.

When considering how radically Socrates is being reconceived in the autobiography, we need to distinguish between his philosophical interests and his current method or practice. According to his self-description his interests were, and still are, very wide. In his youth he was eager to discover why things come to be, cease to be and are (96a8–9). His subsequent remarks show that this includes the questions of why things come to have, have, and cease to have certain properties: he gives as an example the causes of a person becoming large and ceasing to be small (96c7–d5, especially d4–5). Such questions could be applied to ethics: how do people come to be good, or cease to be bad, or (if we choose to word the question as the generation of a new item) how does virtue come to be present in people?[25] But these ethical questions are not among the examples Socrates gives. The objects of his curiosity are rather numbers, size, life and intelligence – a very diffuse group.[26] And evidently he retains this range of interests: when he concludes that he was not qualified for that kind of inquiry, he renounces not these objects of inquiry, but merely his initial way of approaching them (97b). He says that he now adopts a different approach of his own to the very same subjects: coming to be, ceasing to be and being (97b4–6).

The reason why Plato makes Socrates have, and retain, such a general interest in causes does not become clear until the last argument for the soul's immortality (102a–107a). That argument will require various causal parallels to the soul. Soul as the cause of life will be paralleled by largeness as the cause of exceeding in size, fire as the cause of being hot, threeness as the cause of being odd. Each of these parallel causes is incapable of taking on the property that is the opposite of the property it causes (largeness cannot become small, fire cannot become cold, threeness cannot become even); similarly the soul, as the

[25] Compare the wording in *Meno* 70a.

[26] Notice that the changes to celestial bodies and the Earth (96c) were merely part of his studies. It is only when the discussion turns to Anaxagoras that Socrates focuses on cosmological questions.

Socratic Discussions of Death and Immortality

cause of life, cannot become dead. As Denyer has shown,[27] these metaphysically diverse parallels enable the argument to accommodate different conceptions of the soul. It does not matter whether soul is corporeal, like fire, or non-corporeal, like threeness, for on either view of the soul the claim about causes has been shown to be true for the relevant kind of item. But then Socrates needs some reasoned commitment to the view that these are the correct causal analyses – that is, that threeness, fire and largeness really are the causes, and so serve as parallels for the soul as the cause of life. Socrates therefore needs to have his own account of causes across all these different areas, and so he needs still to have a correspondingly broad interest in causes. In retrospect we can see that the autobiography has been carefully preparing for the discussion of soul and its parallels in the last argument, for at the start of the autobiography the youthful Socrates is curious about the causes of being alive, having a certain number, and becoming larger (96a–d), the very properties that will return in the last argument.

This feature of the last argument requires Socrates to be given a surprising range of underlying interests. By contrast, the autobiography's description of Socrates' current philosophical *practice* – his so-called 'second voyage' – exploits something more recognizably Socratic: the use of dialectic and attention to logical relationships, particularly that of 'being in harmony' and 'disharmony' (συμφωνεῖν). The second voyage will be illustrated by means of a causal hypothesis about Forms, but from the perspective of a Socratic readership it is introduced in the far less controversial terms of a recourse to λόγοι (theories, claims and arguments).[28] To quote from Socrates, 'I thought I had better take refuge in arguments and consider the truth of things in them' (99e4–6). After Socrates has set off on his second voyage he considers arguments or theories and the relationship between them – not only on the subjects of Forms and causes, but on every other subject too:

---

[27] Denyer (2007) 92–3.
[28] Compare Kanayama (2000), where it is called 'the *logoi* method'.

Alex Long

> On every occasion I hypothesize whatever theory I deem most robust, and then I set down as true whatever I think harmonizes with it – both about cause and about everything else – and as false whatever doesn't. (100a3–7)

The account of Socratic inquiry puts the scrutiny of logical relationships at its centre, and it is hardly eccentric to suggest that Socrates brings claims or theses into relation with another and examines how well they stand together. In Plato's writing this is thematized with particular prominence in the *Gorgias*. Each of its three main exchanges contains some comment on logical 'harmony'. In Socrates' conversation with Gorgias he draws attention to the 'disharmony' between Gorgias' claims about rhetoric (οὐδὲ σύμφωνα, 457e).[29] Socrates then shows Polus that avoiding 'disharmony' (480b) with their previous agreements requires them to accept a claim that Polus would otherwise find incredible (namely that a man guilty of injustice must seek out punishment). Shortly afterwards Callicles is told that Socrates would prefer to have disharmony in a lyre or chorus than to have it within himself – that is, as he explains, to contradict himself (482b–c). The first two passages show how 'disharmony' can be used when challenging interlocutors or when giving them a compelling reason to accept Socrates' conclusion. But it is not only for use against interlocutors: the last passage, where Socrates talks about his own internal harmony, indicates that he examines the fit between *his own* statements. We might compare Xenophon's contrast between Socrates and the sophist Hippias (*Memorabilia* 4.4.6). Hippias mocks Socrates for always saying the same thing, to which Socrates replies, in ironic self-criticism, that he even says the same thing on the same subject, whereas a man as learned as Hippias no doubt never does this. The point is that Socrates, unlike Hippias, takes care not to contradict himself.

In the *Phaedo* the account of the second voyage suggests that the discussion of the soul and its immortality depends on this Socratic preoccupation with logical 'harmony' and

---

[29] At 461a Socrates uses the different phrase οὐ συνᾴδειν as if it were equivalent. Compare *Protagoras* 333a–b (οὐ γὰρ συνᾴδουσιν οὐδὲ συναρμόττουσιν ἀλλήλοις).

70

Socratic Discussions of Death and Immortality

'disharmony'. Before we turn to those arguments, let us see what else Socrates reveals about his second voyage. In the sentence quoted above Socrates has said that he sets down as true what he thinks harmonizes with the most robust hypothesis; he then offers to explain himself (100a7–8), and the term he clarifies is not 'harmonize' but 'robust'. (Modern scholarship has usually found his use of 'harmonize' more puzzling.)[30] He returns to the hypothesis that there is a Beautiful, or Fine, in itself, a Good in itself and so on, and tries to explain what makes explanation in terms of Forms more 'robust' than the alternatives. He envisages a dialectical context, which may perfectly well be an exchange with oneself (100e1–3).[31] The best hypothesis is the one that avoids the objections or difficulties that would be raised, in such a context, against the alternatives (101a5–6). For example, it is 'safe' for Socrates to reply to himself, or to somebody else, that the cause of an object's beauty is the Beautiful or Fine, whereas if he held responsible the object's colour or shape (100d1–2) he himself, or someone else, might object that the very same shape or colour would make a different object ugly.[32] The shape of a fine pipe would be impractical for a lyre, and a face as purple as an iris would not be beautiful.[33]

Socrates thus starts each inquiry by considering which hypothesis will be, in the dialectical context, least open to objections. He then considers the relationship between that hypothesis and other claims, accepting as true what 'harmonizes' with it and rejecting as false what is in disharmony. It is frustrating that Socrates does not explain the musical terms 'harmony' and 'disharmony' as well as 'robustness', but the following at least should be uncontroversial. If two theses are in disharmony, they cannot both be true, for the disharmony between

---

[30] Robinson (1953) 126–36, Gentzler (1991), Bailey (2005).

[31] For further discussion, see A. G. Long (2013) 80–6.

[32] That this would be the objection is suggested by the parallel with size: somebody might object if the suggested cause of largeness could also make something smaller (101a8–9).

[33] The discussion of beauty or fineness in *Hippias Major* (290d–291a) suggests that practicality may be just as relevant as aesthetic appeal. Compare the famous discussion of Socrates' beauty in Xenophon *Symposium* 5.

71

the most robust hypothesis and some other thesis is enough for Socrates to reject the second thesis as false (100a). On the other hand, as scholars have long recognized, if the method is to be at all workable, the presence of 'harmony' cannot be mere consistency: when Socrates has decided which hypothesis is most robust, he does not set down as true *everything* that is consistent with it. But whatever exactly 'harmony' means, this minimal assumption about 'disharmony' – two disharmonious claims cannot both be true – will take us some way in our understanding of the passage.

It is worth emphasizing that Socrates' new practice can be used to expose falsehoods as well as to put together a 'harmonizing' set of claims, even though he sometimes dismisses claims without actually finding them false. For example, when he selects his own causal hypothesis about Forms, the alternative explanations – such as that beauty is caused by colours or shapes – are dismissed (100d2–3) not as false but as less 'safe', and more disturbing for Socrates (100d3), than the hypothesis about Forms. In this passage Socrates is looking for the safe thesis for him and his interlocutors to advance, and he says that Cebes should be wary of offering any alternative explanation, not that each of the alternatives is actually false.[34] This might give the impression that his practice is to construct, albeit selectively, but not to refute, which would be a strange thing to say of Socratic philosophy. But he has said previously that he sets down as *false* the claims that are in disharmony with his chosen hypothesis (100a7), and so obviously the second voyage can be used to refute as well as to construct. The fact that he does not reject, as false, explanation of beauty in terms of colour or shape suggests that these kinds of explanation are not actually in disharmony with his own hypothesis about Forms.[35] And of course they are not in *harmony* with the

---

[34] He suggests that Cebes will admit no other explanation (101a1–5, 101c2–6) not because he has found each of the alternatives false, but merely because the difficulties to which they are open makes him 'fear' endorsing them (101a5, b2, 5, 8). They are not refuted but left for wiser heads to defend (101c8).

[35] Compare the later introduction of more sophisticated explanations (admittedly they are not actually called 'causes', as Denyer (2007) 93 notes), such as that fire is responsible for heat in bodies (105b8–c2). That explanation is not incompatible with

Socratic Discussions of Death and Immortality

hypothesis either, for if they were they would be found true, as the procedure described at 100a3–7 requires. So some pairs of claims stand in neither relationship, 'harmony' or 'disharmony'.[36] One such pair, as we will shortly see, is 'the soul is immortal' and 'the soul is corporeal', which can be contrasted with the disharmonious pair 'the soul is immortal' and 'the soul is the attunement of qualities in the body'.

This suggestion that the second voyage can be used critically is confirmed by a later passage where Socrates tells Cebes how to deal with someone else who is 'clinging' to a hypothesis (ἔχοιτο, 101d3–4): Cebes should consider whether he finds the consequences of the hypothesis to be in 'harmony' or 'disharmony' with each other. That sounds a peculiar test, until we remember that within a dialectical context other premises, to which both parties agree, may be included to show 'disharmony'.[37] (See the discussion of the attunement theory on p.74.) It is tempting to translate the verb as if the other person were *attacking* Cebes' hypothesis, but, as has already been noted,[38] the verb has been used elsewhere in the passage (100d9, 101d2) of commitment to a hypothesis, rather than an attack on it. So, in the situation Socrates imagines, the other person is committed to, or championing, his own hypothesis, not attacking Cebes' hypothesis. Socrates says that in this situation Cebes should consider, before he answers, what follows from the other person's thesis. It is rather odd that Cebes is represented as giving an answer – presumably the point is that Cebes, on being asked whether he too accepts the hypothesis, should consider first what it entails, and only then say yes or no. And if his answer is no, he can surely explain his answer by drawing the interlocutor's attention to the disharmony.

---

holding hotness responsible for their heat; it is less 'ignorant', or, as we might say, more informative. More than one analysis is possible, although the passage gives us no reason to think that Socrates would actually accept explanation of beauty in terms of *colour* or *shape*, particularly given that one and the same shape could cause beauty in one object and ugliness in another, whereas fire can never cause coldness.

[36] So Gallop (1975) 181, although according to Gallop Socrates thinks that explanations of beauty in terms of colour or shape are actually false.

[37] See Robinson (1953) 131–3; Gallop (1975) 166.

[38] See Gallop (1975) 235.

Alex Long

Attunement and the Soul's Immortality

Once it is appreciated that the second voyage can be used to refute as well as to construct, it becomes clear that the discussion of Socrates' practice, especially his looking for 'disharmony', looks backwards as well as forwards.[39] Socrates does not embark on his second voyage for the very first time during the last argument for immortality; it is supposed to have been his procedure ever since his disappointing encounter with Anaxagoras.[40] Directly before the autobiography Socrates argues against the theory of the soul as an attunement, and his arguments rely on the incompatibility between that theory and other claims about musical attunement and the soul. The discussion of attunement may seem a comparatively unimportant passage, but it too is part of the rescue of Socrates' friends that wins him high praise from Phaedo in 88e–89a. The attunement theory (85e3–86d3) was initially used as an analogy to resist an inference from the soul's invisibility and incorporeality to its immortality: Simmias objects that a musical attunement is similarly invisible and incorporeal but nonetheless has a finite duration. But it then becomes more than an analogy: Simmias suggests that the soul really is an attunement of the opposed qualities (hot, cold, wet, dry) in the body, and if so it will be destroyed even sooner than the body at death.

When Socrates argues against the attunement theory he first considers its relationship with claims that they have already accepted, namely (a) learning is recollection of knowledge acquired before birth, and (b) the soul must have existed before birth. The attunement theory – according to which the soul is the blending of hot and cold, wet and dry *in the body* – is incompatible with the thesis that the soul pre-existed the body. As Socrates puts it, using in a pun musical language that obviously prefigures that of the second voyage, the attunement theory is 'discordant' with (συνᾴδειν, 92c3, c6) the theory of recollection and the soul's pre-existence.[41] Simmias

---

[39] Compare Gallop (1975) 157 and 166.
[40] So Kanayama (2000) 96.
[41] It is true that Socrates uses different musical language here (συνᾴδειν rather than συμφωνεῖν), but it would be out of character for Plato to confine himself to one term,

74

Socratic Discussions of Death and Immortality

therefore faces a choice between the theories of recollection and attunement, and his criterion for making the choice is the credibility of the 'hypothesis' on which the recollection theory rests: the Forms exist. The attunement theory is rejected.

Socrates then tries to show independently of the doctrine of recollection that the attunement theory must be false. Now the identity of the hypothesis changes: the attunement theory is itself treated as the 'hypothesis' (93c10, 94b1), and the question is whether this hypothesis should be accepted. Socrates' approach is to consider what follows from it, and to show incompatibility between its consequences and other, more secure claims about the soul.[42] First, if the soul were an attunement of the qualities present in the body, it could never oppose the body, given that the character and 'actions' of an attunement depend on the condition or actions of its components (93a). But in fact the soul not only acts independently of the body but sometimes opposes it. For example, characteristically of the *Phaedo*, thirst is attributed to the body, not the soul (94b), and the soul sometimes resists thirst and prevents drinking. The second argument (93a–94a) is rather more elaborate, and relies on the claims that (a) there are not degrees of being a soul and (b) there are good and bad souls. Again, these claims are treated as being so plausible as to need no further defence. Socrates suggests that advocates of the attunement theory have no way of accounting for bad souls without implying degrees of being a soul: the only way to characterize an attunement is in terms of its being more tuned or less tuned, and so if souls were attunements, the only way to mark the differences between them would be to make them *souls* to a greater or lesser degree.[43] But that is impossible: no soul is less a soul than another soul is. The attunement theory

---

and in *Gorgias* 457e and 461a the two verbs are used as if they were equivalent. See n. 29.

[42] Compare p.73. The sequence of the passage is complicated; Gallop (1975) 158 provides an analysis.

[43] A more tenacious proponent of the attunement theory could perhaps suggest that a certain level of attunement is required for there to be a soul at all, and that more and more precise tuning above that level would make a soul become more wise or virtuous, not become *a soul* to an even greater degree.

thus makes it impossible for one soul to be inferior, morally or cognitively, to another soul; its consequences are incompatible with the obviously true claim that not all souls are equally good. By looking for this kind of incompatibility Socrates is able to reject an account of the soul without making reference to the doctrine of recollection.

As we have seen, the last argument for the soul's immortality (102a–107a) requires, in addition to the study of logical 'disharmony', the broad study of causes that Socrates supposedly started in his youth. Socrates needs a sufficient range of causal examples to establish a general claim: any item, corporeal or incorporeal, that always causes one of a pair of opposite properties never itself becomes the *other* member of the pair (105a). To this extent, soul, the cause of life, resembles other such causes: like fire or largeness, the soul does not take on the property that is the opposite of the property it causes. But soul is nonetheless a special case. The other causes have the two options of retreating and perishing, but for soul to perish, and so become dead, would precisely be for it to take on the opposite property of life, the property it causes. So retreat is the only option. Socrates shows the soul to be incapable of perishing by considering the logical fit between the thesis 'a soul can perish' and his account of causes, and showing them to be incompatible. Searching for 'disharmony' thus proves extremely versatile: it enables Socrates to establish claims as well as to refute them.

I have argued that Plato is trying to offer a Socratic discussion of the soul's immortality by showing how the familiar Socratic preoccupation with logical relationships can be applied outside ethics. This makes it easier to understand why Socrates argues against the attunement theory and not some other theory of the soul. Plato could have written a far more comprehensive discussion of the soul, with a definition of soul, a defence of its incorporeality and a reasoned rejection of any theory of soul as corporeal. Instead he targets only the attunement theory, even though Socrates' autobiography mentions several corporeal explanations of life and intelligence, where blood, air, fire or the brain are held responsible (96b). One of these

Socratic Discussions of Death and Immortality

candidate explanations, air, is mocked when Socrates describes the soul being blasted apart as it leaves the body – particularly if there happens to be a strong wind (77e, cf 70a). But there is no argument in the text against a corporeal conception of the soul, and, as we have seen, the last argument is designed in such a way as to accommodate a corporeal view of the soul.

Perhaps the humorous tone of 77e gives us all the explanation that is needed: Plato thought that corporeal conceptions of soul are so implausible that they need no discussion. But the interpretation followed in this chapter suggests a different explanation: discussing such a conception of the soul does not fit a *Socratic* approach. Socrates' recourse to theories and arguments relies on logical relationships, such as inconsistency. The attunement theory (at least as Plato presents it) is incompatible with the soul's immortality, and so in a discussion of immortality attunement has to be confronted; fortunately for Socrates, the attunement theory is also incompatible with less controversial claims, such as that there are bad souls but not degrees of being soul, and these incompatibilities enable him to refute the theory. By contrast, a straightforwardly corporeal conception of the soul is compatible with the soul's immortality, and so there is no need for Socrates to refute it. And he may be unable to refute it, given that a corporeal view of the soul is also compatible with the further claims on which Socrates relied in his arguments against the attunement theory. A corporeal soul could have contrasting moral and intellectual properties, could pre-exist its presence in the body, and could control and resist the body. However, crude or unattractive Plato may find corporeal views of the soul, Socrates cannot use this kind of argument against them. That suggests that the attunement theory was chosen as a target not only because of the challenge it poses to the thesis of immortality, but also with a view to enabling Socrates to offer a reasoned position on the fate and nature of the soul.

CHAPTER 4

A SUPERANNUATED STUDENT: ARISTOTLE AND AUTHORITY IN THE ACADEMY

DOROTHEA FREDE*

Introduction: The Value of Background Information

In view of the modern age's obsession with biographical details, experts in ancient philosophy sometimes regard the absence of such information with secret relief. But if this lack of information creates the feeling of liberation from the obligation to take the philosophers' personal lives and views into consideration, this feeling does not extend to the inner life in the philosophical schools. In that regard we are lacking vital information and that lack represents quite some impediment to our treatment of the extant texts and fragments of texts. We have only scant information about Plato's dialogues, how they were received by his contemporaries, and what role they played in his school.

Many scholars nowadays prefer to concentrate on Plato's dialogues themselves. All the same, if we had a clear view about the nature and intention of Plato's dialogues throughout his long life this would help to solve unavoidable questions about the dialogues, such as the order in which they were composed, the 'progress' they reflect, and the nature and intention of difficult late work. Because the dialogues themselves provide no safe answers it is advisable to put to good use all the extra information that is available to us. So let us turn to the information we have about his interaction with his students and peers.

---

* This article has no pretences to originality or ground-breaking innovations; it merely provides a survey of well-known facts, with an occasional special twist and emphasis, as a contribution to this volume's topic in gratitude for many years of David Sedley's friendship and collegiality. Considerations of length have prevented discussions of the views proposed by a long line of distinguished predecessors.

Aristotle and Authority in the Academy

Plato's School – Its Organization and Members

With respect to the Academy we are on no safe ground at all. Although there are various 'facts' reported about the school's name, location, and organization, many of these are only what one might call 'well-informed conjectures'. It is likely that Plato founded the school after his return from Sicily, around 387 BC, because he had come to realize that more was needed than philosophical discussions with like-minded friends.[1] Though it is uncertain when Plato started to write and who were the addressees of his first writings, it stands to reason that he was first prompted by the need to vindicate Socrates in the eyes of the world, as he does in the *Apology* and the *Crito*, and to illustrate the character of Socratic questioning and concern for an 'examined life'.[2] During those years Plato must have come to the conclusion that a permanent institution was necessary, especially in view of the need for reliable leaders in politics. His resolution must have been strengthened by the fact that Isocrates had founded a school with similar intentions, but with a significantly different conception of 'philosophy' in 390 BC. But there is next to no information about the early years of Plato's school. This fact is often ignored in accounts of the Academy. There is also little consideration of the fact that its character must have changed through Plato's long philosophical life, just as his philosophy, its character, and aim, did change, as witnessed by his dialogues. It therefore stands to reason that the intellectual life in the school in its earlier years was rather different from what it was at the time when in 367 the 17-year-old Aristotle joined an institution that had already existed for twenty years.[3]

To what extent the organization of the Academy in its early years was intended to realize the ideas about education that Plato expressed in the *Republic* is hard to say. For little is

---

[1] The *VIIth Letter*, whether genuine or not (which I am inclined to think), does not provide any clues on these questions.
[2] A report that Plato had started to write Socratic dialogues already during Socrates' lifetime – so that Socrates shook his head at the confabulations he found in the *Lysis* (DL 3.35) – clearly must be a late invention, even if it has some adherents nowadays.
[3] Jaeger (1923) 12ff.

known about its organization and virtually nothing is known about the curriculum that was used for the education of young students in the school. As other authors have pointed out, it is highly unlikely that Plato's programme mirrored that of the education of the philosopher kings. But the 'liberal arts' must have played an important role in the students' actual instruction and so must a certain kind of training in philosophical argument.[4] How much leeway the students had to pursue interests of their own remains an open question. For nothing is known about Plato's interaction with students and other members of the Academy. It is likely that Plato did not act alone, but had associates, such as his nephew and successor Speusippus. But most of those members whose names are known to us must have joined the Academy later, because they would have been far too young to work in the Academy during its fledgling years. We can only assume that Plato started out with a few assistants, and that over the years the Academy increasingly attracted not only intelligent students but also collaborators and associates with philosophical interests of their own. But these assumptions largely depend on the information we have on the Academy in its heyday, when people such as the mathematician Theaetetus, the philosopher and astronomer Heraclides Ponticus, and the famous astronomer and mathematician Eudoxus had either joined the Academy or at least become associates of it.

These later developments suggest that Plato's institution had not been designed from the beginning as a tightly knit organization of higher education but to give quite some leeway to the collaborators and students. But this is, again, a conjecture that is based on reports about its later development. It is, at any rate, very likely that the division into two groups of members existed from early on: Plato's peers and collaborators, the so-called *presbyteroi*, and the young students who needed

---

[4] According to Merlan (1954) 73: 'In all probability the *Antidosis* and the *Panathenaicus* describe the main features of the Academic, the late Platonic, and the post-Platonic curriculum adequately. It contained discussions of poetry, instruction in rhetoric, geometry, astronomy, and eristics.'

Aristotle and Authority in the Academy

basic education, the so-called *neaniskoi*.[5] There is some evidence that the beginners were taught in the gymnasium of the Academy, while the discussions with advanced students and other members were held in the garden of the nearby house that Plato had purchased for that purpose.[6]

This distinction between two kinds of members provides no information, however, about the function and reception of Plato's dialogues within the Academy, nor about his personal involvement in the education of the younger students.[7] For, if we do not want to assume that Plato wrote nothing until the tender age of forty, some of the early dialogues must have preceded the foundation of his school and therefore cannot have been written for the purpose of advertising the Academy. In addition, many of the later dialogues are so hard to penetrate that they presuppose a readership well familiar with Plato's philosophy; uninitiated readers would feel repelled rather than attracted.[8] A similar verdict applies to other general claims about the dialogues, e.g. that they were presented orally in the Academy. Not only must some of them have preceded its foundation, but only some of the early-middle dialogues contain lively discussions that lend themselves to oral presentation and are likely to engage intelligent students and colleagues in discussion. In the case of some of the longer and difficult writings such use is unlikely. While it is feasible that the *Republic* or the *Theaetetus* was read out in instalments, it is hard to imagine

---

[5] Philodemus *Index Academicorum* (*PHerc.* 1021 and 164) VI.41–VII.5 and XVIII 1–8 Dorandi (1991). For how long the *neaniskoi* remained in that position is unclear. On this issue, cf. Lynch (1972); Natali (2013) 17–31. Natali does not aim at supplanting learned studies like that of Düring (1961) but concentrates on information on the school itself.

[6] See Aelian *VH* 3.19.

[7] The Tübingen school, headed by K. Gaiser and H. Krämer, assume that Plato's dialogues had a protreptic and paraenetic character, i.e. that they were designed to attract a wider public to his philosophy; though the writings contain vestiges of his philosophy, the 'real doctrine' was reserved for oral discussion. The Straussians, the adherents of Leo Strauss, treat the texts as crucial but in need of subversive interpretation that goes beyond the apparent meaning. Neither of these two schools will be discussed further in this article.

[8] Many may have shared Isocrates' verdict that Plato's school was a community of logic-chopping sophists (*Antidosis* 169–79; cf. his polemics against Plato and Aristotle as '*eristikoi*' in *Letter to Alexander* 5; *Helen* 1 and 6).

an audience capable of following a reading of the *Parmenides* (even if Plato's half-brother Antiphon allegedly managed to reproduce it to the letter), the *Sophist*, the *Statesman*, the *Timaeus* or the *Philebus*.

More information about the inner life in the Academy would help not only to clear up some of these uncertainties but also to provide valuable clues about the dialogues themselves, for whom Plato wrote them, and how they were received. For, as everyone who has ever taught Plato to undergraduate students (let alone to explain him to laypeople) must have experienced, even the short aporetic and seemingly 'easy' early dialogues are full of traps that require careful analysis and intellectual patience. Even the short and early dialogues therefore presuppose a sufficiently trained readership, able and ready to work out problems on their own that Plato merely sketches.

This diagnosis, finally, leads to the topic that is up for discussion in this volume: authority. What kind of authority did Plato exert in his school? What kind of authority did he want to exert in his school? What role did his dialogues play? That Plato exerted quite some authority in his school cannot be doubted, as is witnessed by the fact that it attracted students and associates from all over the Greek world and even beyond, if the respective sources are to be trusted.[9] Among the intelligent young students was the 17-year-old Aristotle who joined the school in 367 and remained a member of the Academy until Plato's death. In addition, the fact that several other 'superannuated' students continued to work as members of the Academy – once their apprentice years were over and they developed philosophical ideas of their own that diverged from Plato's and sometimes were openly critical of them – is a strong witness not only to the reputation of Plato and his school, but also to the liberal spirit in which the school must have been organized and to the high level of discussion and research that prevailed within the institution.[10]

---

[9] According to Diogenes Laertius (3.25) Mithradates, a Persian, set up a statue of Plato in the Academy.

[10] On the terms designating students and other members cf. Baltes (1999) 255: visitor (*phoitētēs*), learner (*mathētēs*), hearer (*akoustēs, akroatēs*), intimate (*synēthēs*),

Aristotle and Authority in the Academy

There are, at any rate, good reasons for the assumption that Plato not only tolerated dissent within his school but also instigated research of all kinds.[11] Thus, Eudoxus famously produced a mathematical model, explaining the trajectories of the planets as a combination of circular movements, in contradistinction to the traditional view reflected in the name 'planet' that these stars are just wandering or erring on irregular paths. That the Academy was a well-established and flourishing institution of research and learning is not just attested by the accomplishments of Plato's collaborators and students and their loyalty, but also by the fact that he could safely leave that institution in the hands of others for protracted leaves of absence (perhaps involuntarily lengthy because of forces not in his control) that he spent in Sicily at the court of Dionysius the Younger.[12] That Plato in his school acted as a benign overseer is in a way confirmed by an – admittedly – very late source. In the *Life of Plato* attributed to Olympiodorus[13] we learn that Plato dropped the Socratic style of irony and of talking to everyone in the marketplace. He also did away with the 'closed door' mentality of the kind practised by the Pythagoreans and the oath of loyalty to the teaching of Pythagoras, and adopted a more open style (*politikōteron*), so that the teaching in the Academy was free of any sectarian atmosphere. He seems to have welcomed scientists such as Eudoxus from other cities – and the fact that he appointed Speusippus as his successor shows that allegiance to Plato's doctrine was not required even among the inner circle of the Academy.

Aristotle as a Witness

It is time to consult Aristotle as a witness. Now, someone might feel prompted to ask: why Aristotle? For Aristotle joined the

---

acquaintance (*gnōrimos*), companion (*herairos*), and friend (*philos*). So there were obviously different degrees of intimacy as well as of advancement.

[11] Cf. Baltes (1999) 252, with reference to Philod. *Index Academicorum* Y.1–7 Dorandi (1991).

[12] The reports vary on the dates of Plato's Sicilian ventures, but the most likely dates are 367–365 for the first expedition, 361–360 for the second.

[13] *In Platonis Alcibiadem commentarii* 2.154 Westerink (1956).

Academy fairly late and at a time Plato was absent, so he must have received his basic instruction from teachers other than Plato. Furthermore, his extant writings were composed at an even later time and are largely critical of Plato, especially when he focuses on so-called 'esoteric' philosophy of which there are hardly any traces to be found in the dialogues. In addition, many references in Aristotle concentrate on dissent within the Academy,[14] and at least some of those works must have been composed much later.[15]

If these reasons threaten to disqualify Aristotle as a fair and informed witness on Plato, it has to be objected that not only is Aristotle the only disciple of Plato's whose work has been preserved, at least in a significant part, but that the attention paid to the critical treatment of Plato in Aristotle's work, most of all because of the controversy about an esoteric Plato, leads to a distortion.[16] For it makes it appear as if Aristotle treated Plato's dialogues with negligence and focused on ill-attested 'oral teaching', some of which seems to have been collected as 'Plato's unwritten doctrine' either in written form or in the collective memory within the Academy.[17] But, as we will see a little later, this focus tends to distort Aristotle's importance as a witness to Plato' work.

---

[14] In *Metaphysics* A.9 Aristotle seems to include himself in a group of Academic dissenters, as the 'we' indicates that he uses there, while in the corresponding chapters in *Met.* M.4–5 he replaces the 'we' by a distant 'they'. On this point, see Frede (2012) 269ff. esp. n. 12.

[15] This applies most of all to the critique of the Form of the Good in *NE* 1.6 (and its predecessor in *EE* 1.7). It is uncertain when, exactly, the critical comments of Plato's Forms in the *Metaphysics* originated.

[16] This controversy has roots in antiquity and was well known to commentators in the nineteenth century, such as Zeller. In the twentieth century it was revived energetically by Cherniss – who wanted to discard all of Aristotle's critical comments as unjustified and the references to an esoteric Plato as fabrications; Cherniss' views were most vociferously criticized by defenders of an esoteric interpretation in the 'Tübingen school' and by adherents of a Neoplatonist interpretation of Plato's work.

[17] Aristotle refers to the so-called *agrapha dogmata* once in *Phys.* 4.2, 209b14–15 in a perfunctory way; some mention is found in later witnesses (Galen *Placita* 3.15, 68) and in the ancient commentators on Aristotle, most of all in Simplicius and Philoponus, who claim that these doctrines originated from discussions (*synousiai*) with Plato concerning 'the Good'. The justification of these claims cannot be pursued here.

Whether Aristotle started out as a faithful disciple of Plato remains a matter of controversy. But given his young age when he joined the Academy, this is likely, and, as the catalogue of his works in in Diogenes Laertius (5.12) shows, he wrote works with titles identical to some by Plato: there was a *Sophist*, a *Statesman*, a *Menexenus*, and a *Symposium*. Since the list contains a bewildering amount of items not otherwise known to us it is hard to tell which of them were composed in the wake of Plato and which were independent works.[18]

It is, of course, only to be expected that Aristotle started to develop his own philosophy while he was still a member of the Academy. At the time of Plato's death, he was 37 years old and it would be more than strange had he adhered to the master's voice until that time. First, there were other dissenters; Speusippus, for instance, rejected the theory of Forms and it seems that no conformity was expected, anyway; and Xenocrates, another disciple and Speusippus' successor, at least modified that theory. As mentioned earlier, Plato, apparently, tolerated such dissent, as is confirmed by the report that he designated Speusippus as head of his school after his death. Second, there is information that Aristotle was given quite some leeway to pursue his own interests already when he was a student.[19] Whether or not Aristotle already had an interest in biology when he joined the Academy is uncertain, just as it is uncertain whether any of his peers shared his interest in that field. And it is hard to evaluate the claim that it was a very young Aristotle who introduced rhetoric as a subject of instruction, against Plato's wishes, because he felt prompted to take up the cudgel against Isocrates. If he did so, it was hardly against Plato's wishes, for though in the *Gorgias* (462b–463c) Plato famously denounces rhetoric as a mere knack, producing gratification and pleasure, comparable to cookery and pastry-baking, in the *Phaedrus* (259e–264e) he advocates the existence

---

[18] If the report in the *Vita Marciana* is correct that Plato was in Sicily in 367, that does not speak in favour of disagreement between the young Aristotle and Plato from the start, as some scholars argue (cf. Lynch (1972) 82, n. 20). It only shows that the Academy was an institution that did not concentrate on the thought of its founder.

[19] Cf. the references in Natali (2013) 20ff.

of a kind of 'scientific' rhetoric that is based on knowledge of both the subject matter and the audience's types of soul.

The Academy must, of course, have changed considerably by the time Aristotle joined it and it must have changed even more while he remained there, first as a student and then as an associate. And it is unlikely that he ignored the fact that the style and spirit of Plato's dialogues had changed over the years.[20]

By the time Aristotle joined the Academy the Socratic spirit of Plato's earlier works clearly had been replaced by a concern for dialectic, the discipline that aims for precise determinations of concepts and questions concerning methodology, as witnessed in the later works from the *Parmenides, Sophist,* and *Statesman* to the *Philebus*.[21] Not only did Plato write such works, but there are testimonies showing that he practised what he preached. A witness to this practice is the famous fragment of the comic poet Epicrates that depicts Plato supervising his students hard at work to determine the nature of the pumpkin in application of the method of division.[22] The depiction must have struck people as familiar, both the method and Plato's friendly but detached attitude when he refrains from comments but gently encourages the students to start all over again. Although Aristotle critically refers to that method in both the *Prior* (1.31) and the *Posterior Analytics* (2.5), because it assumes what it is supposed to demonstrate, he later grants that the method has heuristic value in the establishment of definitions (*APo.* 2.13 and 14).

Are there any signs that Aristotle drew a clear line between Plato's earlier, Socratic, dialogues and those of his later years?

[20] This is, of course, what all those scholars deny who are either wedded to a 'unitarian' conception of Plato's works or reject the thought that Plato's works display any trajectory of development at all. A unitarian position is, for instance, defended by Kahn (1996); examples of 'anarchic' interpretations with respect to development are contained in Annas and Rowe (eds.) (2002).

[21] On this point, cf. Jaeger (1923) 12ff.

[22] See Athenaeus *Deipnosophists* 59d–f. The depiction of those divisions reminds me of my high school exercises in biology with attempts to determine the species of plants with the help of *Schmeil's Textbook of Botany for Institutions of Higher Learning*. We usually got lost after the third step, despite the careful enumeration of the criteria of division.

Aristotle and Authority in the Academy

And: how familiar was Aristotle with Plato's early works? The evidence concerning the presence of Plato in Aristotle's work was collected in a systematic way in Bonitz' *Index Aristotelicus*, s.v. Platon in 598a9–599b38. Bonitz makes a general distinction between (1) passages where works are referred to and (2) passages where Platonic doctrine in general is addressed. Bonitz further subdivides (1) into works where: (a) both the title and either the name of Socrates or Plato is referred to; (b) the name of Plato is not added to the work; (c) Plato's name is referred to but the work is uncertain; (d) neither Plato's name nor the work is given but where the work ascribed to an anonymous authority (*phasin, oiontai, nomizousi tines*) can be identified with certainty or high probability. Class (1) refers to practically all the undisputed works. The only omissions are the *Euthyphro*, the *Crito*, and the *Parmenides*, but these omissions may be accidental, especially in view of the fact that not all of Aristotle's works are extant.

The lion's share of these references are to Plato's political works, the *Republic* and the *Laws*, because Aristotle explicitly discusses them in *Politics* 2. Next in line is the *Timaeus* because Aristotle refers to it directly or indirectly both in his works on nature and in his metaphysics. The context of these references varies, and their evaluation would require an article of its own. Some of the dialogues that are not referred to by name, but clearly presupposed, serve as the butt of Aristotle's criticism, such as the doctrine of pleasure in the *Philebus* that comes under fire in both *EN* 7 and 10. It is also generally assumed that Aristotle's discussion of friendship relies heavily on the discussion in Plato's *Lysis*. That dialogue is not mentioned by name, but it seems to have served as a repository of arguments in the discussion of friendship in *EN* 8 and 9, as well as in *EE* 7. Aristotle does not openly criticize any of the arguments, but in his own treatment he quickly passes by one of the main obstacles to a satisfactory treatment of friendship in the *Lysis*: reciprocity as a condition of friendship is discarded there all too soon and for insufficient reasons.[23]

---

[23] A mere quote from a poem of Solon is treated as a refutation, in exploitation of the ambiguity that some things can be dear to a person that cannot be her friend (*Lys.* 212d–e).

Aristotle, in his own account of friendship, makes mutuality the basic condition right away (*EN* 8.2, 1155b27–1156a5). The example of the use of the *Lysis* makes it at least likely that some of Plato's work were used as material for the exercise of the students, perhaps in class, and were not supposed to contain Plato's well-considered views. About such agreements and general understanding we have no information; Aristotle seems to have presupposed it. More information may have been contained in Aristotle's lost early work that seems to have been more directly influenced by Plato than his later 'esoteric' work. For some of those works were dialogues and some of them may have been imitations of the kind that other students composed as well.[24] This assumption explains the character of some of the spurious or dubious works that have found their way into the *Corpus Platonicum* and that were not removed by later editors despite the fact that they recognized that Plato was not their author.[25] These dialogues may not have been written with the intention to deceive but as exercises in imitation of Plato's earlier works. This is, again, rather speculative, for there is no information about the authors and their intentions. It is the style and content of some of the *dubia* and *spuria* that suggest that they were more or less successful imitations of Plato's dialogues and that diagnosis might also apply to some of Aristotle's earliest works.

The ample references to Plato's work show that despite the changes of spirit in the Academy, Plato's dialogues continued to play an important role in the school's intellectual life. Aristotle refers to the full span of Plato's works, but neither where he agrees nor where he disagrees does he explicitly distinguish between early and late works or refer to such a distinction.

---

[24] We should keep apart here the works by other followers of Socrates and those of the *disciples* of Plato. For as Kahn (1996) has argued persuasively, the composition of 'Socratic discussions' constituted a genre among the 'Socratics' of Plato's own generation, i.e. Antisthenes, Aeschines, Aristippus, Phaedo, and Euclides.

[25] The origin, date, and explanation of many of the recognized spurious dialogues (in contradistinction from dubious works) is still a matter of debate. Some of them may have been composed as mere exercises, without any intention to deceive or any claim to originality. Others may have been later forgeries, once the famous libraries paid high prices for manuscripts. On Platonic pseudepigrapha: Erler et al. (eds.) (2005).

This is not contradicted by the fact that in the *Politics* (2.6, 1264b26–28) he mentions that the *Laws* were written much later than the *Republic* and points up significant differences in the conception of the constitution that is proposed in the *Laws*: it is not monarchical, but represents, rather, a mixture of oligarchy and democracy (1266a1–30). But Aristotle does not clearly state that Plato thereby meant to replace his earlier conception of the best state; for although he acknowledges that Plato tried to make the state in the *Laws* more attainable by actual city-states, yet 'he gradually turns it back towards the other constitution', i.e. to that of the *Republic* (6, 1265a2–4). To his criticism he adds, somewhat incongruously, a praise of the extraordinary, subtle, innovative, and investigative character of all 'Socratic' dialogues (6, 1265a10–13). The incongruity is that Aristotle clearly overlooks the fact that the speaker in the *Laws* is not Socrates but the Athenian Stranger, just as Aristotle seems to ignore the fact that in some other dialogues Socrates is no longer the main speaker.

As some commentators have suggested, that 'lapse' may be due only to Aristotle's habit of designating all of Plato's work as '*hoi tou Sokratous logoi*'. Though there are no parallels to this phrase in Aristotle's other works it may indeed reflect a convention within the Academy when referring to Plato's dialogues. It is a sign that Plato's works had become fixtures in his school (even while he was still adding to them), a repository of arguments and positions one could refer to, in the way we still refer to the views of famous philosophers including Plato and Aristotle. 'Plato says ...' is as familiar to us as it was to Aristotle. Further, it is a sign that the knowledge of Plato's dialogues was a prerequisite in the Academy, and that it continued to be so not only in Plato's later years but also in Aristotle's. For, it is unlikely that Aristotle would have referred to Plato's works unless he could expect his own disciples to be familiar with them. Plato was, then, treated as an authority in his life and beyond his life, an authority one could haggle with, but nevertheless an important, if not *the* most important authority. There is no other philosopher to whom Aristotle refers as often as he refers to Plato.

Dorothea Frede

These observations do not settle the question about whether Aristotle was concerned with changes in Plato's doctrine and how much of a historian Aristotle cared to be in that respect. I am not here raising the question of how *good* a historian Aristotle was when it comes to reconstructing his predecessors' doctrine *tout court*, including that of Plato. The question is only whether Aristotle was aware of changes in Plato's doctrine and, moreover, whether and to what degree he distinguished between the Socratic and the Platonic side in Plato. A lot hinges on the question of what to make of Aristotle's short summary of the distinction between Socrates and Plato in *Metaphysics* A.6, 987b1–10: 'Socrates was busying himself about ethical matters and neglecting the world of nature as a whole but seeking the universal in these ethical matters, and fixed thought for the first time on definitions; Plato accepted this teaching, but held that the problem applied not to any sensible thing but to entities of another kind – for this reason, that the common definition could not be a definition of any sensible thing, as they were always changing. Things of this other sort, then, he called Ideas, and sensible things, he said, were apart from these and were called after these.'[26]

This text has been the object of much controversy.[27] Although more than thirty years had passed since Socrates' death by the time Aristotle joined the Academy, it is highly unlikely that nothing was ever said about Socrates as a philosopher and as a person – and that an intelligent young man with a lot of intellectual curiosity would never have tried to obtain more information about him. It would also have been odd if Plato, who dedicated so much effort to the vindication of Socrates, never talked about him to his students and associates. The Academy was a small institution whose members knew each other intimately, not a large and anonymous organization like modern universities. In addition, Athens was a small township, and memory of prominent citizens in such communities lasts much longer than it does in modern mass societies. So whatever we

---

[26] Trans. by Ross in Barnes (ed.) (1984).
[27] For an extensive discussion of this chapter, cf. Steel (2012b).

are to make of some other aspects of Aristotle's reports on Plato and their justification, there is no reason to reject the simple narrative in the passage quoted above.[28] There is other evidence that the historical Socrates was concerned with ethics rather than with natural philosophy and with the definition of general concepts. Xenophon is a clear witness to that fact and the same must have been true of some of the other 'Socratics'.[29] There are good reasons for assuming that the separation of the Forms was a theory that Plato developed as a consequence of further reflections on the status of general concepts and their counterparts and there is no reason why his students should not have been informed of that fact.

That the young Aristotle would be so totally unconcerned with the Academy's past and with Plato's own background as simply to accept what certain people found fit to report seems quite unintelligible. That Aristotle was no historian who tried to give precise reconstructions or to treat the still available texts with the utmost care is quite another matter. But he was clearly not unconcerned with his predecessors' views – even if he sometimes used them only as a foil to show that his own theory is right – and theirs deficient. So while it would certainly be wrong to overrate Aristotle as a source, it is just as wrong to underrate him.

That Aristotle had information of a distinction between Socrates and Plato does not immediately justify the assumption that he made a division between truly 'Socratic' dialogues and those dialogues that continue to use Socrates as the main interlocutor but that contain Platonic doctrine concerning

---

[28] We shall leave aside here Aristotle's report on Plato's so-called unwritten doctrine and his discussion of Plato's, in all likelihood, late tendencies to 'mathematize' the theory of Forms, for that is an altogether different kettle of fish that has been the subject of long controversies during the last decades.

[29] Cf. Xenophon, *Mem.* 1.1, 11 – on Socrates' rejection of discussions on nature; on his concentration on human beings and on general moral concepts, see 1.16 *et passim*. Although Xenophon's personal encounters with Socrates must have been of short duration and he clearly made use of Plato's dialogues, he must also have made use of other information about Socrates. Aristotle does not mention Xenophon who had been banished from Athens until 365 BC. But since *Gryllus*, Aristotle's early work on rhetoric was an encomium on Xenophon's son who died in the battle of Mantinea in 462, it is likely that he met Xenophon and had access to his work.

the Forms as separate entities, as adumbrated in the *Meno* and explicated in the *Phaedo*. The fact that Aristotle globally addresses Plato's work as 'Socratic discourses' would prima facie speak against the assumption that he made a separation of that kind. But there is reason for caution on this point, for he does refer to Socrates in two distinct ways. He sometimes refers to Socrates with the definite article '*ho Sokratēs*', and sometimes without the article, '*Sokratēs*' and, as one theory has it, the latter refers to Socrates when he is supposed to speak in his own voice, while the former refers to his role as the proponent of Platonic doctrine. This theory was first proposed by William Fitzgerald and has become known as 'Fitzgerald's canon'.[30] The 'canon' was seemingly refuted by the famous philosopher and Platonist A. E. Taylor[31] but it was rehabilitated by W. D. Ross, who called it 'a minor but interesting question'.[32] As Ross points out, by a careful review of the references to Socrates and other persons in Aristotle (such as Parmenides and Aristophanes), the practice of inserting the article where only the figure in Plato's dialogues is meant is the rule – while omissions are exceptions that confirm the rule.[33]

When Ross calls the distinction 'interesting but minor' this is clearly an understatement. For it is significant not only that Aristotle makes such a distinction at all, but even more significant that he tacitly presupposes that his audience/readership understands the point of that linguistic distinction. For it

[30] Fitzgerald (1850) 163. The book is, unfortunately, accessible only in rare book collections like those of the University of Cambridge.

[31] Taylor (1911) 41–89.

[32] Ross (1924) vol. 1, xxxix–xli.

[33] This is not the place to review the evidence again and to reply to various objections. Cf. Deman (1942), Vlastos (1991) 97 n. 67, Nehamas (1999), 92–4. Nor can the question be investigated as to what extent Aristotle is right when he makes that distinction and where he prima facie seems to be wrong. There is one very prominent case where Aristotle omits the article and assigns the doctrine of a Platonic dialogue to the historical Socrates: the denial of the phenomenon of *akrasia* in *NE* 7.2, 1045b23–7. The evidence that this is an exception to the 'canon' is not compelling. The *NE* contains, incidentally, several references to the historical Socrates. They concern either Socrates' 'intellectualism' that virtue is knowledge (6.13, 1045b23–7; 28–30) or his 'irony' in the sense of mock-modesty (4.7, 1127b22–6). The only exception is 3.11, 1116b4–6; the Socratic tenet that courage is knowledge must be a reference to the *Laches*.

Aristotle and Authority in the Academy

is a clear indication that the difference between the 'Socratic' Socrates and the 'Platonic' Socrates was part of the general understanding not only in the Academy but in the Peripatos as well. Unfortunately, we have no other texts that could confirm that assumption. When later authors refer to Socrates using the article they do so in the sense, common in Greek, that emphasizes the person's importance, 'the (famous) Socrates'. Had Aristotle meant to use it in that sense, the 'canon' would have been reversed and the historical Socrates been designated as 'the' Socrates.

Plato's Avoidance of Authority

The assumption of so much enlightenment concerning Plato's work within his school seems to fit badly with a different but quite pronounced phenomenon: the remarkable insecurity concerning Plato's dialogues among his students and associates that manifests itself in disagreement about his intentions. The example that comes to mind right away concerns the interpretation of the *Timaeus*. While some of the members of the Academy understood the 'myth of creation' and its divine craftsman in a literal sense, others treated it as an allegory only. In *De caelo* 1.10 Aristotle clearly presupposes a literal interpretation. Although he does not mention Plato's name and refers to the *Timaeus* only as if in passing (280a28–32), it is clear that the butt of Aristotle's criticism is the statement in *Timaeus* that the world has been generated but is indestructible. The refutation of that possibility is continued through *DC* 1.11 and 12 and clearly is aimed at Plato. Other members of the Academy adopted an interpretation that treats the talk of the creation of the universe by a divine craftsman as a metaphor. Aristotle mentions them anonymously, summing up their explanation as follows (*DC* 10, 279a32–280a2): they claimed that 'generation' is to be understood as it is in the case of the construction of a geometric figure where the geometer does not assume that his figures are in truth generated but pretends to generate them only for didactic reasons (*didaskalias charin*). Aristotle rejects this comparison on the grounds that while geometrical figures display all parts of the construction simultaneously this does not apply to processes of generation where order follows disorder. For nothing can be at the same time ordered and in disorder (280a2–10). There is later information confirming that Speusippus and Xenocrates tried to defend Plato against Aristotle's attacks on such grounds.[34]

Similarly, there obviously was quite some disagreement about the interpretation of the 'receptacle' or 'nurse' of all becoming that constitutes the 'third kind' of being in the *Timaeus* (48e–51b). Aristotle objects to that conception, quite extensively, in his discussion of place in *Physics* 4.2, 209a31–b17, on the grounds that Plato identifies space (*chōra*) and matter (*hylē*) in the *Timaeus;* against this Aristotle points out that these entities have to be kept separate, because the substrate of a body and its place (*topos*) should not be confused. Aristotle in that connection mentions that the account of the receptacle in Plato's so-called unwritten doctrine (*agrapha dogmata*) is a different one, but insists that Plato, nevertheless, identified place and space. The justifiability of Aristotle's criticism is not our topic here. Whatever we make of his unsympathetic treatment of Plato's *Timaeus* and other aspects of his philosophy, it seems that he was following his own lights. That fact speaks for the assumption that there was no agreement about how to read Plato's dialogues, and it also speaks for the assumption that Aristotle was not much concerned with that fact nor went to any lengths to ascertain that he got Plato right.[35]

Be that as it may, such uncertainty and disagreement among Plato's students and associates suggests that he did not assume any authority concerning the interpretation of his works within his school during his lifetime. And that must strike us as an

---

[34] The most important information on the controversy is contained in Proclus' commentary on the Timaeus. On Aristotle's attitude towards Plato, cf. Sedley (2007) ch. 6. On the disagreement within the Academy, cf. Dillon (2003b). For further discussion, cf. Mohr and Sattler (eds.) (2010). Though for a while allegorical interpretations dominated the field, 'creationism' in recent years has had strong supporters (cf. Johansen (2004), Broadie (2012)).

[35] Cf. Steel (2012b) 169.

Aristotle and Authority in the Academy

astonishing abstemiousness on his part. For, though some of those reconstructive interpretations may have arisen only after Plato's death, some of them must have been proposed while he was still alive. It seems inconceivable that Aristotle, as well as some of Plato's older collaborators, started to comment on his dialogues only after his death. For it is highly unlikely that all the agreements Aristotle professes in the name of a group of Plato's followers in *Metaphysics* A.9 originated at Assos, during the short period of Aristotle's stay at that place. The claims he makes in the name of that group ('we') are substantial and they seem to have resulted from quite some discussion: that there are no Forms of relatives, that there are no Forms of the objects of certain sciences, that there are no Forms of artefacts, that the assumption of Forms leads to the infinite regress of the 'Third Man Argument'.[36] Aristotle refers to the Third Man Argument in other places as well,[37] without ever mentioning that its origin is in Plato's *Parmenides* (where 'large' rather than 'man' is used, *Parm.* 130c–d). It is unclear whether Aristotle is aware of the fact that in the *Parmenides* it is a very young and inexperienced Socrates who professes himself unable to defend separate Forms and that Parmenides expresses the conviction that the problems will be solved by a great mind; for otherwise the power of dialectic must be altogether destroyed (135a–c). The 'laborious game' that follows is supposed to provide the kind of training that is the prerequisite for the solution of the problems. Though Aristotle must have known the *Parmenides*, it seems that the 'Third Man Argument' had become a topic of discussion independent of its origin, and perhaps in ignorance of it. But this fact speaks for the assumption that the debate had been going on for quite a while and therefore must have started during Plato's lifetime, for both *Met.* A and *SE* are

---

[36] This is just an excerpt from the barrage of arguments Aristotle enlists against the Forms in the chapter's first part (990a33–991b9), before launching an attack on the numerological interpretation of the Forms in the chapter's second part (991b9–993a10). For a discussion of these two difficult pieces of text, cf. Frede (2012), Crubellier (2012).

[37] The argument is referred to in *SE* 22, 178b36–8, in *Met.* Z 13, 1039a2ff. and, without name, in Z.6, 1031b28–1034a4.

early works. If Plato was aware of those discussions, he seems not to have interfered with them and his disciples seem not to have consulted him, just as they did not consult him on the question of how to read the *Timaeus*.

There is more evidence in Aristotle that confirms that there was a surprising lack of information or insecurity about Plato's intentions. Aristotle complains in *Politics* 2 that both the discussion in the *Republic* and in the *Laws* abounds with obscurity, unsettled points, and open questions. Thus in 2.5, 1264a11–b6 Aristotle presents a catalogue of questions that 'Socrates' has left open in the *Republic*, such as the arrangement of the family life and property within the third class, whether it is also supposed to be communal or not, and he objects to Socrates' confidence that life will function without many laws despite the fact that he has not said anything about the education of the citizens of the third class. With respect to the *Laws* Aristotle raises similar complaints about the lack of sufficient information concerning the organization of the state, its constitution, the participation of the citizens in government, and in military matters.[38]

One feels prompted to ask: Why did they not ask Plato? To be sure, this possibility was not open in the case of the *Laws*, if the reports are correct that this work has been 'edited' only after Plato's death so that his disciples did not have access to that work.[39] But the *Republic* must have been available long before Aristotle's arrival at the school. And though we cannot be sure about the date of composition of the *Timaeus* it is likely that Plato composed it and made it accessible during Aristotle's time at the school. That there was uncertainty concerning Plato's intentions among his students and associates suggests, then, that there was an agreement among the members of the Academy not to ask Plato about the meaning and intention of his dialogues. Whether the master had refused outright to respond or whether there was just a general understanding that

[38] *Pol.* 2.6.
[39] DL 3.37 states that there is a report that Philip of Opus edited the *Laws* after Plato's death because they were still written only on wax tablets.

Aristotle and Authority in the Academy

he was not to be bothered is anyone's guess. The dialogues were, then, available for study and discussions among the members, but they were not the subject of discussion with Plato. This may sound strange to us, given that the Academy was an institution of small size, but Plato must have preferred not to act as his own interpreter, once his school had been established. Otherwise he would have been obliged to explain his works to every new generation of students for nearly forty years.

There may be more to his reluctance than such practical considerations. Of course, this is not the place to start a proper discussion of the mysterious story of Plato's lecture *On the Good*, as reported by Aristoxenus, the later disciple of Aristotle.[40] But, if Simplicius' report on the circumstances of that lecture is correct, i.e. that Aristotle, Heraclides Ponticus, Hestiaios, and other friends had been present at that occasion and taken 'notes' on what was expressed in an enigmatic way (*ta rhēthenta ainigmatōdes*), it appears that asking Plato was not an option. This supports the assumption that there was a general understanding that Plato was not to be disturbed with questions concerning his philosophy.[41] Perhaps there existed a general etiquette in the Academy on the proper subjects of discussion with Plato. For, as the caricature in Epicrates indicates, he was neither invisible nor unfriendly.

If his dialogues were accessible to every member of the school and there was no authoritative reading or orthodoxy, Plato may indeed have acted in accordance with the conviction he lets (his) Socrates famously pronounce in his critique of writing in the *Phaedrus*, 274b–277a. Ammon, the god-king, reprimands Theuth for his invention of writing because it will not provide wisdom but only its appearance: 'Your invention will enable your students to hear many things without being properly taught, and they will imagine that they have come to know while for the most part they will know nothing.' According to Ammon, the fate of written documents is rather dire: 'When it once has been written down, every discourse

[40] *Harm.* 2.39–40.
[41] Simplicius *In Phys.* 454,18.

97

rolls about everywhere, reaching indiscriminately those with understanding no less than those that have no business with it. And when it is faulted and attacked unfairly, it always needs its father's support; alone it can neither defend itself nor come to its own support.'

This depiction of the reception of written work would suggest, then, that Plato did not feel called to give his dialogues any 'fatherly support' but left them intentionally to the mercy of all comers – not only in the Academy but to posterity as well. Whether he assumed that their artistic form, the dialogue, would provide protection against misuse, as some interpreters have suggested, is dubious, and if he did assume so, the reception of his writings during his lifetime must have shown to him that this assumption was wrong. For even highly intelligent students like Aristotle did not treat them with the kind of consideration that they deserve in the eyes of sensitive readers. Did Plato not care about the fate of his offspring? He may, indeed, have written the dialogues with the attitude that he somewhat facetiously expresses in what follows in *Phdr.* 276d: 'When he writes, it is likely that he will sow gardens of letters for the sake of amusing himself, storing up a treasury of reminders for himself when he reaches forgetful old age and for everyone who wants to follow in his footsteps.' He must have assumed that some readers will get his message and some will not.

Plato's Treatment of Other Authorities

If the sometimes disrespectful tone of Aristotle's criticism of Plato strikes one as peculiar, we must keep in mind that Aristotle's critique is the only direct witness we have concerning the treatment of Plato's work in the Academy. The fact, however, that Aristotle more than once appears to speak for an entire cohort of critics justifies the view that a critical discussion of Platonic views was not the exception but rather the rule in the Academy. This impression is confirmed by information that other disciples disagreed with Plato on important issues. Thus Speusippus seems to have rejected the theory of

Forms summarily – and others may have gone their separate ways as well.

It should also be noted that Plato's treatment of his own predecessors must have represented a kind of model that encouraged a certain degree of outspokenness in the expression of dissent with the authorities of old. Outspoken criticism, on Plato's side, is not confined to the treatment of the sophists, including the most respected representatives of that group of migrating teachers, Protagoras, Prodicus, and Gorgias. His criticism includes the most respected figures in Greek culture: the poets, starting with Homer, and at least implicitly including Aeschylus, Sophocles, and Euripides.

Plato also includes in his criticism the major representatives of the Presocratic tradition. Thus Heraclitus and Heracliteanism come in for some quite critical treatment in the *Cratylus* and in the *Theaetetus*. The deficiencies of Anaxagoras' account of causality in nature are made responsible for Socrates' rejection of philosophy of nature howsoever in the *Phaedo*. And even father Parmenides is subjected to a major revision of central tenets concerning both being and not-being in the *Sophist*. Thus, if the dialogues were treated as models of philosophical discussion in the school, they clearly invited criticism rather than discouraged it.

The critical attitude in Plato's dialogues is not limited to earlier authorities. It also – in its own way – includes Socrates. Though Socrates is usually the questioner and not the person questioned, and he is signally unsuccessful when he encourages his partners to question him in turn, Socrates' procedure is not always beyond reproach, and it is unlikely that Plato did not give that impression intentionally at certain occasions, even if he regarded Socrates as 'the best, and also the wisest and the most upright' (*Phaedo* 118a). Even admirers of Socrates – i.e. the Socrates in Plato – admit that he sometimes plays a less than admirable role in his treatment of his partners.[42] Indeed, the role that Socrates plays in Plato's dialogues varies greatly, from whimsical and cunning to deeply serious and painstaking. This is one

---

[42] E.g. Vlastos (1956), esp. xxiv–xxvi.

of the reasons why it is not only hard to say who the historical Socrates was but equally hard to sum up who Plato's Socrates is. He never acts exactly the same in two dialogues and one of the reasons for his Protean personality is that he treats others as 'authorities' in as many ways as he represents an authority himself. Thus Plato presented his students with quite different models of how to deal with 'authorities' and it should therefore come as no surprise to see from our witnesses that he was treated in his school as quite an authority – but not as an authority that is beyond questioning or criticism in the way Pythagoras seems to have been within his school. Plato seems to have encouraged a critical spirit among his disciples and he would probably have been quite nonplussed had anyone predicted to him that for centuries his works would be regarded as beyond criticism or questioning, as sacred territory where even angels fear to tread.

Postscript: Authority in Aristotle's School

What about Aristotle's school? Did he, likewise, not only tolerate criticism by his students but invite it and encourage independent study and research? When it comes to the organization of Aristotle's school we are worse off than we are in Plato's case. For we have next to no information about his disciples' reaction to his teaching and research in general. Theophrastus is, of course, a witness to a certain amount of dissent – as can be concluded from his fragment that discusses the shortcomings of Aristotle's metaphysics.[43] But Theophrastus was a near contemporary of Aristotle's as well as a close friend and collaborator and may therefore have been the exception in the Peripatos, not the rule. How much discussion Aristotle permitted or encouraged in his classroom in lectures for beginners – and in personal encounters with his peers – is hard to say, given the impersonal tone of his extant works that represent his lecture notes or working manuscripts. For even where Aristotle refers to problems and to objections to his own views, as he does very often, it is unclear whether they represent actual objections or his own fabrications.

[43] Cf. van Raalte (1993), Laks et al. (1993).

Aristotle and Authority in the Academy

But occasionally he provides at least a glimpse of his personal style of teaching. Thus in the famous passage *On the parts of animals* Aristotle pleads for the study of the lowlier subjects in biology – as if he had to persuade his students not to turn up their noses when it came to getting their hands dirty in biological research. He compares there the 'lofty studies' of the celestial bodies and their divine nature – that are far away and for which evidence is hard to come by – with the ample material on, and the nearness of, the phenomena in the world of animals and he recommends that students not shy away from the latter: *PA* 1.5, 645a15–25.

Aristotle's use of the endoxic method as an accommodation of common opinions may not be as extensive as has been assumed in recent years; in most of his treatises it is Aristotle himself who defines the subject matter and lays down the law of the land. But he does so in quite an unobtrusive way. It is therefore likely that his audience – just like many of his readers – felt guided rather than dictated to. For all the attention is given to the subject that is under consideration and none to the treatise's author. Aristotle only rarely refers to himself as an authority, as he does, for instance, in *NE* 2.2 when he explains that the intention of his ethics is to help make his audience and readers better.[44] In the same work Aristotle mentions that what he submits is only an outline and expresses the expectation that 'everyone' will be able to fill in the details (1.7, 1098a20–26). His frequent use of '*legō*' is no evidence to the contrary, for it means no more than: 'by that I mean'. Aristotle did not, then, assign supreme authority to himself even though he must have been conscious that, with the exception of Theophrastus in some areas, none of his collaborators or disciples could hold a candle to his achievements in all the areas he worked in. That, one might say, is the sign of true authority. And in that respect Plato must have set a model to Aristotle.

---

[44] He does, however, refer to the great difference between teachers of philosophy and the students in his discussion of unequal friendships; their worth cannot be measured in money but only in honour – in the way gods and parents are (*NE* 9.1, 1164b6).

CHAPTER 5

WORDS, DEEDS, AND LOVERS OF TRUTH IN ARISTOTLE

SARAH BROADIE*

The contrast of words and deeds in connection with Aristotle might label more questions than one. After first encountering Aristotle through his philosophical texts one might also ask whether he was involved in any historically significant deeds – aside, of course, from whatever he did in elaborating his ideas and putting them into writing. Such a question would be answered – depending on what one brings under the vague qualification 'historically significant' – through a retelling of all or some of what we know of the rest of Aristotle's biography, such as the times and places of his birth and death, his various connections with the court of Macedon, his long sojourn in the Academy, his time in Assos and Lesbos and friendship with the ruler of Assos, his return to Athens and foundation of his own school, his marriage or marriages, and his children. Another kind of question about words and deeds in Aristotle would focus on the content of his philosophy: lining up 'words' with theory and 'deeds' with practice, it would be looking to explore his famous distinction between theoretical and practical reason and their respective virtues. And interest in this could be powered by either or both of two motives: the historian's desire to know, from the corpus that has come down to us, what Aristotle actually said and taught, and the philosopher's desire, using Aristotle as stepping stone, irritant, or sparring partner, to explore *in propria persona* the nature of reason in general, the contributions of the different kinds to human life, the epistemic norms relevant to each kind, and so on.

---

* In appreciation of David Sedley's massive and many-branched contribution to the study of ancient philosophy.

Words, Deeds, and Lovers of Truth in Aristotle

This paper, however, is not about either of the mentioned types of word–deed antithesis. Instead, it mainly comments on some ethically centred thoughts of Aristotle's concerning authorial authenticity – which is a matter closely bound up with the question of authorial authority. The relevant general sort of antithesis is therefore the ancient one in which someone's deeds – conduct – are seen as belying or not belying their words.[1] But we need to narrow this further.

The kind of inauthenticity at issue is not the one where someone pretends to a standing or expertise which they lack, nor the one in which they make a promise knowing that they will not carry it out. It is more like that in which the ailing doctor refuses to take the medicine he or she prescribes to others. If you break (without excuse) a promise to me, I judge *you* dishonest and untrustworthy, but your behaviour does not impugn the value or usefulness to me of what you would have delivered if you had kept the promise. On the contrary, when you renege I not only lose reason to trust you but am normally also disadvantaged by not receiving what you promised: which implies that what you promised would have been a good thing or a good thing for me. But if someone coolly[2] fails to follow advice which they press on others in the same situation, this fact, if detected, not only shows the adviser up as knowingly untrue to their word (since normally in advising S to do A one knowingly conveys to S and to others present that oneself would do A in the corresponding situation) but also casts doubt on the value of

---

[1] In Robert Wardy's phrase, this is 'a defining polarity of the ancient Greek culture'. The form of it that concerns us here, namely the opening up of gaps between what moralists teach and how they live ('Physician, heal thyself') must be everywhere a captivating topic for debunkers and potential source of anxiety to moralists themselves. Certainly, in and around ancient Greek philosophy there was a veritable tradition of comment on such gaps. A particularly conspicuous and concrete example is the making of a last will and testament by Epicurus, on which see the fascinating detailed study by Warren (2004), ch 5. In Aristotle's case, in addition to the question of gaps between moral prescription and practice, there is the question whether his scientific writings measure up to his methodological prescriptions on scientific procedure. This paper, however, is only about the first question.

[2] That is, not under duress or acratically. I also mean to rule out the case where the excellence of what is advised is not in question but through some extraneous circumstance the adviser would be morally or prudentially at fault in carrying out what she prescribes.

whatever course is being advised, and therefore also on the value of taking the advice. Thus, unlike the promise-breaker's failure to match her words with deeds, the adviser's failure to do so, if revealed, may actually benefit potential advisees by flagging up the worthlessness of the course advised when they would otherwise have embraced it perhaps at significant cost to themselves. More generally, the potential advisees will draw a disjunctive lesson: either the adviser knows her field, hence knows e.g. that what she prescribes as a nutritious diet is in fact a primrose path to obesity or worse, or she is aware of being ignorant and incompetent to advise, hence without a trustworthy message.

What has this to do with Aristotle? It is meant to frame investigation of a handful of related passages, all, as it happens, occurring in the *Nicomachean Ethics*. Very near the end of Book 10 he writes:

> These sorts of considerations too, then, do carry a certain conviction; but in the practical sphere the truth is judged (*to alēthes krinetai*) on the basis of the way <someone's> life is actually lived (*ek tōn ergōn kai tou biou*), for this is decisive. So when one looks at everything that has been said up to this point, one should be bringing it to bear on the life as actually lived (*epi ta erga kai ton bion*), and if it is in harmony with what is actually done (*tois ergois*), it should be accepted, while if there is discord, it should be supposed mere words (*logous*). (*NE* 10.8, 1179a17–22)[3]

This appeal to life as actually lived comes just before Aristotle's final step in the series of positive reasons why the theoretical ideal of happiness is superior to its practical counterpart. In the final step he will argue that the gods love most, and are readiest to reward, those human beings who, as well as living correct and admirable practical lives (*kai orthōs te kai kalōs prattontas*), esteem and value most what in us is closest in nature to them, namely our intellect in active theoretical mode. So the *sophos* is the one most beloved of the gods (*theophilestatos*), and this is yet another reason for counting him the happiest of mortals (1179a22–32).[4]

---

[3] The translations from the *NE* follow Rowe in Broadie and Rowe (2002), although with slight changes.

[4] In placing this theme of who is most loved by the gods very near the end of the *NE*, Aristotle may be following Plato, who brings it in at *Republic* 612e–613a, just before the myth of Er.

Words, Deeds, and Lovers of Truth in Aristotle

The previous positive reasons for this conclusion (referred to at the start of the quoted passage as 'These sorts of considerations') were presented in two stages. First came a list of pre-eminent features of theoretical intellection such as its greater continuousness, its greater pleasantness, its lesser dependence on external resources, its finding its end solely within itself, and its freedom from external pressures (1177a17–26; see also 1178a23–b5). Then came the argument that the life of those paradigmatically happy beings, the gods, must be theoretical rather than practical, from which it follows that the human activity most akin to theirs is the greatest source of happiness for us (1178b7–23). After this second stage, Aristotle emphasises again that the *sophos* needs only very moderate external resources; but in contrast to what he said in the first stage he now extends this point so as to include virtuous agents in general (1178b33–9). Whereas before he brought out ways in which the dependence of practical virtue on external goods far exceeds that of theoretical virtue (1178a28–b4), now he seems to want to underline the similarity: in both cases virtue or virtuous activity is the core of happiness, and neither kind of virtuous activity needs great wealth or power. And for confirmation he cites the authority of Solon and Anaxagoras, presumably representing practical and theoretical wisdom, respectively (1179a9–17).

The allusion to Anaxagoras is, I suggest, the pivot whereby Aristotle swings back to his main theme in this part of the *Ethics*: the superiority of theoretical happiness. He is almost about to produce the final and clinching argument for this ranking – the argument about the type most loved by the gods; but first we are given the lines 1179a17–22, quoted above. These lines are couched in wholly general terms. But if the immediately preceding mention of Anaxagoras (1179a13–15) is the moment when Aristotle's re-focuses on the superiority of theoretical happiness, then 1179a17–22 is in some way a contribution to that particular theme. It contributes to it, as I see the matter, by being a declaration about Aristotle himself.[5] It brings to the table the fact that this teacher, who for

---

[5] This is the interpretation of Dirlmeier (1960) 597.

some time now has been explaining that and why excellent theoretical activity is ultimately the most perfect good attainable by human beings, has himself lived and continues to live a mainly theoretical life. The ideal for which arguments are being propounded gets further support when the audience is made to notice the propounder's own investment of life and work in that same ideal.[6]

By bringing to the table this fact of his own biography, Aristotle is not, I think, adducing positive evidence for the superiority of the theoretical mode of happiness. Rather, he is defeating a possible defeater. Suppose, holding other things constant, that outside his ethical and political writings and lectures he lived in a way that was plainly not centred on achieving knowledge and understanding for their own sake: this would have tended to defeat the position presented near the end of the *Ethics* through impersonal philosophical argument; however, he implies, the audience need only consider the actual facts of the life of the one who spins these ethical arguments in order to see that there is no ground here for doubting the arguments: they are not just clever spinnings untethered to their author's concrete biographical reality. The counterfactual situation would have cast doubt on them because Aristotle like all human beings seeks happiness; so if we found him in his life choosing not to follow in the footprints of his own final arguments about happiness, we should be entitled to infer that he did not trust them to lead in the right direction; and why should we be more trusting than he?

The issue at 1179a17–22 is the convincingness of Aristotle's arguments for the primacy of the theoretical ideal: the issue

---

[6] This differs from the interpretation of 1179a17–22 in Broadie and Rowe (2002) 446–7. There I took the passage to be telling the audience to check whether they take Aristotle's arguments seriously by considering how they themselves are willing to live. On that view, the 'life' side of the contrast is a test of whether the audience do believe the conclusion, not a test of whether to take it as true, i.e. whether they *should* believe it, as on the present interpretation. The latter is a better explanation of the reference to truth at 1179a18. Cf. the reference to true *logoi* at 1172b4, where the context indicates that *logoi* about the nature of the good do not count as *alētheis* unless their proponents live accordingly.

Words, Deeds, and Lovers of Truth in Aristotle

is not their author's sincerity.[7] It would, of course, be true that the counterfactual discrepancy between the life and the pretended sincerity of the arguments would prove the arguer's lack of integrity. This would be a moral failure, one that perhaps comes under Aristotle's treatment of the social virtue of truthfulness about oneself (*NE* 4.7, 1127a13–b18). We learn from the opening of that discussion (1127a13 referring back to 1126b11–12) that the typical sphere for truthfulness about oneself is informal conversation, including conversation about trivial matters (cf. 1127a33–b5). But I do not think Aristotle's concern at 1179a17–22 over the match between life-deeds and philosophical words is geared in the least to whether he himself might be revealed as sincere or not. Either way this would simply be a fact about *him* as a particular ethical subject. Instead, rather, the care being voiced is solely lest the impression of a mismatch should undermine the didactic force of his carefully argued ethical position – thereby weakening any practical impulse in his audience to take up the life of *theōria* themselves or support such a choice in others. Of course, this concern does presuppose that a philosophy of the highest human good is seriously didactic. According to the individualism that wants each of us to work out our own answer to the 'What is the greatest happiness?' question, where the most anyone can seek is 'the answer that is right for me', the fact that someone fails to live up to their answer may be sad news about *them* but has no authority to affect what others in their own lives think or do.

Although, as I have argued, Aristotle in 1179a17–22 is in fact referring to himself – to his own life as test for his arguments – we might think that he does so in a distinctly veiled fashion in order to avoid the invidiousness of openly claiming, in the immediately ensuing argument at 1179a22–32, that the most

---

[7] What is at stake is the convincingness of *those* arguments. Aristotle's arguments on theoretical topics in metaphysics, physics, or astronomy would not be made less credible simply by the discovery that he did not live the life of someone who believes that the activity of theorising is the locus of the highest human happiness. Only 'in the practical sphere' is truth judged on the basis of deeds and the life as lived (1179a18–19).

107

god-beloved of all human types is exemplified by himself. But regardless of how he expects his audience to understand 1179a17–22, it cannot escape him that he himself, given his signal devotion to theoretical philosophy, is close to fitting his own profile of the *theophilestatos*, nor that his audience too is bound to take this in. So a veiled approach in 1179a17–22 will not have managed to blur the implied self-reference for them. In my view, the logical generality of 1179a17–22 is not a gesture of (transparently) false modesty, but is just what it seems, namely logical generality. That is: in this passage, which, as I have indicated, has a somewhat different dialectical role from that of the surrounding direct arguments for the superiority of theoretical happiness, Aristotle is saying that *whoever* is the author of the direct arguments, the audience should not allow themselves to be argumentatively convinced before checking that author's life choice. The Aristotle who issues this warning (which after all is just common sense, in itself showing no special intimacy with *theōria* – one would sooner expect such advice from shrewd Solon than from otherworldly Anaxagoras) is only incidentally the same human being as the one whose life choice he says should be the touchstone. So in 1179a17–22 he does, by obvious implication, speak of himself, the particular individual who authored the direct arguments, and of course the self-reference will have registered with his audience; but he is speaking of this individual *qua* other, like the doctor doctoring himself (*Physics* 2.1, 192b24–27) – and the audience ought to be able to register this too.[8] This analysis brings out the difference between what is at issue here, and the *NE* 4 topic of the imposter, the self-deprecator, and the truthful. These three characters all talk about themselves as such, not merely *per accidens* or *qua* other. Accordingly (to take a more modern version of the triad), Aristotle is not either being or failing to be suitably modest about himself in 1179a17–22; for suitable modesty and its opposites (boastfulness, and excessive or tiresomely tendentious modesty) all presuppose someone talking or avoiding talking about himself as

---

[8] I am assuming that they are not 'the crowd'; see caveat 2 in the next note.

Words, Deeds, and Lovers of Truth in Aristotle

such – about his own excellences, achievements, or assets *qua* his own. It is, moreover, Aristotle the ethico-political philosopher, not Aristotle the theoretical sage, who argues for the theoretical sage's supremacy in respect of happiness: so it is also only incidentally true that he, the arguer, matches the profile of the *theophilestatos* outlined in the final argument.[9]

Deeds matching or not matching philosophical words seems to be quite a recurring theme of *NE* 10. For instance:

> ... what people say (*hoi logoi*) about matters in the sphere of affections and actions carries less conviction than what they actually do (*ta erga*), so that whenever their pronouncements disagree with what one can see before one's eyes, they [i.e. the pronouncements] earn contempt ... (10.3, 1172a34–6)

Aristotle is talking about moralists who revile all pleasure indiscriminately but are seen sometimes sliding back to it (1172b1–2). He continues:

> It seems, then, that true statements (*hoi alētheis tōn logōn*) are the most useful ones in relation not only to knowledge but to life (*pros ton bion*); for since they are in agreement with what is seen to happen (*sunōidoi ontes tois ergois*) they carry conviction, and so encourage those who comprehend them to live accordingly. (1172b3–7)

Then comes a passage that seems to reverse the very point just made. Aristotle is discussing the philosophical hedonism of his associate in the Academy, the mathematician and astronomer Eudoxus of Cnidus:

> Eudoxus's pronouncements (*logoi*) carried conviction more because of the excellence of his character than in themselves; for he was regarded as a person of exceptional moderation, and so it was not thought that he made them as a lover of pleasure, but that things were truly as he said. (1172b15–18)

---

[9] Two caveats: (1) I have used '*per accidens*' and 'incidental' in the Aristotelian fashion, hence without implying any causal claim as to whether Aristotle could have been the genius he was in ethical philosophy without being the genius he was in theoretical philosophy. (2) In emphasising the difference between his roles of ethical and theoretical philosopher I do not mean in the least to suggest that any of the ethical arguments in this part of the *NE* are not to be taken as philosophically serious. Some commentators, embarrassed by the *do ut des* element of the *theophilestatos* argument (*anteupoiein*, 1179a28), have held that Aristotle here just aims to get 'the crowd' on his side by invoking popular beliefs which he himself rejects (see e.g. Gauthier and Jolif [1970], vol. II. 2, 898, strongly criticised by Bodéüs [2001] 10–11). See Broadie (2003).

109

Aristotle gives Eudoxus a beta for ethical philosophy and an alpha plus for moral virtue. His ethical arguments to the effect that pleasure is the highest good were, says Aristotle, accepted (to the extent that they were, which the passage seems to leave open) less because they were strong arguments than because people took his exceptional moderation as a proof that he was judging objectively, not as a mindless partisan whom pleasure itself had charmed into singing its praises. If Eudoxus had been known as a libertine, people's reaction to his philosophical hedonism would have been 'Well, he would say that, wouldn't he?' (the issue this time being the speaker's unreliability, not mendacity – as it was in the case which made those words proverbial).

So is Aristotle saying that the exceptionally temperate Eudoxus gave credibility to his ethical philosophy precisely by *not* living in accordance with it? This may be a neat witticism, but shouldn't Aristotle be afraid of its converse being applied to his own case when he sings the praises of the theoretical ideal later in this same book of the *NE*? That is, shouldn't he worry lest his own very visible adherence to the theoretical life be taken as evidence that he is prejudiced in its favour and argues for it simply because he likes it or it has a hold on him? And what are we to make of his first noting that wholesale opponents of pleasure undermine their own credibility by inevitably failing to live up to their doctrine, and then only a few lines later talking about Eudoxus in a way that seems to make the opposite point, i.e. the point that by not living up to his hedonist position Eudoxus rendered it *more* credible, not less?

Rather than trying to tackle each of these questions head on, let us make a few observations. First, our word for Eudoxus's stance in his argumentative defence of hedonism is 'objective'. He did not mouth his arguments because pleasure herself was his ventriloquist or as someone intoxicated by pleasure like the drunk who mechanically repeated verses of Empedocles (*NE* 7.3, 1147b12). Eudoxus formulated his arguments as a pathway to the truth.

Words, Deeds, and Lovers of Truth in Aristotle

Secondly, when the topic is an area of life where, notoriously, many of us are hijacked by impulse and hence by the second-order impulse to defend or justify the kind of choices that ensue, maintaining objectivity about the value of taking such a path is something that people admire, and rightly so. But there may be people who admire it so much that they automatically believe that the objective person's stated position is correct, and they leave the matter at that. The final sentence of the last quoted passage shows the admirers of Eudoxus passing straight from 'He is unprejudiced' to 'Things are as he says'.

The third point, of course, is that being objective is not the same as actually getting hold of the truth, and does not guarantee it. One great lesson Aristotle carried away from his study of earlier thinkers in every branch of philosophy and science was that truth can elude even the most serious investigators. When it comes to elucidating the best way to live, Aristotle is aware that human beings are beset by two kinds of difficulties, moral and intellectual. On the one hand they are not automatically mature enough to try to think objectively about 'matters in the sphere of affections and actions', or to notice it when objectivity deserts them. On the other hand, even when the passionate part of the soul has been trained to reliable silence, the path to truth is intellectually hard to negotiate: one can be genuinely looking for the way and get lost even so. On this level, the morally decent person – the *spoudaios* – is certainly not, as such, a 'canon and measure of the truth' (cf. *NE* 3.4, 1113a22–b2).

Fourthly, on the question of whether a philosopher should live in accordance with his ethical philosophy, it surely makes a difference whether the ethical philosophy at issue ought to be lived up to – whether by its author or anyone else. Now, Aristotle obviously thinks that his own arguments for the supremacy of the theoretical ideal are good ones: they get closer than anyone else has got to the ethical truth. So *these* arguments, as arguments, *deserve* not to be betrayed by their author's failing in his life to live up to them. But inferior arguments about the *summum bonum*, however objective in spirit, arguably fail to deserve to be borne out by the author's

111

life in the same way. As when conscience tells a person to do what in fact is evil: something is wrong with them if they obey even though something else is wrong with them if they do not. So if, inhibited by his own moral decency, Eudoxus did fail to live up to an objectively embraced, but in Aristotle's view mistaken, philosophical hedonism (on this see more below), we can fault Eudoxus for inauthenticity, but the Aristotelian response would be: 'The position is too unsound to deserve its author's practical loyalty. Also, it is better to be inauthentic and a poor advertisement for one's own personal integrity than authentic and a good advertisement for a false ethical position.'

Fifthly, we can imagine for Aristotle a reply to the objection that he himself only gives arguments for the theoretical ideal because as a matter of personal fact he is anyway addicted to theorising. He could answer that if the ethical arguments are good and strong as arguments – which we assume he thinks they are – this is so regardless of his personal predilection. If the arguments were weak one might fall back on biography to explain why he gives them the time of day: 'Since early childhood he has been insatiably curious about physical and metaphysical reality.' This sort of personal and pre-rational fact would not make weak arguments strong. Correspondingly, if the arguments stand up for themselves in their own right, the same personal and pre-rational fact does not make them weak.

As for Eudoxus: does Aristotle in fact regard him as a case of the philosopher's lifestyle failing to harmonise with his account of the *summum bonum*? Aristotle does not say so. He represents people who knew Eudoxus as reasoning: 'Eudoxus is exceptionally moderate; therefore he is not a friend of pleasure; therefore his philosophical endorsement of pleasure as highest good is objective, not due to a *parti pris* in favour of pleasure.' But Aristotle makes it clear later in Book 10 that he himself sees no tension between being moderate and being a great friend of pleasure. The tension disappears if true or logically unqualified[10] pleasure is construed as pleasure in virtuous and

---

[10] Things that only the brutish or morally corrupt take pleasure in are not pleasant or pleasures *simpliciter*, but only 'to them'.

Words, Deeds, and Lovers of Truth in Aristotle

refined activities (see especially 1176a15–29, the peroration of his Book 10 discussion of pleasure). And Aristotle may have understood Eudoxus as sharing that construal, hence equating pleasure with the highest good in accordance with a refined interpretation of pleasure. If so, Aristotle objects to that Eudoxan equation because it is not well founded on argument, not because it is a philosophy that could not be lived by decent people like Eudoxus.

Our word for the quality of Eudoxus's unprejudiced stance towards hedonism is 'objectivity'. The nearest equivalent for Aristotle and his associates would be 'love of truth'. *NE* 10 has many motifs in common with *NE* 1, love of truth being one of them and, by implication, piety another. According to Aristotle's final argument for the theoretical ideal, the *sophos* is *theophilestatos*. That is, as we know from the *Euthyphro* (14a–c), the *sophos* has to a superlative degree a property – that of being dear to the gods – which although not identical with the virtue of piety (*to hosion*) is the immediate and essential consequence of piety alone. Thus we can infer that Aristotle's *sophos* is a person of pre-eminent piety;[11] a conclusion confirmed by taking the statement that the *sophos* is the type that most of all 'devotes itself to (*therapeuōn*) intelligence' (1179a22–3) together with the statement that intelligence is 'either divine or the most divine thing in us' (1177a13–16).[12] But those who devote themselves to intelligence, i.e. cultivate it and exercise it for its own sake, are identical with the lovers of truth – even when, as in the case of Eudoxus arguing for hedonism, their arguments (anyway according to Aristotle) do not hold water. The view that emerges from Aristotle's lines seems to be that actively caring about the truth for its own sake is what entitles you to be considered pious and god-beloved, whether or not you always get it right.

[11] I am, of course, assuming that Aristotle had read the *Euthyphro*, but, as Christopher Rowe (2013) has pointed out, while this is a plausible assumption, there is no independent evidence for it.

[12] I tend to think, although this is a discussion for another occasion, that someone could fit the template of Aristotelian piety without subscribing to Aristotle's theologism about intelligence and intellectual activity.

Sarah Broadie

And that is surely how Aristotle saw things when it came to Plato. Thus we arrive at the famous passage in *NE* 1.6 where Aristotle is about to issue a series of unsparingly negative comments on the Platonist Form of the Good. Piety and love of the truth are explicitly conjoined here:

> ... perhaps we had better discuss the universal good, and raise difficulties about how 'good' is predicated – although such an investigation goes against the grain because it was friends of ours who introduced the forms. But it would seem perhaps better, even imperative, certainly when it is a matter of saving the truth, to destroy even what is one's own, especially if one is a philosopher; for while both friends and the truth are dear, the right thing (*hosion*) is to honour the truth first (*protiman tēn alētheian*). (1096a11–17)[13]

Why is Aristotle so ceremoniously apologetic here towards Plato or the Platonists when so often elsewhere he argues against them abrasively and with what may appear to us a stunning lack of hermeneutic sympathy or sensitivity? There are two questions here: why, when disagreeing with the Platonists elsewhere, is he often so aggressively polemical and uncharitable in representing their views, and why on the contrary does he here (and uniquely here) display such compunction before stating his objections? On the first question, Julia Annas seems to me to make the right judgement when she writes (speaking here about *Metaphysics* M and N, but her judgement applies more generally):

> No doubt there are many points in *M-N* where Plato's position is stated in a form in which Plato would not wish to hold it. But this is not the unfairness of malice, or lack of insight. (Aristotle does sometimes have lapses, but they are clearly recognizable, and often understandable.) Aristotle is interested in the truth, and his polemic comes from a desire to see the argument through.[14]

That is: he uses Plato as stepping-stone, irritant, and sparring partner for the development of his own conclusions. I would only add, in deference to this volume's title (even though it has probably been said many times before), that Aristotle like Plato seems to have had an extraordinarily heightened sense

---

[13] A perfect translation of *hosion* here would land between the attenuated 'the right thing' and the overwrought 'it is a sacred duty'.

[14] Annas (1976) 77. See also Fine (1993) 28–9.

114

Words, Deeds, and Lovers of Truth in Aristotle

of the human tendency to suck in views about values, life, the universe, uncritically from other people. Plato saw his culture as forever looking for authority in Homer or Simonides etc. Aristotle, in the context of the philosophical circles he was part of, seems to have had a similar attitude especially about Plato and the early Platonists. He fought, sometimes indecorously, to prevent their dicta from simply being accepted by future students of philosophy. In general he may have thought that human beings have a natural tendency to assimilate famous people's dicta just as they stand, whether written down or not.[15]

A connected point is this: if Aristotle takes it that you, like him, have a paramount interest in finding out about physics and chemistry or about the ontology of mathematics or about psychology, then from his point of view the *only* reason you could have for patiently and charitably trying to reconstruct a predecessor's view on any of these topics would be because through laziness or bedazzlement you have swallowed the assumption that this predecessor *already has the truth on whatever it is*. So: if you seek and encourage your students to seek to listen to that predecessor more carefully, with a deeper concern to do justice to what he really thought or thinks, this must be because you regard him as your authority on whatever you are hoping to learn more about— the tides, the material of the heavenly bodies, the nature of ultimate substance, etc., etc. But (always the problem for uncritical reception of a supposedly authoritative source) how do we know that the supposed authority is reliable? And in any case there are many predecessors and they say conflicting things on the same subject. Only a demented child desperate for a world where all is really peace between his quarrelling parents could suppose that if we reconstruct each of their views sympathetically, trying to establish what each author was *really* trying to get across, we shall find that they harmonise and between them give us the truth.

---

[15] As Dorothea Frede in this volume makes abundantly clear, Plato was probably the last person to desire the kind of unreasoning adherence that Aristotle is resisting. See especially Section 3 of her chapter.

I think the reasoning I have just attributed to Aristotle is more or less on the right track. If your exclusive concern is to get closer to the truth about first-order things, you will take account of the handed down views of others to just the extent and in just those manners (positive, negative, accepting, rejecting, brusque, admiring) that seem to advance your own inquiries. But if (on the same hypothesis) you invariably, with gentle patience, do your best to understand what your sources meant by what they said in the context in which they said it, this could only be because you had taken on board the conviction – a truly weird conviction – that this is our best method for finding out about those first-order things. (It would only not be weird if, under some science-fiction scenario, we were forever cut off from direct access of our own to those things and were also devoid of memories acquired through earlier direct access. The things, in other words, would have to be on the other side of some sort of veil impenetrable by us.)

If we cannot find ourselves in the picture sketched above, it is because we are not there. The picture was of people who, like Aristotle, really only want to discover the truth about the stars, the tides, the perishability of this cosmos, the number of elements, the nature of substance, the nature of the highest good, etc. but who are wedded to a very strange method. We, when we engage in the scholarly study of Aristotle and other ancient philosophers, are not trying to find out about those first-order things.

The second question is: why is it in the *NE* that Aristotle displays such compunction about rejecting the Platonist Form of the Good? I think that the answer lies in the fact that this is an ethical work, and friendship and received wisdom about friendship are topics for ethics.[16] Consider the following: (a) it is well entrenched popular wisdom that 'What is friends' is shared in common' (*koina ta tōn philōn*: Euripides *Orestes* 735 and *Andromache* 376–7; Plato *Lysis* 207c, *Republic* 424a and 449c; Aristotle *NE* 8.9, 1159b31 and 9.8, 1168b7–8); (b) Aristotle

---

[16] This raises the question of why no such expression of compunction occurs in the *Eudemian Ethics*. See note 19 for a possible reason.

Words, Deeds, and Lovers of Truth in Aristotle

utterly rejects the Platonist Form of the Good; (c) Plato famously held in the *Republic* that the happiest human beings are philosophers who have discharged their political responsibilities and now lead lives devoted entirely to thinking and studying (*Rep.* 540b–c; cf. 517c; 520e); (d) Aristotle of course fully agrees with this, even though he draws the line between practical and theoretical differently from Plato; (e) hence Plato's authority adds important confirmation to the *NE* 10 position about the superior happiness of the thinker. The original *NE* audience would of course have known the *Republic* and some of them alongside Aristotle may have studied with Plato. So Plato is or should be a silent positive presence in the background of the *NE* 10 arguments about the *sophos*.[17] But (a) together with (b) yields the result that Plato and Aristotle are *not* friends. At the beginning of *NE* 1.6 Aristotle emphatically denies this inference, declaring that the Platonists and he *are* friends although they disagree fundamentally on metaphysics. Friends, he implies, do not have to have theories of metaphysics in common. So what *do* they have to have in common in order to be the strongest and best kind of friends? We can already see the answer: they have to have fundamental values in common; they have to approve and want to live the same kind of life.[18]

Aristotle will explain all this in detail in Books 8 and 9 on friendship. He will explain there that the like-mindedness essential for friendship, whether political or personal, is not like-mindedness about e.g. questions of astronomy (9.6, 1167a22ff.). There he will provide some explicit guidance on how 'What is friends' is in common' is to be taken. He cannot explain all this in the first book of the *NE*. But here, just as he rolls up his sleeves to take on the Platonist Form of the Good, he makes a gesture of homage to the underlying ethical reality,

---

[17] See Sedley (1999b) esp. 324–8, on the Platonic origin of Aristotle's elevation of the contemplative life.

[18] The *Eudemian Ethics* has a parallel critique of the Platonic Form of the Good (*EE* 1217b2–1218b7) unframed by apology. The difference may be because the *EE* contains little or nothing about the superior happiness of the *sophos*, hence has less reason to be conscious of any sharing of values with Plato. The *Magna Moralia* stands with the *EE* in this.

which is that the distinctive common possession of paradigmatic friends consists in the values by which they live, and that the present case exemplifies this since both sides share the love of truth.

How does Aristotle convey all this? By means of his famous dictum:

while both friends and the truth are dear, the right thing (*hosion*) is to honour the truth first (*protiman tēn alētheian*). (1096a16–17)

For this is an amalgam of parts of two memorable sentences spoken by Socrates in *Republic* 10:

(1) a man is not to be honoured more than the truth (*ou ... pro tēs alētheias timēteos anēr*). (595c3–4)

and:

(2) to betray what one believes to be the truth is impious (*ouch hosion*). (607c7–8)

Aristotle commandeers Plato's own words to speak for himself, and thereby gracefully shows, not says, that Plato and he share fundamental priorities on how to live (*bios* and *erga*) despite their radical disagreement on metaphysics (*logoi*).[19] Aristotle also, I think, hints at how one might indeed have found Plato's influence enthralling. For when Plato has Socrates say that a man is not to be honoured more than the truth, in this case the truth is that Callipolis has no place for mimetic poetry, and the man is Socrates's beloved and revered Homer whose hold on him since childhood makes it hard to speak that truth (*philia ge tis me kai aidōs ek paidos echousa apokōleuei legein*, 595b9–10, echoed by Aristotle's 'such an investigation goes against the grain because it was friends of ours who introduced the forms', *prosantous tēs toiautēs zētēseōs ginomenēs dia to philous andras eisagagein ta eidē*, 1096a12–13). And at 607c7–d2 Socrates confesses to the spellbinding power of such poetry, above

---

[19] We can imagine him extracting a syllogism from the two passages: 'Honouring a man more than the truth is betraying the truth; betraying the truth is impious; therefore (or that is why) honouring a man more than the truth is impious.' I am assuming that Aristotle takes those passages as expressing Plato's own attitude, not just ascribing it to the Socrates-character.

Words, Deeds, and Lovers of Truth in Aristotle

all when exercised by Homer. In short, given the context in Plato of Aristotle's amalgamated quotation one can hardly fail to entertain the analogy: 'As Homer to Plato, so Plato to Aristotle'. Aristotle need not mean this to be taken with full seriousness; it is enough that he floats the thought in front of us. Finally, given that his *NE* 1096a16–17 declaration is manifestly a *borrowing from* Plato, Aristotle may intend by it to declare not merely the convergence of his and Plato's attitudes towards the truth, but also a certain dependence of his own intellectual independence on Plato's example and encouragement.[20,21]

But there is all the difference in the world between deferring to an authority and learning from an exemplar.[22,23]

---

[20] Cf. Wardy, this volume, xxx.

[21] Highly pertinent, despite the many interpretative problems, is the fragment preserved by Olympiodorus, in his commentary on the *Gorgias*, of Aristotle's elegiacs to Eudemus:

> Coming to the fair land of Cecropia
> he piously (*eusebeōs*) founded an altar of holy friendship
> for a man whom the wicked may not properly even praise [or: mention];
> he, alone or the first of mortals, showed clearly
> by his own life (*oikeōi te biōi*) and by the courses of his arguments (*kai methodoisi logōn*)
> that a man becomes good and happy at the same time:
> but now none can grasp this any more (Fr. 673 Rose).

Whether or not it is *himself* that Aristotle describes as having piously founded the altar of holy friendship, it is clear from Olympiodorus that the 'man' of the ensuing lines is Plato and that these lines express Aristotle's own attitude. Aristotle endorses both his subject's personal life and 'the courses of his arguments'. Were the latter non-technical ethical arguments, i.e. ones that did not depend on questionable Platonist metaphysics? Or does *methodoi logōn* mean something more like 'the *ways* he argued', referring to qualities such as objectivity, seriousness, thoroughness etc. but not necessarily implying acceptance of all the arguments? For a recent discussion of fr. 673, with references to previous scholarship, see Ford (2011) 160–4.

[22] A conceptually exact laying out of the difference may itself be quite a task, to which Robert Wardy's chapter in this volume offers a thought-provoking protreptic. Wardy draws attention to a surprising fact: 'Research easily yields voluminous materials on the philosophical theme of political authority; but one looks in vain for the self-reflexive move, philosophers asking themselves what, if anything, would constitute authority within the philosophical sphere itself?' (Wardy, 316)

[23] My thanks to the editors and to Alex Long for helpful suggestions.

CHAPTER 6

ARISTOTLE'S *CATEGORIES* 7 ADOPTS PLATO'S VIEW OF RELATIVITY

MATTHEW DUNCOMBE*

Since the 1960s, scholars have thought that the *Categories* is an anti-authoritarian work. Aristotle engages with Platonism, rather than straightforwardly rejecting or blindly adopting any element of it.[1] In particular, Owen argued that the *Categories* evinces an anti-Platonic linguistic theory.[2] That theory enables further objections against Plato's philosophy.[3] Owen stressed

---

* I am grateful to audiences in Durham and Oxford for feedback on this paper – especially Lesley Brown, George Boys-Stones, Luca Castagnoli, Phil Horky and Thomas Johansen – and to Mabel Duncombe and Robert Wardy for improvements to the final version. Most of all, I am grateful to David himself, for always supporting my work with characteristic insight, good humour and generosity. The paper originates in my doctoral work on relativity in Plato, which David supervised. Although he was particularly enthusiastic about Plato's influence on Aristotle, in the end, I barely touched on that theme in my thesis. So I am delighted that I can offer this piece for his *festschrift*.

[1] Owen (1966) gives the classic statement of this view. He reacts against Jaeger et al. (1962) 53, especially, but also De Vogel (1965), with critique by Düring (1966) and (Owen 1966, 128–30). Jaeger's view is part of a wider tendency to see Aristotle's work as emerging from Platonism: Jaeger (1962) and Case (1910). Case (1925) applied this reading primarily to Aristotle's *Eudemus, Protrepticus, Metaphysics, Nicomachean Ethics* and *Eudemian Ethics*. For a similar suggestion with *De Caelo*, see Guthrie (1939) xxix–xxxi cited and developed by Ross (1957) 74–5. For this sort of treatment of the *Organon* as a whole, see Solmsen (1929). For the *Poetics*, see Solmsen (1935). More recently, Frede (1987b) 27–8 argues for the view that species and genera in Plato's *Sophist, Parmenides* and *Philebus* exert a strong influence on the *Categories*. But even here Frede's claim is that Aristotle adapts, rather than adopts, the Platonic view, since Aristotle reverses the Platonic view which holds that the genera and species are primary. Menn (1995) 318–19 also connects the genera of the *Sophist* to the *Categories* but claims that the *Categories* give an exhaustive list of the highest genera for use in inquiry.
  We should also be aware that scholars debate whether the *Categories* is a single work and whether it is by Aristotle. Frede (1987b) 13 has questioned whether the discussion of relativity at *Cat.* 11a20–37 is by the same author as the discussion of *Cat.* 6a36–8b24. To avoid tricky issues of authenticity and unity, I confine my claims to *Categories* 7 6a36–8b24, which is usually thought to be genuine Aristotle.

[2] For example, an anti-Platonic theory of predication, as Owen (1966) 134–9.

[3] See, for example, Owen (1966) 146; Owen (1960a); Owen (1965).

120

Aristotle's *Categories* 7

that Plato influenced Aristotle's early work and that Aristotle's account of predication in the *Categories* reacts against the Forms.[4] Plato influenced the *Categories*, not by his authority, but by setting the background against which Aristotle developed his theories.

On the micro-level of *Categories* 7, scholars take a similar anti-authoritarian attitude. After defining relatives at 6a36, Aristotle draws out some formal features of them: some relatives have a contrary (6b15–19); some come in degrees (6b19–27); all reciprocate with their correlatives (6b28–7b14); some are simultaneous with their correlative (7b15–8a12). Aristotle then raises a worry: some substances are relatives (8a13–28). A hand is a substance, since a hand is part of a secondary substance, but a hand is also a relative, since a hand is said of something. To address this worry Aristotle introduces a second account of relatives (8a31–2). He then describes a test for whether a relative falls under the second account (8a35–b21).

Some commentators argue that Aristotle rejected the first account in favour of the second, but neglect the possible influence of Plato on *Categories* 7.[5] Another group holds that Aristotle develops his views of relativity against a 'Platonic background', but decline to say whether Plato directly influenced Aristotle.[6] But many commentators hold that Aristotle sets up Plato's view of relativity in the first account, only to replace it with the second.[7] Against the first group, I argue that Aristotle takes the *Categories* 7 notion of relativity from Plato. Against the second group, I argue that Aristotle

---

[4] Owen (1966) 134–9.

[5] See Husik (1904) 525; Ackrill (1963) 102; Mignucci (1986) 107–8.

[6] Jansen (2006); Harari (2011) 536. Hood (2004) 26 mentions the ancient view that Aristotle explicitly rejects Plato's view, but does not endorse it herself. Sedley (2002a) 348–51 argues that *both* definitions originate in Academic debate.

[7] Simplicius *In Cat.* 159, 10–20 follows Boethus of Sidon in claiming that the first definition that Aristotle gives (*Cat.* 7 6a36) derives from Plato. Simplicius later reads Aristotle as rejecting the first definition and replacing it with a second definition (*Cat.* 7, 8a32–5), which he takes to be Aristotle's settled view on the matter (*In Cat.* 198,12–199,1). Bodéüs (2001) 117–18, 129 follows this ancient tradition.

121

takes the view directly from Plato. Against the third group, I argue that Aristotle cleaves to that Platonic position.

In part I, I argue Plato and Aristotle share a view of relativity. First, I give textual evidence that both share the 'intensional' view of relatives. Second, Aristotle's formal features have antecedents in Plato. In the second part of the paper, I argue that Aristotle draws directly on Plato's view. For relativity, there is neither a shared source nor an intermediate source. In the third part, I show that Aristotle retains the first account of relatives.

Plato and Aristotle Share the Intensional View of Relatives

The term 'relativity' covers many sins. I begin with two distinctions to show how Plato's and Aristotle's views are alike. First, I distinguish 'relatives' from 'relations'. Take a relational state of affairs: Achilles is faster than Hector. We can distinguish two types of item here. On the one hand, there are items that relate to something: Achilles and Hector. Call these 'relatives'. Proper names, like 'Achilles', can pick out relatives, but so can descriptions, such as 'the faster man'. 'The faster man is faster than the slower man' is true, if stilted. On the other hand, there are items that relate things: call these 'relations'. The relation 'being faster' relates Achilles to Hector. We pick out relations either with a gerund (e.g. 'being faster than') or with a schematic expression (e.g. '... is faster than ...'). In principle, of course, relational expressions can have more than two gaps. For example, '... is between ... and ...' picks out a relation. Ancient philosophers use relations often. But when analysing relativity Plato and Aristotle start from relatives, even though relations enter into the analysis. Plato and Aristotle use the notion of a relation, but share an analysis based on relatives.[8]

---

[8] Relations, rather than relatives, ground 'analytic' treatments of relativity. Frege (1893) and Russell (1938) §§28–30 take relations as primitives in their formal systems. Several treatments of Plato also begin from relations: Castañeda (1972); Castañeda (1978); McPherran (1983). Criticism can be found in Matthen (1982) and Matthen (1984). For an alternative reading of Plato, see Scaltsas (2013). Hood (2004) argues that Aristotle has a view of relations, rather than relatives.

Aristotle's *Categories* 7

Second, I distinguish between extensional and intensional relatives. Some item is an extensional relative just when that item relates to something:

(EXT) *a* is a relative iff *a* relates to some *b*.[9]

On the extensional view, Achilles is a relative simply in virtue of being faster than Hector. Achilles is faster than Hector; so, Achilles relates to Hector; so, Achilles relates to something. So, Achilles is a relative. The extensional account of relatives is permissive. EXT does not restrict which relation is invoked, so everything is a relative. After all, everything is the same or different relative to something. Moreover, under the extensional view, the same relative can bear different relations to different things. For example, Achilles can bear the relation '... is faster than ...' to Hector and '... is the son of ...' to Thetis. EXT allows a relative multiple relations.

The intensional view builds a specific relation into being a given relative entity:

(INT) *a* is a relative iff being *a* involves relating to some *b*.[10]

Take a relative like a brother. Relating in some way to something does not suffice for being a brother. A brother must be *a brother* of something. Being a brother depends on bearing the '... is a brother of ...' relation to something. A named individual brother, Hector, does bear the '... is a brother of ...' relation to someone, Paris. But being a brother of Paris is not what it is to be a brother: Agamemnon is a brother, but not a brother of Paris. To avoid such counter-examples, we might specify that we are interested in being a brother *as such*, rather than some named brother. Plato and Aristotle (*Symp.* 199e3–4; *Parm.* 133c–134e; *Theaetet.* 204e11; *Cat.* 6a36) follow that strategy.

---

[9] EXT is found in antiquity (DL iii 108–9) and Owen (1957) 109 detects this view in Plato. Barnes (1988) takes EXT to be a commonplace in antiquity.

[10] Compare INT with a certain notion of 'internal' relations. A relation, R, may be said to be 'internal' iff Rxy is essential to x and essential to y. This formulation is due to Marmodoro and Yates (2016) 8, but the 'essentialist' reading of internal relations is found in Bradley (1897) 347; Ewing (1934) chapter 2; Bosanquet (1911) 277; Blanchard (1939) 452; Rorty (1967) 125 and Schaffer (2010) 349 from whom I took these citations. See also Mignucci (1986) and Mignucci (1988) which advocate a similar reading of relatives in Aristotle and Plato.

Matthew Duncombe

EXT contrasts with INT in the cases of named individuals. On EXT, Hector is a relative, since '... is a brother of someone' is true of Hector. However, on INT, Hector will not be a relative, since relating to something is not part of being Hector. The contrast also comes out in cases like being a human. If we assume that 'a human' is defined as 'a rational animal', under EXT, a human can be a relative, since a human can relate to things. On INT, however, a human is not a relative, since bearing a relation to something is not part of what it is to be a human. A human can be a rational animal even alone in the universe. Furthermore, unlike on the EXT view, on the INT view, the same relative cannot be encountered in different relations. A brother, as such, is brother of something; a faster thing, as such, is faster than something. No scope here for a brother, as such, being faster than something.

Aristotle and Plato are committed to the intensional view of relatives. First, both use intensional language to discuss relatives. In particular, both thinkers use an expression (ὅπερ ἐστίν) to specify a relative 'as such', precisely what we would expect if the intensional view were in play. Aristotle uses ὅπερ ἐστίν extensively in *Cat.* 7, in particular in his initial definition at 6a36–b6:[11]

(T1) We call relatives (πρός τι) all such things as are said to be just what they are (αὐτὰ ἅπερ ἐστίν) of or than other things (ἑτέρων) or in some other way in relation to something else. For example, what is called larger is called what it is than something else (it is called larger than something) (οἷον τὸ μεῖζον τοῦθ' ὅπερ ἐστὶν ἑτέρου λέγεται, τινὸς γὰρ μεῖζον λέγεται); and what is double is called what it is of something else (it is called double of something).

In this passage, Aristotle defines relatives:

R1: x is a relative $=_{def}$ x is said to be what it is in relation to some y and x is different to y.[12]

Aristotle wants to pick out a class of items, rather than a class of properties of items, so focuses on relatives, rather than

---

[11] Translations of the *Categories* are taken from Ackrill (1963) unless otherwise noted.
[12] Aristotle calls R1 a definition at 8a28.

124

Aristotle's *Categories* 7

relations; on 'the larger thing' (τὸ μεῖζον) rather than the relation 'being larger than'. Furthermore, Aristotle defines not entities that happen to relate, but rather relative entities as such. ὅπερ ἐστίν indicates this emphasis. The larger, as such, is called larger than something. Suppose that Ajax is larger than Achilles. Aristotle's point is not that Ajax is called larger than Achilles (although this is no doubt true). Aristotle's point is that the larger thing, in so far as it is a larger thing, is called larger than something. Ajax, as larger, is called larger than something. But, Ajax, as a larger thing, is not called larger than Achilles. Rather, Ajax, as a larger thing, is called larger than a proper correlative (the smaller).

The language Aristotle uses suggests the intensional view of relatives. We might choose qualifications such as 'as such' to mark out that the intensional view is being invoked. Aristotle uses Greek equivalents of this expression several times. T1 uses ἅπερ ἐστίν and ὅπερ ἐστίν: singular and plural forms of the same expression. The former means 'the very things which are' and the latter means 'that very thing which it is'. In T1, Aristotle uses one to qualify 'relatives' (πρός τι) and the other to qualify 'larger' (τὸ μεῖζον). In the *Categories*, the only use of τοῦθ' ὅπερ ἐστίν, or equivalents, in Aristotle is in *Categories* 7, discussing relatives (6a38, 6a39; 6b4).[13]

Further evidence that ὅπερ ἐστίν picks out an intensional relative is found when Aristotle says, at *Categories* 7, 6b4, that certain terms are of 'other things' (ἑτέρων) when specified as just what they are (τοῦθ' ὅπερ ἐστίν) and not when specified as 'something else' (οὐκ ἄλλο τι). He then gives the example of knowledge (ἐπιστήμη). Knowledge, when specified as what it is (i.e. knowledge), is of something else. Knowledge, specified as something else (ἄλλο τι), say, a mental state, is not of something else. The τοῦθ' ὅπερ ἐστίν qualification focuses on taking

---

[13] ὅπερ ἐστίν occurs only once within the *Categories*, but outside *Categories* 7, at *Cat.* 3b36. There, Aristotle says that substances 'τοῦθ' ὅπερ ἐστίν' do not admit of a more or less. Even this uses τοῦθ' ὅπερ ἐστίν in the context of relatives. Aristotle's point is that a human, as such, is not more a human than another human, but a pale thing, as such, can be paler than another pale thing.

125

Matthew Duncombe

the relative as the relative it is. That is, reading relatives in an intensional, rather than extensional, way.[14]

Plato also uses ὅπερ ἐστίν to specify intensional relatives. In the *Symposium*, after Agathon speaks in praise of Love (*eros*), Socrates poses the following question:

> (T2) Is Love such as to be a love of something or of nothing? ... it is as if I were to ask the same about a father – is a father a father of something or not (ἆρα ὁ πατήρ ἐστι πατήρ τινος ἢ οὔ;)? You'd tell me, of course, if you wanted to give me a good answer, that it's of a son or a daughter (ὑέος γε ἢ θυγατρός) that a father is the father. Wouldn't you?
>
> 'Certainly,' said Agathon.
>
> 'Then the same goes for the mother?' He agreed to that also.
>
> 'Well, then,' said Socrates, "answer a little more fully, and you will understand better what I want. If I should ask, 'What about this: a brother just in so far as he *is* a brother (ἀδελφός, αὐτὸ τοῦθ' ὅπερ ἐστιν), is he brother of something or not?' He said that he was.
>
> 'And he's of a brother or a sister, isn't he?' He agreed.
>
> 'Now try to tell me about love,' he said. 'Is Love the love of nothing or of something?'
>
> 'Of something, surely!'
>
> (*Symp.* 199d1–199e8. Trans. Nehamas/Woodruff, modified, my brackets).

As Socrates tells us later (200e), (T2) aims to show that Love is the love of something. Love is a relative with a special sort of object, a correlative; all relatives are of, in some sense, their correlatives; so, all relatives are of something. Love is a relative entity, so, Love is of something. Socrates gives two analogical examples. First, if x is a father, then y is the son or daughter of x. Second, if x is a mother, then y is the son or daughter of x. In these cases, the relative is a parent and the correlative an offspring. These are relatives under the INT account of relatives,

---

[14] Cf. *Theaetetus* 204e11; *Sophist* 255d7; *Parmenides* 133c8. Although controversial, I think that the same idea can be found at *Sophist* 255c–d. Duncombe (2012) argues for this in detail. Duncombe (2015) discusses an occurrence of this expression at *Republic* 439a2. These two paragraphs, modified, appear in my Duncombe (2015).

126

Aristotle's *Categories* 7

since the fatherhood relation is part of what it is to be a father. On this reading what we know about the entity, x, and all we know about x, is that x is a father. Given that, we know that the father has a correlative (a son or daughter).

Socrates shifts to the example of 'a brother'. A brother, just in so far as he is a brother, is brother of something ('ἀδελφός, αὐτὸ τοῦθ᾽ ὅπερ ἔστιν, ἔστι τινὸς ἀδελφός᾽ (*Symp.* 199e2–4)). Language of 'ὅπερ ἐστίν᾽ recurs in the context of relativity.[15] Here it specifies that Socrates does not mean some individual brother, e.g. Hector, with various properties, but rather a brother as such, a brother *qua* brother. There are various differences between Hector and a brother *qua* brother. First, a brother is essentially a brother, while Hector is only contingently a brother. Second, we know and are able only to know that a brother is a brother but are able to know a great deal more about Hector than that he is a brother. But, as with Aristotle, the language of ὅπερ ἔστιν specifies that a relative is intensional. Linguistic and conceptual similarity encourages us to think that Plato and Aristotle share a view. Shared formal features will give further evidence.

Each relative has a correlative. The most common example of a relative in Plato is larger (μεῖζον).[16] When larger is mentioned as a relative, larger always relates to smaller (ἔλαττον). Another common example, double (διπλάσιον), always comes with its partner, half (ἥμισυ).[17] In general, relative–correlative pairing uses a stable terminology. One common example of a relative, knowledge (ἐπιστήμη), always has a partner, but the label for that partner changes.[18] But clearly both Plato and Aristotle hold that each relative has a special correlative.

---

[15] In Plato 'τοῦθ᾽ ὅπερ ἐστίν᾽ occurs without a 'λέγεται᾽, unlike in Aristotle's *Categories* 7. However, Aristotle does use the expression without a 'λέγεται᾽ at *De Anima* 430a23.

[16] *Charmides* 168b; *Republic* IV 438b; *Theaetetus* 155a; *Phaedo* 101a–d, 102c; *Statesman* 283–5. Large and small are given as a pair at *Rep.* vii 523–4; *Phaedo* 96d–e; *Statesman* 283d. Aristotle gives the example of larger and smaller at *Cat.* 7 6a36–b10.

[17] *Charmides* 168c; *Republic* IV 438b.

[18] Cf. *Charmides* 167c; *Parmenides* 133a–134a; *Parmenides* 142a. Aristotle coins a term for the correlative of knowledge, 'knowable' (*Cat.* 7), but Plato prefers natural language, even if it is not quite consistent.

Not only that, but each relative has a correlative to which it exclusively relates. Aristotle discusses this at length in *Categories* 7 at 7a31–b9. A master should relate to a slave *not* to a human and when we 'strip away' all the features incidental to being a slave, such as being a human or being a biped, we will see that master relates only to slave. T2 shows correlativity in Plato. The correlative of father is offspring and the correlative of brother is sibling. Socrates chooses the disjunctive cases 'son or daughter' as the correlative of 'father' and 'brother or sister' as the correlative of 'brother'. These disjunctions should not be read as 'either a son or a daughter but not both' nor as 'either a son or a daughter or both' but as 'son or daughter, i.e., offspring'. The disjunctions indicate that the relative always relates to this correlative, no matter what.

This commitment to exclusivity confirms that relatives in Plato and Aristotle are intensional. After all, father *as such* does not relate to a son. There are some fathers who only have daughters. Similarly, a father as such does not relate to a daughter. There are some fathers who only have sons. Only the exhaustive correlative, 'offspring' or 'son or daughter' taken exhaustively, gives a correlative for a father as such.

Aristotle shares with Plato a commitment to reciprocity. Not only do relatives relate only to their proper correlative, but the correlative also relates to the relative. A master is called master of a slave and a slave is called slave of a master (7b6–7). Where x and y are a relative–correlative pair:

REC: if x relates to y, then y relates to x.

Aristotle makes the point explicitly:

(T3) All relatives are spoken of in relation to correlatives that reciprocate. For example, the slave is called slave of a master and the master is called master of a slave; the double double of a half, and the half half of a double; the larger larger than a smaller and the smaller smaller than a larger and the rest too. (Trans. Ackrill. *Cat.* 7, 6b28)

Although Plato does not rely on this principle in the *Symposium* (T2), reciprocity operates at a crucial point in Plato's *Parmenides*. Between 133c and 134e, Parmenides raises what he calls the 'greatest difficulty' with the Theory of

Aristotle's *Categories* 7

Forms. One step in Parmenides' argument is that at least some relatives hold only between Forms and never between Forms and things in our realm. The class picked out is 'all the Ideas which are what they are in relation to each other' (ὅσαι τῶν ἰδεῶν πρὸς ἀλλήλας εἰσὶν αἵ εἰσιν) (*Parm.* 133c8–d2).[19] Similarly, the corresponding items in our realm are what they are in relation to each other (*Parm.* 133d2–5).

The central examples are master, slave, knowledge and knowledge's object, truth. Parmenides' point is that each item in each pair is what it is relative to the other. Master is what it is in relation to slave; slave is what it is in relation to master.[20] Knowledge is what it is in relation to its object, the object of knowledge is what it is in relation to knowledge. But these pairs reciprocate only within either the Form realm or our realm. With this agreed, Parmenides proceeds with a *reductio*, which I will discuss further below. But for now, I stress that reciprocity is a key part of the greatest difficulty.

In short, Plato and Aristotle share some core commitments about relativity. For both: analysis of relativity starts from relatives; relatives are intensional; each relative has an exclusive correlative; each relative reciprocates with its correlative. However, this does not yet show that Plato directly influenced Aristotle. Both could be drawing on a shared tradition or there could be an intermediate source between the two. The next part of the paper eliminates these possibilities.

---

[19] Relatives, taken intensionally, are in play here: notice the use of εἰσὶν αἵ εἰσιν, simply another variation on ὅπερ ἔστιν, this time a feminine plural. To specify reciprocity, Plato uses πρὸς ἄλληλα. Plato often uses the expression πρὸς ἄλληλα to describe a relation that things that are the same have to each other, especially things that are of the same kind (for example: *Theaetetus* 195c8–d1; *Sophist* 228c4, 253a2 and 253b9; *Parmenides* 136b1 and 158d2), even when the specific ideas of correlative are not at stake. Plato uses the expression πρὸς ἄλληλα to specify the reciprocal feature of relatives in the *Statesman*: 'we must not say, as we said a little while ago, that [greater and smaller] are only relative to each other [πρὸς ἄλληλα], but rather that, on the one hand, they are relative to each other [πρὸς ἄλληλα], while, on the other hand, relative to the measure' (*Statesman* 283e). The third comes from an alternative manuscript reading of the *Sophist* at 255c14. I defended this as the correct reading in Duncombe (2012).

[20] Cf. Aristotle *Cat.* 7 6b28–7a21. Aristotle is clear that relatives reciprocate (6b28–35) and even uses as examples master and slave (6b29–30) and knowledge (6b34–5).

129

Matthew Duncombe

Plato Directly Influenced Aristotle

As well as some core ideas about relatives, Plato and Aristotle also share a key set of examples of relative entities. Alone, shared examples do not show that Plato influenced Aristotle.[21] However, these examples of relatives serve particular philosophical purposes in Plato. Since Plato introduced these examples to serve his philosophical needs, it is unlikely that Plato is drawing on another source for his views of relatives and hence likely that Aristotle draws on Plato.[22] I will discuss two sets of examples. First, master, slave and knowledge (*Parmenides* 133d7–134b1. Cf. *Cat.* 7 6b1–3; 6b28–b35). Second, desire (*Rep.* IV 437c. Cf. *Topics* 146b12; *SE* 173a39–40; 173b4–5).

To see the case of master, slave and knowledge, I need to return to the 'greatest difficulty'. We saw above that the basic strategy is a *reductio*. The Forms, as outlined by the young Socrates, lead to absurd consequences, when combined with some further plausible premises.[23] In particular, when we posit Forms corresponding to certain relative entities, absurd consequences follow. The examples chosen for the *reductio* are relatives, but are not chosen at random. Parmenides draws out three absurd consequences.[24] The first absurd consequence is epistemic. The Forms cannot be known (133b4–6, 134b11–c2).[25] The second 'astonishing' (θαυμαστός) (134e7) consequence is that the divine, or the gods, could not know human matters (134e5–6).[26] Parmenides draws one further absurd consequence, often overlooked in the literature on the

---

[21] Cf. Owen (1966) 144). Owen points out that Plato (in the later dialogues) and Aristotle share a suspicion of over-simplification, but declines to draw the conclusion that Plato influenced Aristotle.

[22] David Sedley suggested this line of argument to me.

[23] There is consensus on the general *reductio* strategy of the argument, although the details are controversial. For discussion, see my Duncombe (2013).

[24] For this reading, see my Duncombe (2013) 48–9.

[25] Many scholars note this consequence: Forrester (1974) 233; Peterson (1981) 1; Rickless (2007) 90.

[26] Also noted by: Lewis (1979) 120–3; McPherran (1999) 55–71; Rickless (2007) 90–3.

130

Aristotle's *Categories* 7

greatest difficulty, namely, that the gods cannot be our masters (134d9–e1).[27]

So Plato does not choose the examples of relatives used in the *reductio* at random. Plato chooses master, slave and knowledge precisely because these examples give rise to the unacceptable consequences just mentioned. Master, slave and knowledge are given as examples of relatives because they do philosophical work in Plato's text, namely, showing that the inchoate Theory of Forms has absurd consequences. So Plato does not simply adopt from some outside source.

Aristotle, on the other hand, does adopt the examples of master, slave and knowledge merely as examples of relatives which do no philosophical work. This is not to say that master, slave and knowledge play no philosophical role at any point in Aristotle. Masters and slaves are key to Aristotle's discussion in *Politics* I.4–6 (1253b25–1255b15) and I.13 (1259b15–1260b25); knowledge relates to demonstration at *Posterior Analytics* 72b5–23 and the cognitive psychology of *De Anima* III. 4, 429a9–10. The difference is that Plato introduces master, slave and knowledge as relatives, but also as playing a key philosophical role, while Aristotle, in the *Categories* treats them as merely relatives, while elsewhere as having a philosophical role. We can tell this because master, slave and knowledge appear indifferently as items on a list of examples of relatives. For instance, at T3 above, master, slave (Cf. *Cat.* 7 6b1–3; 6b28–b35) and knowledge (Cf. *Topics* 114a17–18; 121a1; 146b2; 149b4–15; *SE* 181a35–6) appear as examples of relatives that exhibit reciprocity.

Unlike Plato's *Parmenides*, master, slave and knowledge in the *Categories* do duty only as examples of relatives. In Aristotle the examples are interchangeable, as they appear on a list with larger, smaller, double, half, perception and percept (*Cat.* 7 6a36–b10). In Plato, the examples are not interchangeable, since Parmenides runs a *reductio* precisely based on worries about mastery and knowledge. Plato has a

---

[27] A similar thought is found in *Phaedo* 62d2–3 where we are the possessions (κτήματα) of the divine.

Matthew Duncombe

philosophical reason to employ master, slave and knowledge, but Aristotle does not. Hence, it is likely that Plato originates the examples and Aristotle adopts them.

Desire is a further case where a certain example of a relative plays a philosophical role in Plato's text, but serves only as an example of a relative in Aristotle. At *Rep.* 436b9–439c9, before arguing that the soul has exactly three parts, Socrates argues that the soul has at least two parts.[28] Socrates argues that the soul has parts because it sometimes relates in opposite ways to the same item (436b9–c2). This suffices for an item to have parts, in particular the soul. Socrates then instantiates this principle with the examples of desire and rejection: desiring and rejecting are opposite relations (437b1–c9). But, as a matter of fact, humans do sometimes desire and reject the same item (439c3–5). So the human soul has parts. Along the way, it becomes clear that Socrates thinks of desire as a relative. At 438a7–b2, Socrates puts desire in the class of things that are 'such as to be of something', which foreshadows Aristotle's own formulation, that 'all things are said to be just what they are of other things' (*Cat.* 7 6a35).

The example of desire as a relative cannot here have been picked at random. Although the argument sketched above only establishes that the soul has parts, not what parts there are, it is ultimately crucial to Socrates' argument that one of the parts performs the function of desiring (439d–e) so that there is a desiring part that corresponds to the money-making class in the city (440e–441a). No other example of a relative could do. So it is highly unlikely that Plato draws this example of a relative from an external source.

Aristotle, on the other hand, probably adopts the example of desire from Plato. Aristotle mentions desire as a relative at *Topics* VI 8, 146b12, when outlining how to test the adequacy of a given definition of a relative term. Aristotle makes the point that when defining a relative term, we should select a correct correlative. Aristotle has a range of examples here,

---

[28] Socrates calls the elements in the soul 'εἴδη' at 435c5, 435e1, 439e1, 'γένη' at 441c6, 443d3 and 'μέρη' at 442b10 and 442c4. These are cited by Brown (2012) 53.

132

Aristotle's *Categories* 7

each of which would exemplify his point equally well. Aristotle has just been discussing 'wish' (*boulesis*) as a relative (*Top.* VI 8, 146b3), which could have made the same point. A further use of 'desire' as an exemplification of relativity arises when Aristotle discusses the 'babbling' fallacy at *SE* 8 173a30–b17. The babbling fallacy can occur with any term, especially any relative term, as Aristotle notes (173a1–2). In the *Topics* and *SE* discussions, 'desire' does no particular work as a relative, so there is no reason to think that Aristotle originates the example. But, as we saw in Plato, the example of desire does play a key role in Socrates' discussion of the parts of the soul, which is reason to think that the example originates with Plato and is adopted by Aristotle, rather than both drawing on a common source.

Finally, I rule out the possibility that Plato indirectly influenced Aristotle's view of relatives. Could there have been an intermediate source influenced by Plato and who influenced Aristotle? There are only two known, if unlikely, candidates for such an intermediary: Xenocrates and Hermodorus. These are rough contemporaries of Aristotle, for whom a view about relatives is attested. Their precise relation to Aristotle is uncertain, but even assuming that either figure was active in the right context to be an intermediary, I argue that neither was an intermediary.

First, Simplicius reports that Xenocrates had a two-category scheme of 'absolute' (καθ' αὑτό) and 'relative' (πρός τι), and rejected the Aristotelian ten-category scheme as having too many categories.[29] Two categories suffice because everything is either an independent item, e.g. Achilles, or it relates in some way to an independent item, for example, by belonging to it. Thus, being a brother would be a relative, since a brother is brother of some one but being pale would also be relative, since being pale belongs to some one. If this is right, Xenocrates had a view of relatives more permissive than the INT view of Plato and Aristotle. Otherwise, items like being pale could not be relatives. But since Plato and Aristotle share the INT view

---

[29] Simp. *In Cat.* 63, 22 Kalbfleisch (=Fr 12 H/95 IP). Citation from Dillon (2003a) 151.

Matthew Duncombe

of relatives, as I have been arguing, Xenocrates cannot be an intermediary.[30]

Simplicius also reports that Hermodorus of Syracuse, another first-generation Academic, has a notion of relativity:

(T4) He says, 'Amongst beings, some are absolute (καθ' αὑτά), such as man and horse, others are relative to others (πρὸς ἕτερα) and of these some are relative to opposites (πρὸς ἐναντία), such as good to bad, while others are relative to something (πρός τι) and of these, some are definite and some are indefinite'. (Hermodorus, Simp. *In Phys.* IX 248, 2–18. =Hermodorus Fr 7 Isnardi Parente)[31]

Hermodorus divides 'relative to others' into 'relative to opposites' and 'relative to something' (πρός τι), but this seems impossible to reconcile with Aristotle's stated view. Hermodorus' relatives (πρός τι) are a sort, amongst other sorts, of things relative to something else (πρὸς ἕτερα). So Hermodorus' relatives (πρός τι) are not identical to, or even co-extensive with, the things in relation to something else. But for Aristotle, a relative (πρός τι) is said to be what it is relative to other things (ἑτέρων) (T1). Aristotle's relatives are identical to things relative to something else. Aristotle contradicts Hermodorus.

Aristotle Does Not Reject R1 in Favour of R2

Plato and Aristotle share the intensional view of relatives and Aristotle took the view of relatives directly from Plato. However, my reading now faces an objection. Aristotle gives two accounts of 'relatives' in *Cat.* 7, R1 and R2. A common reading since antiquity claims that Aristotle rejects R1 in favour of R2. For my argument to stand, I must rebut this reading. Scholars often think that Aristotle rejects R1 in favour of R2 because R1 seems to Aristotle to allow some substances, such as parts of secondary substances, to be relatives. Aristotle,

---

[30] As an aside, Xenocrates' view would also be less permissive than the EXT view. The EXT view allows, but Xenocrates blocks, substances from being relatives. Thus, Xenocrates' view has an extension strictly between INT and EXT.

[31] For discussion of this fragment, see Cherniss (1945) 286–7; Krämer (1959) 284–7; Isnardi Parente (1982) 439–44; Dillon (2003a) 203–4, who cites these authorities.

134

Aristotle's *Categories* 7

the thought goes, rejected the possibly Platonic R1 for the extensionally narrower R2. Scholars point to some explicit evidence that Aristotle intends to switch definitions.[32] After outlining the extensional adequacy objection, Aristotle says (*Cat.* 7, 8a32–5, trans. Ackrill, modified):

(T5) If it [R1] was not adequate, and if [R2] those things are relative for which being is the same as being somehow relative to something (τὸ εἶναι ταὐτόν ἐστι τῷ πρός τί πως ἔχειν), perhaps some answer may be found. The previous definition (ὁ δὲ πρότερος ὁρισμός) does, indeed, apply to all relatives, yet this – their being called what they are, of other things – is not what their being relative is.[33]

Despite the traditional reading, Aristotle claims neither (a) that there are two definitions nor (b) that the earlier account has a wider extension than the later. Aristotle does mention one definition. But he does not call it a 'first' definition. πρότερος can mean 'first', but the basic meaning is 'earlier', a sense conveyed by Ackrill's translation. Aristotle simply refers to an earlier definition, at 6a36–7 (T1). If there is no first definition, only an earlier one, the account given at 8a31–2 may not be a definition at all. Indeed, if R2 were intended as a definition, the *definiens* would contain the *definiendum*.[34]

Secondly, and more importantly, Aristotle does not assert that the earlier definition (R1) covers more items than the later account of relatives (R2). He says that the earlier definition covers all relatives and that it is not what being relative is. But this does not imply that R1 has an extension strictly wider than R2, merely that R1's extension is at least as wide as R2's. This, of course, leaves open the possibility that R1 and R2 co-extend.[35]

---

[32] Mignucci (1986) 101–7; Morales (1994) 250; Bodéüs (2001) 129; Sedley (2002a) 332; Harari (2011) 535. Ackrill (1963) 101 avoids committing himself by calling what we find at 8a33–5 a 'criterion'.

[33] Phil Horky pointed out that we find πρός τί πως ἔχειν in Arcytas in the first century BC. For further discussion of the later history of this expression, see Sedley (2002a).

[34] The circularity of R2 has been recognised since ancient times: Porphyry, *in Cat.* 123.35–124.1 Busse; Simplicius, *in Cat.* 201.34–202.3 Kalbfleisch. Among modern commentators, Bodéüs (2001) 129 presses the circularity.

[35] Mignucci (1986) 107 misses this point, and asserts that R2 is strictly narrower than R1; erring in the other direction, Frede (1987b) 23, in a throwaway remark, asserts

Aristotle, then, does not tell us that he abandons R1 for R2. Just as well, since Aristotle moves back and forth between R1 and R2 throughout his corpus.[36] In particular, Aristotle wavers in the *Categories*. He apparently forgets R2 in the immediately following chapter of the *Categories*. At *Cat.* 8, 11a20–3 Aristotle worries that the category of quality might contain some relatives, such as states and conditions. He then gives an argument (11a23–36) that, although some genera, like knowledge, may be relatives, their species, such as grammatical knowledge, are not, strictly speaking, relatives.[37] Aristotle intends to defuse the worry about cross-categorical items. But if the traditional reading of *Categories* 7 were correct, Aristotle's move here would not make sense. Aristotle could preserve the integrity of the categories of quality and relative simply by saying that state, condition and knowledge are relatives according to definition (R1) but not according to the later, strict definition (R2). State, condition and knowledge would, strictly speaking, just be qualities.

When Aristotle writes *Topics* 6.8, he denies that R2 is narrower than R1. Aristotle discusses how to test whether a relative has been correctly defined. He explains at 146b3–4 that 'for each of the relatives (πρός τι), being is the same as being somehow relative to something (πρός τί πως ἔχειν)'. This statement first picks out all relatives, using πρός τι, the characteristic designation of R1 relatives. But then Aristotle asserts that being an R1 relative is the same as being somehow relative to something. This latter expression designates R2 relatives (as

---

that '*pros ti*' is narrower than '*pros ti pos echein*'. Ackrill (1963) 101 is more cautious, committing himself only to the claim that 'whatever satisfies the second criterion also satisfies the first'. Cf. *Topics* 1.5, 101b37–102a31, where Aristotle distinguishes 'definition' from 'unique property'. These two have the same extension – they pick out all and only items that fall under a term – but definition picks out the essence, while 'unique property' does not. The above four paragraphs are taken, modified, from my Duncombe (2015).

[36] In *Nicomachean Ethics* 1.12, 1101b13; *Physics* 7.3, 246b8; *Topics* 6.4, 142a26–31 and 6.8, 146a36, Aristotle uses the characteristic R2 expression πρός τί πως ἔχειν to describe relatives, but in *Metaphysics* Δ.15, Aristotle's other official discussion of relatives, they are called simply πρός τί.

[37] Scholars acknowledge this crux (e.g. Ackrill (1963) 108–9), but none press it as an objection to the traditional reading.

136

Aristotle's *Categories* 7

in T2). So Aristotle asserts that being an R1 relative is the same as being an R2 relative which entails that R1 and R2 co-extend.

I have defended elsewhere a reading which makes R2 compatible with R1.[38] Briefly, I suggest that R1 tells us what it is to be a relative, while R2 tells us what it is to be a specific relative. Take the example of a master. R1 tells us that a master is a relative. A master is said to be what it is of something, so a master is a relative. However, R1 does not tell us how to distinguish within the class of relatives. For example, how would one distinguish between a master of students and a master of slaves? A master of students is said to be just what it is of something, and a master of slaves is said to be just what it is of something. R2 tells us how we distinguish between the former and the latter case. R2 stresses that being, for a master, just is being relative to something, a correlative. So to distinguish between a master (of students) and a master (of slaves) one must specify what the correlative is.

This also explains how R2 relates to the so-called 'Principle of Cognitive Symmetry' (8a35–7): If someone knows definitely a relative, that person knows definitely its correlative.[39] I know definitely a master, when I can distinguish it from other similar items. To distinguish a master of slaves from a master of students, I need to know what the correlative is. That is, I need to know whether slaves or students are the correlative in question. When I know definitely which the correlative is, I know definitely which sort of master the relative is.[40]

Conclusion

In sum, Aristotle engages with Platonic views of relativity, but, given the arguments I have made here, Aristotle's attitude is direct adoption, rather than critical engagement. Indeed, where

---

[38] See my Duncombe (2015).

[39] Sedley (2002a) coins the expression. This principle has proved rather worrisome: Ackrill (1963) 103; Morales (1994) 263; Mignucci (1986) 109; Bodéüs (2001) 131–2.

[40] There is much more to be said to make this reading convincing. See my Duncombe (2015).

we find in Plato a set of thoughts about relativity, in Aristotle we find those ideas repeated in a more coherent and explicit form. But Aristotle expresses the same ideas in the same language. Even if the *Categories* as a whole is anti-authoritarian, *Categories* 7 adheres closely to Plato's views of relativity.

CHAPTER 7

THEOPHRASTUS AND THE AUTHORITY OF THE *DE SENSIBUS*

KELLI RUDOLPH*

Authorship and authority are often in tension when we consider philosophical commentaries from which we hope to obtain information about Presocratic philosophy. Authorial elements such as methods of summary, additions of example and explanation, applications of concepts or decisions about presentation can be used to decipher which elements of a so-called doxographical text belong to the commentator and which to the philosopher upon whom he is commenting. Sometimes, however, such elements are treated as impediments to excavating the genuine or authentic thoughts of the earlier thinkers, or are used to repudiate or exculpate a commentator on charges of distortion, inaccuracy or unreliability. The tensions between authority and authorship do not, then, arise from the text itself, but rather from the pressures of what modern scholars ask the text to reveal.

Theophrastus' authority in antiquity is well known and often remarked upon,[1] but his authority as a source for the Presocratics has concerned modern scholars eager to glean details from our few textual remains. His *de Sensibus,* one of the research-based texts of the Peripatos, has been an important source for the Presocratics, since it is among the earliest reports we have of early Greek perceptual philosophy. Importantly, Theophrastus includes Plato among his

---

* For David Sedley, from whom I have learnt more about ancient philosophy than from any other scholar. My views on Theophrastus' *de Sensibus* were largely formed in discussion with him.

[1] Diels' (1879) views regarding Theophrastus' authority have been challenged in recent scholarship, not least by Mansfeld and Runia (1997). On Theophrastus' influence, see FHSG and van Ophuijsen and van Raalte (1998).

Kelli Rudolph

predecessors, and his report of Plato's sensory theory derives mainly from the *Timaeus*. This gives us special insight into Theophrastus' authorial methods, excerpting techniques and criticisms. Scholars vary in their judgements about the Peripatetic's accuracy and reliability. However, what is meant by 'reliability' and 'accuracy', and how modern expectations and standards influence the way the text is read, threaten to make studies of this text anachronistic. If we expect a report closely attuned to the intricacies of his predecessors' text, we will be largely disappointed. If, instead, we approach this as an outline of early Greek sensory theories, written within a Peripatetic framework, with specific parameters in mind, our judgements about the 'accuracy' and 'reliability' of the text may shift.

In *de Sensibus*, Theophrastus divides the examination of the perceptual theories of Aristotle's predecessors into two sections: the first concerns sensation (περὶ αἰσθήσεως; *DS* 1–58) and the second, sensory objects (περὶ τῶν αἰσθητῶν; 59–91).[2] In the first, Theophrastus classifies his predecessors according to an inherited Aristotelian distinction that views perception as arising from either similarity or contrast.[3] In the second, Theophrastus dismisses most of the Presocratics for giving insufficient explanations (*DS* 60) and focuses instead on Democritus, Plato and their commitment to explanations by affection or by nature.

Theophrastus remains broadly loyal to Aristotle's philosophy, most obviously in continuing 'to ask questions and raise difficulties'.[4] He devotes himself to exposing inconsistencies in, and raising questions about, earlier doctrines through a combination of report and critique.[5] He emphasises Aristotelian topics like the doctrine of the mean (*DS* 29), disposition,

---

[2] Theophrastus, *On the Senses (de Sensibus)*, hereafter *DS*; all numbers refer to text printed in Diels (1879).

[3] See, for example, Aristotle, *On Generation and Corruption* 323b1–324a9 and *On the Soul* 404b16–18.

[4] Sharples (1998) 279.

[5] On Theophrastus' basic methodology, see Huby (1985); Long (1996); van Ophuijsen and van Raalte (1998); Baltussen (2000); Laks (2007).

140

Theophrastus and the Authority of the *de Sensibus*

qualitative change and mixture[6], as well as concepts of natural place (*DS* 83), inherence (*DS* 4, 22, 69) and the conformity of perceptual processes to nature (*DS* 31, 43, 70, 83–4). But Theophrastus also distinguishes his hermeneutic remarks from direct reporting with such phrases as 'he tries to say' (*DS* 2, 7, 27, 40, 49) and 'he wants to say' (*DS* 35, 46, 48, 54, 55, 66, 72, 91).[7] Without specifying his own preferred explanation, he offers criticisms and identifies deficiencies without pronouncing a particular philosopher to be wrong or making strong judgements.[8] As elsewhere, Theophrastus values observation and examination, and praises those who supply reasons and a consistent account.[9]

Modern scholars have, nevertheless, been critical of Theophrastus' presentation in the *DS*, focusing on his adherence to Aristotelianism[10] and his general claims, which, according to Long, may be 'inaccurate either by omission, inappropriate addition or by failing to fit the data precisely'.[11] Standards for treating texts have changed dramatically over the last 1,500 years, and we must be cautious about how we judge the reliability of our ancient sources.[12] Criticisms levelled against Theophrastus' adherence to Aristotelianism fail to clarify why this is to be frowned upon, when we consider that his purpose is not to preserve the opinions of pre-Aristotelian philosophers for posterity. Rather, accepting that Theophrastus is a Peripatetic philosopher, we must ask whether

---

[6] On disposition, see *DS* 4, 19, 35, 39, 64, 72; cf. Theophrastus, *On the Causes of Plants* (hereafter *CP*) 6.2.2; Aristotle, *On the Soul* 429a31–b2. On qualitative change: *DS* 2, 23, 31, 63, 72. On mixture: *DS* 32, 35, 39, 41, 46, 58.

[7] See Baltussen (2000) 72–94 for detailed analysis.

[8] For example, at *DS* 72 he expresses uncertainty rather than a preferred interpretation. See Baltussen (2000).

[9] Theophrastus, *On Weather Signs* 59; *On Odours* 64; *CP* 1.21.4 and 3.2.3–5; cf. *CP* 1.1 and 6.15.1. See Steinmetz (1964) 17–18, 325; Baltussen (2000) 60–2.

[10] See Heidel (1906). Cherniss (1935) xiii–iv and McDiarmid (1953) 129–33 and (1959) 59–60, 70 argue that Theophrastus' evidence is primarily from Aristotle's own analysis and critique of Plato. Cf. Guthrie (1957); Kahn (1960) 17–24. Sedley (1992a) 29, by contrast, considers Theophrastus a 'prisoner of an over-schematised doxographical view' resulting from excessive adherence to Aristotelian distinctions; Baltussen (2000) 134–5 concurs.

[11] Long (1996) 362.

[12] Long (1996) and Baltussen (2000) 134–5 issue similar warnings, but draw negative conclusions.

141

we can separate his Aristotelianism from his reports, and to what extent his authorial choices colour his presentation of his predecessors. Does the material he has chosen to report allow us to discern the theory of his predecessors? Even without the added Peripatetic parameters of similarity and contrast, the dichotomy of Theophrastus' report, unlike a straightforward summary of perceptual *doxai*, requires careful reading in order to understand his use of omission and interpretation.

The *Timaeus* is an excellent test case, since a comparison between our text and Theophrastus' account of its contents provides a clear indication of his treatment of his predecessors.[13] In what follows, I look carefully at Theophrastus' use of paraphrase, indirect speech and quotation, examining his abbreviations of Platonic phrases and theory. If we accept Theophrastus' selectivity, and do not expect him to provide a précis of his predecessors' work, we can then assess how accurately his text represents Plato's specific views.

One may question the suitability of Theophrastus' treatment of Plato, perhaps one of his early teachers, as a comparison for his treatment of the Presocratics. While Theophrastus would certainly have been well versed in, and had access to, Plato's texts, we do not know what his sources for the Presocratics might have been. We cannot know how Theophrastus obtained his material,[14] but the comparison in this chapter gives us a clearer sense of his authorial habits, from which we can extrapolate when we examine the range of extant evidence for the Presocratics.

Plato's *Timaeus* offers two accounts of αἴσθησις. Seeing and hearing (45–7) are part of Timaeus' explanation of the human soul and man's creation, since these senses allow us to access

---

[13] Theophrastus comments on Plato and the *Timaeus* elsewhere; see Stratton (1917) 11, 203; Runia (1986) 47, 53, 482 n. 37; Long (1996) 346 n. 5; Baltussen (2000) 256–8. Theophrastus never names the *Timaeus* as his source, but see below and Stratton (1917) 159; *pace* McDiarmid (1953), (1959).

[14] Stratton (1917) 203 n. 203 imagines Theophrastus with the *Timaeus* before him; Baltussen (2000) 132 is sceptical. He may have worked directly from original texts, notes, an epitome or some combination thereof.

Theophrastus and the Authority of the *de Sensibus*

reason. Later in the dialogue (61c2–d5), Timaeus turns to the perceptual affections, distinguishing the first set of (tactile) affections as those 'common to the whole body' (65b4), whereas the others are located in particular sensory organs (65b5). This later section provides the focus for Theophrastus' own account. Within his own sensation/sense object division, Theophrastus follows Plato's order from the common to the particular objects of perception in the latter half of the *DS*, but it is only sight and hearing that feature in the section on sensation proper.[15] I will follow this order in my subsequent analysis before returning to the question of Theophrastus' authorial method and the *de Sensibus'* authority as a source for Presocratic philosophy.

The *Timaeus* opens with a description of hot and cold. Fire causes the sensation of heat[16] by dividing and cutting the body, producing a kind of sharp feeling (ὀξύ τι τὸ πάθος). All of this is caused by the thin edges, sharp angles (γωνιῶν ὀξύτητα), smallness and rapidity of heat particles responsible for fire's intensity, keenness and ability to cut sharply. Cold, however, affects by its fluidity (*Timaeus* 62a6-b6). Larger particles enter the body, driving out the smaller, resulting in the compression (σύνωσις) of the moisture within the body. The non-uniformity and motion of heat is thus replaced by the immobility (ἀκίνητον) and density of cold. When the body, thus contracted, puts up a fight we call this 'shivering' (ῥῖγος) or 'trembling' (τρόμος), while the affection and the cause are both termed 'cold'.

Theophrastus' paraphrase of hot and cold, although brief, retains much of the Platonic terminology, even where minor inconsistencies point to a lack of attention to Plato's own naming process.[17] First, Plato's list of heat-related properties is truncated to ὀξύς when Theophrastus summarises: 'a

---

[15] Perhaps because it is a distinction shared by the Peripatetics.

[16] *Timaeus* 61d4–62a5.

[17] *DS* 83.2–4: [Plato says that a substance is] 'cold whenever by their fluidity the larger particles expel the smaller, and being unable to enter among them, encompass and compress them. "Shivering" is the name for the conflict; while the affection is called "chill".' Theophrastus reduces elaborate phrasing (*Timaeus* 62a6–7) to simple and abstract forms. Cf. *DS* 84, discussed below.

143

substance is hot when it divides by the sharpness of its angles'.[18] The preponderance of ὀξύς in the Platonic passage, and Plato's emphasis on the physical form of heat, justifies Theophrastus' assumption that this term is a good general descriptor for the cause of heat. Although Theophrastus' selectivity strips the report of the rich Platonic details, it preserves the most important aspects, including the agency of the particles producing the bodily heat sensation. Second, when explaining cold, Plato makes ῥῖγος and τρόμος names of 'the fight between the particles', and says that this process *as well as* the affection is called ψυχρόν. Theophrastus transmits both names, but suggests τρόμος is the *cause* of feeling cold, whereas ῥῖγος is Plato's name for it. Although not as precise as Plato's distinction, ῥιγοῦν can mean to 'feel cold' even in Plato.[19] Theophrastus may have simply thought the meaning was clear, since he introduces the explanation as Plato's definition of ψυχρόν.[20]

Theophrastus' critique, that Plato defines hot, but not cold, by shape (*DS* 87) corresponds to his initial hypothesis that the absolute nature of Plato's sense-objects is undercut by his relative explanations. By contrasting Plato's explanation of cold affects, with his shape-focused account of hot, the criticism strengthens Theophrastus' main thesis by drawing on key emphases in his reports. Although a more charitable interpretation of Plato's position is possible, Theophrastus' critique does not mislead us in our reading of the report. We can still see from its main features that Plato intends heat to bring about division and cold to cause condensation in the perceiver, an outline consistent with Plato's *Timaeus*.

As with hot and cold, Theophrastus preserves the essential information about hard and soft feelings and the most

---

[18] *DS* 83.1. Cf. *DS* 87.2–3. *Pace* McDiarmid (1959) 61, Plato does not need a strong linguistic distinction between affections and qualities, since he uses θερμός to signify both the sensation and hotness.

[19] LSJ s.v. ῥιγόω; Plato, *Euthyphro* 4d.

[20] Long (1996) 353–4 judges it a 'fairly accurate paraphrase', and yet sees a 'revealing instance of accurate quotation combined with error' particularly regarding Plato's notion of compression; see also Baltussen (2000) 109–11. See Taylor *apud* Stratton (1917) 204 n. 205; McDiarmid (1959).

Theophrastus and the Authority of the *de Sensibus*

basic principle underlying the shape of soft objects in his almost verbatim report of *Timaeus* 62b6–c3.[21] He omits Timaeus' comments about the quadrangular bases of hard objects, although this is easy to infer as the opposite of what causes softness. This approach to the *Timaeus* corresponds to what we find elsewhere in Theophrastus' methodological statements; he tends to leave out things that people are good at supplying.[22] Theophrastus' critical remarks (*DS* 87.3–7) betray his Aristotelian commitments, focusing as they do on the impossibility of calling water, fire and air soft and equating depth rather than density with softness.[23]

At *DS* 83, Theophrastus amplifies Plato's rhetorical line that rough and smooth can be easily explained by anyone, leaving out the details Timaeus asserts are obvious: namely, that roughness is caused by hardness combined with irregularity, and smoothness by regularity and density (*Timaeus* 63e8–64a1). Baltussen and Long take παραλείπει at *DS* 83.8–9 to represent a complaint that Plato 'does not deal with' or 'passes over' these properties.[24] However, παράλειψις, like *praeteritio*, is the technical term for purposeful exclusion, and Theophrastus may instead mean that Plato 'purposefully omits' an explanation.[25] Theophrastus clearly focuses on the first clause rather than the second, but downplaying Plato's antithesis may be motivated by benign considerations, both because Theophrastus admits leaving out what he believes is self-evident and because he believes Plato purposefully passes over it as well.[26]

Plato's elaborate argument about relative weight (*Timaeus* 62c3–8, 63c5–e8) is reported in extremely abbreviated form by Theophrastus, who condenses fifty-three lines in Burnet's OCT to a mere two-and-a-half lines in Diels' *Doxographi Graeci*,

---

[21] *DS* 83.4–5.
[22] See Theophrastus, *On Weather Signs* 59; cf. 362A, 711 FHSG; *DS* 36, 54, 89 and 91.
[23] Cf. Aristotle, *On the Heavens* 299 a30–b14.
[24] Long (1996) 355 and Baltussen (2000) 112.
[25] LSJ s.v. παράλειψις 3. We find scant discussion of rough and smooth in Peripatetic accounts of contact. See Aristotle *GC* 329b17–19; *Metaphysics* 1042b34–6; Theophrastus, *On Odours* 64.9–11.
[26] *pace* Baltussen (2000) 112.

Kelli Rudolph

managing nonetheless to retain the most pertinent information.[27] Theophrastus accurately reports the movements of heavy and light objects παρὰ φύσιν, and his summary of the relativity of up and down is correct. More information about the intricacies of Plato's approach to heavy and light are also found in the critique, although this portion of Theophrastus' text comes under fire as a misleading interpretation of Plato's position for two reasons.

First, Long argues, Theophrastus 'very misleadingly' states that Plato gives only an account of weight with respect to what is earthy. However, the phrase ἐπὶ τῶν γεωδῶν (*DS* 88.2) need not express such a specific claim. Before standardised page and line numbers, this phrase could indicate whence Theophrastus drew his report or whither he directed his reader. Timaeus' description is complex, explaining weight with respect to various locations, including earth; Theophrastus assists his readers by specifying this. Timaeus' thought-experiment about lifting heavy and light portions (*Timaeus* 63b–c) asserts that 'this is the very thing we must detect ourselves doing in our own region when we stand on the earth and weigh out one earth-like thing against another' (63c–e). Only here does Plato deal specifically with the actual measuring of weight. Theophrastus' penchant for observation, and his repetition of Plato's παρὰ φύσιν and ἑλκόμενον (*DS* 83.8) from the section on moving earth (*Timaeus* 63c), bear this out.[28] Moreover, Theophrastus later discusses the relative heaviness and lightness of fire (*DS* 88.1–89.3), which would clarify any confusion caused by the opening statement, even if we did not have the *Timaeus*. With this in mind, we could also read ἐπὶ τῶν γεωδῶν as metonymic for 'relative', since it is paired with Theophrastus' preferred alternative, namely, an explanation that is ἁπλῶς. None of this misleads us about Plato's theory of weight itself.

Second, Long argues that by summarising Plato's account of the light as anything easily drawn to a place opposed to its own nature (*DS* 83), Theophrastus implies that 'heavy' and

---

[27] *DS* 83.6–8.
[28] See *DS* 61–2, 63, 71 for similar references.

146

Theophrastus and the Authority of the *de Sensibus*

'light', unlike the relative terms 'up' and 'down', are objective properties. However, Theophrastus carefully clarifies the relativity of the weights of earth, fire and air, and his criticisms (DS 88–9) are straightforward examples of Peripatetic objections to Plato's non-relative explanation of weight. As is often the case, Theophrastus delays key elements of his predecessor's theory to the critique in order to make his own position more cogent.[29] A full account of Plato's theory is spread over report and critique, which should encourage readers to be more holistic in approaching Theophrastus' text.

After a brief introduction (*Timaeus* 64a2–6) to the topic of pleasure and pain, Plato's Timaeus discusses the relation between perception and motion (65a6–c7) before explaining pleasure and pain, partially by example (64c7–65b3). Theophrastus bypasses the first two sections, unsurprisingly choosing to report the explanation:

> With regard to pleasure and pain, he explains the former as a sudden feeling towards the natural state (εἰς φύσιν ἀθρόον πάθος); pain, as a feeling of violence and contrary to the natural state (παρὰ φύσιν καὶ βίᾳ); while the intermediate feelings (τὰ μέσα) are also imperceptible (ἀναίσθητα) to a proportionate degree (ἀνὰ λόγον). Which is also why in the case of sight there is no pain or pleasure from the dilation and contraction.[30]

Theophrastus paraphrases the opening, retaining its terminology and key antitheses. Plato's mild (ἠρέμα) and gradual (σμικρὸν) affections become intermediate (μέσα) here, where Theophrastus associates such relatively neutral feelings with Plato's 'imperceptible' (*Timaeus* 64d). Baltussen argues that Theophrastus' terms make Plato's meaning 'unintelligible'.[31] However, this problem only arises because Baltussen mistakenly interprets Plato's mild (ἠρέμα) and gradual (σμικρὸν) as referring to a motion rather than an affection (πάθος). Although specific distinctions between intense and mild affections go unmentioned, Theophrastus' ἀνὰ λόγον is a good

---

[29] Cf. *DS* 51, 52.
[30] *DS* 84.1–4. Oddly, this is the only Platonic section that Theophrastus refrains from critiquing.
[31] Baltussen (2000) 114.

147

Kelli Rudolph

gloss of Plato's more puzzling τὸ δ' ἐναντίον τούτοις ἐναντίως ('and the opposite [sc. affection] to these in an opposite way', *Timaeus* 64d3). Baltussen finds Plato's phrase 'rather repetitive', but Theophrastus sees the point: the extent to which something can be perceived, whether pleasant, unpleasant or intermediate, is proportionate to its suddenness, force or calming effect. Timaeus' visual example illustrates the latter point, and Theophrastus' abbreviated presentation of it marks out his preference for what is immediately relevant to perception. Two elisions further reveal his method. First, leaving aside visual details in the example illustrates how extensively his divisions between perception and its objects govern his reporting style, and second, his omission of Plato's description of 'bodies composed of larger parts' (64e4–5), presumably occurs because it substantially repeats the general explanation he has already summarised.

Turning now to flavour, the first of the particular senses, we find Theophrastus refers to two sections of the *Timaeus*. The first, concerning composite waters and the four named savours of earth-grown plants (*Timaeus* 59e5–60b5), he demarcates with the phrase ἐν μὲν τοῖς περὶ ὕδατος (*DS* 84.4), and the second, Plato's discussion of flavour proper (*Timaeus* 65c1–66c7), he introduces with a corresponding δέ clause (*DS* 84.5–6). Baltussen thinks the περὶ ὕδατος[32] in the μέν clause is 'odd', but it is as precise a reference as one could give without standardised textual references. Although Timaeus' discussion of composite waters does not deal specifically with flavour, the flavour section (*Timaeus* 65c1–3) opens with an allusion to this earlier section.[33] Theophrastus, then, is not only justified in highlighting these four savours as part of Plato's description of flavour. In addition, by following the reference, he proves himself a perceptive reader of Plato's text.[34] Drawing on 60a, Theophrastus condenses Plato's explicit reference to naming

---

[32] Baltussen (2000) 116.

[33] *Timaeus* 65c1–2: ... τῶν χυμῶν πέρι λέγοντες ἐν τοῖς πρόσθεν ἀπελίπομεν ...

[34] *pace* Long (1996) 356. Theophrastus occasionally neglects other Platonic allusions, but with one exception (64d refers to visual rays at 45c), they are irrelevant to sensation. See *Timaeus* 62a referring to 56a–b (cf. 53d) and 64b to 57d–e.

148

Theophrastus and the Authority of the *de Sensibus*

while preserving the Platonic distinctions and terminology. Moreover, he clarifies that these four are not the *only* kinds of flavour, merely those discussed in the section on water.

Theophrastus concentrates on the Platonic flavours proper (*DS* 84.6–11) and their affections.[35] Summaries of astringent (στρυφνός), harsh (αὐστηρός), salty (ἁλμυρός) and bitter (πικρός) closely paraphrase those of the *Timaeus*, and the account of sweet (γλυκύς) preserves references to the tongue as well. The explanations of pungent (δριμύς) and acid (ὀξύς) are condensed to their general characteristics. In one minor departure, Theophrastus reverses Plato's order of exposition with regard to πικρός and ἁλμυρός. While this may reflect Theophrastus' preferred order of the flavours (*CP* 6.1.2), it also makes a more logical progression within the Platonic system, since Plato's ἁλμυρός more weakly cleanses the pores than πικρός.

Long asserts that the earthy flavour (τὸν γεώδη χυμόν) in *DS* 84.6 'has no authority in Plato's text'.[36] Although Plato does not categorise earthy flavours as such, earth-particles constitute the genus of flavours covered by his descriptions of στρυφνός, αὐστηρός and ὀξύς. The prevalence of γεώ- terms in Timaeus' descriptions suggests that Theophrastus' attribution of earthiness to these flavours may have resulted from a hasty reading of the text or from an attempt to unify Plato's twofold explanation of tastes. Nevertheless, Theophrastus correctly paraphrases the effects of Plato's earth-particles, which through a process of contracting and compacting, produce στρυφνός when the particles are rougher and αὐστηρός when less rough. Thus, Theophrastus' treatment of Plato's flavours illustrates another important positive feature of his approach: his willingness to draw on different passages to produce an integrated account of his predecessor's theory. Additionally, Theophrastus' distinction between sense objects and their affections is at it starkest here, mirroring his analysis of Democritus.[37]

---

[35] Cf. Theophrastus, *CP* 6.1.3.
[36] Long (1996) 356.
[37] *DS* 65–8. See Rudolph (2018).

Kelli Rudolph

Turning now to flavour's companion sense – smell – Theophrastus presents a careful summary of Plato's odours in a close paraphrase of *Timaeus* 66d1–67a6.[38] This is one of the best examples of Theophrastus' doxographical skill.

> Odours [he says] have no 'kinds', but are differentiated by means of painfulness and pleasantness. Odour is subtler than water, though less refined than air. The proof (σημεῖον) of this is that if we inhale through obstruction, the breath enters without odour. Hence odour is a kind of invisible vapour or mist from bodies; vapour is a transition from water to air, mist the transition from air to water.[39]

Theophrastus' introduction integrates material drawn from the beginning and end of Timaeus' account to clarify that odours are classified by pleasantness and painfulness rather than by kind.[40] Introducing the example of how obstructions strain odours from the air, Theophrastus' σημεῖον mirrors Plato's δηλοῦνται (66e).[41] No significant information is lost in reporting the odours themselves, and he is making no more than a trivial addition when, unlike Plato, he specifically mentions the Peripatetic view concerning the invisibility of the vapour that causes odour. In his critique,[42] Theophrastus hints at the possibility of further distinguishing kinds of odours, a project he pursues elsewhere.[43] Rather than criticising Plato's general analysis, he marshals the evidence from the *Timaeus* to support his own position against those who make vapour and mist identical, citing Plato's description, introduced by λέγει (*DS* 90.6), nearly verbatim.[44]

Thus far, I have concentrated my analysis of the *de Sensibus* on the section concerning Plato's objects of sensation. No corresponding treatment of Plato's account of the sensations of touch, taste, or smell is found in the earlier half of the *DS*. Indeed, Theophrastus asserts that 'in short, concerning

---

[38] Long (1996) 359 lauds this passage as an 'impeccable account of Plato's text, accurate, clear and ... full'.
[39] *DS* 85.1–6.
[40] See Baltussen (2015); Sharples (1985) and Sedley (1985) on smell and taste.
[41] Cf. σημεῖον at *DS* 64. Baltussen (2000) 59, 180; cf. Burnyeat (1982) 193–4.
[42] *DS* 90.1–8.
[43] See Theophrastus, *On Odours* and *CP* 6.1.1, 6.3.1.
[44] Cf. *DS* 53.6, 73.2, 80.1, 84.4 and φησί at *DS* 53.4, 71.7, 80.7, 83.1.

Theophrastus and the Authority of the *de Sensibus*

smell, taste and touch, [sc. Plato] says nothing', before adding that 'concerning the sense objects, however, he is more exact (ἀκριβολογεῖται)' (*DS* 6.3–5).

In the case of touch, what little information Plato supplies is bound up with his descriptions of the sensory affections. Theophrastus follows his teacher, presenting Plato's tactile affections in contrast to explanations suggesting a more 'absolute' nature, because there is no other clearly identifiable information to extract regarding touching itself.

For smell and taste, however, Plato does articulate distinctions between sensations and sensory objects. In the case of odours, the closely attuned reader could excerpt physiological details about veins in the nostrils (*Timaeus* 66d), the straining of smells (66e) and the portion of the body between the head and the navel affected by smells (67a). Plato's details about the tongue's veins (65c–66a) and their functional role in tasting could also be harnessed as physiological evidence. We would expect that a reader of the *Timaeus*, capable of the kind of sophisticated reading and concentrated summaries we have seen from Theophrastus, would be able to isolate and report such physiological details from Plato's object-focused account of the senses. It is striking that Theophrastus demonstrates just such an ability to excise precisely these elements in relation to smell and taste, but rather than reporting them in the first half of the *de Sensibus*, he omits them entirely. In both cases the omission impoverishes our knowledge of Plato's sensory theory, since it leaves us in the dark about the physiology and function of the sense organs.

With this in mind, Theophrastus' judgement at *DS* 6.3, that Plato says nothing about touch, smell and taste, seems manifestly false. How are we to explain this omission? Theophrastus has no reason for maliciously making such a claim, but in light of his definitive denial of Plato's treatment of these sensations, neither can we assume that this omission occurs accidentally or because the *DS* was incomplete. Theophrastus' caveat at *DS* 6.5, about Plato's more exact or accurate account of the sense objects may be the key. Details concerning the veins of the tongue and nostrils are intricately connected to

151

Plato's affection-based account of the sense objects, and must be picked out and re-written to form a coherent summary.[45] Plato's explanations of hearing and sight are treated very differently. While these descriptions, too, derive from his teacher's account of the sense objects, Theophrastus excerpts them from sections of the *Timaeus* where Plato explicitly distinguishes the processes of hearing and sight from the way sense objects affect the body. In other words, the absence of an explanation of smell and touch as perceptual processes arises in Theophrastus' text because he finds no explicit distinction in Plato's *Timaeus* between the organ and process of perception and their qualities.

Scholars interested in Theophrastus as a source for Presocratic philosophy must take his hasty and ill-expressed evaluation of touch, smell and taste as a cautionary tale. When Theophrastus specifies an omission in his predecessors or a more exact account of one thing than another, interpreters have often been quick to trust the reported omission. Instead, we should question these strong assertions, since such claims may, in fact, signal that the topic is implicit or bound up in a larger discussion, but not presented with the kind of specific demarcations that Theophrastus uses or would like to see.[46] On the positive side, however, these clear-cut claims of omission stand in stark contrast to the material Theophrastus does transmit. What he chooses to include represents what Plato explicitly had to say on the topics in which Theophrastus is interested. In the case of Plato and Democritus (the only two philosophers he discusses in the latter section of the *DS*) Theophrastus makes clear that the ontology and aetiology of the sensible objects are the primary concern in his analysis, but he takes few liberties with what these authors may say. Theophrastus' approach to his sources is, then, relatively straightforward, and such transparency should provide some

---

[45] Theophrastus may also have Plato's lack of uniqueness in mind, since he shares the view with Alcmaeon (*DS* 25), on which see Rudolph (2018) 48–59.

[46] See *DS* 54 for a similar omission of Democritus' explanation of the imaging of sizes and distances. For discussion, see Rudolph (2011).

Theophrastus and the Authority of the *de Sensibus*

grounds for establishing the *DS* as an authoritative source for Presocratic perceptual theories.

Let us now turn to hearing and sight. In the first half of the *DS*, Theophrastus says Plato 'defines hearing διὰ τῆς φωνῆς' (*DS* 6.1), before adding details about motion extending through the head and liver. This 'definition' supports his account of the perceptual process with a clear and succinct summation of Plato's description of hearing. Long sees a connection between Plato's reported 'definition' and Theophrastus' remarks regarding Empedocles' theory of sound (*DS* 9.1). Long takes *DS* 6.1 to mean 'Plato defines hearing through sound', which he thinks gives 'the erroneous impression that Plato takes hearing to be *itself a sound* [sic],[47] since it gives an implicit explanation by likeness. This interpretation is problematic, since the Empedoclean notion of sound being within is missing from *DS* 6, and διὰ alone is too weak to suggest similarity of the sort Long's argument requires. Although initially categorising Plato among the likeness theorists, Theophrastus never refers to his teacher's account of harmony and sound (*Timaeus* 47c–e), where the like-by-like nature of hearing can restore order and concord by facilitating the soul's association with the divine. The absence of such references here and in his report of Platonic vision is noteworthy.

It is more likely that διὰ signals the section of the *Timaeus* from which Theophrastus drew his report on hearing.[48] On my reading, the opening phrase at *DS* 6.1 means: 'He defines hearing in the course of his explanation of sound'. In this way, Theophrastus provides a reference to *Timaeus* 67a7–c3, where Plato draws his reader's attention to the third organ of perception. Such a specific reference to the sensory organ gives Theophrastus another reason to include these details in the first half of the *DS*, but his textual reference makes clear that this is not separate from Plato's discussion of the sense objects.

In his report of sound (*DS* 85.7–9), Theophrastus reprises his summary, only substituting δὲ for γάρ. He omits

---

[47] Long (1996) 347, 352.
[48] LSJ. s.v. διά.

153

Kelli Rudolph

process-related details, choosing instead to synthesise the concordance of swift and slow sounds described at *Timaeus* 80a3–b8. As in the case of smell, Theophrastus integrates the complex details of Plato's theory of sound into a coherent explanation of the sense-object that we would be hard pressed to summarise better.

The repetition of the so-called definition of hearing at *DS* 85, however, is curious. Baltussen argues that Theophrastus 'seems to reproduce the "definition" mechanically with a view to its physiological functioning only'.[49] However, Theophrastus has very good reasons for repeating this account. First, strictly speaking, the repeated section is an explanation of sound, not hearing, but because Plato explicitly marks it as an account of hearing and includes the physiological process, Theophrastus uses it in the first section of *DS*. Second, since it is the only cause of sound Plato presents, Theophrastus must also include it in his section on sense-objects because of his interest in aetiology. If these were Theophrastus' only reasons for the repetition, one might wonder why he did not simply include his own back-reference to *DS* 6.1. It is the criticism (*DS* 91.1–4) which clarifies Theophrastus' third motivation for the repetition: he must explicitly show that Plato describes our *perception* of sound, rather than the sensible object itself. For Theophrastus, an account of sense-objects should not limit itself to describing the sensory affections, when the proponent of the theory holds sense-objects to be absolute things in their essences (καθ᾽ αὐτὰ ποιῶν ταῖς οὐσίαις, *DS* 61), as Plato does. However, Plato's account of sound does precisely that. By opposing Plato's subjectivity, Theophrastus' criticism highlights his interest in explanations that give the cause of perception *in a particular way*. Theophrastus is particularly interested in highlighting instances in which Plato focuses on perceptions or affections to the exclusion of the absolute nature of the sense-objects because this, he argues, is Plato's greatest contradiction (*DS* 60).

[49] Noted by Baltussen (2000) 117 but with no further explanation.

Theophrastus and the Authority of the *de Sensibus*

Scholars have criticised Theophrastus' report (*DS* 5.2–7) of Plato's visual theory for its weak correlation with the account of sight at *Timaeus* 45b–d.[50] As we have seen, Plato's own words pervade Theophrastus' report elsewhere, and it would be odd for Theophrastus to suppress everything but the most general references to πῦρ (45b7) and συμφύω (45d5) here. The lack of verbatim citation or close paraphrase is even more surprising when we consider the predominance of likeness in this section of the *Timaeus* alongside the similarity/contrast framework into which Theophrastus attempts to fit Plato at the beginning of the *de Sensibus*. If Theophrastus had *Timaeus* 45b–d at hand, it would be absurd for him to omit details found there in favour of a parenthetical remark about commensurability (*DS* 5.3–4).

If, however, we compare *DS* 5.2–7 with *Timaeus* 67c4–68b8, we find precisely the kind of paraphrase and quotation we have come to expect from Theophrastus.

> Vision he makes of fire, which is why he also makes colour a kind of flame coming from bodies, having its parts commensurate with vision on the grounds that the effluence occurs and they must fit into each other. It passes out of the eye for a certain distance and coalesces with the effluence, and that is how we see. Thus, it is as if he were placing his opinion half way between those who say that vision falls upon its object and of those who say that something is carried from the visible objects to sight.[51]

Theophrastus' initial claim on Plato's behalf is that vision is made of fire; this can be inferred from the account of 'brilliant', where Timaeus describes the 'sharper' (ὀξυτέραν, 67e6) moving body, being itself a fire, meeting the fire from the opposite direction (i.e. vision), which 'leaps out like a flash' (68a2–3). Theophrastus need not have drawn this statement from Plato's association of vision with fire at 45c. Theophrastus'

---

[50] Stratton (1917) ad loc. See also Sedley (1992a) 30; Long (1996) 350–1; Baltussen (2000) 132.

[51] *DS* 5.2–7: καὶ τὴν μὲν ὄψιν ποιεῖ πυρός, διὸ καὶ τὸ χρῶμα φλόγα τιν᾽ ἀπὸ τῶν σωμάτων σύμμετρα μόρια τῇ ὄψει ἔχουσαν, ὡς ἀπορροῆς τε γινομένης καὶ δέον συναρμόττειν ἀλλήλοις. ἐξιοῦσαν <δὲ> μέχρι τινὸς συμφύεσθαι τῇ ἀπορροῇ καὶ οὕτως ὁρᾶν ἡμᾶς· ὥσπερ ἂν εἰς τὸ μέσον τιθεὶς τὴν ἑαυτοῦ δόξαν τῶν τε φασκόντων προσπίπτειν τὴν ὄψιν καὶ τῶν φέρεσθαι πρὸς αὐτὴν ἀπὸ τῶν ὁρατῶν. Sedley's (1992a) text and translation, modified.

155

Kelli Rudolph

accompanying explanatory clause (διὸ ... συναρμόττειν), Sedley suggests, is 'not strictly speaking a report of Plato, but his own explanation, in terms of the like-by-like principle, of why Plato, having made vision consist of fire, did the same for its object, colour'.[52] According to Sedley, the διό clause is not *itself* a report of Plato's text, rather it is Theophrastus' own conjecture about how *Timaeus* 67c linked to 45b–d. However, setting aside the assumption that Theophrastus draws from 45b–d, we see that this is, in fact, a close paraphrase of *Timaeus* 67c6–7.[53] Theophrastus may very well take the later passage as evidence that Plato was a likeness theorist, but he has not made the mistake of 'conflating symmetry of particles to likeness of substance' as Long suggests.[54] The Peripatetic does not assert an identity relation between vision and fire, and he equivocates on the substance of colour, going only so far as to report that it is a 'kind of flame'.

Theophrastus may have taken the allusion accompanying Plato's statement of commensurability (67c7–8) to refer to Timaeus' example of vision in the section on pleasure and pain (64d), from which our author may have drawn his συμφύεσθαι (*DS* 5.5). However, there is no clear sign that he follows the subsequent back-reference (64d5) to *Timaeus* 45b–d, where Plato describes vision and the eye's physiology in a way that would clearly situate him among the like-by-like theorists. His disregard for this section is particularly odd, not only because it contains a substantial explanation of the visual organ, but also because Plato's language of similarity and commensurability is at its most obvious here. This omission suggests that Theophrastus draws his information for the *DS* only from the second half of the *Timaeus,* where Plato's theory of sense perception is clearly not, *stricto sensu,* a theory of like-by-like correspondence. Although similarities and opposites occasionally play a role in Plato's account

---

[52] Sedley (1992a) 30.
[53] *Timaeus* 67c6–7: ... ἃ σύμπαντα μὲν χρόας ἐκαλέσαμεν, φλόγα τῶν σωμάτων ἑκάστων ἀπορρέουσαν, ὄψει σύμμετρα μόρια ἔχουσαν πρὸς αἴσθησιν.
[54] Long (1996) 351.

156

Theophrastus and the Authority of the *de Sensibus*

of Necessity, it depends more upon the notion of proportion (συμμετρία).[55]

In the *DS* Theophrastus uses no passages of the *Timaeus* before the 60s, even when they would support his like-by-like categorisation of Plato. One must then ask why Theophrastus would omit the sensory-related evidence from *Timaeus* 45a–47e. When we consider the structure of Plato's work, two possibilities arise. First, the relevant sensory material from the 40s comes immediately before Plato's second beginning at 47e, where there is a clear break in both the text and its content. Perhaps Theophrastus undertook a hasty reading of the *Timaeus*, worked from an imprecise epitome[56] or intentionally chose to restrict himself to the section of the speech where Timaeus addresses the physiology rather than the teleology of perception. Alternatively, it may be that the text of the *Timaeus* was divided into two scrolls, of which Theophrastus consulted only the second (which would begin in the mid-50s).[57] Regardless, it is not clear that Theophrastus, as Baltussen suggests, has the whole work in mind.[58] Once we limit the source material to the second part of the *Timaeus*, the oddities Baltussen highlights (for example, the absence of any mention of Plato's division or rearrangement of evidence from the first and second parts) are not difficulties at all. Rather, they turn out to be necessitated by the text with which Theophrastus worked, or by his own interest in the physics of perception.

A second omission in the report of sight is notable, namely that of daylight and the transmission of movement back to the eye. Long suggests that the report at *DS* 5 credits Plato 'with a misleadingly crude theory of seeing as the contact between two fires outside the eye'. The omission of daylight is a difficulty, even if I am correct in thinking that Theophrastus only

---

[55] Cf. hot and cold (*Timaeus* 61e1–4), taste (66a2–5), smell (66d2–3), harmonious sound (47d2–3) and vision (45b–46a2) where 'like by like' seems to express proportionality rather than a strict like-by-like correspondence. See Brisson (1997).

[56] See Huffman (2005) 586–8 on Aristotle's epitome of the *Timaeus*.

[57] Theophrastus is aware of the earlier section of the *Timaeus* (cf. 150 FHSG); I merely suggest he is not using it here. On papyrus scrolls, see Pliny, *Natural History* 13.74–82, especially 77. See Lewis (1974); Skeat (1982); Menci (1988).

[58] Baltussen (2000) 105, 130.

Kelli Rudolph

draws from *Timaeus* 64d–e and 67c–68d in his visual report. Daylight is clearly mentioned at 64d7, although its role is less articulated than at 45b–d. Coming as it does in an example of pleasure and pain, Theophrastus may not have deemed it necessary to include details of this example in his summary of Plato's visual theory. Rather, Theophrastus may have omitted daylight because Plato does not mention it specifically in *Timaeus* 67c–68d, or because it resembles the Peripatetics' own view of daylight as the actuality of the transparent, and was, therefore, easy to supply.[59] Thus, we see two potential motivations for omission in this section of the *DS*. First, it appears that Theophrastus has limited himself to the latter half of the *Timaeus,* and second, Theophrastus relies on explicit markers in his source text to guide his selection of material on the senses and their objects.

Finally, turning to Theophrastus' treatment of colour (*DS* 86.1–8), we find our author repeating the information about the commensurability of the visual process and object, where it is, once again, important for the critique. The initial reference to commensurability at *DS* 5.3–4 gives Theophrastus grounds for critiquing Plato's visual theory alongside Empedocles' (*DS* 91), enabling him to make the general point that likeness should not have been limited to vision. This observation again renders his own similarity/contrast framework explicit, but more importantly, it reveals Theophrastus' awareness that Plato does not precisely fit in the like-by-like camp. Moreover, the repetition of τῶν σωμάτων ... ὄψει at *DS* 86.2 substantiates Theophrastus' claims about the greatest discrepancy (*DS* 60) in Plato's account by explaining colour as that which has its parts commensurate with vision, whilst simultaneously calling it a flame.[60] As in the critique of sound, we see that repetitions allow Theophrastus to emphasise difficulties in his predecessor's explanation.

---

[59] Perhaps this explains Theophrastus' omission of the transparent from his summary of colour or, remembering *Theaetetus* 156d3–e7, he may assume that daylight's role is minor when the two 'parents' coalesce and join in mid-air. An echo of the *Theaetetus* may also account for Theophrastus' summary of Plato as 'halfway' between visual-ray and effluence theorists; *pace* Stratton (1917) 161. The latter may also explain why Theophrastus elides Democritus' account of the role of sunlight at *DS* 54.

[60] *DS* 91.5–6 is corrupt.

158

Theophrastus and the Authority of the *de Sensibus*

At *DS* 86.6–8 Theophrastus quotes, nearly verbatim, Plato's assertion (*Timaeus* 68b6–8) that dilation is responsible for white, while contraction is responsible for black. He preserves Plato's multi-modal comparison (the analogous cases of hot/cold and astringent/pungent), as well as his claim that the proportions responsible for mixed colours cannot be stated or known because we have no likely account or proof of them. Although Plato outlines (68b8–d2) the main principles of the ratios of colour mixtures, Theophrastus takes Plato at his word and omits them from his report. Baltussen maintains that Theophrastus' use of εἰκότα λόγον 'looks like a mechanical repetition of the source instead of a sensible paraphrase', but does not explain why this might be. So far, Theophrastus has carefully selected material from the *Timaeus* to serve his own methodological purposes, and it would be odd for him to report this passage without some purpose in mind. It is unlikely that Theophrastus overlooked the description of mixed colours, since Plato's final statement about experimentation and the power of god, which Theophrastus does report, follows directly after the account of the mixtures. Instead, Theophrastus seems to take Plato's remarks as a sign that he can omit this section as mere speculation, since it cannot be explained or verified. This confirms the picture we have been building of Theophrastus' authorial style: he takes his source material at its word regarding inclusion and exclusion of material and he privileges observation, ontology and aetiology.

Nevertheless, we are left asking why Theophrastus mentions Plato's methodological details in a treatise focused exclusively on perception. The answer comes in the final lines of Theophrastus' critique (*DS* 91.4–10), where, despite a corrupt text, he clearly responds to Plato's methodological remarks (68b6–8). Theophrastus reports the εἰκὼς λόγος in order to set up another contradiction. By reporting the obvious impossibility of offering either a likely or a necessary account, Theophrastus asserts that Plato is unable to provide an aetiology of colour. Plato can neither explain the ratios needed to reproduce colour-mixtures nor replicate god's work. Theophrastus' subsequent λόγος and πίστις (*DS* 91.9–10) picks

159

Kelli Rudolph

up these points. Although raising an aetiological point by way of a methodological one is unique in the *DS*, Theophrastus' emphasis on causality is not.[61]

We have established some merits in Theophrastus' authorial method. First, he rarely distorts the information that he selects for report, and he almost invariably follows the order of his source material. More importantly, Theophrastus retains items of Platonic terminology even though he rarely marks them as such. Employing verbatim quotation and close paraphrase in both report and critique, he proves himself a careful reader, both by following references and by identifying his source passages when appropriate.

If we have also discovered some warning signs, they concern the incompleteness of his coverage. Theophrastus prefers to concentrate on a single source-text, and, even within that text, on certain parts at the expense of others. Moreover, when paraphrasing a passage, he is ready to omit aspects the author identifies as dispensable, either because he considers them to be obvious or because they are less germane to Theophrastus' own agenda. Finally, the methodological concerns guiding his selection of material (e.g. causality, objective properties, subjective affections) limit his scope and may distort the coherence and breadth of his predecessors' themes.

With these elements in mind, we return to Theophrastus' accuracy. First, we must note that the Aristotelian framework of likeness and contrast does not distort our view of Plato's theory. Although initially placed in the likeness camp, Theophrastus does not manipulate reports in order to emphasise Plato's place among these theorists. Even when it would serve these larger aims, he avoids sections of the *Timaeus* that do not strictly pertain to perception, in favour of presenting precise summaries of Plato's physical sensory accounts. In instances where he postpones his predecessors' material to his critique in order to highlight discrepancies, these passages exhibit the same level of consistency – paraphrase and even verbatim quotation – found in the report. Theophrastus'

---

[61] Cf. *DS* 15, 40, 71. See also Baltussen (2000) 206.

160

Theophrastus and the Authority of the *de Sensibus*

approach to his source material is, at times, so precise that he omits elements marked as dispensable. Without explicit signalling, he is reluctant to extract from descriptions of sense-objects information relevant to sensation. If Theophrastus were our only source on Plato's sense-objects, our conception of them would not differ markedly from that found in the *Timaeus* itself. However, our understanding of his sensory organs, particularly those of smell and taste, would be greatly reduced. We would also be hard pressed to distinguish Plato's unique link between vision, hearing, and reason, but on the particulars of vision and hearing themselves, we could glean the general theoretical outlines, devoid though they would be of Plato's rich detail.

This analysis largely rehabilitates Theophrastus as an authority for pre-Aristotelian philosophy. Many of the authorial elements displayed in the Platonic section feature elsewhere in the *DS*. However, with the original sources lost, any conclusions regarding the Presocratics are provisional until a detailed study of the *de Sensibus* within the broader context of the extant fragments has been undertaken for each of these thinkers.

CHAPTER 8

PSEUDO-ARCHYTAS AND THE
CATEGORIES

MYRTO HATZIMICHALI

The history of ancient philosophy poses many questions relating to authorship and authority, and they are especially pronounced in the case of a group of writings that, although produced in the Hellenistic period, circulated under the names of sixth- to fourth-century Pythagorean philosophers. There seems to be little doubt that the authors of these texts deliberately published their works under false attributions and that it was not a later development in the course of transmission. At first glance it is not at all clear what they were hoping to gain by the association with, for instance, the obscure Sthenidas of Locri or Charondas of Catane, or even with thinkers like Archytas of Tarentum, who was much more prominent as an expert in the exact sciences than for his views on philosophical questions. The contents of these pseudo-pythagorica are equally a source of perplexity, because they are dominated by ideas more closely associated with Platonism and Aristotelianism than with anything we know about the Pythagorean tradition. In what follows I propose to approach some of these questions by looking at one specific text, namely the *On the Universal Logos* (or *On the Whole System*, Περὶ τοῦ καθόλου λόγου), that was circulating and was cited by the ancient commentators on Aristotle's *Categories* under the name of Archytas of Tarentum.[1]

This text is a particularly fertile ground for such investigations, as it presents a complex web of relations and

---

[1] For the suggestion of this as a possible topic under the theme of 'Authors and Authorities' I am indebted to David Sedley, just as I am for much else. I am therefore grateful to the editors for the opportunity to contribute to a volume in his honour.

162

Pseudo-Archytas and the *Categories*

dependencies when it comes to the construction of authority. In addition to the usurpation of authority through the falsified Archytan authorship, the text evokes the authority of Pythagoras while relying on a popular Aristotelian treatise, the *Categories*. It was granted, in turn, authoritative status by Neoplatonists who commented on the *Categories* and claimed to find 'Archytas'' work highly illuminating for the purposes of explicating Aristotle. In this chapter I will try to disentangle some of these points, and come to some conclusions about the consequences this whole affair has for the interpretation of Aristotle's *Categories*.

Pythagorean Background and Hellenistic Pseudo-Pythagorica

The only certain thing about the Pythagorean tradition is that there can be no definitive history of Pythagoras, his disciples and his 'sect', whatever that might mean.[2] The older view, revived in some quarters,[3] was that of Pythagoras as a scientist and mathematician. It was seriously challenged in Burkert's seminal work, which presented an alternative picture of Pythagoras as a religious leader or shaman, with the transmigration of the soul as his only distinctive doctrine.[4] In fact our evidence itself seems to point in two quite distinct directions: on the one hand, we have information on individual Pythagoreans, notably Philolaus and Archytas, who made important scientific discoveries on harmonics, mathematics and cosmology.[5] On the other hand, we have different types of evidence for Pythagoreanism as a way of life (Plato, *Rep.* 10 600a refers to the 'Pythagorean way of life', Πυθαγόρειος τρόπος τοῦ βίου) following the authoritative precepts of the

[2] See Lloyd (2014b).
[3] Guthrie (1962); Zhmud (2012), (2014).
[4] Burkert (1972).
[5] See Huffman (1993) and (2005), respectively. Our understanding of both Philolaus and Archytas is complicated by persistent problems with the reliability of the evidence, the attribution of the fragments etc. See also Graham (2014) and Schofield (2014).

163

founder in terms of conduct, diet, clothing and religious observance.[6] This situation makes it almost impossible to achieve consensus on which type of evidence should be chosen as representative of 'true' Pythagoreanism, or (if neither) on how they are to be combined.[7] This problem is not new: already in antiquity there was talk of a division into two distinct groups of Pythagoreans, the *mathematici* and the *acousmatici*, with interests diverging along the lines just described.[8]

There is little evidence of Pythagorean activity in the Hellenistic period or, rather, the evidence that may relate to it is contested in terms of dating. But it is legitimate to speak of a sort of revival for Pythagoreanism in the first centuries BC and AD.[9] With this revival we may connect figures such as Nigidius Figulus at Rome, who is explicitly credited by Cicero with reviving the creed that had faded away at its main bastions in Italy and Sicily (Cic. *Tim.* 1). There was an interest in Pythagoreanism on the part of intellectuals such as Cicero himself (e.g. *Tusc.* 3.36, 4.55; *Rep.* 1.16; *Fin.* 5.87) as well as Ovid,[10] and we must also include here the work of Alexander Polyhistor, a scholar and polymath who, according to Diogenes Laertius (8.24–35), found and transmitted the *Pythagorean Commentaries*.[11]

This renewed interest in Pythagoreanism must also be connected to the emergence of an extensive corpus of texts

---

[6] Huffman (1993) 10–12. Many of the precepts are preserved by later sources such as Aristoxenus (esp. frs. 33–41 Wehrli), Diogenes Laertius (8.34–5, including the famous ban on beans), Iamblichus (*VP* 82–6), Porphyry (*VP* 42–5), under the headings ἀποφάσεις ('assertions'), ἀκούσματα ('oral instruction') or σύμβολα ('secret codes').

[7] Centrone (2014) 315 opts for a chronological approach: 'originally a way of life (*bios*), it later acquired the features of a philosophical doctrine, initially thanks to Philolaus and Archytas but then largely through the influence of the Academy and the biographical tradition'. Zhmud rejects any dichotomy, (2012) 169–75; (2014), and looks for overlapping characteristics and a scientific, not religious, background informing the activity of known Pythagoreans.

[8] See Iamblichus. *De Communi Mathematica Scientia* 25, 76.16–78.8; *VP* 81–6; Porphyry *VP* 37; Clement *Strom.* 5.9.59.

[9] Trapp (2007) 348–9; Flinterman (2014).

[10] Cf. *Met.* 15.1–478 on the founding of Croton, with a long speech by Pythagoras discussing metempsychosis, avoidance of bloodshed etc.

[11] On this material see A. A. Long (2013) (arguing that it was composed by Alexander himself), Laks (2014).

Pseudo-Archytas and the *Categories*

purporting to be by early Pythagoreans, but in fact dating from the late Hellenistic period.[12] A comparison with the renewed engagement with dogmatic Platonism and with Aristotle and the strong textual focus of these other revivals ('back to the ancients' meant 'back to the texts'[13]) could go some way towards answering the question of the motivation of our mysterious authors. We can imagine, for instance, that Pythagoreans sensed a gap in their own tradition, given that Pythagoras himself left nothing in writing,[14] and the mathematical/scientific investigations of the early Pythagoreans were not sufficient for addressing topics that were prominent in contemporary philosophical debate.

The texts survive mainly through indirect transmission (primarily in Stobaeus), with the exception of very few that have been preserved in mediaeval manuscripts.[15] In the contents of the corpus, a pronounced twofold distinction is once again apparent. On the one hand, there are writings attributed to Pythagoras himself or members of his family that are written primarily in Ionic prose and refer directly to the great man and his teachings, often with mystical or cultic overtones, reminiscent of the precepts preserved by Aristoxenus and other early sources. On the other hand, we have writings in Doric prose (a literary, artificial version of the dialect that was used in the centres of early Pythagoreanism in Magna Graecia and Sicily) attributed to other Pythagoreans, a large proportion of which purports to be by Archytas, while other names include Occelus of Lucania and Timaeus of Locri. These latter writings cover ethical and religious topics, some arithmology, as well as cosmology and doctrines of causes and principles, thus addressing many of the topical issues in late Hellenistic philosophy. The text by 'Timaeus' is especially interesting, because it is essentially a summary of Plato's *Timaeus*, thus claiming to provide the original doctrine from where Plato drew the material for

---

[12] This dating is not entirely uncontroversial, but is accepted by most scholars, cf. Centrone (2014) 319–20 with n. 18; Huffman (2005) 93–4.
[13] Frede (1999) 783–4; Sedley (2003) 36; Hatzimichali (2013b) 1–5.
[14] According to some, cf. DL 8.6–7.
[15] They are collected in Thesslef (1965).

165

Timaeus' speech in his own dialogue. In this sense it is parallel to the text that concerns us here, which is a reworking (in fact an amplification rather than a summary) of Aristotle's doctrine of the ten categories.

Problems of Philosophical Allegiance

These two texts bring to the fore very emphatically an important general feature of the corpus of Doric pseudo-pythagorica: their doctrinal content 'consists of a mix of Platonic and Aristotelian doctrines' (Centrone (2014) 319) or is 'a mishmash of Academic and Peripatetic ideas' (A. A. Long (2013) 139). This raises a fundamental question on the subject of authority, as we are invited to wonder what is the point of forging *Pythagorean* treatises if one is not looking to provide the missing textual pedigree for Pythagorean ideas but aims to discuss, or even copy, Plato or Aristotle. In other words, who is supposed to be the authority?

There are two main approaches to this question. One can opt for a faithfully Pythagorean allegiance for these authors by arguing that they in fact intended to *lay claim* to the contents of e.g. the *Timaeus* or the *Categories* and to persuade their readers that Plato and Aristotle effectively copied or were dependent on Timaeus and Archytas, respectively. This would be a particularly expedient strategy also because, as indicated above, Pythagoreanism did not have much to show on the major theoretical questions that dominated first-century philosophical debate. These included the moral end, the fundamental principles in physics/metaphysics and indeed the theory of the ten categories, which was receiving a lot of attention from philosophers from different schools in the first century BC. As Schofield notes concerning pseudo-Archytas' *On the Universal Logos*: 'to put into circulation a text designed to use a fashionable philosophical engagement with the *Categories* for promoting interest in the idea of that treatise's fundamental indebtedness to Pythagoreanism was an ingenious stroke at such a historical juncture'.[16] Huffman takes a similar line in

---

[16] Schofield (2014) 79.

Pseudo-Archytas and the *Categories*

arguing that the purpose of the pseudepigrapha was to 'glorify the Pythagoreans at the expense of Plato and Aristotle'.[17]

An alternative, more subtle and complex, approach that has gained ground in recent scholarship is to argue that the main focus and purpose of these texts is a Platonist one, namely to bolster dogmatic Platonism by finding support in an even more ancient predecessor, drawing on the genuine Pythagorean interests of Plato himself and particularly his early successors.[18] Moreover, according to this line of interpretation, the appeal to Pythagoreanism also resulted in a successful integration of Aristotle into the Platonic system, by supplying a venerable common ancestry for the two.[19] Such tactics ultimately diminish the Pythagoreans' authority, by exploiting just their names to add a veneer of antiquity to doctrines that actually have little to do with Pythagoreanism. The assumption must remain, however, that Pythagoreanism was a desirable tradition to be associated with, remarkably even without its doctrines: Kahn speaks of the 'enduring prestige of the Pythagorean name', while Centrone appeals to a 'cultural interest in Pythagorean teachings'.[20]

It is also worth noting that the only voice from antiquity who expressed any doubt as to the authenticity of the *On the Universal Logos*, the fourth-century AD orator and philosopher Themistius, proposed yet another rationale. He thought it was forged by a Peripatetic who wanted to confer authority upon his new work by associating it with an ancient name: *Peripateticum aliquem Archytem, qui nouo operi auctoritatem uetustate nominis conderet*, 'a certain Peripatetic called Archytas, who was intending to establish authority for his new work by means of the antiquity of his name' (Boethius *In Cat.* 162A Migne). It would have to be a rather imprudent Peripatetic, though, because his action resulted in centuries

---

[17] Huffman (2005) 95. He considers other possible motivations, such as financial profit or the production of rhetorical exercises.

[18] Bonazzi (2013a) 166. The role of the 'Pythagoreanising Platonist' Eudorus is highly significant in this respect. See also Bonazzi (2013b) and Ulacco (2016) 203–4.

[19] Centrone (2014) 338.

[20] Kahn (2001) 79; Centrone (2014) 315.

167

of commentators believing that Aristotle was not the original author of the doctrine of the ten categories!

These alternative interpretations indicate that it is very difficult to reach a definitive final answer on the philosophical allegiance and motivations of the authors who composed the Pythagorean pseudepigrapha. In what follows I will limit myself to Pseudo-Archytas' *On the Universal Logos*, acknowledging that, despite a number of unifying features that suggest a common intellectual milieu,[21] we cannot expect all the treatises to follow the same rationale when it comes to their detailed attitudes to Aristotle's (or indeed Plato's) texts and ideas.

'Archytas' and the *Categories*

The work by pseudo-Archytas entitled *On the Universal Logos* is part of a cluster of three related treatises ascribed to the same author and closely related to Aristotle's *Categories*. The *Universal Logos* has a direct transmission in the form of one manuscript, where the Doric dialect has been 'translated' into *koine* Greek, while substantial extracts of the Doric version are preserved by Simplicius.[22] A shorter *Ten Universal Logoi* (Καθολικοὶ λόγοι δέκα) also survives in one manuscript and an early printed edition from 1561, but has been shown to be a much later work.[23] Finally, Simplicius' commentary on the *Categories* makes reference to an *On Opposites* (Περὶ ἀντικειμένων) by Archytas when commenting on the relevant section of the *Postpraedicamenta*. A note of caution is required at this point, arising from the fact that we are dealing with falsified authorship: we cannot assume that pseudo-Archytas is one person, responsible for all the texts circulating under his name, not even for all the material on the categories. Of course no modern scholar makes any such claim explicitly, and

---

[21] Centrone (2014), esp. 319–20.
[22] See Szlezák (1972) 2.
[23] Szlezák (1972) 20–4.

Pseudo-Archytas and the *Categories*

at most there is an appeal to a common or similar doctrinal system permeating the Doric treatises ascribed to Archytas. Even this, though, does not permit us to say that the fact that the *On opposites* is a separate treatise from the *Universal Logos* 'reflects' the opinion of Andronicus of Rhodes that the *Postpraedicamenta* do not form part of the *Categories* (Simpl. *In Cat.* 379.8–10).[24] There could be two completely different authors dealing with the ten categories and the opposites respectively due to their different interests, and not due to any awareness of a specific form in which the text of Aristotle should or should not be engaged with. In fact, the author of *On opposites* is very selective and does not seek full coverage of the *Postpraedicamenta*. Similarly, the author of the *Universal Logos* all but ignores the early chapters of Aristotle's text (*Cat.* 1–3), focusing exclusively on the theory of the ten categories, whereas Andronicus accorded great importance to that preliminary section.[25] It is clear, therefore, that the contents of these pseudo-Archytan texts were dictated by thematic rather than editorial choices.

The work under consideration does, however, legitimately form part of the story of the early commentators on Aristotle's *Categories* even though it is not a commentary at all, but in a sense a reworking of the central portion of the Aristotelian text, namely the part that deals directly with the ten categories. It gives examples and brief definitions of the ten categories, some remarks on their order, a detailed account of *differentiae* within each category as well as lists of their common and individual features. Crucially, it offers this systematic information in an exhaustive way for the last six categories (where, when, being-in-a-position, having, doing, being affected), which had received no treatment in Aristotle. Thus the pseudo-Archytan work is to an important extent an exercise in tidying up loose ends left by Aristotle, in the spirit of doxographical systematisation that characterised many philosophical enterprises

[24] This statement is found in Szlezák (1972) 15; Huffman (2005) 93; Centrone (2014) 324–5; Ulacco (2016) 207, with a caution in n. 13.
[25] See Griffin (2015) 57–71.

Myrto Hatzimichali

in the first century BC.[26] In this effort, it shows clear signs of engaging with and making use of the products of the contemporary debate on the *Categories*, and in particular the contributions of the Peripatetic Boethus and the Platonist Eudorus.

The *Skopos* of Aristotle's *Categories*

A question that preoccupied the commentators from the earliest times was that of the *skopos* of the *Categories*, namely what it is that Aristotle divides into ten categories. The evidence that we can date to the first century BC or thereabouts concerns first of all the Stoic Athenodorus who, along with Cornutus, believed that Aristotle categorised 'words insofar as they are words' (περὶ λέξεων οἰόμενοι τὸν σκοπὸν εἶναι καθὸ λέξεις εἰσίν, cf. Simpl. *In Cat.* 18.27–19.1). Furthermore, we have some evidence on the views of Boethus, who seems to have been aware of the three main candidates for the *skopos* (words, things, concepts – φωναί, πράγματα, νοήματα) and, according to Simplicius, was in the camp that favoured a combination of the three:

> The *skopos* is appropriate to the study of logic, and concerns simple, primary and general words, insofar as they signify beings (περὶ τῶν ἁπλῶν καὶ πρώτων καὶ γενικῶν φωνῶν καθὸ σημαντικαὶ τῶν ὄντων εἰσίν). By all means there is concurrent instruction about the things that are signified by them and the concepts (τὰ σημαινόμενα ὑπ' αὐτῶν πράγματα καὶ τὰ νοήματα), insofar as things are signified by words. (Simpl. *In Cat.* 13.11–15)[27]

Elsewhere Boethus appears to refer to the relationship between words and beings only (Simpl. *In Cat.* 11.23–12.1), but Simplicius also indicates that he did envisage a role for 'concepts' or 'intellections' (νοήσεις, equivalent to διάνοιαι a couple of lines later): they constitute what is said and signified

---

[26] This scholastic tendency with a taste for classification and systematisation has been identified as a common feature of the Doric pseudo-pythagorica, cf. Centrone (2014) 320.

[27] Boethus is named as a supporter of this view at 13.16, alongside Alexander of Aegae, Alexander of Aphrodisias, Herminus, Porphyry, Iamblichus and Syrianus.

170

Pseudo-Archytas and the *Categories*

(λεγόμενα καὶ σημαινόμενα) and are the bearers of truth and falsehood (41.28–32).

Naturally we may not expect pseudo-Archytas to pronounce on the *skopos* of the Aristotelian treatise, but what he says about the aims of his own work is illuminating (22.8–14).[28] He divides the 'universal *logos*' into thought and speech (διάνοια and λέξις), corresponding to signified and signifier respectively (σημαινομένη and σημαίνουσα).[29] He is quite clear that he is not directly concerned with things/beings, but with an analysis of the *logos* that permits humans to express and know them. His analysis of *logos* has a strong Stoic flavour: it is noteworthy that he identifies the signified with thought and not with the things themselves, which appears to reflect the focus on the role of signified concepts and thoughts that we found in Boethus. It is also tempting to think here of Stoic *lekta* – in fact Simplicius fills what appears to be a gap in the transmitted text of the *koine* version (at 22.12) with an enumeration of 'simple and compound and complete and incomplete' (*In Cat.* 43.29, no noun provided), which is reminiscent of the types of *lekta* at DL 7.62–3.[30]

Having made this twofold division of the universal *logos*, our author gives the familiar list of the ten categories as corresponding to what is signified: λέγω δὲ τὰ μὲν σημαινόμενα οὐσίαν, ποιότητα, ποσότητα, πρός τί πως ἔχον· ἔτι δὲ ποιεῖν, πάσχειν, ἔχειν, κεῖσθαι, ποῦ, πότε, 'I say that the things signified are substance, quality, quantity, relative; moreover, doing, being affected, having, being-in-a-position, where, when' (22.13–14).[31] A few lines later he indicates that the examples falling under each of the categories are in fact the signifiers. For pseudo-Archytas, therefore, the ten categories divide the universal *logos* into ten general kinds of signified (which correspond to διάνοια, 'thought'), under

---

[28] References to pseudo-Archytas are to Thesslef's (1965) page and line number for the *koine* version, while the Doric fragments will be cited directly from Simplicius.

[29] διάνοιαν μὲν εἶναι τὴν σημαινομένην, λέξιν δὲ τὴν σημαίνουσαν, 'thought is what is signified, and speech is what signifies' (22.11–12).

[30] Szlezák (1972) 99.

[31] Cf. Arist. *Cat.* 1b25–2a4. On the differences in the sequence, see p.173–4.

171

which all the relevant expressions can be classed. Aristotle's text offers very good precedent for this approach (e.g. *Cat.* 1b26; 3b16–21; 5b27), and it is also acknowledged in the more complex later formulations of the *skopos* involving 'words insofar as they signify things/concepts' (see above). We should note that in our text the ontological aspect is not very pronounced, featuring only through an epistemological pathway:[32] the elements of the *logos* enable us to utter and know things, but it is not things that are divided into ten categories. We cannot exclude that our author was influenced by the Stoic theory of *lekta* and sought to understand the ten categories as a system for classifying *lekta*; but he would have to operate with a similar interpretation of the theory to that of Sext. Emp. *M* 8.11–12, where the *lekton* is more or less the meaning of an expression and even the expression 'Dion' has a corresponding *lekton*.[33]

Ordering the Ten Categories

The order of the categories was a significant preoccupation for the commentators, despite the fact that it does not play an important role for Aristotle himself, who shows no interest in providing a rationale for a particular sequence (cf. Simpl. *In Cat.* 340.26). In fact, Aristotle is inconsistent about the order both within the *Categories* and in other treatises.[34] Pseudo-Archytas, however, does try to offer a specific order as well as a justification for it:

Their order is as follows: substance has been placed first because it is the only one that underlies the others and we can name it by itself, whereas we cannot (speak of) the others without it (αὐτὴ(ν) καθ' ἑαυτήν δύνασθαι λέγειν, τὰς δὲ ἄλλας

---

[32] Ulacco (2016) 208–9 acknowledges the epistemological component, but supports an ontological emphasis based on the *per se – per accidens* distinction.

[33] For the problems of this account see Frede (1994) 118–20. See also Griffin (2015) 170–1 for the possible application of the theory of *lekta* to the *Categories* by Cornutus.

[34] At 1b26 quality is mentioned before relatives, but its detailed discussion in chapter 8 follows that of relatives in chapter 7. Cf. Szlezák (1972) 108–9, citing also the order quality-quantity at *Metaph.* 1069a20.

Pseudo-Archytas and the *Categories*

μὴ ἄνευ ταύτης).[35] For they are either predicated of it or said to be in it as substrate. Quality comes second; because at the same time as being 'what it is' it is impossible (for a substance) not to be somehow qualified. Quantity comes third; for, since substance is natural, it is not without body, and body does not come without size (ἐπειδὴ γὰρ ἡ οὐσία φυσική, οὐκ ἄνευ σώματος· τὸ δὲ σῶμα οὐκ ἄνευ μεγέθους ἐστίν) – and this is a continuous quantity (for it is of a certain magnitude; and magnitude belongs to quantity? and size?).[36] So it is reasonable that quantity should come third. It is followed by the state of being in certain relation to something else; for substance and what co-exists with it (<τὰ> συνυπάρχοντα αὐτῇ) must come first, and so it is with being in a certain relation to something else. (23.17–24.5)

It is often remarked that pseudo-Archytas is here in agreement with Eudorus in placing quality and not quantity immediately after substance.[37] In the relevant passage (Simpl. *In Cat.* 206.10–15) Eudorus does not give any explicit reasons for the sequence, other than that both quality and quantity co-subsist with substance (the term is συνυφίστασθαι, perhaps echoed by συνυπάρχοντα at 24.4). Pseudo-Archytas appears to be more informative, pointing to a direct link between the 'what-it-is' and the 'qualified'.[38] Quantity's third place and proximity to substance is justified in terms of physical, bodily substance, a point that was exploited by later commentators, as we shall see below. The relative concludes the privileged group of 'substance and what co-exists with it' (note how these four categories were also separated from the rest by ἔτι δέ at 22.14). Proximity to substance is therefore the reason for the early ranking of quality, quantity and relative, but we are not given sufficient grounds for their internal ordering, nor indeed for the inclusion of relatives in this group. Throughout pseudo-Archytas' discussion of the order of the categories, a lot of work is done by the idea of pre-requisites or necessary conditions, i.e. what is presupposed if we are to conceive of what follows. This

---

[35] As Szlezák (1972) 109 points out, in order to make sense this would require a richer-than-normal understanding of λέγειν, like the twofold λόγος which includes διάνοια. Simplicius has νοεῖσθαι in the corresponding quotation (*In Cat.* 121.16).

[36] The Greek text is uncertain here.

[37] Cf. Szlezák (1972) 109–10, with some suggestions on Eudorus' possible Platonist rationale.

[38] This is absent, however, in Simplicius' quotation at 121.17–18, which reads ἄνευ τῶ τί ἐστιν instead of the ἅμα τῷ τί ἐστιν that we find in the *koine* version at 23.21.

Myrto Hatzimichali

emphasis is reflected in the language used, with the frequent recurrences of the expression 'not without' (οὐκ ἄνευ, μὴ ἄνευ).

We cannot help suspecting that Aristotle's text lies behind the privileging of the first four categories, as they are the only ones that receive some discussion and analysis. In terms of the remaining six categories, 'possession of acquired things' (ἡ τῶν ἐπικτήτων σχέσις) follows after the text quoted above, presumably due to the cognate nature of possession and relation (they are both σχέσεις). Our author may be influenced here by the arguments of Boethus, who reacted to Stoic attempts at incorporating having under their own category of relative (πῶς ἔχειν). Boethus pointed out that σχέσις is said homonymously in three different senses that were erroneously conflated by the Stoics, including something external in relation to oneself that is pertinent for the category of having (Simpl. *In Cat.* 373.7–32).[39] Pseudo-Archytas' account of the order of the categories concludes by explaining that place is a necessary condition for moving and being moved, and therefore for doing and being affected, suggesting the order place – doing – being affected – time for the last four categories.[40]

This attempt to provide a fixed order for the ten categories is not entirely persuasive, largely because of the lack of sufficient argument, but also because of inconsistencies with other passages in the *Universal Logos*. Its main significance lies in the fact that such an attempt was made in the first place, even with questionable success; pseudo-Archytas' list reflects his preoccupation with order, systematisation and exhaustiveness, all features that are lacking in Aristotle's *Categories*.

---

[39] See also 334.15–22, where 'Archytas' is said to have considered the types of σχέσις as outlined by Boethus (who is not named) for the purposes of ranking having before being-in-a-position. But nothing along these lines survives in the directly transmitted text. Cf. Szlézak (1972) 113.

[40] Elsewhere in his text, however, pseudo-Archytas follows the order having, being-in-a-position, doing, being affected, place, time for the last six categories (25.13–26.15 where he lists their subdivisions). Simplicius remarks on this discrepancy (*In Cat.* 340.28–341.2, where he proposes the 'equal right to precedence', ἀντιπλεονέκτησις, of these categories as a possible explanation), as well as on the fact that 'Archytas' often neglects the category of being-in-a-position, which is indeed missing from his account of the order here at 23.17–24.16 (*In Cat.* 335.4–5).

174

Pseudo-Archytas and the *Categories*

Between Two Worlds

This modest assessment of the significance of pseudo-Archytas' ranking of the categories is at odds with the role he played in later debates, especially for Iamblichus and his followers, including Simplicius.[41] We will shortly look at Simplicius' remarks directly following his report of the Doric version of lines 23.17–22, quoted above from the *koine* version. One crucial difference in Simplicius' quotation is that instead of 'substance ... we can name it by itself, whereas we cannot (speak) of the others without it', Simplicius reads 'substance ... can be thought of (νοεῖσθαι) by itself, while the other <categories> cannot be thought of without it'.[42] Simplicius understands this reference to substance as 'by itself' (καθ' ἑαυτήν) in terms of the twofold ontological division into absolute and relative, which derives ultimately from Plato, *Sophist* 255c, and was probably used and emphasised by Xenocrates. The binary distinction featured in the debate on the *Categories* since Andronicus of Rhodes (Simpl. *In Cat.* 63.21–4) and Eudorus (173.14–16).[43] Simplicius or his source assume that 'Archytas' must have intelligible being in mind when he speaks of what is 'thought of by itself', and interprets his ranking of the categories accordingly:

> On this point it is the duty of anyone who is intellectually curious to ask further what each of the two philosophers [sc. Archytas and Aristotle] had in view when the one put Quality, the other Quantity, first <after Substance>. It seems, then, that Archytas postulated that which is knowable *per se* (τὸ καθ' αὑτὸ νοητὸν ὄν), which truly produces completion in all genera, which is present in an undivided manner to all things and which is participated in by them – that this is pre-existent; and he seems to have given the genera their status according to their kinship with it. For that very reason he puts Substance before all else [...] Now the only way in which we recognise intelligible substances is according to kinds (κατὰ τὰ εἴδη), and, if we are to recognise the sensible substances by referring them to those (to the intelligible ones), we will come to know them from the specific features and the marks which characterise Substance, which are considered according to Quality (κατὰ τὴν ποιότητα); hence Quality will quite reasonably have pride of place after Substance over the others. (Simpl. *In Cat.* 121.13–122.1, trans. Fleet)

[41] For Simplicius and Iamblichus, see Baltussen (2008) 153–6.
[42] See n. 35.
[43] On this debate, see Griffin (2015) 48–54, 82–7.

175

Archytas is said to have placed quality before quantity because of its greater affinity to the 'kinds' (εἴδη) by which we recognise intelligible substances and, derivatively, sensible ones too. His interest in the intelligible realm is thus proposed as the motivation for his order/rank of the first two categories, with the implication that, by contrast, it was Aristotle's focus on bodily sensible substances that led him to assign the second place to quantity. This is an interpretation that goes well beyond the sparse rationale in the transmitted text of the *Universal Logos* itself, and passages of this kind are indicative of the important role that our text was made to play in the debate about the relationship of the categories (and the *Categories*) to the intelligible world, which was a major Platonist preoccupation.

As we have seen, no ontological rationale was explicit in pseudo-Archytas' ordering of the ten categories. There are, however, other passages that do indicate a distinction between two ontological levels, for instance when our author claims that the full range of the categories is applicable only to particulars, not to things 'in themselves': τὴν ἐφαρμογὴν ἁπάντων τούτων οὐκ αὐτὸς ὁ ἄνθρωπος, ἀλλ' ὁ τὶς ἄνθρωπος ἐπιδέχεται, 'all these things apply not to man himself but to some particular man' (30.19–20).[44] By contrast, 'man himself' is said here to admit the 'primary meaning' (τὴν πρώτην ἐπιδέχεται σημασίαν), and this primary meaning signifies 'what-it-is in accordance with the form' (τὸ τί ἔστιν κατὰ τὴν ἰδέαν); it is neither qualified, nor quantified, nor in a relation to anything else, nor doing or undergoing anything, it does not have anything, and is not in place or time (30.23–31.3). The twofold ontology is clearest in the sentence that concludes our author's main account of the categories: πάντα γὰρ ταῦτα φυσικῆς οὐσίας καὶ σωματικῆς συμβεβηκότα ἐστίν, ἀλλ' οὐ νοητῆς <καὶ> ἀκινήτου καὶ προσέτι ἀμεροῦς, 'for all these things are accidents of physical and bodily being, but not of the intelligible and unchanging and moreover indivisible (being)' (31.3–5).[45]

---

[44] This is very clear in the case of quantity, which is explicitly said to apply to (and require) bodies, 23.22–3 cited p. 173.

[45] Cf. Simpl. *In Cat.* 378.1–379.2.

176

Pseudo-Archytas and the *Categories*

From such remarks it is apparent that pseudo-Archytas was operating with the Platonic dualist framework, so it becomes important to clarify his standpoint with regard to the scope of the ten categories across the sensible and intelligible realms. This was a pressing matter for Platonist readers of the *Categories*, who criticised Aristotle for presenting an incomplete division that ignores intelligible beings, 'beings to the highest degree' (Plotinus, *Enn.* 6.1.1.28–30, cf. Simpl. *In Cat.* 73.15–28) and thus admitting an incoherent category of substance that lacks unity (76.13–17). Chiaradonna has argued that this was not the strategy of Eudorus, generally thought to be the earliest Platonist interpreter of the *Categories*.[46] His argument relies on the section from pseudo-Archytas discussed above, where the distinction is drawn between 'some particular man' and 'man himself' (30.19–31.5), and where the nine categories other than substance are twice listed as pertaining only to sensible beings.[47] Taken together with the association of 'man himself' with the 'first signification', i.e. the first category of substance, this suggests that pseudo-Archytas' category of substance applied also to intelligible being, unlike his remaining nine categories.[48] Chiaradonna goes on to emphasise how the pseudo-Archytan text formed part of an early Platonist strategy of appropriating Aristotelian doctrines into a Pythagorising-Platonist system, where Eudorus was the central figure.[49]

This integration of intelligible being into the category of substance could be successful in reassuring Platonists that the doctrine of the ten categories, and thus perhaps also Aristotle's *Categories* when read through an Archytan prism, was not actively hostile to their metaphysics.[50] But the fact that the intelligible world was pertinent for substance only, to

---

[46] Chiaradonna (2009) 99–108.

[47] The second time around, at 31.1–3, being-in-a-position is omitted (cf. n. 40).

[48] See Chiaradonna (2009) 102, with Szlezák (1972) 142 and Ulacco (2016) 209. This was precisely Simplicius' interpretation of 'Archytas' (*In Cat.* 378.1–3).

[49] Chiaradonna (2009) 106–8; see also Bonazzi (2013a) and (2013b); Centrone (2014).

[50] Such hostility is detected in Aristotle's *Categories* by modern interpreters; see e.g. Shields (2014) 178–84.

the exclusion of the other categories, means that the tenfold division was at best irrelevant for Platonist metaphysics and ontology. Porphyry allowed as much for Aristotle's work, while critics like Lucius, Nicostratus and of course Plotinus were not swayed by Eudorus' appropriating tactics and remained polemically opposed to the *Categories*. A much more radical integration of the ten categories into a two-world ontology was attempted by Iamblichus, another Platonist with strong Pythagorean interests, and the use to which he put the *Universal Logos* is of great interest for our purposes.

The emphasis on 'Archytas'' alleged anticipation of the theory of the ten categories was a major part of Iamblichus' interpretative strategy towards the Aristotelian text, in line with his goal of investing the unified Platonic-Aristotelian philosophical tradition with a strong Pythagorean background. More specifically, Iamblichus was able to use 'Archytas'' text in support of his own view (*contra* Plotinus) that *all* the proposed genera (and not just substance) are equally applicable to the intelligible realm, and thus Aristotle's *Categories* could be read as a work of Platonic ontology in its entirety. He proceeded to show this for each category individually, applying his 'intellective theory' (νοερὰ θεωρία), as Simplicius calls it.[51] This type of theory goes well beyond Porphyry's view, whereby the *Categories* was a semantic work categorising the way in which we speak about the sensible world, compatible with, but not representative of, Platonic metaphysics.[52] Moreover, Iamblichus' constant appeals to 'Archytas' go well beyond and occasionally contradict what we actually find in the *Universal Logos* in terms of metaphysical content, while at the same time they constitute the basis for our author's ascendancy to authoritative status.

Iamblichus' approach was endorsed by Simplicius in yet another move of deference to authority, evident in the reverence with which he treats the 'divine Iamblichus'. In the proem to his commentary on the *Categories*, where he gives an account

[51] On this theory, see Dillon (1997).
[52] Griffin (2012) 175.

Pseudo-Archytas and the *Categories*

of the predecessors on whom his own work will be based, Simplicius explains how Iamblichus both followed but also diverged from Porphyry's long commentary *To Gedaleius*: he removed Porphyry's punctilious nit-picking (τὴν ὡς ἐν σχολαῖς πρὸς τὰς ἐνστάσεις μακρολογίαν, 'the scholastic long-windedness in dealing with objections', 2.13–14) and replaced it with his own 'intellective theory'. Simplicius clearly suggests that 'Archytas' was the source for a large part of Iamblichus' additions to and departures from Porphyry.

> In addition, he (sc. Iamblichus) also added something else to his writing which was useful: for even before Aristotle, the Pythagorean Archytas, in the book he entitled *On the All*, had already divided the primary genera into ten, and had clearly explained, with the help of examples, their distinctive tokens, and had indicated the order they occupy with regard to one another, and the specific differences of each [genus], as well as their common and individual properties. (Simpl. *In Cat.* 2.14–20, trans. Chase)

Simplicius goes on to explain that Iamblichus adduced 'Archytas'' remarks under the relevant categories, amplifying what had been 'intellectively concentrated' (νοερῶς συνεσπειραμένα) and indicating the agreement between Aristotle and 'Archytas'. In effect, Iamblichus proceeded to distinguish multiple levels of reality relating to each category, thus creating ontological space for intelligible versions in each case and making the ten genera metaphysically far richer and more complex than Aristotle could have ever imagined. For example, Iamblichus endorses from pseudo-Archytas (25.1–3) the inclusion of weight (ῥοπή) as a third type of quantity alongside size and number. This allows him to construct hierarchies of both corporeal and incorporeal beings based on weight, from the four elements that have weight all the way to incorporeal Intellect that is weightless (Simpl. *In Cat.* 128.16–129.7).[53]

Iamblichus' intellective use of 'Archytas' is particularly prominent in the case of place and time: unlike Aristotle, who classed them under quantity and had separate categories for where and

---

[53] As we saw above (p. 176 with n. 44) Archytas was very clear that quantity pertains to body only. On Iamblichus' exploitation of weight, see also Dillon (1997) 71–2.

when, pseudo-Archytas treated them as separate categories, perhaps following Andronicus (Simpl. *In Cat.* 342.21–5). Archytas' grounds for doing so were ontological according to Simplicius/Iamblichus, to be contrasted with Aristotle's allegedly semantic considerations: 'on the one hand Aristotle, paying heed to the differences in their meanings, puts the [concept] when in another category [from time]; and on the other hand Archytas, having regard to the kinship in respect of their objects (πρὸς τὴν κατὰ τὰ πράγματα συγγένειαν ἀποβλέπων), arranged the [concept] when together with time' (347.13–15, trans. Gaskin). However, as we saw above (p. 174), pseudo-Archytas' rationale for these two separate categories was based on their role as prerequisites for acting and undergoing. Nevertheless, Iamblichus proceeded to make use of 'Archytas' in order to elaborate further on the ontological status of time and place:

> In conveying the nature of time more theoretically, Iamblichus again chooses as his guide Archytas, who says that 'time is the number of a certain movement, or, more generally, the extension of the nature of the universe too' ('ἐστὶν ὁ χρόνος κινάσιός τινος ἀριθμὸς ἢ καὶ καθόλω διάστημα τᾶς τοῦ παντὸς φύσιος'). In this he does not conflate together the opinions of Aristotle and the Stoics, as some think, because Aristotle says that time is the number of movement [sc. without qualification], whereas of the Stoics Zeno said that time is the extension of all movement simpliciter, while Chrysippus [called it] the extension of the movement of the world. Now [Archytas] does not join these two definitions together, but establishes a single definition, one which is special [to time] and goes beyond the assertions of the other [definitions]. (Simpl. *In Cat.* 350.10–18, trans. Gaskin)

Iamblichus once again exploits pseudo-Archytas for the purposes of his own innovative account whereby there are two kinds of time, a superior one that is static and generates the subordinate one, which flows and 'resides' in the events that take place in it. He was able to derive this from Archytas' definition of time in the passage just cited, which conveniently has two legs (i) the number of a certain movement and (ii) the extension of the nature of the universe. Further grist to Iamblichus' mill was offered by pseudo-Archytas' specification of the distinctive properties of time as 'indivisible' and 'insubstantial'

Pseudo-Archytas and the *Categories*

(τὸ ἀμερὲς καὶ τὸ ἀνυπόστατον, 29.12), which Iamblichus took to refer to different levels of time (Simpl. *In Cat.* 353.19–356.7; cf. *In Phys.* 792.20–793.23).[54] On the passage just quoted, it is noteworthy that there were interpreters who identified a combination between Aristotelian and Stoic ideas (cf. 'as some think'). One immediately wonders whether this might be a reference to Themistius, just because we know of no one else who doubted the Archytan authorship. Interestingly, Simplicius/ Iamblichus feel they have to argue in detail for the unity of the definition instead of having the confidence to go for a simple argument from chronological impossibility.

Iamblichus' 'intellective theory' was at work again in the case of place, where he latched on to pseudo-Archytas' reference to ultimate place as the limit of the whole world in order to develop his notion of the 'divine *ousia* of place' with an active limiting role, applicable even in the intelligible realm:

> For the principal things have always embraced the [position in the] order belonging to the eldest place (τοῦ πρεσβυτάτου τόπου). Archytas too assigns this special feature to place, saying: 'The distinguishing mark of place is that other things are in it, but it itself is in nothing: for if it were [itself] in some place, then the place [sc. containing it] would again itself be in some other [place], and the process would go on to infinity. It is therefore necessary that while other things are in place, place [itself] is in nothing, but rather relates to existents as limits relate to the things which are limited: for the place of the whole world is the limit of all things that exist' (ὁ γὰρ τῷ παντὸς κόσμῳ τόπος πέρας ἁπάντων τῶν ὄντων ἐστίν). Iamblichus remarks: '[Archytas] clearly states here that the special feature of place is to be the limit of things limited in any way at all, unless, that is, by "things that exist" he means the bodies with which the categories are concerned.' (363.20–9, trans. Gaskin)

Iamblichus assures readers that 'Archytas' does *not* have in mind only bodies, but that 'the dynamic conception of place as what preserves a thing by surrounding it does apply, and applies first and foremost, to the intelligible world.'[55]

---

[54] Dillon (1997) 75–6. For an analysis of Iamblichus' theory of static and flowing time, see Sorabji (1983) 33–45.
[55] Sorabji (1988a) 206.

181

Myrto Hatzimichali

Conclusions: the 'Archytan' Categories

At this point we may draw together the main results that have emerged from the discussion so far. In terms of an overall impression from the *Universal Logos*, the key aspect has to be the ordering and systematising project, in particular the meticulous provision of subdivisions as well as common and individual properties for each of the categories. Significantly, pseudo-Archytas fills the 'gaps' left by Aristotle, especially in connection with the last six categories. To this end our author appears to have kept himself fully abreast of developments in the scholarly interpretation of Aristotle's *Categories*, where Eudorus and Boethus were the most prominent figures.[56]

We have seen that our author did distinguish sensible from intelligible being and sought to encompass both under the category of substance, but he otherwise did not invest his work with any strong ontological focus, even though it was heavily used to back up the elaborate ontological edifice endorsed by Iamblichus and, through him, Simplicius. If anything, pseudo-Archytas' categories have a semantic orientation, highlighted by the Stoic distinction between signifier and signified. This is coupled with an interesting epistemological approach, which makes the most of 'Archytas'' Pythagorean credentials:

He says that all art and science is something ordered and a definite reality, but that such a thing is determined in number (ἐν ἀριθμῷ ἀφορίζεσθαι). Now, the overall number is the decade (τὸν δὲ σύμπαντα ἀριθμὸν δεκάδα εἶναι), and therefore it is reasonable that all things should be divided into ten, and that all forms should be ten, and that the ideal numbers should be ten; and further that the extremities of the body should have ten parts. Thus, he says, the elements of the account of the All are also ten. (68.24–8, trans. Chase)

Simplicius typically prefaces this with a metaphysical remark ('Archytas, arguing Pythagorically, reduces the cause of all beings to the principles of the number ten', 68.22–3), but pseudo-Archytas' main focus is on man's ability to know an infinite amount of things through enumeration of a finite number of elements (32.10–14). Most opportunely, the system

---

[56] Szlezák (1972) 15–17.

182

Pseudo-Archytas and the *Categories*

of the *ten* categories provides an ideal such number, and man whose extremities have ten parts (fingers, used for counting) is ideally suited to this epistemic task of knowing through numbering (cf. 31.32–32.2: 'man is the measure and rule (κανὼν καὶ στάθμη) of real knowledge and has been born to survey the whole truth of beings').[57]

Despite the good Pythagorean pedigree of all these references to number, limits and unlimiteds, we will never be entirely certain about our author's philosophical allegiance, as there are too many authorities in play in this text: to begin with, Aristotle's *Categories* is copied, interpreted and supplemented where required. Archytas is claimed as the author, but as most scholars agree (and often assume without any discussion) this amounts to an indirect appeal to Pythagoras' authority. Finally, Plato's *auctoritas* is also at stake, especially if we accept that pseudo-Archytas' text is part of a Platonist movement looking to colonise both Pythagorean and Aristotelian intellectual territory. In any case, we should not underestimate the fact that out of all these authorities it was the association with philosophical/scientific Pythagoreanism that our author chose to emphasise through the assumed name, unlike Eudorus who wrote under his own name and was known as an Academic. Whoever our author was, his text was taken very seriously by Iamblichus and his followers and thus, despite being parasitic on earlier authorities, it managed to achieve a peculiar authoritative status of its own,[58] even at the price of being distorted in order to back up the purposes of those who relied on its authority.

---

[57] See also Griffin (2015) 99.

[58] This may have contributed to its attaining some direct manuscript transmission, unlike most of the other pseudo-pythagorica.

CHAPTER 9

NUMENIUS ON INTELLECT, SOUL, AND THE AUTHORITY OF PLATO

GEORGE BOYS-STONES

Introduction

In an influential pair of articles, one in each of the two *Philosophia Togata* volumes, David Sedley shed new light on the issue of philosophical 'authority' and its importance for understanding school identity in the Hellenistic and post-Hellenistic age.[1] An assumption had prevailed before his work that the appeal to authority was characteristic of religions, something found among philosophers only insofar as they were more 'religious' than philosophical in spirit. The prime example was taken to be the Epicurean school whose members were supposed, on the basis of a double-edged compliment in Numenius, to have exhibited an unwavering and quasi-religious devotion to Epicurus.[2] But what David Sedley convincingly demonstrated is that the Epicureans were not the exceptions that Numenius had been taken to suggest: in fact every one of the Hellenistic schools subscribed, ostensibly at least, to the authority of their founder. No Stoic, for example, is ever caught suggesting that the founder of Stoicism, Zeno, was *wrong* about something: on the contrary, a Stoic might go to some lengths to show how their own view was consistent with that of Zeno.

This insight had a number of very important consequences for scholarship. First of all, it opened up a new range of questions that could be brought to the study of Epicureanism as a tradition – just because if (*pace* Numenius) Epicurean

---

[1] Sedley (1989), (1997).
[2] Fr. 24.22–31 (here, as throughout the paper, references are to the edition of des Places (1973)). Numenius himself uses the language of religion here: Epicureans, he claims, view it as an impiety, ἀσέβημα, to oppose Epicurus.

184

Numenius on Intellect and Soul

devotion to Epicurus was no more extreme than Stoic devotion to Zeno then, by the same token, the possibility for finding serious philosophical debate within the Epicurean school was no less than it was within Stoicism. Secondly, it undoubtedly helped in the slow process of rehabilitating interest in post-Hellenistic Platonism, by normalising to some extent what might otherwise seem to be their alarming obsession with the views and *ipsissima verba* of Plato. So, for example, the striking turn to commentary, exhibited by Platonists as well as others of the period, can on Sedley's view be seen as a natural extension of Hellenistic school practice rather than an epochal deviation from it: Platonist commentaries served precisely the purpose of maintaining the identity of a tradition founded by Plato at a time when the mechanisms of the institutional school were no longer there to do it (Sedley (1997)).

But it seems to me important to make sure that this normalisation does not come at the price of excessive homogenisation. Plato may play a role for Platonists comparable *in some respects* to that of Zeno or Epicurus for their followers; but I am not so sure that the relationship is quite the same, just because it is not obvious that Platonists at this period see themselves as a 'school' or a 'tradition' in quite the same mould as the Stoa or Garden. There is scope to think that their interest in Plato is much more direct, and much more directly to do with a belief in his epistemic authority, and less to do with deference which he might be owed as the founder of their putative 'school'. One might put the point by suggesting that it is wrong to think that deference to Plato is a posterior entailment of subscription to the community of his followers, but rather that Platonism exists in the first place as a community of philosophers who put their faith in Plato.

One reason why one might want to consider matters in this light is the remarkable lack of interest that Platonists show in the school that Plato actually founded. Platonists never identify themselves as 'Academics', for example.[3] This cannot be

---

[3] This is true, at least, for all of our evidence after Antiochus and Eudorus, both consistently called 'Academics'. But even if one allows that one or both are properly

explained by supposing that the word 'Academic' had acquired inalienable association with the Scepticism of the New Academy: on the contrary, the epithet is left free to default to this sense just because it is discarded by later dogmatic Platonists. (If it were the other way round, then it becomes inexplicable how Antiochus or Eudorus could be known as 'Academics'.)[4]

Historically minded Platonists were interested in where the Academy fitted into the story, of course; and someone like Plutarch could argue that the Academy had in fact remained in faithful doctrinal alignment with Plato, and was thereby able to appropriate it to his own view of a continuous Platonic tradition.[5] But this is, I suggest, a *constructed* view – a retrospective appropriation of the Academy to a particular view of the history of philosophy – and not the description of a 'golden chain' by which Plutarch tries to legitimise his own connection to Plato. If Plutarch's view were more widely shared, and especially if it also carried that weight of identity, we should certainly expect to hear more from those Platonists who disagreed with it – those who do *not* think that the Academy always remained faithful to Plato as well. After all, they would have at least as much investment in what is and what is not part of the pure 'school' tradition. To put this another way: if Plutarch were doing what Philo of Larissa was doing to assert his philosophical legitimacy by arguing for the unity of the Academy, then we should expect to find other Platonists doing what Antiochus was doing when he argued against it as a way of asserting his. We do not.

---

thought of as 'Platonists' (a term which attaches to neither in our evidence), it is easy enough to bracket them as exceptions in the very fact that they would be first-generation Platonists, operating when the Academy is still alive and well. Later on, the term 'Academic' might refer to a Platonist's education (e.g. Plutarch, *On the E* 387F; Apuleius, *Florida* 15.26), but is never used of their affiliation. See in general Glucker (1978) 206–25.

4 See previous note. For the use of 'Academic' to mean 'sceptical', see esp. Anon. *in Tht.* col. 54.40.

5 This is suggested by the title of his lost work *On the Unity of the Academy* (*Lamprias* 63); cf. argument in *Against Colotes* 1121F–1122A with Brittain (2001) 225–36.

Numenius on Intellect and Soul

The fact is that most Platonists show no discernible interest in the Academy at all. There is a very telling passage in Alcinous' *Didaskalikos*, at the beginning of his discussion of ethics (27.1):

> He [sc. Plato] thought that the most honourable and the greatest good is not easily found, and those who find it cannot express it to everyone without risk of misunderstanding [cf. *Tim.* 28c]. He himself passed on his teaching about the good to a very few, carefully chosen pupils. But if you read his writings carefully he placed our good in the knowledge and contemplation of the first good, which one might call god or first intellect.

It looks like Alcinous might be having a 'Tübingen' moment here, when he says that the best account a person could possibly have of the good would come from Plato's own mouth. But it does not occur to him that a good source for the rest of us might be through teachings and traditions preserved in the Academy – or even that there might be traditions in the Academy that could help to interpret Plato's writings. As far as Alcinous is concerned, Plato's school might as well not exist. It is irrelevant. His own project is evidently to get as close as possible to direct contact with Plato himself: the closest for us that that can be is to read what he himself wrote.

When I tried to get to grips with this subject once before (Boys-Stones 2001), I argued that the difference between the Hellenistic schools and Platonism is that, for Platonism, the scholarch's authority is not only a matter of identity, but *also* a question of *philosophical methodology*. Platonists, I wanted to say, do not look to Plato because he was the founder or figurehead of the tradition in which they are working; they came to Plato and worked with him because (in brief) they believe that he knew the truths that it is the purpose of philosophy to seek. I tried to show that this was a reasoned move, not a matter of fideism; but the upshot was somehow the same: Plato's authority is the *prior reason* for becoming a 'Platonist'; it is not, as in Sedley's picture of the schools, a badge one assumes by virtue of joining a particular tradition. In this paper, I would like to suggest that we can get to the same sort of conclusion by another route as well. My idea here is that a different view of philosophical 'authority' is more or less bound to accompany the particular views that Platonism has about the *aim* of philosophy, i.e. the cognitive achievement which constitutes success in philosophy. The basic point is that, unlike the broadly 'empirical' schools of the Hellenistic era, Platonism does not think that philosophical understanding amounts to the acquisition of a body of *propositional* knowledge – the sort of knowledge that can, in principle, be preserved in a school tradition even by those who have an imperfect grasp of it. Rather, it is constituted by the achievement of a higher cognitive state (intellection) which has *non*-propositional objects (Forms), objects which can only be known 'by acquaintance'. In these circumstances, the authority one wants is precisely someone, some individual, who has themselves achieved a grasp of the Forms, and who can try to articulate something of what the experience is like and how they came to achieve it. But this sort of account does not constitute a body of scientific knowledge of the sort that can be tested or improved by others, so that there is no value that can be added to it by the subsequent tradition. Plato is an 'authority' for someone who believes that Plato had seen the Forms, and that they have access to what he was able to say in the light of the experience: there is no Platonism without these beliefs; but they have nothing to do with the existence or activity of any subsequent school or tradition. This alignment between epistemological theory and the question of authority is something that seems to have been quite consciously explored in the work of Numenius in particular. Indeed, their connection is so intimate that, as I hope to show in the next section, Numenius' history of philosophy, and the reflections on philosophical authority that arise in the course of it, can actually help us to trace and understand the intricacies of his cognitive theory.

Numenius on Soul and Thinking

Three Forms of Thought

I said that Platonists think that *success* in philosophy is constituted by intellection of the Forms; but that is not to

Numenius on Intellect and Soul

deny that what one might call 'applied' philosophy, philosophy as a *dialectical practice* in a particular social context, involves chewing over propositions, just as it does for Stoics or Epicureans. Even a sage may have to deal with students or enemies, who do not (yet) share his vision of the Forms; and any embodied philosopher at all needs to have true rather than false beliefs about the world in order to move about it successfully. So if we are thinking about the *dialectical practice* of philosophy and how it will help us (the sort of thought that might lead us into the history of philosophy, indeed), one technical question which we might have early on is how exactly *discursive* thinking (διανόησις) relates to the sort of intellection (νόησις) that we are in pursuit of. In particular, what is the relationship between these two modes of thinking such that the former has any hope of leading us towards the latter?

The beginnings of an answer to that question for Numenius can be found in what he has to say about the relationship between the three *deities* of his metaphysical system – whose characteristic activities are described precisely in epistemological terms. Commenting on *Timaeus* 39e ('*Intellect* sees how many and what sort of ideas there are in the *essence of animal*, and *decided* that this [sc. the cosmos] should have just the same number and kind'), Numenius says this (fr. 22):[6]

Numenius aligns his first intellect with 'essence of animal', and says that it thinks by using the second. The second he aligns with 'intellect', and says that this, again, creates by using the third. The third he aligns with 'deciding'.

The easiest place to start in unpacking this is with the second god, the creator of the cosmos.[7] It seems reasonable to suppose that, like the creator-god in other Platonist systems, this god is an intellect which contains, or is even identified with, the

---

[6] Proclus, *On the Timaeus* iii.103.28–32. Des Places' rather severe excerption omits the lemmatic context, and has led to a great deal of unnecessary controversy over the meaning of this fragment – including attempts at emendation by Krämer (1964) 85–90 which look plausible enough without the context, but unthinkable with it.

[7] This identification is supported by frr. 12, 15–17, 21; but commentators have sometimes sought the creator with the world soul (or the third god insofar as it helps to constitute the world soul): e.g. Dodds (1960); Opsomer (2005) 64–5.

189

George Boys-Stones

Forms[8] – and as such, we can think of it as representing the ideal model, or perhaps the limiting case, for the sort of intellection to which even human beings can aspire – namely, the contemplation of the Forms. The first god is an intellect *above* this one, probably to be identified with the Form of the good. (This is not a mode of intellection to which we can aspire: if the second intellect is the limiting case of our cognitive abilities, the first god is the limiting case of what can be grasped by them: cf. esp. fr. 2.) Meanwhile, the third god, below the second, is identified with discursive thinking (διανόησις). As we shall soon see, this third god has a role in organising the empirical world as its soul (or one of its souls) – so the association with discursive thinking seems quite appropriate.

My question about the relationship between discursive thought and intellection, insofar as it is relevant to us, can be rephrased, then, as a question about how Numenius' second god stands in relation to his third. This is something addressed in a fragment from Numenius' lost work *On the Good* (fr. 11):

> The first god, being in himself, is simple (ἁπλοῦς), and being together with himself throughout can never be divided. The god who is the second and third, however, is one (εἷς).[9] He comes into contact with matter, but it is dyadic and, although he unifies it, he is divided by it, since it has an appetitive and fluid character. Because he is gazing on matter, he is not intent on the intelligible (for in that case he would have been intent on himself); and by giving his attention to matter he becomes heedless of himself. And he gets to grips with the perceptible and is absorbed in his work with it, and by devoting himself to matter he takes it up even into his own character.

The basic scheme in this passage seems clear enough: the first god (the intellect that I am suggesting is more or less beyond us) lacks complexity of any sort (so, is 'simple', ἁπλοῦς). The second god, which represents an intellect furnished with Forms,

---

[8] Although some place the Forms with the first god: e.g. Ferrari (1995) 255; (2012) 122; Trabattoni (2010).

[9] For this translation, which trades on the difference between 'simple' and 'one', see Frede (1987a) 1057 with Plotinus, *Enn.* 5.6.4.1. This difference is overlooked by the alternative, which finds a Pythagorean system of three 'ones' by translating: 'The second god is also a third "One"' (see e.g. Moderatus ap. Simplicius *In Phys.* 230.34–231.5 with Brenk (2005) 37; Turner (2006) 32). Note, however, that on any account the second god ends up in an identity relationship with the third.

Numenius on Intellect and Soul

presumably loses points for simplicity for that very reason, but it nevertheless manages to be an essential unity (a 'one', εἷς; maybe what Plotinus will call a 'one-in-many'). Perhaps surprisingly, the third god – which we can now see takes the role of a world soul – *also* qualifies as a unity (εἷς), although it is, I take it, what Plotinus would call a 'one *and* many'. It deals with, and attempts to bring unity to matter, and does so by the explicit articulation of the Forms present in the second god: their distribution in the realm of nature, as it might be. So, while the activity of the second god is *noetic* (stable contemplation of the Forms), that of third is *dianoetic* – discursive.

So far so good. But note that Numenius does not just claim that the second god is a unity and the third god is a unity, but that they are *the same unity*. In some sense, the second and third gods – or rather, 'the god who is the second and third', is *the same god*.

Discussions of this passage have acknowledged (and worried about) the claim, but the temptation has always been to overlook it in practice.[10] Insofar as there is any consensus on the matter, the tendency is to imagine that the third god is engendered when the second god as it were 'sinks' into matter. In the process it is divided into the part that remains outside (the second god) and the part that is sunk (the third god).

But this view seems to me untenable. Apart from anything else, it suggests that intellect is 'divided' so that there really are two different gods – one in matter, one outside it, which is exactly what is denied when Numenius say that the third god *is* the second god. (The second god is produced in some way from the first god too – and whatever the process in that case, it does not *even* involve matter or the possibility of spatial distinction; yet Numenius does not say that the first and second gods are the same. How can division at the hands of matter preserve identity?) Conversely, of course, if the third god *is* the second god, why does Numenius not simply say that the second god enters the material realm – without bringing a *third* god into the picture at all?

---

[10] E.g. Frede (1987a) 1057–8; Tarrant (2004) 186–7; Reydams-Schils (2007) 252–5.

George Boys-Stones

The Role of Matter

In addressing the relationship of the divine with matter, it is important not to be too easily seduced by Numenius' own metaphors of contact and absorption – or at least, we should remember that metaphor is precisely what they are. And we should remember too that, in Numenius' system, matter contains its *own* principle of movement, which is presumably what is implied by his insistence that it is the source of evil in the cosmos (fr. 52, esp. 52.44–64). So there is a bottom-up story to be told about the cosmogony, not just a top-down story. Perhaps what we should think is something like the following. The Forms that exist eternally and without change in the second divine intellect effectively stipulate the patterns by which anything beyond them – any unified plurality – can exist. They do not as it were *force themselves* on matter willynilly, but it turns out that matter, which is inherently in motion, moves according to these patterns just because *they are only patterns to move according to*. (In this sense, the radically chaotic motion in terms of which it is described is purely analytical: after all to move without *any* order is not really to move at all, just as to have no unifying structure is not really to be any thing at all.) This is a situation that we can describe equally well from the top down: Forms bring order to matter. But all the 'moving parts' are – as they should be – at the bottom of the system. The 'grappling' of Numenius' second god with matter is *really* matter's (imperfect and fluid) assumption of the standard that this god embodies.

As far as this goes, Numenius is not all unique for his age: Atticus seems to think something similar, and so does Plutarch.[11] But Numenius does not follow Atticus and Plutarch to the easy conclusion that matter ends up in possession of a single source of *orderly movement* – a single *world soul*. (Plutarch for example, thinks that the world soul just is the principle of motion in matter, namely radical world soul, but moving now in the light of the Forms.) Numenius is evidently concerned

---

[11] See esp. Atticus *ap.* Proclus, *On the Timaeus* i. 392.8–17; cf. Plutarch, *On the Procreation of the Soul* 1014B–E.

Numenius on Intellect and Soul

that, if we say *this*, then we lose the explanation for there being evil and chaos in the world, as well as order and unity. The principle of evil is, as it were, neutralised out of existence in a cosmology like Plutarch's.[12] This leads Numenius to his famously eccentric claim that the process of cosmogony does not result in the transformation of matter's principle of movement into world soul, but that, instead, the principle of movement inherent to matter – call it 'evil world soul' – is *joined* by a good principle of movement – a good world soul. What we normally call 'soul' (whether in the case of world soul or, as it happens, individual soul) is really two souls: one evil, one good.[13]

It is often assumed that Numenius has in mind that these two souls are two distinct substances, or two actual motions which are in competition with each other. That seems to me implausible – as if in the analogous case of the human being the claim that there are two souls (fr. 44) amounts to the claim that there are two competing centres of will or consciousness. We can get away with something less drastic and more interesting if we assume that Numenius is rather insisting on an analytical point about the way matter moves under the influence of Forms. He may be saying, not that there are two *actual* motions, but that there are two actual (i.e. actually operative) *causes* of motion – which explain what (single) motion the ensouled body happens to have. The movement of an ensouled body in his view might be something like what we would call a compound motion, resulting from conflicting tendencies: a tendency towards plurality which is native to matter; and a tendency towards unity (order) which is given to matter by the Forms, or second god. In this case, the evil soul is the native impulse actually active within matter towards plurality and chaos; the good soul – the third god – is the acquired impulse actually active within matter towards unity and order.

Why put it the way Numenius does – why talk about there being *two world souls*? I suggest that one reason is precisely

---

[12] See again fr. 52, which makes just this case.
[13] Fr. 52.64–75. Jourdan (2015) is unnecessarily sceptical about this claim, which can be seen to do real philosophical work for Numenius.

to keep isolated in our minds that aspect of movement in the cosmos which is good, *and only that aspect*: because, if you think about *that* in sufficient abstraction from the cosmos, it turns out that you are thinking precisely of the Forms.

And that is the basis for Numenius' claim that the good world soul (the third god) is identical with the second god. The third god is not an *imitation* of the second god, or a new substance mysteriously produced from it. *It is precisely the order that the second god is* – but insofar as it is a principle of the movement displayed by matter.

History of Philosophy

From Metaphysics to Epistemology

The foregoing may seem to have been a lengthy digression through the thickets of Numenius' metaphysics; but given the defining associations between modalities of thought and Numenius' second and third gods, it should start to be obvious that we now have in hand the tools for addressing the crucial question for philosophical practice in Numenius' epistemology, namely the relationship between discursive and intellective thought. If I am right that Numenius' third god just *is* his second god, insofar as he manifests as a principle for order in the material world, then it looks like we should conclude that successful discursive thinking (i.e. the activity associated with the third god) just *is* intellection (i.e. the characteristic activity of the second), but intellection insofar as it is the ordering principle involved in our comprehension of the empirical realm.

In other words: *insofar as* our discourse about things successfully reduces rebarbative empirical subject matter to sense and unity, it is identical with intellection. This is an important result, not least because it allows us to give an answer to the old problem of whether, and how, a Platonist philosopher can maintain that intellection of the Forms has any bearing on our dealings with the empirical world – whether and how it can improve our scientific or, indeed, our ethical understanding. On my account, what Numenius can say is that someone with

Numenius on Intellect and Soul

their eye on the Forms will be able to make *the best sense* of the empirical world too – and precisely in virtue of their grasp of the Forms. The reason for this is that, *insofar as* their discursive thought has veridical value, it is identical with their grasp of the Forms. At the same time, someone in search of knowledge can be led there through their discursive thinking, because the greater the veridical value in their thoughts about the world at this level, the nearer they come to cognition of the Forms themselves (which turns out to be something like the limiting case of veridical thought about the world). This is the process, in fact, that we call 'recollection'.

From Epistemology to the History of Philosophy

Plato

So Numenius' metaphysics yields an epistemology that frames his understanding of philosophical practice. But what is especially interesting about Numenius is that he goes on to use this framework to reflect on actual philosophical practice – to construct a history of philosophy, which he put to work in a book attacking what was, in his view, the failure of the Hellenistic Academy to remain focused on Plato – in the way that (as he anyway claims) the Epicureans remained focused on Epicurus.

Consider what Numenius had to say in this book about the background to Plato's own work, for example (frr. 24.47–55 and 73–9):

But long before them [sc. the Stoics], the same thing happened with those followers of Socrates who took different lines – Aristippus his own, Antisthenes his own, the Megarians and Eretreians variously their own, and whoever else there might have been with them. The reason is that Socrates posited three gods, and discussed them in rhythms appropriate to each. Those who heard him did not understand, and thought that he was saying it all without order, directed by the winds of chance as they blew here and there at random.

…

As a man who struck a mean between Pythagoras and Socrates, he [sc. Plato] reduced the solemnity of the one to make it humane, and elevated the wit and playfulness of the other from the level of irony to dignity and weight. He made this mixture of Pythagoras with Socrates, and proved himself more accessible than the one and more dignified than the other.

195

The picture we are presented with is Plato as a force for *unity* at a time when those around him were shooting off in different directions, 'taking different lines' (ἀφελκύσαντες διαφόρους τοὺς λόγους, 24.48–9). The dynamic between a unified truth on the one hand and forces of diversity on the other recalls that in Numenius' metaphysics between intellect (the second god) and the evil world soul: Plato appears here as the 'good world soul' that emerges in their encounter.

One thing to notice here is the curious emphasis on Plato's *style*: the 'mean' that he is meant to have struck between Pythagoras and Socrates concerns expression rather than content. (Indeed, Numenius is quite clear that both Pythagoras and Socrates had a complete and perfect grasp of the truth: there was no improvement to content that Plato might have made.) Numenius' point seems to be that, in the face of the disruptive challenge to the truth represented by Socrates and Pythagoras, Plato, the perfect philosopher in his own age, produces *new discursive material* – philosophical discourse appropriate to the times and the dialectical context, the particular attacks that philosophy then faced. His intellection remains steady and unmoved, but the way this translates into discourse depends on the nature of his 'material' context.

This is not the only passage in which Numenius shows an interest in how Plato's dialectical context affected his expression: for example, Numenius argues that Plato manages safely but also frankly to criticise Athenian theological views by representing them in the obnoxious person of Euthyphro (fr. 23). In other words: the Pythagorean/Socratic *truth* which Plato also has comes out in his engagement within a particular context as the *dialogues* we know and love. *The second god is the third*: his discourse *just is* the application of Pythagorean/Socratic truth in a realm of Athenian discord.

After Plato

But Numenius' history has a second chapter, and the dynamic traced for the post-Socratic generation recurs in the post-Aristotelian age. In his own time, Plato played third god to Pythagoras' second; relative to subsequent generations, *he* is now

Numenius on Intellect and Soul

the second god, the more accessible embodiment of the truth; and the forces of division – the Hellenistic schools take over from the minor Socratics – operate with respect to him (fr. 24.55–73):

> But Plato had Pythagorean training, and knew that Socrates derived it all from no other source than that, and that he understood what he said. So he too bound his subjects together in an unconventional manner, and did not set them out clearly. Treating each as he saw fit, he hid them in between clarity and obscurity. So he wrote in safety, but himself provided a cause for later dissension, and distortion of his doctrines, which happened not through envy or malice. But I don't want to speak dishonourably of the venerable. Now we have learnt this, we should apply our thought elsewhere and, as we set out to distinguish Plato from Aristotle and Zeno, so now, with the help of god, we shall separate him from the Academy, and let him be in his own terms, a Pythagorean. As things stand, he has been pulled to and fro in a frenzy more crazed than any Pentheus deserved, and suffers in each of his limbs;[14] but as a whole he never changes into something different from himself as a whole, or change back.

And so I take it that the message is that *we*, Numenius' readers, are now being invited to take on the mantle of 'good world soul': the philosophy that we are to do is aimed at applying unity (the unity that Plato embodies) to the factionalism of the Hellenistic schools. This is borne out by Numenius' explicit methodological recommendations to us in fr. 1a (a quotation, perhaps programmatic, from the first book of his *On the Good* 1):

> On this matter, when one has set out a position and drawn one's conclusions, it will be necessary to retire into the testimony of Plato and bind it all together by the words of Pythagoras; and to call on the aid of those nations held in honour, as Plato did, adducing their rites and ordinances and their rituals of consecration – whatever Brahmans and Jews and Magi and Egyptians have organised.

Plato's Authority

But consider, finally, the implications of this. The second god *is* the third: Plato's dialogues *were* Socrates' philosophy (and

---

[14] It is interesting to note that Atticus, making a similar point about the unifying effects of Plato's work, uses Pentheus as an emblem of *philosophy itself* (fr. 1.19–23). If we are to read these two deployments of the image against each other, in whichever direction, it suggests a close identification of Plato himself with the philosophical truth, an identification which plays to my argument that Platonists are interested in Plato the philosopher, not Plato the scholarch.

Pythagoras'); ideally, our philosophising, then, *is Plato's*. If successful, our philosophising has the same identity relationship with Plato that the work of the good world soul has with divine intellect. Our philosophising will be Plato's truth, as properly expressed relative to the forces of division in our world. And it is this way of understanding what it is for us to do philosophy that underpins what is distinctive about the notion of authority invested in Plato.

First of all, it explains what Sedley characterises as the 'religious' language which Platonists apply to Plato: Plato is commonly referred to as 'divine' for example; or as a 'hero' (i.e. exactly, a divinised human being). Now, this could be conventional hyperbole; Lucretius talks about Epicurus as a 'god' as well. But the language *ought* to have special resonance in the context of a philosophy whose formal definition of the end is *assimilation to god* (Alcinous, *Did.* 28.3 just for example). After all, if Plato was an ideal philosopher, then a Platonist would be bound to think that he actually had *become like god* – namely and concretely the divine intellect which sees, and perhaps contains, the Forms by which the world was made. By the same token, of course, it means that coming to be like Plato will be one way of *our* coming to be like god. But we have seen that our aspiration is precisely to engage in philosophy which replicates Plato's position. Numenius calls us to 'become like' Plato, just as Plato became like Socrates and Pythagoras.

Next, this all explains in turn the general lack of interest among Platonists in Plato's school as such, and it explains the position expressed by Alcinous in *Did.* 27.1. A Platonist is not at all interested in the sort of information that a school could preserve. A Platonist is concerned only about what *Plato* himself, as Plato, has in mind. That is why Alcinous' impossible dream is to have been one of Plato's chosen pupils; and why, failing that, his recourse is to the works that Plato wrote: it is as near to the man as it is possible to get.

If I am right that Plato's authority for Platonists is not tied to his role as the founder of a school, a third thing that is explained is that, although his epistemic authority is considered to be absolute, it is not considered to be unique. Unlike Stoics and

Epicureans, Platonists are able, both in principle and practice, to recognise other figures who are *as authoritative as Plato*, figures who might serve equally well as the reference point for their identity. According to Numenius, as we have seen, Plato himself looked to Socrates and Pythagoras as authorities: presumably the only thing that prevents us from doing so is the limited independent access we happen to have to them.

In fact Numenius himself, despite the cardinal role he gives to Plato in the history of philosophy and the absolute epistemic authority with which he invests Plato, and despite being treated by later Platonists to all intents and purposes as one of their own, apparently thought of himself as a Pythagorean, and was almost always referred to as such by others. This is a challenge to a rider David Sedley gives to his, 'school'-oriented definition of authority. Sedley formulated the rule that: 'acknowledged forerunners of one's primary authority could themselves bear secondary authority-status' (Sedley (1989) 101): a Platonist, for example, can recognise Pythagoras as an authority too. But Numenius' case is the other way round: the authority by which he constructs his identity, the 'primary' authority in Sedley's sense, is Pythagoras; Plato is supposed to *inherit* his authority in a subsequent generation. That he is no less authoritative for Numenius is explained if the notion of authority involved here is purely epistemic.

This last point has a corollary: if there can be multiple authorities, and if it is epistemic authority that is at issue here (perhaps with some qualifications concerning access), then there is no principled reason why *new* authorities should not arise. And in fact it seems that Platonists are unusually relaxed about this possibility. Take for example, the work of Nicomachus of Gerasa, another second-century philosopher known as a Pythagorean. His work achieved adulation among Platonists – which stops short of being 'authoritative' to be sure, but which comes remarkably close it, especially for someone who is not a self-describing Platonist. His *Introduction to Arithmetic* was translated into Latin in his lifetime (by Apuleius) (and again in the sixth century by Boethius); it attracted commentaries by Iamblichus (who is prepared

George Boys-Stones

to correct him), Proclus (who is not),[15] and by Asclepius and Philoponus, who in turn took their interest from their teacher Ammonius. If John Dillon (1969) is right, a remark in Marinus' biography of Proclus is meant to make us think that Proclus might have been a reincarnation of Nicomachus. That would be remarkable. We know that Platonists were not shy to praise one another as reincarnations of *Plato* himself[16] – and Marinus is not one to hold back. So if it is right that Marinus wants us to think that Proclus was a reincarnation of Nicomachus, then he is thinking about Nicomachus (and Proclus in turn, of course) as a reasonable proxy for Plato.

And finally, of course, there are the Chaldaean Oracles – another product of the second century AD. In a way these constitute an even clearer and more remarkable example of the phenomenon; there is no sense in which someone could argue that their authority derives from Plato (or Pythagoras), since they are supposed to derive from Apollo himself. It is true that not everyone takes them up, and we do not know if there were people in the second century who were aware of them but treated them with suspicion. On the other hand, we also never hear of anyone testing them against Plato and approving or rejecting them as a result. When they are used, they are used alongside Plato, but with an authority that is all their own.

Epilogue

In another important article, dealing with the status of the Athenian schools in the post-Hellenistic era, David Sedley (2003) makes a distinction between movements that have their ancestry in the Hellenistic Athenian schools and those that do not. (The immediate example is Pyrrhonism.) Different rules, he allows, may apply in the latter case. I think that this is a tremendously important insight, because it allows that there are different things going on in the post-Hellenistic age: that movements appear which do not have their feet in

[15] Cf. Vinel (2014) 19, 51.
[16] E.g. inscriptions to Ofellius Laetus: *IG* II² 3816; *IK* 17.2 3901.

the Hellenistic schools alongside those that do. (It is a serious impediment to the appreciation of the period that this diversity is not always recognised, with regrettably Procrustean results.) I think the principle applies, however, at a point in our evidence where we, at least sometimes, part company. One strand of Sedley's view of the post-Hellenistic period has been an insistence that Platonism should be seen as a continuation of the Academy – or, conversely, that the Academics are helpfully thought of as 'Platonists' too.[17] I am not so sure that they were, or that it should. Given how well developed even our earliest evidence for Platonism is, I suspect that the movement predates the 'end' of the Academy – or, perhaps, that its immediate ancestor in the Hellenistic age is not the Academy at all, but the 'Pythagorean' movement (about which we know far too little). In any case, I do not think that Platonism *is* one of those movements with its ancestry in the Athenians schools. (Seneca, who evidently knew about Platonism, quite clearly says that in his day neither the 'new' *nor* the 'old' Academy had surviving representatives: *NQ* 7.32.2.)

But *even if it is*, I have argued that it quickly came to think about many things – and philosophy itself – in such a radically different way that it would actually be rather surprising if it inherited the 'school' sense of authority. Platonism brings into the post-Hellenistic age – or discovers it then, if you prefer – a notion of 'authority' that transcends historical narratives just as the truth to which they aspired transcended any historical context for the practice of philosophy. Plato is not 'authoritative' because his school matters: in fact, the identity *he* creates for Platonists, and the authority he represents for them, mean that his school does not matter at all.

---

[17] So, for example, one of the 'three Platonist interpretations' of the *Theaetetus* in Sedley (1996) is an interpretation supporting the Scepticism of the Hellenistic Academy.

CHAPTER 10

DEMETRIUS OF LACONIA ON EPICURUS
ON THE TELOS (US. 68)

JAMES WARREN*

The text I want to consider is just one sentence long. It is important, nevertheless, because it is one of the few citations we have from Epicurus' work *On the Telos* (Us. 68 = Long and Sedley 21 N, Bailey fr. 11, Arrighetti fr. 22.3). It was clearly a well-known phrase in antiquity since it appears in full or in part in various sources and it was taken to be an important expression of a central Epicurean tenet. It might even be fair to say that it became something of a 'proof text' cited regularly in support of a certain critical picture of the Epicurean ethical goal. And, in fact, it continues to be taken as an important piece of evidence in various modern interpretations of Epicurean hedonism. It is one of a group of fragments, including also the notoriously difficult phrase from Epicurus' *On Choices* preserved at DL 10.136, which are regularly deployed to support various interpretations of his views on the good life and, in particular, the relationship between bodily and psychic pleasure.[1]

I aim to shed some light both on ancient discussions of Epicurus the author and also on the curious status that Us. 68 has enjoyed since antiquity as an authoritative statement of

---

* I hope that this is an appropriate topic in honour of someone who has transformed our understanding of Epicureanism. Working on this essay brought me back to one of David's earlier articles, which is also one of my favourites: Sedley 1976. My thanks to all those whose questions provoked various improvements to the essay, in particular: Malcolm Schofield, Robert Wardy, Michael Pakaluk, David Butterfield, Simon Gathercole, and Thomas Bénatouïl.

[1] For example: Erler and Schofield (1999) 656: 'Our best clue to how that other kind of pleasure [sc. katastematic pleasure] was conceived by Epicurus is supplied by another extract from *On the Goal* [Us. 68 *ap.* Plut. *Non Posse* 1089D] ...' Purinton (1993) and Nikolsky (2001) both make extensive use of evidence from Plutarch – including this fragment and its context in the *Non Posse* – for their respective accounts of Epicurean hedonism.

202

Demetrius of Laconia on Epicurus *On the Telos*

a central claim in Epicurean hedonism. A problem with such 'proof texts' is that they are often cited without reference to their original context and Us. 68 certainly suffers this fate. An additional problem with this text is that we have no access to its original context and, what is more, the precise meaning of the sentence itself is somewhat obscure. It was even unclear to some ancient readers just what the phrase means.

Plutarch *Non Posse* 1089D

Here is the most complete citation of the phrase we have, from Plutarch's *Non Posse* 1089D.[2] Plutarch is illustrating an absurdity which he thinks the Epicureans are forced to admit. He thinks that Us. 68 reveals their misguided commitment to the priority of bodily needs and bodily pleasures over the pleasures of the soul.

That's why, having noticed these absurdities, they seem to me to take refuge in painlessness and the good settled-state of the flesh, as though thinking that this has been and will belong to the pleasant life in the case of some people. 'τὸ γὰρ εὐσταθὲς σαρκὸς κατάστημα καὶ τὸ περὶ ταύτης πιστὸν ἔλπισμα τὴν ἀκροτάτην χαρὰν καὶ βεβαιοτάτην ἔχειν τοῖς ἐπιλογίζεσθαι δυναμένοις' (Us. 68). Notice, first of all, the sort of thing they are doing by measuring out pleasure or painlessness or the good settled-state back and forth from the body to the soul and then back from the soul to the body, because they are forced by the fact that the body cannot retain pleasure as it flows away and slips past, to attach it to its origin ...

I leave the quotation untranslated for now so as not to predetermine some of the interpretative questions I want to raise later. But we might start by comparing the more familiar *Vatican Saying* 33, which is clearly expressing a similar thought.

The cry of the flesh is not to be hungry, thirsty, or cold. Whoever has these things and expects to have them might rival even Zeus in happiness.

Note the shared emphasis on the flesh and on a combination of possessing and expecting to possess a certain state of comfort as a major contribution to human happiness.

---

[2] Plutarch also provides the evidence for assigning this fragment to Epicurus' work *On the Telos*: 1091A.

James Warren

Without taking a stand on the more controversial issues of interpretation and translation, we can see that in Us. 68 Epicurus asserts a set of relationships between three items:

(1) a certain bodily state (τὸ εὐσταθὲς σαρκὸς κατάστημα),
(2) a future-directed attitude (τὸ πιστὸν ἔλπισμα), and
(3) the 'highest and most secure joy' (ἡ ἀκροτάτη χαρά καὶ βεβαιοτάτη).

Epicurus asserts that these relationships hold in the case of those things able to engage in a certain kind of reasoning (*epilogizesthai*) and therefore must hold in the case of humans. Just how these three items are to be related to one another, however, is not clear. Plutarch, for his part, thinks that his quotation from *On the Telos* shows yet again how the Epicureans are reprehensibly focused on simple bodily satisfactions and therefore are to be censured for two related errors. Not only do they mistake the absence of pain for pleasure – indeed, the highest pleasure – but they mistakenly subordinate the soul to the body and reduce the pleasures of the soul to the mere anticipation or recollection of bodily painlessness.[3]

Other Sources

In due course I will look more closely at our only citation of the phrase in an Epicurean source – the account from Demetrius of Laconia – which is in fact also our earliest surviving discussion. But before then, let us consider the other ancient contexts in which it – or some part of it – is cited and notice the uses to which it is put. In short, these sources report a connection between Epicurus' assertion of hedonism and the tag: 'the well-settled state of the flesh', presumably hoping to characterise Epicureanism in the familiar guise of a philosophy concerned entirely with the body and with bodily indulgence. For example, when he introduces a list of various earlier accounts of the nature of pleasure, Aulus Gellius comments at *Noct. Att.* 9.5:

---

[3] For more on Plutarch's criticisms of Epicurus in the *Non Posse*, see Warren (2011) and (2014a).

204

Demetrius of Laconia on Epicurus *On the Telos*

The old philosophers offered different views about pleasure. Epicurus set it up as the highest good and defines it as 'the well-settled state of the flesh' (ita definit: σαρκὸς εὐσταθὲς κατάστημα).

Here, just one phrase is reported and is taken to be a clear and simple definitional claim. Indeed, given that it is not unlikely that this phrase occurred more than once in Epicurus' work we cannot be sure that Aulus is intending to cite *On the Telos* in particular, nor indeed that he had any knowledge of the work beyond this tag. But the switch from Latin into Greek shows that Aulus is taking care to report Epicurus' own terminology.[4]

A much more extensive use of the fragment is found in Cleomedes' astronomical work *The Heavens* (*Meteōra*) and here we can be much more confident that our particular phrase from *On the Telos* is being discussed. The first chapter of Cleomedes' second book is devoted to a lengthy criticism of Epicurus for his claim that the sun is only as large as it appears.[5] Towards the end of his demolition of the Epicureans' view, Cleomedes diagnoses Epicurus' blindness to the obvious fact of the sun's enormous size as a symptom of a more general affliction. These hedonists simply cannot recognise plain truths:

No wonder, since pleasure-loving fellows certainly cannot uncover the truth in what exists. That is for *men* who are naturally disposed to virtue and value nothing ahead of it, not for lovers of a 'tranquil condition of flesh' (σαρκὸς εὐσταθὲς κατάστημα) and the 'confident expectation regarding it' (καὶ τὸ περὶ ταύτης πιστὸν ἔλπισμα). (Cleomedes *The Heavens* 2.1 410–13 Todd, trans. Bowen and Todd)

Here, phrases from our sentence from *On the Telos* are sufficient to show the miserable Epicurean devotion to bodily pleasure, which is in turn a good indication of their general inability to spot the truth.[6]

A little later, Cleomedes uses some phrases from this fragment when he wonders whether Epicurus ought to be

---

[4] σαρκὸς εὐσταθὲς κατάστημα appears as the *capitulum* to Lucretius *DRN* 2.14 in the Oblongus MS.

[5] See Algra (2000); Bowen and Todd (2004).

[6] Algra (2000) 178–9 argues for a stronger connection: 'Since the ἀρεταί are interconnected, one cannot be a good logician or physicist if one is not a morally virtuous person as well.'

James Warren

compared with Homer's Thersites since both are boastful but ugly and both claim to deserve great honours although they are in reality quite worthless. But then Cleomedes argues that in at least one respect Epicurus is inferior even to Thersites:

That is why I would believe it to be quite wrong for someone to say to *him*: 'Babbling Thersites, clear orator though you are, hold off!' For I would not also call *this* Thersites 'clear', as Odysseus does the Homeric one, when on top of everything else his mode of expression is also elaborately corrupt. He speaks of 'tranquil conditions of the flesh' (σαρκὸς εὐσταθῆ καταστήματα) and 'the confident expectations (πιστὰ ἐλπίσματα) regarding it', and describes a tear as a 'glistening of the eyes' (λίπασμα ὀφθαλμῶν), and speaks of 'sacred ululations' (ἱερὰ ἀνακραυγάσματα) and 'titillations of the body' (γαργαλισμοὺς σώματος) and 'debaucheries' (ληκήματα) and other such dreadful horrors. (Cleomedes *The Heavens* 2.1 493–8 Todd, trans. Bowen and Todd)

Homer's Thersites was at least not a bad orator. Epicurus, on the other hand, uses all sorts of disgraceful phrases. Epicurus' ugly prose style was regularly criticised by his opponents and Demetrius of Laconia too seems on occasion to be attempting to fend off complaints about his master's particular choice of words.[7] Here, however, it seems that Cleomedes is concerned not only about the aesthetic failings of Epicurus' form of expression but also by the fact that Epicurus is happy to talk openly and positively about things that are in fact quite unseemly: Epicurus' prose matches the base subject matter. (Cleomedes goes on to wonder whether these are expressions that derive from the kind of talk you hear in brothels or at the women's festival of the Thesmophoria or even from Jewish synagogues.) For example, Epicurus' expression 'σαρκὸς εὐσταθῆ καταστήματα' is not only an unpleasant piece of prose but is also perhaps a rather perverse construction. It is similar, in that case, to the way in which Epicurus uses the phrase 'glistening of the eyes' (λίπασμα ὀφθαλμῶν) as a tortured way of saying 'tear'. Certainly, Cleomedes enjoys being able to list a number of cases in which Epicurus has chosen to use a noun with a –μα or –μος termination and the cumulative effect of his

---

[7] For complaints about Epicurus' style, see Cic. *Fin.* 1.14, DL 10.13, Aulus Gellius *Noct. Att.* 2.9.4, Athenaeus 187e (cf. Usener (1887) 88–90).

Demetrius of Laconia on Epicurus *On the Telos*

little list is quite striking. Cleomedes even makes plural some of the nouns which our other sources retain in the singular and which Cleomedes himself quoted in the singular just a page or two earlier: κατάστημα and ἔλπισμα in the quotation from *On the Telos* here become καταστήματα and ἐλπίσματα, perhaps to emphasise still more the ugliness of the expression.

In the next example, Origen cites the first part of the phrase during his response to Celsus' anti-Christian attacks (*Contra Celsum* 3.80). Celsus apparently claimed that Christians were indulging in vain hopes for the afterlife (3.80.1). Origen replies by mounting a 'companions in guilt' argument: he notes how many of Celsus' preferred pagan philosophers might similarly be subject to the same criticism. What is more, this holds not just for Pythagoreans and Platonists, who do have some idea that the soul might be immortal, but even for the Epicureans. Of course, their hopes are not for some kind of post-mortem future but they are nevertheless just as guilty of making a good life dependent on some kind of hope for something yet to come (3.80.23–7). Here Origen twists the knife just a little by noting that the Epicureans – among whose supporters he counts Celsus – vainly have faith in Epicurus' promises of future well-being as well as a faith in their own future well-being itself.[8]

> Will, then, Celsus and the Epicureans not say that the hope for their goal of life – pleasure – is vain also? That's what they think is the good: the well-settled state of the flesh and Epicurus' firm hope for it (τὸ τῆς σαρκὸς εὐσταθὲς κατάστημα καὶ τὸ περὶ ταύτης πιστὸν Ἐπικούρῳ ἔλπισμα).

There are three further passages that cite our sentence, but they attribute it to Metrodorus rather than to Epicurus. Körte makes these reports sources for the content of Metrodorus' *On the fact that we are more responsible for our own happiness than external objects are* (frs. 5 and 6 Körte) and there is no particular reason to doubt that Metrodorus may have borrowed his master's expression in a work of his own. The first of these is a brief mention in Cicero's *Tusculan Disputations* 2.17 which is perhaps no more than a paraphrase of the general sentiment

---

[8] See also Markschies (2000) esp. 195–8.

207

James Warren

of the first part of the sentence. Nevertheless, it is like the other passages in that it concentrates on the importance of the good state of the body and the expectation of the continuance of this bodily state. Indeed, it asserts that this is what constitutes the state of someone living a complete and blessed life.[9] The second example is something of a paraphrase of the fragment in Plutarch's *Adversus Colotem* 1125B which Plutarch uses as further evidence for the familiar idea that the Epicureans are disgracefully reducing all goodness to the base pleasures of the flesh.[10]

The last example is more interesting. Clement of Alexandria comments at *Stromata* 2.131.1:

> But Epicurus thinks that all joy of the soul comes about based on the prior experience of the flesh. And Metrodorus says in *On the fact that we are more responsible for our own happiness than external objects are*, that the good of the soul is nothing but 'the well-settled state of the flesh and the secure expectation concerning it' (τὸ σαρκὸς εὐσταθὲς κατάστημα καὶ τὸ περὶ ταύτης πιστὸν ἔλπισμα).

This is interesting for two reasons. First, Clement takes the view that Epicurus is here interested in identifying the good – and therefore, in his terms, the pleasure – that belongs to the soul. (Indeed, some texts include 'ἀγαθὸν ψυχῆς τί ἄλλο ἢ' as part of the quotation, although that seems unlikely.) Disappointingly, it turns out that Epicurus considers the soul's pleasure to derive entirely from some earlier pleasant affection of the flesh. The evidence for this interpretation is the reference to the secure expectation of some state of the flesh in the second part of our sentence. Clement therefore thinks that there are two claims made by Epicurus: the first identifies the good of the body with a certain well-settled and pleasant state of the flesh; the second identifies the good of the soul with a pleasure derived from the

---

[9] Cicero *Tusc.* 2.17, *Metrodorus quidem perfecte eum beatum putat, cui corpus bene constitutum sit et exploratum ita semper fore.* Cf. Cic. *Fin.* 2.96: *ipse enim Metrodorus, paene alter Epicurus, beatum esse describit his fere uerbis: cum corpus bene constitutum sit et sit exploratum ita futurum.*

[10] Plut. *Adv. Col.* 1125B: καθάπερ οἴεται δεῖν ὁ σοφὸς Μητρόδωρος, λέγων τὰ καλὰ πάντα καὶ σοφὰ καὶ περιττὰ τῆς ψυχῆς ἐξευρήματα τῆς κατὰ σάρκα ἡδονῆς ἕνεκα καὶ τῆς ἐλπίδος τῆς ὑπὲρ ταύτης συνεστάναι καὶ πᾶν εἶναι κενὸν ἔργον, ὃ μὴ εἰς τοῦτο κατατείνει.

208

Demetrius of Laconia on Epicurus *On the Telos*

expectation of this same well-settled state of the flesh.[11] This notion that Epicurus is making a pair of claims about, respectively, the pleasures of the body and of the soul, has a descendant in one of the modern interpretations of this fragment and we shall return to it shortly.

Second, the reference to a work by Metrodorus which appears to cite and discuss this phrase from Epicurus' *On the Telos* suggests that the phrase was already in the very early history of the Garden taken to be an important claim in the proper general understanding of Epicurean hedonism. Evidently, both Metrodorus and Epicurus included this claim in their writings and perhaps Metrodorus did so by first citing Epicurus as an authority and then going on to expand on the proper understanding of what his master intended.[12]

Why was Metrodorus doing this? Although we cannot determine the chronology for certain, it is likely that early on in the history of the school Timocrates of Lampsacus – once a member of the school himself – was able to foster a critical picture of Epicurean hedonism in part through the circulation of carefully excerpted or manipulated parts of Epicurus' own works.[13] The evidence for this comes mainly from a passage early in Diogenes Laertius' *Life of Epicurus* which details various slanderous accusations against Epicurus made by Timocrates and others and includes another brief citation from Epicurus' *On the Telos* at 10.6 (= Us. 67) in which Epicurus notoriously says that he 'cannot conceive of the good in the absence of the pleasures of taste, sex, sound, and beautiful shape'. Obviously, that work was a good source for those looking for shocking claims to excerpt and publicise.

Metrodorus was Timocrates' elder brother and was apparently engaged in attempting to counter these accusations. We know that he wrote a work *Timocrates* which contained some

---

[11] Clement's interpretation may well have been an influence on Origen. Clement himself also cites Us. 68 at *Strom.* 2.119, commenting: τί γὰρ ἕτερον ἡ τρυφὴ ἢ φιλήδονος λιχνεία καὶ πλεονασμὸς περίεργος πρὸς ἡδυπάθειαν ἀνειμένων;

[12] Cf. Körte (1890) 540.

[13] See DL 10.5, Plut. *Adv. Col.* 1126D; Sedley (1976) esp. 127–32; and Gordon (2012), esp. 14–17.

James Warren

discussion of the Epicurean theory of pleasure and, in particular, an account of the distinction between kinetic and katastematic pleasure, perhaps to put right a misunderstanding or misinterpretation of that distinction being fostered by his brother.[14] It would not be a surprise in that case if our sentence from *On the Telos* were another one of those used in Timocrates' smear campaign since, as we have seen, it lends itself to a certain negative evaluation of Epicurus' approval of bodily pleasure. And it would therefore not be a surprise if this same sentence also attracted the attention of Epicureans keen to clarify and defend Epicurus' position. It is also quite possible that Timocrates' writings, or sources dependent on them, were used by Plutarch in composing his own anti-Epicurean treatises and may even have been Plutarch's source for the quotation from Epicurus' *On the Telos* with which we began.[15] It is similarly possible that Timocrates' work was the principal means by which this phrase became known to Aulus Gellius, Cleomedes, and Origen. What is more, we shall see that Demetrius of Laconia spent some time looking into this sentence, determining the precise terminology and wording used, and considering various possible interpretations and misinterpretations.

In sum, it appears that this sentence from Epicurus' *On the Telos* – or some more or less distant echo of it – was a favourite both for Epicurus' immediate followers and also for his critics. It may even have been a passage over the interpretation of which Metrodorus and his brother Timocrates fought in the very first generation of the school. It was evidently a favourite piece of evidence for critics of Epicurean hedonism because of the references not merely to a certain well-settled state but also to a well-settled state of the *flesh*, which encouraged two different complaints: that the Epicureans mistake a simple absence of disturbance for pleasure and that they concentrate on the baser aspects of our animal nature rather than our higher psychic and reasoning capacities. The reference to the

---

[14] Cf. DL 10.136 (= Körte fr. 29); Plut. *Non Posse* 1098B.
[15] Sedley (1976) 153 n. 34 suggests that *Adv. Col.* 1124E–1127E and *Non Posse* 1097A–1098D contain material likely to derive from Timocrates.

hope or expectation that a certain bodily state will continue is sometimes included in critical citations of the sentence both in order to provide scope for additional critical remarks about the limited nature of Epicurus' hedonism and also for the tortured and unpleasant nature of Epicurus' prose style. In particular, it is regularly taken as evidence that when Epicurus does consider something like the pleasure of the soul rather than the body, he foolishly understands psychic pleasure simply as some expectation of a future bodily state of painlessness.

Demetrius of Laconia on Us. 68

We cannot be sure of the original title of the work by Demetrius of Laconia now preserved as *PHerc.* 1012 but the remaining material includes a series of interpretative questions concerning various passages in Epicurus' works over which there was some dispute between different groups of Epicurean readers or which gave rise to criticisms from non-Epicurean readers. It is sometimes difficult, unfortunately, to tell whether the problem to which Demetrius is responding is generated by an internal disagreement between Epicurean groups over the proper interpretation of a text or by an external critic taking issue with a certain form of words or offering a critical interpretation of a section of Epicurus' writings. From what we can tell, the approach in the work is relatively straightforward: Demetrius introduces each problem and offers his own view, defending Epicurus against charges of obscurity or inconsistency, sometimes by presenting examples of similar practice in acceptable writers such as Euripides and Homer. In presenting his preferred view, Demetrius also seems to have spent some time checking various versions of a given text and recording variations and scribal errors.[16] Although much of the text is badly damaged, some examples of the kind of discussion we find elsewhere in the surviving columns give a flavour of his interests and approach.[17]

[16] See e.g. Cols. XXXIV, XXXXIX.
[17] On Demetrius' use of citations of Epicurus and his general attitude to the Master's *auctoritas*, see Parisi (2015).

James Warren

At Cols. XXXI–XXXII Demetrius comes to discuss the phrase from Epicurus' *On the Telos* cited by Plutarch at *Non Posse* 1089D. The fact that Demetrius discusses this sentence at all suggests both that already by the late second century BC this was a phrase that had claimed the attention of various critics and detractors of Epicurus and also that Demetrius himself was well aware of the difficulties involved in giving a simple and clear interpretation of it. Here is the full context of the discussion in the relevant columns of *PHerc.* 1012 in Puglia's edition:

XXXI 8. - - - ἐκ τού]||των τῶν ἐπων το[ι]οῦτο [τι] γέ[[γο]]νος τῆς ἀμφι[βο]λίας ἐν|τροχάζε[ι]·
«Νάστης Ἀμφίμα|χος τε Νομείονος ἀγ[λα]ὰ τέ|ˢ[κ]να
[ὃς] καὶ χρυσὸν ἔχων πό|λεμ[όνδ᾽ ἴε]ν».
Καὶ τα[ῦτα τὰ] | ἀμ[φίβολ]α τῶν προεκκε[ι|μένων ῥη]μάτων [λύοιτ᾽ ἄν, εἰ] | γρ[αφικὸ]ν ἁμάρτη|μ᾽ ἔξεσ]||¹⁰τιν [εὑ]ρεῖν παρ᾽ Ἐπικου[ρωι]. | Κἀ[κ το]ῦ [π]ρώτου κάταρ[χ᾽ ἐξ|ε]τ[άζων ἀ]ντίγραφα ἅ[παν|¹³τα - - -]|¹⁶. | [τ]ῆς γραφῆ[ς ... ... | .] HCEN[- - -|...]HC[- - -

XXXII - - - ἀλλάξαν]||τες τὸ μὲν «ἔλπισμα» καὶ ποή᾽σαν᾽|τες «ἐνκατέλπισμα», τὸ δὲ «πε|ρὶ ταύτης» [ἀλλά]ξαντ[ες κ]αὶ | ποήσαν[τες τ]ὸ «περὶ τού|ˢτου» [... ἀγ]ανακτοῦντες |

... from these verses an ambiguity of just such a sort occurs:
'... Nastes and Amphimachos, noble sons of Nomeion, the one who went to battle decked in gold ...'
And the ambiguities in the lines before us might be resolved if it were possible to find some kind of error in the copying of Epicurus. And beginning from the first [book one?] examining all of the copies ... ... having altered 'expectation' (*elpisma*) and inserted 'anticipation' (*enkatelpisma*), and having altered 'about this' (*peri tautēs*) and inserted 'about that' (*peri toutou*) ...

What is the problem that Demetrius thinks he has to settle and why does it matter? The problem is likely to be the fact that there is a syntactical ambiguity in this sentence of *On the Telos* and it matters because the syntactical ambiguity might be exploited by critics intent on finding that the Epicurean view of the good life is grounded in mere bodily satisfaction.

Some kind of syntactical ambiguity appears to be the problem at hand since, although the papyrus is quite damaged at this point, Demetrius of Laconia offers as an illustration

212

Demetrius of Laconia on Epicurus *On the Telos*

of the difficulty a pair of lines from Homer (*Iliad* 2.871–2). In these lines it is unclear which of the two sons of Nomeion mentioned in line 871, Nastes and Amphimachos, is the subject of the relative clause in 872 'who went to battle decked in gold'. The ambiguity was noted by ancient scholiasts: according to Aristarchus it was Amphimachos who wore the gold, while Simonides thought it was Nastes.[18]

We noted at the outset that there are three items in this sentence from *On the Telos* that need to be related to one another:

(1) a certain bodily state: τὸ γὰρ εὐσταθὲς σαρκὸς κατάστημα
(2) a future-directed attitude: τὸ περὶ ταύτης πιστὸν ἔλπισμα
(3) the highest and most secure joy: τὴν ἀκροτάτην χαρὰν καὶ βεβαιοτάτην.

What is the syntactical ambiguity in the case of the sentence from Epicurus' *On the Telos*? Two suggestions have been proposed.

The first possibility is that it is unclear whether the well-settled state of the flesh and the confident expectation of its continuing combine to provide the greatest joy (perhaps in the sense that they are jointly sufficient and individually necessary) or whether each of the well-settled state of the flesh and the confident expectation of its continuing is individually responsible for the greatest joy: one in the sense of the greatest bodily pleasure and the other in the sense of the greatest psychic pleasure. In other words, it is unclear whether (1) and (2) should be taken together as a unit governing the verb ἔχειν and having (3) as their object or whether (1) and (2) should be taken individually as each in turn governing the verb ἔχειν and having (3) as its object.[19] This would be similar to the Homeric example in so far as it is unclear what the subject of the verb is but different from the Homeric example in so far as here the question is not which of the two is the subject of the verb but rather whether they are jointly as a pair or each taken individually the subject of the verb.

---

[18] See: Schol. vet. in Hom. *Il.* 2.871a1.
[19] This is the interpretation proposed by Purinton (1993) 286 n. 8.

James Warren

According to Pohlenz's apparatus, some texts of Plutarch's *Non Posse* 1089D have ἔχει rather than ἔχειν.[20] With this alteration the ambiguity just outlined would remain: (1) and (2) will become nominative rather than accusative and the whole sentence would change from *oratio obliqua* to *oratia recta*. But since the noun phrases in (1) and (2) are both neuter they might still govern the finite verb ἔχει and might still do so either individually or taken together as a single noun phrase.

The second possibility takes (1) and (2) together as a unit. The ambiguity in this case concerns which of the following is the subject of ἔχειν and which is its object:[21]

(1) and (2): τὸ γὰρ εὐσταθὲς σαρκὸς κατάστημα καὶ τὸ περὶ ταύτης πιστὸν ἔλπισμα

(3): τὴν ἀκροτάτην χαρὰν καὶ βεβαιοτάτην.

Since either of these could be the subject and either could be the object of ἔχειν, the sentence then becomes ambiguous in the following way. It could mean either of the following:

(A) 'The settled condition of the body and the sure expectation of this contain the highest and most reliable joy for those who are capable of reasoning.'
(B) 'The highest and most reliable joy contains the settled condition of the body and the secure expectation of this for those who are capable of reasoning.'

(A) does indeed seem to emphasise the role of a certain state of the body for the maintenance or production of 'the highest joy'. More precisely, it makes the settled state of the body and the expectation of its maintenance sufficient for such 'highest joy'. (B), on the other hand, emphasises how a state of highest joy will contain or will involve the settled state of the flesh and the expectation of the continuance of that state. We might put the point most succinctly by saying that (A) points more to the idea that this state of the flesh now and in the future is a sufficient condition of the highest joy, while (B) says that this state

---

[20] Π: 'codices Planudei'. Bailey prints ἔχει, as do Arrighetti (1970) and Diano (1974) 53; Long and Sedley (1987) vol. 2, 122–3, retain ἔχειν.

[21] This is the interpretation of Puglia (1988) 226–32.

214

Demetrius of Laconia on Epicurus *On the Telos*

of the flesh is a necessary part or perhaps a necessary consequence of the highest joy.

This second possible ambiguity is less likely but not very much hangs on which interpretation we prefer.[22] What is more important is that we recognise that the text is potentially ambiguous and, moreover, that Demetrius is clearly aware that the phrase has been the focus of critical attention and is concerned to set out a text and interpretation in reply. It matters to him that the text is established correctly and the syntax of the phrase is properly understood. But before turning at last to the philosophical importance of the sentence, let us dwell briefly on two more philological points. There seems to have been some doubt early on over the precise text since Demetrius himself records two variants in the different copies he has consulted. First, some of them have ἐνκατέλπισμα rather than ἔλπισμα. And second, some have περὶ τούτου rather than περὶ ταύτης. The first variant is less significant. Although ἐνκατέλπισμα is the *lectio difficilior* and Epicurus does have a penchant for compounding prefixes – consider ἐγκατάλειμμα ('residual trace') at *Ep. Hdt.* 50 – there is little reason to think it should be included here. Our other surviving ancient reports of the phrase retain the simple ἔλπισμα and that reading is also supported by the use of the simple ἐλπίζων in *Vatican Saying* 33.[23]

The second variant – περὶ τούτου for περὶ ταύτης – was presumably motivated by the thought that the only feminine noun in the preceding part of the phrase is σάρξ and the idea that what is being anticipated is, strictly speaking, the balanced condition of the flesh rather than the flesh itself. Nevertheless, περὶ ταύτης is probably correct: it is the reading preserved in Clement, Origen, and Cleomedes, and Plutarch himself confirms that this is his understanding of the sentence at 1090F

---

[22] If we read ἔχει rather than ἔχειν then (B) is not possible and, in any case, it might be thought that the word order favours (A) even if we retain the infinitive form. Notice that (A) is still subject to the first proposed form of ambiguity since it remains ambiguous whether the settled condition and the expectation taken together are the subject of the verb or whether each individually 'contains the highest joy'.

[23] *SV* 33: σαρκὸς φωνὴ τὸ μὴ πεινῆν, τὸ μὴ διψῆν, τὸ μὴ ῥιγοῦν· ταῦτα γὰρ ἔχων τις καὶ ἐλπίζων ἔξειν κἂν <Διὶ> ὑπὲρ εὐδαιμονίας μαχέσαιτο.

where he paraphrases the expression in complaining that the Epicureans have learned to take pleasure only in 'the flesh and expectation concerning the flesh' (... ἅνπερ ἐπὶ σαρκὶ καὶ τῇ περὶ σάρκα ἐλπίδι μάθωσιν ἄλλῳ δὲ μηθενὶ χαίρειν καὶ θαρρεῖν).

The Philosophical Importance

Let us start with the referent of περὶ ταύτης: Epicurus is drawing attention to the confident expectation of a certain ongoing state of the flesh (περὶ ταύτης sc. σαρκός) as a source of great pleasure. Some modern commentators interpret the phrase as giving an account of two kinds of highest pleasure – the highest bodily pleasure based on some kind of well-settled state of the flesh and the highest pleasure of the soul based on a certain kind of confident expectation for the future. And these two can then be related to a distinction between *aponia* and *ataraxia*, the two terms used for 'katastematic pleasures' in the fragment of Epicurus' *On Choices* cited at DL 10.136. (We have already seen an ancestor of this view in Clement.) For those commentators, it ought to be something of a difficulty that the confident expectation appears to be restricted to a confident expectation of a certain ongoing state of the flesh.[24] To be sure, Epicurus does elsewhere emphasise the importance for a good life of having confidence that a state of bodily painlessness can be guaranteed in the future: *Vatican Saying* 33 is a prime example. But it would be odd for him to define the highest state of psychic pleasure exclusively as a confidence that hunger, thirst and other kinds of bodily pain will be warded off in the future.

First, Epicurus himself notoriously claimed that, despite feeling considerable bodily pain as he lay sick and dying, he nevertheless was living a good life because he could set against

---

[24] For example, Purinton (1993) thinks that Us. 68 gives us Epicurus' account of both the highest bodily and the highest psychic pleasure. He comments (285): 'Now, there can be little doubt that Epicurus is referring here to the katastematic pleasures, respectively, of the body and of the soul when he speaks of "the well-balanced *katastema* of the flesh and the confident expectation about it".' This specification in Us. 68 of what the confident expectation is about is therefore a problem for his general view.

216

those bodily disturbances various pleasures he could conjure from memory of past philosophical conversations.[25] Whatever the plausibility of that claim, it suggests that the absence of bodily pain is not necessary for living a good life in the sense of achieving and maintaining a state of psychic *ataraxia*. Nor, it seems, is it plausible to think that as Epicurus lay dying he had a confident expectation that the state of his flesh would remain well settled in the future. So we should infer that neither the absence of bodily pain nor the expectation of a well-settled bodily state in the future is necessary for the highest psychic pleasure: *ataraxia*. And yet, it does seem to be a specific kind of confidence for the future state of the flesh that this sentence from *On the Telos* is interested in emphasising. Second, we have good reason to think that the highest state of psychic pleasure depends on plenty of things other than a simple confidence in being free in the future from disturbances to the flesh. After all, much of the Epicureans' therapeutic philosophical enterprise is targeted at ridding us of such concerns as anxieties about the harm of mortality and non-existence. There are other pains such as concerns about one's reputation or desires for political power or fame that also afflict many people and are not at all concerned with the state of one's body. So the confident expectation of a well-settled state of the flesh in the future will not be sufficient for *ataraxia* either; someone might have no anxieties at all about his future bodily state but be subject to all sorts of painful anxieties.

Of course, on occasion Epicurus may well have emphasised the importance for our general well-being of living as far as possible without hunger, thirst, cold, and other bodily discomforts. The first part of Us. 68 doubtless provides an account of what is elsewhere described as *aponia*: the absence of bodily discomfort.[26] But it is very unlikely that this sentence from *On the Telos* is intended to stand as a simple and clear official definition, as it were, of both the highest pleasure of

---

[25] See DL 10.22 (*Letter to Idomeneus*); Cicero *Fin.* 2.96 (*Letter to Hermarchus*), *Tusc.* 5.74, 88; Sen. *Ep.* 66.47.
[26] See e.g. Purinton (1993) 285; Erler and Schofield (1999) 656 and 665.

the body and the highest pleasure of the soul, even though it was so presented by ancient critics and used as a 'proof text' in their criticism of the Epicureans.[27]

To be sure, the fragment does refer to the 'highest and most secure pleasure' and for a hedonist like Epicurus this ought to be some kind of ideal state. The parallel claim in *SV* 33 makes a similar point by reference to rivalling Zeus in happiness. And yet this should not bear too much weight.[28] Epicurus is not a stranger to exaggeration or to deliberately provocative claims, as other evidence for the contents of *On the Telos* shows. The other fragments we have from the work appear to be part of Epicurus' defence of his identifying the good with pleasure and are often outrageous and shocking. They include, for example, the notorious claim that he cannot conceive of anything good that is stripped of the pleasures of taste, sex, hearing, and seeing (Us. 67) and, apparently just a little earlier in the work, the claim that those who assert that the good is something else, such as virtue, are merely voicing empty platitudes and are simply misguided or insincere (Us. 69). The virtues are to be valued only in so far as they produce pleasure (Us. 70).[29] All of these provocative claims were pounced upon by writers interested in emphasising the image of Epicureans as devoted to physical pleasures, but they need not exhaust what Epicurus had to say in the work. Nor should we assume that the whole work was characterised by this consciously combative tone. For example, we know that elsewhere in this work he also said something to the effect that there are kinetic and katastematic pleasures of both body and soul (DL 10.136) and it is therefore reasonable to think that he included some positive explanation

---

[27] That some ancient critics of Epicureanism read this as claiming that the highest psychic pleasure just is some expectation of a state of the flesh is perhaps why some Epicurean texts sought to de-emphasise the reference to the flesh by preferring the reading περὶ τούτου to περὶ ταύτης, as Demetrius notes.

[28] I leave aside for now the tricky question of whether χαρά has some specific reference distinct from other related terms for 'pleasure'. But cf. Warren (2014b) 72–4, for a brief account.

[29] Us. 67 = Athen. 546e; DL 10.6; Cic. *Tusc.* 3.41, *Fin.* 2.7, 2.20, 2.23, 2.29, 2.30, 2.64, *ND* 1.111, *In Pisonem* 69. Us. 69 = Cic. *Tusc.* 3.42, *Fin.* 2.48. Us. 70 = Athen. 546f.

Demetrius of Laconia on Epicurus *On the Telos*

of these and their relationship to one another alongside his more strident general defence of pleasure as the good and his insistence that we should not overlook the contribution of satisfying basic physical needs for food, water, warmth and the like.

My suggestion is that in Us. 68, and elsewhere in texts such as *Vatican Saying* 33, it is far more likely that Epicurus is interested in emphasising the ability of the soul to take pleasure not only in the present state of one's body but also in recalling and anticipating past and future such excellent states. Understanding that ability will be an important aspect of the wise man's approach to life's misfortunes, but this sentence is in no way a 'definition' of the Epicurean *telos* and it is in no way a complete description of the nature of katastematic pleasure, whether of the body or of the soul. Ancient authors with an interest in casting Epicureanism in a poor light may well have presented Us. 68 – together with Us. 67, 69, and 70 – as if it were Epicurus' definition of the highest pleasure and the phrase thereby acquired a kind of authoritative status. But there is no reason for us to follow their lead in our own reconstructions of his hedonist theory. Rather, Us. 68 comes from a discussion of how anticipating future states of well-being can provide pleasure in the present and the importance of that human ability for maintaining well-being. Compare, for example, the following passage from a work by Philodemus which also appears to be a quotation from Epicurus himself and is quite possibly also taken from *On the Telos*.[30]

ὡς γὰρ | ἐλπίδος ὁ καιρὸ[ς ἐ]ψιλώθη | καὶ τῆς κ[ατὰ σάρκα ἡδονῆς | καὶ ἐπιμ[ονως] ἀ[π]ελείφθη | τῆ[ς τῶν γεγονότ]ων χάριτος, ἆρ᾽ [ἂν ἔτι τη]ρήσαιμι, ὦ| Μητ[ρόδωρε, τοιοῦτ]ον κατάστη|μα ψυ[χῆς; ... Philodemus *On Epicurus* (*PHerc.* 1232). (XVIII.10–17 Tepedino)

For when the (present) moment has been stripped of expectation and of bodily pleasure and has permanently been deprived of the pleasure of past [experiences], could I still, Metrodorus, maintain such a state of the soul?

---

[30] For discussion, see Tepedino Guerra (1987) and (1994) and Purinton (1993) 298–9. Cf. Warren (2014a)) 204–6.

Here, Epicurus is explaining how the ability to recall and anticipate a settled state of the flesh is sometimes necessary for maintaining a good state of the soul. And this is not an implausible claim: when I am unwell I can alleviate my mental distress and anxiety by recalling and anticipating a state of health. But that falls short of the claim that this anticipation of a future well-settled bodily state is the highest psychic pleasure since there are also psychic pains other than simple anxieties about one's bodily state. After all, the Epicureans insist that the vast majority of us are subject to damaging misconceptions about what is to be pursued and avoided that generate all manner of painful disturbances. In that case, Us. 68 fits very neatly alongside this passage since there Epicurus says that it is possible to generate pleasure not only in the sense of having in the present a well-settled state of the flesh but also by holding a firm conviction about such a state continuing in the future. That second kind of pleasure is something we are able to enjoy because we are thinking creatures able to consider our futures. The use of *epilogizesthai* in Us. 68 further suggests that Epicurus has in mind a rather specific point: this term is generally used in Epicurean texts to mean a certain kind of rational activity, namely a rational appraisal, often of a comparative kind. In this case, the appraisal seems to involve a comparative assessment of a present and expected future state of well-being, but it may also involve a general appraisal and appreciation of those things that are and are not necessary for living a good and painless life. This sort of appraisal is likely to be possible only for those who have a reasonable appreciation of the principles of Epicurean ethical practice.[31]

The passage from Philodemus' *On Epicurus* adds the thought that grateful recollection (*kharis*) of past pleasures is possible for us too, providing the past-directed counterpart to the confident expectation for the future emphasised in Us. 68. Most

---

[31] Compare Epicurus *Ep. Men.* 133, *KD* 20 and 22. Schofield (1996) surveys the evidence and discusses Plut. *Non Posse* 1089D, concluding that (225): 'The case that it contains at least a reminiscence of *epilogizesthai* as a term of art is that Epicurus presumably refers implicitly to the *sort of* assessment or appraisal which can be adequately conducted only in accordance with Epicurean principles.'

Demetrius of Laconia on Epicurus *On the Telos*

importantly, these anticipations and recollections are under our control. After all, that is a topic we would expect to be treated in a work such as Metrodorus' *On the fact that we are more responsible for our own happiness than external objects are* which, as we saw, certainly discussed and endorsed this same claim.[32] It is evident, therefore, why Epicurus should refer to the 'joy' he mentions in Us. 68 as 'most secure', precisely because, once we have arranged our desires to aim only for natural and necessary objects of pursuit, we do not merely hope for but rather 'confidently expect' to be able to fulfil them in the future. This pleasure is therefore as impervious as it can be to frustration by chance circumstances.

We have good reason, therefore, to set aside the suggestion that the fragment Us. 68 from *On the Telos* is intended simply to give a clear definition of the highest pleasures of the body and of the soul, respectively. Instead, Epicurus is explaining how we humans who are capable of reasoning can take enormous pleasure not only in recognising the presence of a certain settled state of the flesh but also in the confident expectation that it will continue. As for Demetrius, he rightly saw that understanding both the text and the syntax of this sentence was important because, if wrongly interpreted, it might lead astray Epicurean students and, perhaps more likely, offer ammunition to their critics.

---

[32] Diogenes Laertius also includes in his catalogue a work by Metrodorus entitled *On Epicurus' Illness* (10.24). Since the power to recollect past pleasures seems to have been emphasised by Epicurus as a means of withstanding the physical discomfort of his terminal illness, it is possible that Metrodorus addressed the topic there too.

CHAPTER II

LUCRETIUS THE MADMAN ON THE GODS

DAVID BUTTERFIELD*

The life of Lucretius will forever remain a mystery: only a few sketchy details can be reconstructed with any confidence, and it is inconceivable that fresh evidence will emerge to shed light amidst the darkness. Beyond his living in the first half of the first century BC, being based at Rome and composing *De rerum natura* (*DRN*), all is conjectural. Yet, in contrast to this paucity of information stands Jerome's unequivocal summary in his adaptation of Eusebius' *Chronicon* (s.a. 94 BC = Ol.171.3):

Titus Lucretius the poet is born, who was afterwards driven mad by a love potion and, although he wrote some books amidst the lulls of his madness, which Cicero later corrected, he killed himself by his own hand in his 44th year.

A well-read Roman, albeit a Christian four centuries after his death, thus makes the remarkable claims that Lucretius was driven mad by a love potion, wrote (what must be) *De rerum natura* amidst lucid spells, and killed himself in middle age.[1] The more colourful aspects of this account have long been dismissed as confusion and/or wilful fiction.[2] What does merit attention is the bold assertion that Lucretius was a madman: if the love potion story emerges from another source,[3] what in *DRN* would suggest that it is the product of

---

* I owe to David Sedley much for which I will always remain most grateful: among the more tangible are my choosing to pursue research in Classics, investigating Lucretius and his survival, and making Cambridge my home. The exemplary model he sets to scholars is one of unparalleled rigour, clarity, honesty and affability: *hunc longe sequere et uestigia semper adora.*
[1] This may be an error for *XXXVIII*: see Butterfield (2013) 1 n. 2.
[2] The major advance in this field was made by Ziegler (1936); see further Bailey (1947) I 8–12.
[3] The confusion could come from the death of Lucullus by love potion in 56 BC (Plin. *HN* 25.3).

222

Lucretius the Madman on the Gods

a man insane? The simplest answer is that Lucretius' poetic persona reveals a man held fast in the throes of not merely poetic composition but also Epicurean philosophical fervour. For many readers, to maintain the convictions of Epicureanism with the uncompromising zeal that Lucretius demonstrates was *ipso facto* to stray outside the realm of sanity. Since this school regularly suffered the charge of madness in antiquity,[4] Lucretius' utter devotion to its uncompromising doctrines represented the height of insanity for Jerome and his contemporaries.[5]

Whereas others detected madness pervading *De rerum natura*, Lucretius himself segregated mental disorder into three distinct categories. The first is the madness of love (*amor* ~ lust, *cupido*), variously described as *furor* (4.1069, 1117) and *rabies* (4.1083, 1117): if this emotion takes control over the human body and mind, man is lost in irredeemable frenzy. This pessimistic attitude to a universal emotion seems a targeted extension of Epicurus' assertions that the sage should not fall in love, marry or raise a family (unless circumstances demand).[6] The second relates to physical illness: *delirus* and *delirare* are used of human delirium induced by disease (3.453, 464, 5.1159). This confused state, arising beyond one's control, is treated without condemnation by Lucretius. The third, and most significant, species of madness is philosophical delusion: rival, and therefore incorrect, views of the world are described in the most forceful terms – *delirus* (1.698, 2.985), *perdelirus* (1.692), *dementia* (1.704), *furiosus* (2.985), *amens* (6.86). Although the language is drawn from genuine mental disorder, as in the other two cases, its application to all non-Epicurean thought is

---

[4] Cf. Horace's *insanientis … sapientiae* (*Carm.* 1.34); Tertullian's *stupor Epicuri* (*De anima* 3); and Lactantius' *stultitia* (*De opif. Dei* 6.1) and *amentia* (ibid. 2.10, 3.21). The most detailed survey of attitudes to Epicureanism in the Roman world remains Ferguson (1990), although there is much of value in Jones (1992) and, more recently, Gatzemeier (2013).

[5] Statius' *docti furor arduus Lucreti* (*Silu.* 2.7.76) may be the first reflection of this attitude. Lactantius later calls Lucretius brainless (*De ira Dei* 10.17) but attributes his philosophical errors to Epicurus (*De opif. Dei* 6.1, 8.13).

[6] Cf. DL 10.118–19. It is unknown whether Lucretius married (cf. 4.1268?) or whether his devotion to Epicureanism necessitated a bachelor's life.

223

David Butterfield

strikingly hyperbolic. But Lucretius makes this the most culpable and inexcusable of these three categories.

Yet amidst these strictures and his unfailing commitment to *ratio* there is a striking paradox. Although Lucretius was supremely confident that he had evaded madness, by taking up the medium of hexametric poetry, he placed himself in the long epic tradition of irrational poetic inspiration, even hymning the divine figures of Venus in his first proem (1.1–43) and Calliope in his last (6.92–5). While these aberrations from Epicurean doctrine may be attributed simply to poetic convention, a problem remains: there is a third figure whose power over the philosopher-poet stretches far beyond the hackneyed literary deities of pagan worship.

The entirety of Lucretius' enthused devotion is channelled towards his philosophical master, Epicurus. So great is his reverence that Lucretius avoids naming Epicurus directly throughout the poem, except on one striking occasion. Initially, he speaks of a *Graius homo* (1.66) who dared to transcend the mortal sphere: his intellectual success defeated *religio* and his victory set mortals alongside heaven (1.62–79). In Book 3 Lucretius intensifies the panegyric: after addressing Epicurus as *Graiae gentis decus* ('glory of Greece') and declaring himself his direct disciple without pretensions of rivalry (3–8), Lucretius addresses him in hymnic terms as *pater* and *rerum inuentor* (9),[7] whose *aurea dicta* (12) deserve *perpetua uita* (13). Furthermore, the *ratio* sprung from his *mens diuina* (14–15) reveals the secrets of the universe: *moenia mundi | discedunt, totum uideo per inane geri res, | apparet diuom numen sedesque quietae* (16–18). Epicurus' mortal vision of truth earns a clear view of the immortal gods. In Book 5 the register of Lucretius' eulogy ascends further. After asserting (somewhat ironically) that no one of mortal stock could do justice to Epicurus' achievements (1–6), a remarkable claim occurs:

> nam si, ut ipsa petit maiestas cognita rerum,
> dicendum est, deus ille fuit, deus, inclute Memmi,

---

[7] Lucretius echoes the proem to Venus: with 3.9–10, cf. *te, dea, te fugiunt uenti, te nubila caeli* (1.6) and *te sequitur cupide quo quamque inducere pergis.* (16).

224

Lucretius the Madman on the Gods

qui princeps uitae rationem inuenit eam quae
nunc appellatur sapientia. (7–10)

> For if one should speak as the very majesty of the things he discovered requires, he was a god, a god, venerable Memmius, who first discovered that reason of life that is now called wisdom.

Epicurus' discoveries demand that he be termed 'god':[8] or rather, he *was* a god for as long as his life lasted. For Lucretius tells us explicitly – in the one instance where his name is spoken – that Epicurus died, as every mortal must (3.1042);[9] this inescapable biological fact is immediately set against the achievements of his intellect, which *genus humanum superauit* and *omnis (homines) restinxit* (1043–4). Epicurus was thus a mortal who partook of the immortal for as long as was humanly possible.

A survey of these three evenly spaced proems (1.62–79, 3.1–30, 5.1–54) demonstrates the gradual advance of Epicurus from foreign *homo* (1.66) to revered *inclutus* (3.10)[10] to *deus* (5.8), a man whose achievements make him truly worthy of godhood (5.51). This hyperbolic deification of Epicurus is supported by other ancient testimony[11] and has been well explored by scholars.[12] Epicurus himself was clear that his philosophy secured a quasi-divine existence (see esp. *Ep. Men.* 135). This doctrine was not just repeated by Lucretius, who asserted that Epicurean *ratio* lets humans *dignam dis degere uitam* (3.322), but adopted in practice when discussing the founding father himself.

In lieu, then, of any genuine religious fervour towards a deity, Lucretius adopted Epicurus as his paragon of perfection – apparently to the exclusion of all other Epicurean epigoni.

---

[8] Later in the proem we read *deus esse uidetur* (5.19) and *nonne decebit | hunc hominem numero diuom dignarier esse?* (5.50–1); in the proem to Book 6 Lucretius speaks of his *diuina reperta* (6.7), a phrase used at 5.13 of the traditional gods' discoveries.

[9] My previous suggestion (Butterfield 2008, 362–3) that Lucretius could have avoided naming Epicurus even here was probably misguided.

[10] The adjective *inclutus* occurs thrice in *DRN*, always in the vocative: of a deity (Venus, 1.40), a venerated human (Memmius, 5.8) and the quasi-divine Epicurus (3.10).

[11] Cicero observed the Epicureans' tendency to take hero worship to a divine level: *Tusc.* 1.48, cf. *ND* 1.43.

[12] See Fauth (1973), Clay (1986), Gale (1994, 191–207) and Erler (2001).

225

As part of his ground-breaking study of Lucretius' method of work, Sedley (1998, 62–93) has developed the persuasive notion that his devotion to Epicurus was 'fundamentalist'. In such a context of unequivocal devotion, one may be led to wonder whether Lucretius' quasi-religious commitment to a fellow mortal was in part responsible for ancient allegations of his madness: does a sane man give uncritical, almost mystical credit to all aspects of Epicurus' teachings, refusing to assimilate any developments of the subsequent three centuries? Although this picture of Lucretius as a hard-line fundamentalist has been broadly accepted, Sedley himself has argued that Lucretius differed signally from his master's teachings on one of the most important subjects: the nature of the gods.[13] Notwithstanding the difficulty of locating the gods in both the spatial and philosophical framework of the Epicurean worldview, investigation of Lucretius' understanding will be a most interesting test case of his fundamentalism. The stakes are high here: was Lucretius really un-Epicurean (i.e. at odds with Epicurus) in his conception of the most Epicurean (i.e. most ataraxic and blessed) entities? Or did his raving enthusiasm to the cause ensure that he followed Epicurus' theories to the letter?

The most detailed account of the gods occurs at 2.646–51, where the first of the *Kyriai doxai* is carefully versified.[14] The gods, we are told, enjoy immortal, undisturbed, self-sufficient existence far removed from human affairs: their nature (Greek φύσις) is separated far (*longe* 2.648) – in spatial terms – from human affairs. Clear confirmation that Lucretius places the physical existence of the gods 'out there' is shown by an important – and insufficiently discussed – passage in Book 6 (68–78). Lucretius explains that human misconceptions about divinity can cause harm: *delibata deum per te tibi numina sancta*[15] | *saepe*

---

[13] For the most detailed account of Sedley's view, see Long and Sedley (1987) §23 and Sedley (2011).

[14] These lines are also transmitted at 1.44–9, where their presence is unintelligible without positing a lacuna or authorial incompletion: see Butterfield (2014) 26–8.

[15] The adjective *sanctus* is used by Lucretius of gods and philosophers: at 1.1015 he likewise speaks of the *diuom corpora sancta*, and twice invokes them in impassioned

Lucretius the Madman on the Gods

oberunt[16] (70–1). This is not because of their wrath, which cannot exist (71–2; cf. 2.651), but because 'you' (i.e. any human) will misconceive them to be wrathful and therefore be unable to visit their shrines in peace (73–5).[17] This line of argument is extended in remarkable fashion:

> nec de corpore quae sancto simulacra feruntur[18]
> in mentes hominum diuinae nuntia formae
> suscipere haec animi tranquilla pace ualebis. (76–8)

> Nor will you be able to receive with tranquil spiritual peace these *simulacra* that are carried from their holy body into the minds of men conveying their divine form.

Lucretius clearly asserts that mental peace, achieved by the correct understanding of the gods, is essential for receiving *de corpore sancto* the atomic *simulacra* that convey their *forma diuina in mentes hominum. de* can here only be understood spatially, i.e. denoting a physical source.[19] Such *simulacra* must reach humans from the gods' physical location somewhere in the infinite Epicurean universe. Tantalisingly, Lucretius records elsewhere that he had more to write about the gods' location. In Book 5 he states that their *sedes* are not *in mundi partibus ullis* (147): because of their *tenuis natura*,[20] which cannot be perceived by the senses (sight included) but *animi uix mente uidetur* (149), and cannot touch or be touched (151),[21] the gods have no place within our world (150–2), with which they

---

asseverations introduced by *pro* (2.434–5, of the importance of touch), 2.1093–6 (of gods not controlling the universe). At 5.309, the gods' shrines possess *sanctum numen*; compare also *diuinum* or *diuom/deum numen* (1.155, 2.168, 3.18, 4.1239, 5.122, 1161, 6.1276; in the plural 4.1233).

[16] Wakefield's certain emendation for the nonsensical and unmetrical *oderunt* (OQ).

[17] On Lucretius' attitude to religion, see Summers (1995).

[18] This is the certain emendation by the *editio princeps* (Brescia, 1473) of the transmitted *fuerunt* (OQ).

[19] For the phrasing, cf. 6.522 [*nubes nimbique*] *omni uolgo de parte feruntur.* For the movement of *simulacra* from their source Lucretius variously uses *a(b)* (4.130, 737), *ex* (4.738, 739, 1032) and *de*, regularly with *corpore* (4.43, 52, 53, 59, 64, 84, 123, 333 [308]).

[20] The phrase *tenuis natura* (148) is used by Lucretius at 4.731 of images striking the mind, and at 5.557 and 561 of the spirit that sustains our body: the gods' nature is received by an analogous substance.

[21] *tactile nil nobis quod sit contingere debet;* | *tangere enim non quit quod tangi non licet ipsum* (151–2); cf. 1.304.

have neither concern nor contact (2.648). Therefore the gods' habitations (again *sedes*) must be different from ours (146–7), and *tenues de*[22] *corpore eorum*, of a tenuous nature that corresponds to their bodies. Unfortunately the account terminates at this point with the promise *quae tibi posterius largo sermone probabo* (155), a claim that is left unfulfilled in the poem that survives to us.[23]

Nevertheless, later in Book 5 Lucretius provides more detail about the information humans receive from the gods, when he treats the origin of religion in the development of early man:

> quippe etenim iam tum diuom mortalia saecla
> egregias animo facies uigilante uidebant
> et magis in somnis mirando corporis auctu. (1169–71)

> For it is the case that even in that age the mortal race with waking mind and especially in sleep saw the outstanding appearances of the gods of wondrous bodily size.

The picture is unambiguous: both in waking visions and (especially) in dreams, humans 'saw' (*uidebant*) the gods with mental vision (cf. 5.149 *mente uidetur*). Lucretius moves to assert that they attributed sensation (*sensus*) to them because 'they were seen (*uidebantur*)[24] to move their limbs and utter august words in proportion to their wondrous appearance and considerable strength' (1173–4). Lucretius next states that humans attributed eternal life to them *quia semper eorum | suppeditabatur facies et forma manebat* (1175–6): the perceived form of the gods was seen to be continuously resupplied and therefore unchanging. Despite continually emitting *simulacra*, the gods were seen not to suffer diminution or eventual

---

[22] There has been longstanding debate about whether the transmitted *de* is correct. Although the sense is not paralleled elsewhere in the poem, it seems acceptable to retain it (in the sense of *OLD* s.v. 5), rather than emend to *pro* after Lambinus.

[23] This is one of the most striking instances of the poem's unfinished state: see Butterfield (2014) 22–4. It is noteworthy that Lucretius also made a similar promise in the work's programmatic opening: 1.54–5.

[24] This is more natural than 'seemed' (noted as 'possibly' intended by Long and Sedley (1987) II 145). For Lucretius' doctrine about *simulacra* being able to convey the movement of limbs, cf. 4.768–76 and 800–6.

Lucretius the Madman on the Gods

destruction.[25] A second reason is given, namely that they thought beings of such strength could not be destroyed by any force (1177–8). Finally, Lucretius states that they deemed them to be pre-eminent in happiness because they did not fear death (1179–80) and felt no distress in carrying out the *multa et mira* that humans *in somnis ... uidebant* (1181–2). He therefore acknowledges that the gods can be perceived mentally by mortals to be of remarkable appearance and size, perform remarkable deeds and be of an unchanging and untroubled nature.

Up to this point there is no suggestion that humans made incorrect inferences about the images they apprehended from the gods. It is only in the subsequent stage, when these primitive men failed to understand the true workings of the heavens, that they mistakenly took refuge (*perfugium*) in supposing such events to happen at the will of the gods (1183–7). As a result they wrongly located them *in caelo* and at the heart of celestial and atmospheric phenomena. Such mistaken conclusions rouse Lucretius to the impassioned lament *o genus infelix humanum, talia diuis | cum tribuit facta atque iras adiunxit acerbas!* (1194–5).

From these disparate reports Lucretius' overall account can be reconstructed. He placed the gods in a physical location beyond our earth and the visible stars, from where we are able to perceive them via the most tenuous of *simulacra*. Their location must therefore lie in the Epicurean μετακόσμια or *intermundia*, the spaces 'between worlds'[26] attested in many accounts of Epicureanism.[27] Philodemus in his *De dis* locates

---

[25] This important detail is supported elsewhere: at 3.23–4 Lucretius says of the gods' abode that *omnia suppeditat porro natura neque ulla | res animi pacem delibat tempore in ullo* (23–4); naturally abundant atomic material supplies all the gods need to sustain their existence. This process of *suppeditatio* corresponds with Epicurus' ἀνταναπλήρωσις (*Ep. Hdt.* 48.4, of στερέμνια). Wigodsky (2004) 217 has argued that the gods could maintain their substance perpetually as an infinite extension of the process Lucretius discusses at 2.1122–43.

[26] In a different context Epicurus glosses the term as μεταξὺ κόσμων διάστημα (*Ep. Pyth.* 89). However, Epicurus could have used this technical term when discussing the location of the gods in Περὶ φύσεως 5 (cf. Philod. *De dis* Book 3, col. 8.31).

[27] Elsewhere Cicero ridicules a *concilium deorum* amidst the *intermundia Epicuri* (*ND* 1.18), a term repeated at *Fin.* 2.75, Sen. *Ben.* 4.4.19 and 7.31.3; cf. also Quint. *Inst.*

229

David Butterfield

divinities (τὰ θεῖα) in a space distinct from heavenly bodies such as the stars so as to be far removed from 'falling obstructions' (πίπτοντα ἐμποδιστικά, Book 3, col. 9.41).[28] Cicero (*Div.* 2.40), although speaking polemically of Epicurus' gods as translucent (*perlucidi*) and perforated (*perflabiles*), describes them as living 'between two worlds, as if between two groves' (*habitantes tamquam inter duos lucos sic inter duos mundos*); the additional explanation that Epicurus so positioned them *propter metum ruinarum* suggests that this let them avoid the fate of all other atomic aggregations in the universe, i.e. eventual dissolution and destruction.

Does this natural and relatively simple doctrine recorded by Lucretius differ in substance from that which was propounded by Epicurus himself? Although Epicurus is known to have written works Περὶ θεῶν and Περὶ ὁσιότητος,[29] and to have treated the gods in Περὶ φύσεως 12, only the scantiest traces of such texts survive. Instead we are forced to work with his epistolary summaries, especially the *Letter to Menoeceus* (DL 10.122–35), in which Epicurus describes (the singular) god as an 'immortal and blessed living thing' (123)[30] and asserts without qualification that (plural) 'gods exist',[31] because the knowledge (γνῶσις) of them is clear (ἐναργής) (*Ep. Men.* 123–4).

Nothing then from Epicurus' *ipsissima uerba* clashes with what Lucretius outlines. Where then is the serious discrepancy supposed to lie? Such problems that have been raised come from a third, albeit non-Epicurean source – the first book of Cicero's *De natura deorum*, composed in 45 BC.[32] Velleius, the

---

7.3.5 (*inter mundos*) and Hippol. *Phil.* 22.3 (μετακοσμίοις οὕτω καλουμένοις ὑπ' αὐτοῦ).

[28] Essler (2011a) offers an invaluable edition of *PHerc.* 152/157, coll. 8–10.

[29] Commentators tend to agree that Lucretius refers to one of these Epicurean works at 5.53: *immortalibus de* (Lambinus: *e* OQ) *diuis dare dicta suerit*.

[30] For the importance of ζῷον, see Mansfeld (1998) 178 n. 12. The difficult following sentence chastises non-Epicureans for reaching incorrect conclusions (ὑπολήψεις) about the gods, thereby harming their quality of life, which tallies neatly with *DRN* 6.68–78.

[31] See also Cicero *ND* 1.85 and Sextus Empiricus *M.* 9.13; cf. too the statement of Demetrius Laco (*PHerc.* 1055 XV) that the Epicurean god τὴν ὑπόστασιν ἔχῃ.

[32] I am convinced by Essler (2011b) that Cicero, despite his polemical stance, was using plural Epicurean sources in his composition of *ND* 1; cf. also Purinton (2001) 182 n. 1.

230

Lucretius the Madman on the Gods

Epicurean spokesman, runs through elements of Epicurus' theology at 1.43–9: (i) the gods exist, because all humans have an inborn πρόληψις[33] of them and their existence (43b–44); (ii) they are blessed, immortal and without emotions (45); (iii) their form (*species*) is human, since no other form appears to us, awake or asleep (46); (iv) yet it is one not of 'body' (*corpus*) but 'quasi-body' (*quasi corpus*), nor of 'blood' (*sanguinem*) but 'quasi-blood' (*quasi sanguinem*) (48); (v) the gods' nature is perceived not like Epicurean στερέμνια but in a distinct way (which I will seek to clarify below) that allows humans to understand what their blessed and eternal life is (49).

There is little to dispute in (i) and (ii), which confirm Epicurus' arguments from universal acknowledgement, and (iii), which tallies with Lucretius. The following claim (iv), that the gods' body and blood is somehow like[34] these substances in humans but different, seems to account for how they are both living beings and immortal. Since the gods are explicitly alive (48 *deus animans est*), I follow Sanders (2004) in taking the terms to mean 'quasi-flesh', i.e. representing a peculiar variation on human σάρξ, and 'quasi-blood' (perhaps not unlike divine ichor?).

Much the most difficult element is the last (v), which treats how the gods are perceived and their blessed immortality recognised. The passage is dense, with Velleius himself apologising *dissero breuius quam causa desiderat* (49). Pease (1955, 312b) called this long sentence 'the most difficult and disputed in the whole work, if not in all the works of Cicero'; more pessimistically, Masson (1907–9, II 149) termed it 'a slough in which ingenious explanations without number have merely been swallowed up'.[35] The passage is transmitted as follows:

Epicurus autem, qui res occultas et penitus abditas[36] non modo uideat animo, sed etiam sic tractet ut manu, docet eam esse uim et naturam deorum, ut

---

[33] The Greek term is used to clarify various alternative terms: *notio, insitae uel potius innatae cognitiones, praenotio, anticipatio* and *informatio*.

[34] Cotta repeats *quasi corpus* and *quasi sanguinem* at 1.74, having spoken of *tamquam corpus* and *tamquam sanguinem* at 1.71.

[35] For the most detailed account of this passage and the various interpretations it has provoked, see Essler (2011a) 67–108.

[36] It may be worth noting that the language here closely corresponds to the opening line of Lucretius' exposition of physics: *res quibus occultas penitus conuisere possis*

David Butterfield

primum (a) non sensu sed mente cernatur (b) nec soliditate quadam nec ad numerum, ut ea, quae ille propter firmitatem στερέμνια appellat, (c) sed imaginibus similitudine et transitione perceptis, (d) cum[37] infinita simillumarum imaginum species ex innumerabilibus indiuiduis existat et ad deos affluat, (e) cum[38] maximis uoluptatibus in eas imagines mentem intentam infixamque nostram intellegentiam capere, quae sit et beata natura et aeterna.

Yet Epicurus, who not only sees secret and wholly hidden things but also grasps them as if by hand, teaches that the force and nature of the gods is such that first (a) it is perceived not by sensation but by the mind, (b) neither through any solidity nor numerically, like those things he calls στερέμνια because of their firmness, (c) but [that] through images being perceived by their similarity and transition, (d) since the infinite form of most similar images arises from the innumerable atoms and flows to the gods, (e) our mind when focused and fixed on those images with the utmost pleasure realises[39] what their blessed and eternal nature is.

The following points are uncontroversial: the essence or nature of the gods (*uis et natura*)[40] cannot be perceived (*cernatur*) by the human sense organs but only internally by the mind (*mente*) (a); it is therefore perceived differently from typical solid objects of our world (στερέμνια), which can be sensed by their solidity (*soliditate*) and numerical identity (*ad numerum*) (b);[41] instead, (c) images are perceived through 'similarity and transition' (*similitudine et transitione*, a phrase to which we must return), which is explained by the clause (d) *cum ... affluat*, just as *ut ... appellat* explained (b): an infinite number of atoms causes *simillimae imagines* to produce

---

(1.145). We of course know that Cicero had read *DRN* a decade earlier (*Ad Q. Fr.* 2.9.3): see further Gatzemeier (2013) 27–42.

[37] *cum* is transmitted, not *cumque* (as printed by several editors, including Davies, Walker, Orelli, Brieger, and most recently Dyck without comment). The clause is best taken as causal: *sed* of the previous clause introduces the positive part of Epicurus' doctrine (*docet*), at which point the construction moves from *ut* + subjunctive to accusative and infinitive (*capere*).

[38] *cum* is transmitted, although *tum* is found in two manuscripts (CB¹).

[39] I support Dyck (2003 ad loc.) in taking *intellegentiam* as the object of *capere*, perhaps reflecting the Greek ἔννοιαν λαμβάνειν.

[40] This hendiadys probably represents Greek φύσις: cf. Schwenke (1882) 619.

[41] The statement that the gods are not perceived *ad numerum* has long been understood to reflect Greek κατ' ἀριθμόν: they do not have numerical identity but (we may presume) identity of form (κατ' εἶδος), like a waterfall or flame. This tallies with their divine matter continually being changed (through replacement) but being of permanent form (cf. n. 27).

Lucretius the Madman on the Gods

an 'unending form' (*infinita species*)[42] that flows 'to the Gods' (*ad deos affluat*: the actual direction of this flow is disputed); finally, the human mind's focus on this *species* allows us to realise what the gods' blessed and eternal nature is (e).

The points that remain at issue are: (i) what does it mean for images of the gods to be perceived *similitudine et transitione*?; and (ii) what source/target was envisaged for this flux?

(i) *similitudine* and *transitione* are most naturally understood as instrumental ablatives explaining how *imagines* are perceived (*perceptae*).[43] The internal 'vision' of the gods arises from the similarity that each *imago* has to the next one, such that their near-identicalness[44] (owing to their scarcely changing appearance) presents an unchanging and unified picture. The meaning of *transitione* is necessarily ambiguous without further qualification but most naturally expresses the process of each *simulacrum* 'transitioning' or 'passing across' the space between it and the preceding one so as to create a single unified image.[45]

(ii) Since the expression *infinita simillumarum imaginum species* must pick up the preceding *similitudine*, the latter half of clause (c) could well be linked with the process of *transitione*. The transmitted text states that the 'form of most similar images' *ad deos affluat*. Although it must be true, as stated above (n. 27), that the gods' atomic structure is maintained by a reciprocal influx of atoms to supply the loss of the *simulacra* emanating from

---

[42] Although Brieger and others have preferred to emend to *series*, the change is not essential. *species* (εἶδος), a regular term in Velleius' account that is repeated in Cotta's summary at 105 (*speciem dei percipi*), may here refer to the unending appearance of divine form, which is not delimited temporally but in eternal flux (thereby incorporating an infinite *series imaginum*). Cf. also *Diu.* 2.137, where Cicero reports Democritus' belief that *nulla species cogitari potest nisi pulsu imaginum*.

[43] The argument is well made by Dyck (2003) ad loc.

[44] I agree with Long and Sedley (1987) I 145, II 149 in understanding their similarity to be in relation to each other, not to gods. *simillimae* (as opposed to *eaedem*) is used of *imagines* in the preceding clause presumably to express their being the same in form but different atomic constructs each time.

[45] This corresponds to Philodemus' ὑπέρβασις τῶν μεταξύ (*De pietate*, col. 12), as was first suggested by Diels (1917) 27–8, discussed in greater detail by Purinton (2001) 184–7 and 203–9 and now accepted by Sedley (2011) 46 n. 46. Cicero's expression supports this notion better than the mind's 'passing between' each successive *simulacrum*, as suggested by Woodward (1989) 40–41, or Philippson's (1916) claim that the phrase meant καθ' ὁμοιότητα μετάβασις, 'inference by similarity'. Although it is possible that *transitione* could simply mean the 'passing' of the *simulacra* through space and eventually through the human mind (as suggested by Aug. *Ep.* 118.30 *frequenter fluunt et transeunt imagines*), this would not itself distinguish the perception of divine *simulacra* from those of any other object.

them, it is difficult to see how or why *imagines* would flow *to* the gods. Nowhere else in Epicurean doctrine do spontaneously preformed films flow towards the object whose form they represent, let alone regularly and continually. The few critics that have sought to defend the text have either treated *imagines* as if it meant simply atoms or have posited an unnatural and tortured account.[46] The great majority of scholars conclude that the text cannot be sound: indeed, it would be very odd if Velleius does not state, directly or indirectly, that *imagines* of the gods reach humans, so that the mental focus discussed in (e) can occur. We therefore expect the text simply to say that *imagines* travel from the gods (to us), so that they are perceived through transition in the mind. The most minor alteration produces the requisite sense: *a deis*,[47] which could be read either with *adfluat* (*affluat*) as transmitted, or *afluat*.[48] This is more probable than Lambinus' *ad nos affluat*, not only palaeographically but also because mention of the gods is required to provide the location in which the *species* arises. Serious consideration may be given to Heindorf's *a de<is ad n>os affluat*, as the mention of *nos* would not be unwelcome before *nostram* in the following clause.[49]

This unforced understanding of the text is supported by the evidence from later passages of *ND* I, in which the Academic Cotta rebuts Velleius' Epicurean theology.[50] At 105, we are told that the 'form (*speciem*) of god is perceived' (a) by thought (*cogitatione*) not sensation; (b) that it neither has solidity (*soliditatem*) nor retains numerical identity (*ad numerum*

---

[46] For instance, Mansfeld (1998, 199–200) made the improbable argument that such *imagines* form and fly to the gods because like moves to like. Yet the notion that such a targeted flux could arise from continuous chance formations is vanishingly unlikely. By contrast, if Long and Sedley are correct (1987, I 145) that divine *imagines* flow to us humans as gods, i.e. proleptically become gods when thought about in our minds, would Cicero have expressed such a complex idea so misleadingly with the unqualified *ad deos*?

[47] This suggestion was first made by Davies (1718); Manutius' singular *deo* does not fit the context so well. Although *ad deos* is read by all codices, it is possible that *adeos*, the initial reading of B (of equal stemmatic authority to PVAC), represents a stage closer to the truth.

[48] At 1.114 *afluant* is required by sense (see below), although most manuscripts (and the citation of Augustine at *Ep.* 118.30) transmit *adfluant/affluent*: see Pease (1955 ad loc.) for the frequent confusion of these verbs.

[49] It should be observed, however, that the direction of travel of these *simulacra* is not directed or targeted *ad nos*; instead, we humans can perceive such ubiquitous flows of divine *simulacra* at any location or point in time.

[50] Again, for the most detailed treatment of the interpretative options these passages allow, see Essler (2011a) 109–31.

Lucretius the Madman on the Gods

permanere); (c) that the vision (*uisio*) of it is perceived by 'similitude and transition' (*similitudine et transitione cernatur*); (d) that the arrival (*accessio*) of similar *imagines* from infinite atoms never ceases; (e) such that our mind when focused on them apprehends the gods' nature to be blessed and eternal. The fact that in (e) the human mind can focus on the incessant arrival of atoms in (d) again shows that these *imagines* reach us in our world: the gods cannot be perceived externally to our world, but as objects of focus need physically to enter our minds.

At 109 Cotta focuses more closely on the means of perception: (a) the transition (*transitio*) of the images in continuous flux allows one to appear from many; Cotta objects that he does not understand this: (b) how can it be proved that images are in motion continuously (*continenter imagines ferri*) and eternally (*aeterne*)? The answer is given that (c) the infinity of atoms supplies it (*innumerabilitas ... suppeditat*[51] *atomorum*). The incessant physical motion of *imagines* (or *uisiones*) is clearly understood to be towards humans from a source (c) that can be infinitely replenished.

Finally, at 114 Cotta challenges the alleged indestructibility of the gods: how can the blessed god not fear destruction (*ne intereat*) (a) since he is struck and buffeted without pause by the eternal incursion of atoms (*atomorum incursione sempiterna*); (b) and since images flow from god continually (*ex ipso imagines semper afluant*). This summation neatly provides confirmation of both directions of atomic motion, which were expressed too concisely at 1.49: (a) mere (unformed) atoms flow continually but at random to the gods; but (b) *imagines* flow continually from them.

It is therefore possible to understand Cicero's account in *ND* 1, without any distortion beyond one minor textual alteration, in a way that tallies neatly with Lucretius' text and Epicurus' surviving comments. Some core contentions of this reconstruction are also supported by the summary attributed to Aëtius (1.7.34 = Us. 355.11-13): Ἐπίκουρος ἀνθρωποειδεῖς μὲν τοὺς

---

[51] For the term, see n. 27.

235

David Butterfield

θεούς, λόγῳ δὲ πάντας θεωρητούς[52] διὰ τὴν λεπτομέρειαν[53] τῆς τῶν εἰδώλων φύσεως ('Epicurus says that the gods are anthropomorphic but that all are intelligible by the mind [alone] on account of the tenuousness of their *simulacra* material.')[54] There remains, however, one important item that requires our attention.[55] This is the scholion, of uncertain date, to the first of the *Kyriai Doxai*:

ἐν ἄλλοις δέ φησι τοὺς θεοὺς λόγῳ θεωρητούς, οὓς μὲν κατ' ἀριθμὸν ὑφεστῶτας, οὓς δὲ κατὰ ὁμοείδειαν ἐκ τῆς συνεχοῦς ἐπιρρύσεως τῶν ὁμοίων εἰδώλων ἐπὶ τὸ αὐτὸ ἀποτετελεσμένων, ἀνθρωποειδεῖς.

In other [works Epicurus] says that the gods are intelligible by thought, some subsisting numerically, others by the similarity that comes from the continual flow of like *simulacra* fashioned upon the same place.

Much of this tallies: the gods are perceived by mental reason (not the senses) and by a continual flux of similar *simulacra* converging (being fashioned)[56] on the same place, and are human in form. The problem arises in the opposition οὓς μὲν and οὓς δέ, which most naturally suggests two types of god. Such a twofold classification is without parallel in Epicurus and Lucretius, and it is incredible that Cicero and other adversaries could have escaped criticising such a peculiar view.[57] In

---

[52] For the phrase λόγῳ θεωρητός, see Epic. *Ep. Hdt.* 62.4 (of minuscule units of time) and cf. ibid. 47.1, 59.7, 62.7, and the scholion on *KD* 1 (below).

[53] It is possible that λεπτομέρεια was the specific term that Epicurus deployed to denote the gods' *tenuis natura* (*DRN* 5.148); for some stimulating ideas about the gods' atomic composition, see Essler (2011a) 354–8.

[54] The following sentence of this passage, in which four Epicurean imperishable natures are listed (atoms, void, the infinite and 'similarities'), has been carefully analysed by Wigodsky (2007) but does not affect the account given here.

[55] For a detailed account of varying interpretations of this text, see Essler (2011a) 131–47. The account of Sextus Empiricus (*M.* 9.43–7) should not be given great weight: Mansfeld (1998) 193–4 n. 55 has shown the account of Epicurean inference about the gods to be ahistorically Stoicising.

[56] This transmitted participle (BP) modifies the 'idols'; Kuhn has suggested ἀποτετελεσμένους (of the gods' being perceived), and Long and Sedley ἀποτετελεσμένην (of the latter type's unity). I disagree with Long and Sedley (1987) II 151 that 'not much appears to turn on the choice', since on my reading neither the 'gods' nor the similarity of their *simulacra* is 'fashioned' or 'produced' at a point in the mind.

[57] Long and Sedley (1987) II 151 argued that the former class are 'human sages who have become ethical models for future generations', but such figures must be mortal and dead, not 'immortal living gods'.

236

Lucretius the Madman on the Gods

fact, Cicero's Velleius reports something similar but crucially distinct at *ND* 1.49: the gods' essence *non sensu sed mente cernatur … nec ad numerum … sed … infinita simillumarum imaginum species … a deis adfluat.* While Cicero discusses the latter class of perception in the same fashion, the former class is explicitly denied: *nec ad numerum.* Accordingly, alteration of the scholion was made as early as Gassendi (1649, III 1697) to οὐ μέν; this necessitates the further change of οὓς δέ to something idiomatic, and we start to rewrite the text significantly. If the text is correct, the scholiast could be confused in his understanding; alternatively, it may be the *perceptibility* of the gods that is being qualified from two perspectives:[58] the scholiast may be attempting to show that, although the gods physically come to our minds by the latter method, they nevertheless can be thought about accurately as being numerically plural in existence (for, as *Ep. Men.* 123–4 demonstrates, 'gods' is meaningful to an Epicurean and distinct from 'god'). This text (of uncertain date and credibility) need not destabilise the consistent account drawn from other evidence.

We may therefore draw together the threads regarding Epicurus' gods. Their privileged location in the *intermundia* allows them to be free from contact with our world, which they cannot touch or be touched by, and which (unlike them) will be destroyed.[59] Being of a refined nature and having a particular species of flesh and blood, they are able to endure eternally, not because they suffer no decay – for like any atomic aggregate they continually emit *simulacra* – but because they are constantly replenished by an incursion of atoms: in the *intermundia*, as opposed to in a given world, there is infinite material to sustain the gods. Any coarser matter can presumably flow through their tenuous nature without harm; those of an appropriately rarefied form, by contrast, are assimilated into their structure and allow eternal renewal.[60]

[58] See especially Mansfeld (1998) 204–6 with n. 78, where attention is drawn to a similar use of μέν and δέ at Hdt. 1.44.2.
[59] I therefore disagree with Konstan (2011) 58–9 that Epicurus could satisfactorily place them within one given world.
[60] Cf. Konstan (2011) 57: 'psychophysical composition capable of appropriating external matter in such a way as permanently to replace what is lost'. Lucretius,

David Butterfield

Although the gods cannot be perceived by the senses, humans can perceive them mentally, awake or asleep: they can 'see' them in their unchanging state of blessedness and divinity. The frequency, regularity, and universality of divine *simulacra* proves their real existence in this state. An additional qualification (Lucr. 6.76–8) is that the recipient has to be in a state of tranquil peace to *suscipere* ('apprehend') these *simulacra*: those with a mistaken conception of the world and a distorted mental state will fail to apprehend them correctly. Lucretius' reading of Epicurus' account seems then to reproduce his master's understanding, at least as reconstructed from his writings. Perhaps every detail of the gods' physical workings was not established with absolute clarity by Epicurus, just as the notorious *clinamen* (παρέγκλισις) was possibly not worked through to perfection. Yet such possible shortcomings in exactitude are no reason to reject the most natural reading of the extant evidence.

By this point it is clear that I do not find evidence, explicit or implicit, to support the so-called 'idealist' position of the gods as thought constructs without physical permanence:[61] no extant source deprives the gods of physical identity or suggests that humans underpin their existence.[62] Would Epicurus have omitted a doctrine so important and distinctive from his systematic summaries? Instead of stating flatly that god should be acknowledged as a living being, and ridiculing as deranged those who deprive gods of real existence,[63] would he not have said that the gods are not real objects of human thoughts but

---

arguing against the soul's mortality at 3.821–3, may have had the gods in mind when considering how an eternally existing atomic aggregation could exist: [*si*] *non ueniunt omnino aliena salutis* | *aut quia quae ueniunt aliqua ratione recedunt* | *pulsa prius quam quid noceant sentire queamus* (cf. Giussani 1896–8 ad loc.).

[61] This counterintuitive reading was first raised by Lange (1866), and fleshed out by Lachelier (1877) and Scott (1883). It gained further momentum when reprised by Bollack (1975) and finessed by Long and Sedley (1987 §23). For further arguments against this position, see Mansfeld (1998), Babut (2005), Konstan (2011), and Essler (2011a, esp. 344–53).

[62] Cf. Purinton (2001, 186): 'if there were no one in the universe who was 'seeing' Zeus at a given instant, Zeus would cease to exist as a blessed immortal'.

[63] Philod. *De pietate* 112.1 Gomperz: 'Epicurus charges those who eliminate the divine (τὰ θεῖα) from existents (τὰ ὄντα) with total madness'.

238

Lucretius the Madman on the Gods

are only thoughts? Why would he bid his disciplines not to link god with anything that could destroy him or his blessedness, if the human race, destined for destruction, is the very basis for the 'immortal' gods' existence?

Further, it seems inconceivable that the clunky framework of Epicurean perception theory would have been posited for the immortal gods if no constant and immortal source was envisaged:[64] both Lucretius and Cicero give considerable focus to the very regularity of divine images. Yet while it is true that *simulacra* can form spontaneously from any atoms or other *simulacra* (*Ep. Hdt.* 48, *DRN* 4.135, 736), there is no credible account of how this process could provide a constant stream of god-shaped (and appropriately tenuous?) images flowing to each responsive human. Even if god-shaped *simulacra* were to form randomly, Lucretius suggests (4.129–42) that, like clouds, their status would be evanescent and prone to sudden change: what could guarantee the incessant arrival of *simillimae imagines*?

Questions about the origin of the human πρόληψις of the gods do not overturn this reconstruction. If Sedley (2011) is correct in regarding this πρόληψις as an innate disposition to forming appropriate thoughts about the gods,[65] could the point simply be that humans naturally have a mental disposition that allows inflowing divine *simulacra* to prompt two appropriate and inevitable conclusions, that the gods exist and that their existence is blessed and immortal?[66] The primary point seems to be that all humans, regardless of their location or cultural conditioning in the world, are able (*qua* humans) continually to receive images of the gods. Any discordant beliefs about the gods arise from individuals' mistaken inferences from these same προλήψεις. The πρόληψις is *innata* (ἔμφυτος) because

---

[64] If, as Long and Sedley argued (1987, I 147), προλήψεις of the gods can have 'an introspective origin in our feelings', why would one need to introduce *simulacra* theory at all?

[65] This develops the earlier view of Long and Sedley (1987) II 148 that 'what is innate is a predisposition for forming an idealized conception of the happy being we ourselves aim to be'; arguments against the innatism of (divine) προλήψεις can be found in Asmis (1984) 68–9, Scott (1995) 190–201, and Konstan (2011) 66–8.

[66] Sedley may well be right that the gods are the only intelligible objects of a πρόληψις.

David Butterfield

humans are ready from birth to receive divine *simulacra* appropriately: such perception of *simulacra* is essential to the process, as Cicero's account in *ND* 1.46–9 shows after 1.43–5.

So where does this survey leave Lucretius' account of Epicurus' gods? Long and Sedley condemned him for his 'naive reading of Epicurus' theology' (1987, II 153 on *DRN* 5.154). Yet this would tally ill with his close and detailed reconfiguration of the Περὶ φύσεως, and alarmingly so on such an important matter.[67] I do not therefore find credible the notion that Lucretius, along with various Epicurean devotees and Epicurean adversaries,[68] misunderstood their master on so crucial an issue as whether or not the gods exist as corporeal gods. To posit active innovation by such a range of figures is indeed to give 'too much inventiveness to the epigoni in so central a matter' (Konstan (2011) 61).

More probable is that Lucretius followed Epicurus on the gods as closely as he could. Epicurus' philosophising could transcend the *moenia mundi* and range through the boundless *intermundia* (1.72–7),[69] where he himself discovered the secrets of the universe and genuinely apprehended the gods with clarity. Although the gods' contribution to the workings of the universe proves to be negligible, Epicurus revealed their major importance for human ethics. In this respect I am in complete agreement with the 'idealists' about the importance of the gods as an object of emulation. Sedley has argued (2011, 29) that such deities 'are our own graphic idealization of the life to which we aspire, and that the simulacra identified with them are simply those on which ... we choose to focus our minds in order to enjoy the image of such perception'. The ideal life to which the good Epicurean aspires is one of complete tranquillity and blessedness, and for inspiration his thoughts

---

[67] Sedley's view (1998, 66, n. 28; 2011, 50 n. 60) that Lucretius' understanding of the gods was independent from Epicurus' in his proems (including 5.146–55) but canonical in his main text seems improbable.

[68] Despite using Cicero as a source for reconstructing Epicurus' doctrine, Long and Sedley (1987) II 148–9 suspect that 'Cicero is here simply translating Epicurus' technical account without understanding it'.

[69] At 2.1044–7 Lucretius advises the reader that *animi iactus* (ἐπιβολὴ τῆς διανοίας) can let the mind wander beyond the *moenia mundi*.

Lucretius the Madman on the Gods

are attuned to divine *simulacra* that convey this image to him;[70] such *simulacra* are not the gods but they are the closest we can get to the gods' eternally remote existence.

When Epicurus tells Menoeceus that one who lives 'among' the immortal gods is not like a mortal being (*Ep. Men.* 133) he envisages the Epicurean contemplating the divine. Epicurus himself could approximate to the divine through such internalised contemplation; his devotees could, by reading his philosophy and emulating his lifestyle, approximate to him and thereby quasi-divinity. Nevertheless, being mortal they must die like him (3.1042), even if philosophical truths merit a life like god (3.322, 5.8): this is the best and final offer available to mankind and one that Lucretius urges his readers to take.

I end by returning to the madness and delusion with which Lucretius has been charged over the ages. It was indeed Lucretius' quasi-religious fervour towards his mortal master that led him to accept such a novel and strange theological doctrine; although he believed that constant information received from the gods allows humans to reach the correct understanding about them, making such an assertion tarnished him with the very charge of madness his work sought to dispel.[71] Furthermore, by treating Epicurus as tantamount to a god, Lucretius' devotional stance emerges to be the most fundamental of all. Yet for such *arduus furor* we must be grateful, as it requires a certain sublime frenzy to tackle Epicureanism head on – and in hexametric Latin verse – something only Lucretius was mad enough to take on.

---

[70] Cf. Long and Sedley (1987) I 146–7, Warren (2000) and (2009) 241.

[71] Cf. Aug. *Ep.* 118.30–1, dismissing Epicurean theology as *deliramenta*. Even as hard-nosed a scholar as Bailey could suspect Lucretian madness: based on Lucretius' account of animals in warfare he supposed that the poet 'was from time to time deranged' (1947, III 1529).

CHAPTER 12

IN AND OUT OF THE STOA: DIOGENES LAERTIUS ON ZENO

A. A. LONG*

David Sedley in his celebrated article on 'philosophical allegiance in the Greco-Roman World' emphasizes the extraordinary authority that founders of schools acquired among their followers, at least after the founder's death.[1] This point pertains to Zeno of Citium as much as it does to Epicurus, who is the main focus of Sedley's study. No card-carrying Stoic, subsequent to the first generation of so-called 'dissidents' (DL 7.167), appears to have ever challenged Zeno or criticized his doctrines, whatever they were taken to be. For Epictetus (3.21.19), lecturing at the turn of the first and second centuries CE, Zeno occupies philosophy's 'didactic and doctrinal chair'. In generic testimonies concerning Stoicism the school is typically designated by such phrases as *hoi peri Zenona* or *hoi apo Zenonos*, and also by expressions that explicitly call Zeno the founder or leader of the sect.[2] Diogenes Laertius appends his huge doxography of Stoicism to the biography of the individual Zeno. Thus he underlines Zeno's authority for the entire Stoic tradition. His seamless account of Zeno and Stoic doctrine is the longest item in his entire set of eighty-two philosopher lives.

Nonetheless disagreement between individual Stoics other than Zeno and difference of emphasis between them are quite marked by Diogenes in his doxography, especially in its introductory pages.[3] Equally noteworthy is the frequency with

---

* For David from Tony, celebrating the first forty-five years of our friendship and collaboration, 1969–2014.
[1] Sedley (1989).
[2] See for instance *SVF* 1.65, 94–6, 124, 158, 164, 250.
[3] See DL 7.40–1, 127, 139, 142, 149, 157.

242

In and out of the Stoa: Diogenes Laertius on Zeno

which, in Diogenes' treatment of physics, Chrysippus' name and works are cited alongside those of Zeno, indicating their community of viewpoint.[4] I take this solidarity to indicate that Diogenes was working in the doxography from sources that wanted to emphasize continuity between the founder and his second and greatest successor. Just occasionally, in late sources, Zeno's name is even preceded by that of Chrysippus (*SVF* 1.142, 153). The most elaborate designation of Zeno himself comes from Theodoret, writing in the fifth century CE: 'Zeno of Citium, son of Mnaseas, the disciple of Crates and the originator of the Stoic sect' (*SVF* 1.85).

This is how Diogenes prefaces the doxography (7.38):

> I have decided to speak generically, in the life of Zeno, about all the Stoic doctrines on account of the fact that he was the founder of the sect. His many books, in which he has talked like no other Stoic, have already been recorded [i.e. recorded by Diogenes himself at 7.4].

Diogenes (7.160–7) positions his lives of three of Zeno's other contemporary followers Aristo, Herillus, and Dionysius between the end of the doxography and the life of Cleanthes, Zeno's official successor. By calling them 'the dissidents', Diogenes again underlines Zeno's authority for the Stoic apostolic tradition. The actual writings of Zeno, however, hardly had the canonical status that the works of Epicurus enjoyed in his school.[5] Diogenes' bibliography of Zeno (7.4) includes twenty titles, from which he cites just two in the doxography. They are entitled *On the human being's nature*, and *On the universe*. Diogenes cites the latter work four times, twice for doctrines he conjoins to the name of Chrysippus, and twice for doctrines he ascribes to Zeno alone.[6]

Given the complexity and chronological range of the doxography, it is risky to draw inferences about any recourse

---

[4] DL 7.134, 136, 142, 148, 149, 150.
[5] As stated by Sedley (1989) 98.
[6] These doctrines concern the world's unity, the four elements, solar eclipses, and lightning. DL 7.134 also refers to a work *On substance*, while Aëtius (*SVF* 1.176) credits Zeno with a work that has the hoary title *On nature*. Neither of these works may actually be different from the well-attested book *Peri tou holou*; see Algra (2002) 177.

243

that Diogenes' sources had to Zeno's actual writings.[7] I will make just two points about that. First, if any of Zeno's works were available to, or part of the required reading of, later Stoics, *On the universe* (*Peri tou holou*) probably topped the list.[8] Second, we may note the absence of Zeno's name from any part of the 'logical' section of the doxography, which includes epistemology and the material on sense impressions and assent that Cicero (*Acad.* 1.40–2) ascribes in detail to Zeno quite specifically. By attaching Zeno's name to the entire doxography Diogenes lets his readers infer that Zeno's thinking was seminal for all Stoic doctrine throughout the school's history. Yet, as Sedley cogently observes in his aforementioned study, 'Zeno, by contrast [with Epicurus], seems to have been an inspirational rather than a systematic teacher, leaving vast areas of unclarity about his teachings for his successors to illuminate, and much virgin territory, including logic, for them to colonize.'[9]

In this chapter I want to develop Sedley's insight by first discussing a striking mismatch between Cicero and Diogenes on details of Zeno's career, and then by exploring in some detail the sources and the structure of Diogenes' vita section. These findings will tell us little that is certain, unfortunately, about Zeno's philosophical career. What they will illuminate is a large gap between how Zeno was perceived by various contemporary authors and how Stoics at the time of Cicero represented Zeno's role as founding father of the school. I am far from being a pioneer in taking this line, which Jaap Mansfeld and David Hahm have already pursued most effectively.[10] Much, however, remains to be said about Diogenes' Life of Zeno, leaving us, if I am right, unsettling questions about the first Stoic's intellectual biography and persona.

---

[7] For further details concerning Zeno's works and citations from them, see Kidd (2002) 354–5.

[8] Aëtius 1.7.33, which is a lemma on generic Stoic notions of god, summarizes Stoic cosmology in language that fully coheres with Diogenes' doxography, including phrases explicitly attested from that Zenonian work, see Long (2018) 439–45.

[9] Sedley (1989) 98.

[10] Mansfeld (1986); Hahm (2002)

In and out of the Stoa: Diogenes Laertius on Zeno

According to Cicero's spokesman Varro, Zeno's entire system (*disciplina*) was a remodelling or rectification (*correctio*) of the Academic philosophy he had learned, along with Arcesilaus, as an assiduous student of Polemo (*Acad.* 1.35). Varro's ensuing outline of Zeno's novelties gives special attention to the Stoic's fundamental and contentious notion of infallible cognition (*comprehensio*). In the other surviving book of the *Academica*, Cicero himself, writing as an Academic sceptic, gives a vivid account of the criticism Zeno's original doctrine elicited from the Academic Arcesilaus, and of the amendments to it that Zeno made in response. Zeno's encounters with Arcesilaus were subsequently given lurid and polemical colouring by the Platonist Numenius, writing in the second century CE; and Cicero's account is also echoed by Augustine.[11] Little that we think we know about Zeno's philosophical biography, or that of Arcesilaus, seems more secure and conceptually significant than their disputatious relationship. As to Polemo, Sedley has invoked Zeno's pupillary relationship to this fifth head of the Academy as a fundamental mediating link between Zeno's physics and contemporary interpretations of Plato's *Timaeus*.[12]

Cicero's authorities for his statements about Polemo, Arcesilaus, and Zeno were the rival Academics of the first century BCE, Philo and Antiochus, who had powerful agendas of their own. These agendas do not of course, by themselves, impugn the historicity of the aforementioned relationships. What must arouse reflection, or rather suspicion, is Diogenes' reticence in his Lives about Zeno's dealings with Academics.

In regard to the association of Zeno and Arcesilaus, Diogenes says absolutely nothing. He makes no mention of their encountering one another in any of his Lives, neither those of Academics nor those of Stoics. Both Arcesilaus and Aristo, however, figure together in each of the Lives Diogenes composed for them (4.33, 40; 7.162–3). Long ago

---

[11] Numenius fr. 25 des Places *ap.* Euseb., *PE* 14.5.11, 14.6.9 (*SVF* 1.11–12); Augustine, *C. Acad.* 2.13, 3.38.

[12] See Sedley (2002b). His thesis on Polemo's formative influence has been supported by Dillon (2003a) 168, 174, and by Gill (2006) 17, 19. Challenges to it have been made by Inwood (2012), Reydams-Schils (2013), and Algra (2016).

245

A. A. Long

I drew attention to the prominence Diogenes accords to the encounters between these two men, who were named the outstanding philosophers of the day by the contemporary intellectual Eratosthenes (Strabo 1.15), and I asked whether perhaps Aristo, rather than Zeno, was actually Arcesilaus's main sparring partner.[13] This is not the occasion to rehash these points, except to say that I continue to find Diogenes' complete silence about Zeno and Arcesilaus worthy of a discussion that it has not yet apparently received.

As to Polemo, Diogenes mentions him twice in his life of Zeno, but without any prominence. First, after naming Crates, Stilpo, and Xenocrates (this last a chronological impossibility) as Zeno's teachers (7.2), Diogenes (to quote Hahm), 'tacks on Polemo as an afterthought'.[14] Diogenes writes expansively about Zeno's time with Crates, as we shall see. He also reports on Zeno's formative meetings with Philo of Megara and the dialectician Diodorus Cronus (7.16). Then, close to the end of the life, he writes (7.25):

> When Zeno was already an advanced thinker but thoroughly modest, he would enter Polemo's school. Consequently, Polemo is reported to have said: 'Well, Zeno, don't think I fail to notice you slipping in at the garden door, stealing my doctrines and giving them a Phoenician clothing'.

Without further comment Diogenes passes on to his next anecdote. One would give much to know exactly what he meant by Zeno's Phoenician clothing. I cannot do better than quote the following comment by Jacques Brunschwig:

> Was it a matter of philosophical doctrine, or a matter of expression, style and vocabulary? I suspect that the second option is the right one, and that the anecdote supports (or has been concocted so as to support) an Antiochean view of Stoicism, according to which there is no real difference between the Stoics and the Old Academy, but only a verbal one.[15]

Brunschwig was surely right to detect an echo of Antiochus' representation of Zeno's deep indebtedness to Polemo, as represented by Cicero. But, far from simply making that point,

[13] See Long (2006a) 106–7.
[14] Hahm (2002) 42.
[15] Brunschwig (2002) 24.

246

In and out of the Stoa: Diogenes Laertius on Zeno

the anecdote strongly compliments Zeno by indicating that he was already an advanced thinker by the time he attended Polemo's classes. The charge of theft, coupled with Zeno's modesty, hardly redounds to Polemo's credit or influence.[16] Strabo also reports, like Cicero, that Zeno was a co-pupil with Arcesilaus of Polemo (13, 614 = *SVF* 1.10).

That relationship, as we have seen, is one way that our evidence characterizes a decisive feature of Zeno's philosophical pedigree. But it is only one way. Theodoret, as I said earlier, calls Zeno the disciple of Crates. Heraclides of Lembos, writing some 100 years before Cicero, calls him a pupil of Stilpo (DL 2.120); that relationship is prominently attested in Diogenes' Life of Zeno itself (7.2 and 24). Before we probe further into the biographical details, I want to say more about the sources and authorities that he explicitly cites, starting with Zeno's earliest followers.

These personages include Persaeus, Zeno's Cypriot protégé and housemate in Athens (DL 7. 13, 36), Aristo, and Cleanthes. Sedley's point about the early followers' need to clarify Zeno's doctrines is tellingly confirmed by the fact that Aristo wrote on that precise subject (DL 7.163), while Cleanthes' bibliography includes two books on Zeno's theory of nature (DL 7.174). Diogenes also reports (ibid.) that Cleanthes recorded Zeno's lectures on oyster shells and the shoulder blades of oxen, because he could not afford papyrus. Chrysippus, we are told, authenticated Zeno's notorious *Politeia* in his own work of that name (DL 7.34). This testimony, to which I will return, suggests that Zeno's social theory had already become quite controversial in his lifetime. How Zeno's fellow Stoics described his doctrines is unfortunately not recoverable from Diogenes because in the biographical part of his vita he attributes no distinctive philosophical contributions to Zeno.[17]

---

[16] According to Diocles of Magnesia (7.162), cited in Diogenes' Life of Aristo, it was an encounter between Aristo and Polemo, while Zeno was suffering from a long illness, that caused Aristo to become a 'turn coat' (*metetheto*), which is the verb used to characterize the renegade Stoic Dionysius, who deserted Zeno for Epicurus. This testimony, like the anecdote about Zeno's thieving, suggests that relations between him and Polemo were far from cordial.

[17] Unless we count Zeno's innovative use of the term *kathekon*, 7.25.

247

What do we learn about Zeno from contemporaries who were not his followers? He figured in two of Timon's *Silloi* (DL 7.15–16). One of these spoofs, which includes a slur about Zeno's dark skin, seems to mock his interest in logical subtleties; the other displays contempt for the poverty and insignificance of his followers.[18] Such racist and elitist prejudice was also present, I think, in the way Antigonus of Carystus represented Zeno in his biography of the Stoic founder (DL 3.66). Antigonus was probably the principal source for Diogenes' lives of the Academics.[19] As we have seen, those biographies are studiedly silent on any connections between Zeno and the Academy. Antigonus was pro-Academy in his biographical stance. He was also pro-Pergamum, the city from where Arcesilaus hailed. In his Life of Zeno Antigonus emphasized Zeno's loyalty to Citium, and seemingly his financial support of Crates, describing Crates as Zeno's 'teacher' (7.12). Zeno's sex life was also a topic Antigonus treated, including the claim that he was an inveterate paedophile with no interest in heterosexual activity.[20] I conjecture that Diogenes' less complimentary anecdotes concerning Zeno, especially those involving his connections with Crates, go back to Antigonus.

Diogenes bespatters the Life with citations from other biographers, ranging in date from about 250–50 BCE. His most frequently cited author is Apollonius of Tyre, who wrote a multi-book work *On Zeno* and also a *Catalogue of the philosophers of Zeno's school and their books*. Apollonius' literary activity is known only from Strabo (16.2.4), who describes him as writing 'somewhat before my time'.[21] From Diogenes' contexts drawing on Apollonius, we can see that this author went out of his way to present Zeno in extravagantly laudatory terms. Signs of that are evident each time Diogenes invokes him. According to Persaeus, who knew Zeno intimately, the Stoic founder was tubby and frail, but Apollonius

---

[18] See my remarks on Timon in Long (2006b) 91–2.
[19] See DL 4.17, 22, and Long (2006b) 98–9.
[20] See Athenaeus 13, 563 (*SVF* 1.247), who cites Antigonus' *Life of Zeno.*
[21] The chronology gives Apollonius an approximate floruit of 50 BCE. He was clearly a strong Stoic sympathizer but probably not an actual teacher of Stoicism.

248

In and out of the Stoa: Diogenes Laertius on Zeno

made him lean and tall (7.1). Similar discrepancy is present in Diogenes' reports on Zeno's death – at the age of seventy-two, according to Persaeus, but at ninety-eight on the word of Apollonius, after a life without a day of sickness (7.28).

Apollonius's eulogistic tone is detectable in the preceding words of Diogenes:

> Zeno surpassed everyone in self-mastery (*enkrateia*) and in dignity (*semnotes*) and yes, by Zeus, in happiness (*makariotes*).

No matter that longevity and good health are indifferent to happiness, according to strict Stoic doctrine, and that no Stoic, even including Zeno, is securely attested to have met the Stoic conditions for wisdom.[22]

We are not yet done with Diogenes' sources, especially Apollonius, but at this point, I turn to his narrative concerning Zeno's actions (7.5):

> Zeno made a habit of presenting his lectures, while walking up and down in the Painted Stoa ... wishing to keep the place free from bystanders ... People went there to hear Zeno, and this is why they [the bystanders] were called Stoics. The same name was given to his followers, who had originally been called Zenonians, as Epicurus says in his letters.

Since Epicurus was a few years older than Zeno, who outlived him, we can probably infer that Zeno's students were already being called Stoics during Zeno's lifetime.[23]

As presented by Diogenes, Zeno is an intriguingly ambiguous figure. We see it immediately in the story about his collecting followers while simultaneously discouraging bystanders. Diogenes does not tell us what Zeno lectured on, but the subject matter must have been lively enough to attract a crowd of curious listeners. We can plausibly identify some of it from Zeno's first and most famous, or rather infamous, publication, entitled *Politeia*. In this work of utopian socio-political theory, Zeno presented proposals that would, if implemented,

---

[22] See Brouwer (2014) 125.
[23] Hippobotus (DL 1.19), late third century BCE, gives 'Zenonian or Stoic' as the name of the school.

have completely undermined the foundations of a Greek polis and its cultural norms, or indeed of any conceivable human community. Currency, courts of law, temples, gymnasia and traditional education would be abolished. The nuclear family would be prohibited. Sexual relations would be based simply on mutual consent. Unisex clothing and partial nudity would be required of everyone. Ethical goodness would be the only criterion for citizenship, freedom, and friendship. From elsewhere we know that Zeno also challenged sexual taboos by permitting incest and recommending virtuous teachers to practise bisexual paedophilia, and elevated Eros to the role of the community's tutelary divinity.[24]

Diogenes reports that Zeno wrote the *Politeia* under the influence of his first teacher, the Cynic Crates (7.4). This testimony rings true; for many of Zeno's proposals recall Cynic contempt for conventional values by advocating 'nature' as the appropriate ethical standard. If Zeno lectured on these themes, we can understand some people's eagerness to hear him. Yet, Diogenes tucks his account of Zeno's shocking *Politeia* into an appendix after ending the Life proper with an incredible account of Zeno's suicide. In the intervening episodes of the ensuing biography there is no trace of the social and sexual iconoclasm of the *Politeia*. Zeno comes across as rather surly, prudish, and caustic, but no radical and intriguing cultural commentator. Notwithstanding Zeno's scarcely engaging personality, Diogenes reports at length on the way Zeno was courted by kings and awarded great honours at Athens in recognition of his sterling character, even though he was an immigrant.

What did Zeno actually do to earn such accolades that included celebration in eulogistic verses by famous poets? How do these honours fit the radical author of the *Politeia*? Diogenes tells us nothing of any special acts of courage or

---

[24] For details see Schofield (1991) Gaca (2003), and Bees (2011). Diogenes' outline (7.33–4) of the contents of Zeno's *Politeia* is mild meat compared with sexual details recorded elsewhere (see Sextus Empiricus, *PH* 3.245–6 and *Adversus mathematicos* 11.190–1). Diogenes' qualms in writing about sex are on view when (7.187–8) he alludes to the similar theories of Chrysippus.

In and out of the Stoa: Diogenes Laertius on Zeno

kindness or civic benefaction. The most striking features of Zeno's character, as it emerges from these pages, are frugality, contempt for money or fame, a sharp tongue, and physical and mental toughness. All Diogenes' leading figures in the Lives are endowed with characters that fit appropriate generic aspects of their philosophies, making them stoical or sceptical in the modern sense of these epithets, as the case may be. But doubts remain about whether Diogenes' portrayal of Zeno's life is fully coherent as a biography, and if not, why it is not.[25]

By way of preface to this topic, I offer a summary of the Life, to which I attach the paragraph numbers in parentheses. I also note the names of the main sources either as cited by Diogenes or those that his sources probably used, together with their approximate BCE floruit dates. The names of Stoic philosophers Diogenes adduces are printed in bold.

A *Nationality and physique* (7.1): Timotheus (? 250), Apollonius of Tyre (50), **Persaeus** (280), and **Chrysippus** (240 BCE).
B *Philosophical teachers* comprising Crates, Stilpo, Xenocrates, and Polemo (7.2): **Hecato** (80) and Apollonius.
C *Conversion to philosophy, interest in Socrates, and attachment to Crates* (7.3–5).
D *List of Zeno's writings.* (7.4).
E *Zeno's lectures in the Athenian Stoa* (7.5).
F *Zeno's honours and decrees at Athens,* and correspondence with King Antigonus (7.6–12): Apollonius.
G *Biographical chitchat* (7.12–16): **Cleanthes** (260), Antigonus of Carystus (240).
H *Anecdotes and anti-Cynic sayings* (7.16–24): Apollonius.
I *Other philosophical teachers, dialectic and ethics* (7.25–6): Hippobotus (200) and **Hecato**.
J *Poets' celebratory verses* (7.27).
K Zeno's age and death (7.28): **Persaeus** and Apollonius.
L *Eulogistic epigrams by various poets* (7.29–30).
M *Epigram by Diogenes* (7.31).
N *Conversion to philosophy again, Socrates, and Crates* (7.31–2): Demetrius of Magnesia (50).
O *Summary, criticism and expurgation of Zeno's Politeia* (7.32–4).

---

[25] Hahm (2002) 33 finds in Zeno's supposed letter to King Antigonus (7.8–9), 'a thinly disguised outline of the Stoic theory of education and moral development'. This text, however, is probably a first-century BCE fabrication.

What are we to make of this biography?[26] The points of greatest interest and puzzlement to me are sections B and I on Zeno's philosophical teachers, and sections C and O on Zeno's conversion to philosophy. Why did Diogenes present this material twice, and why did he intersperse these sections with quite different subject matter? Rather than account for these issues as due to random methods of composition, we should take them as evidence, drawn from Diogenes' multiple sources, of disagreements and uncertainties about how to present the life of Stoicism's founder in the years after Zeno's death. From Diogenes himself we learn that Zeno bequeathed a fragmented school. Three of his prize students joined other philosophers or started schismatic movements. Zeno's chosen successor, Cleanthes, kept the school going as a formal establishment, but it was only under the next leader Chrysippus and his successors that Stoicism began to acquire the dominance it would achieve by the time of Cicero, 200 years after Zeno had ended his life. By then Stoics wanted to look back to Zeno as the school's illustrious founder, but was the record of Zeno's life and teaching, especially his shocking and Cynic-influenced *Politeia*, appropriate for fashionable Stoic teachers like Panaetius and their wealthy and respectable Roman patrons?

The pertinence of this question will emerge when we review Zeno's teachers and conversion to philosophy (sections B, C, I, N), and also some anti-Cynic remarks attributed to him (section H). The principal source of this latter material seems to have been the eulogistic biographer Apollonius of Tyre. Apollonius evidently wanted to present Zeno in a light that would appeal to elite Roman citizens by minimizing the effect of Cynic non-conformity on Zeno's philosophy and lifestyle. Thus in section C, we are told that Zeno left Crates out of embarrassment at his teacher's crudity. And in section H Diogenes presents a string of anecdotes to confirm Zeno's mature distance from Crates: for instance, that Zeno scolds a

---

[26] Hahm (1992) dissects the episodes and sources with far greater detail than I can offer here.

252

In and out of the Stoa: Diogenes Laertius on Zeno

man identified as a Cynic, rebukes a pederast, gives conventional lessons in rhetoric, urges conformity on young men, praises chastity, and, as explicitly reported by Apollonius, resists the efforts of Crates to 'drag him away' from Stilpo with whom Zeno was now studying. Unfortunately for Apollonius, however, and for Stoics who disapproved of Cynicism, Diogenes could not, or would not, erase the tradition that Cynic teaching had been the primary influence on Zeno's philosophical makeup and lifestyle. Moreover, a minimally Cynic Zeno is in stark tension with the literary context Diogenes assigns to his biography.

Immediately before starting the Life of Zeno, Diogenes discusses a 'succession' of Cynics, starting with the Socratic philosopher Antisthenes, and ending with a summary of 'the doctrines they [Cynics] held in common' (6.103–5):

> They also hold that the goal is to live in accordance with virtue, as Antisthenes says in his *Heracles*: exactly like the Stoics. For these two schools have much in common. Hence it has been said that Cynicism is a shortcut to virtue. And it was in the manner of the Cynics that Zeno of Citium lived his life. They also think that one should live frugally, eating only for nourishment and wearing only one garment; and they despise wealth, fame and noble birth. Some, at any rate, eat nothing but vegetables, drink nothing but cold water, and use whatever shelters or tubs they find, like Diogenes, who used to say that it was characteristic of the gods to need nothing, and of godlike men to need very little. They hold that virtue can be taught, as Antisthenes says in his *Heracles*, and once acquired cannot be lost; that the wise man is worthy of love, has no flaw, and is a friend to his like, and that nothing should be entrusted to fortune. They maintain, like Aristo of Chios, that that which is intermediate between virtue and evil is neither good nor bad. These, then, are the Cynics. We must turn to the Stoics, whose founder was Zeno, a student of Crates.

What immediately follows this passage is the very first line of Diogenes' Life of Zeno, stating his name and birthplace (section A).

Diogenes' readers, then, if they read his work in its book sequence, will not only come to Zeno with the information that he was a student of Crates.[27] They will have also learned

---

[27] On the continuity between Cynics and Stoics, as presented by DL, see Mansfeld (1986) 356ff.

253

that Zeno actually lived a dignified version of the Cynic life, consisting of extreme frugality, and contempt for wealth, fame, and noble birth. Diogenes' anecdotal material concerning Zeno's lifestyle illustrates Zeno's adoption of these principles (for instance 7.16, 7.26).[28] The doctrine that virtue is the goal of life also comes up repeatedly (7.7, 7.8, 7.10, 7.30). And the eulogistic epigrams (section L) emphasize such Cynic attributes as self-sufficiency, poverty, and freedom, and even credit Zeno with virtual apotheosis. Diogenes, then, leaves no doubt, that Zeno was strongly influenced by Cynicism, and Cynicism as specifically taught by Crates. Yet he does not quite say that Zeno exemplified every Cynic trait mentioned in the passage I just translated. Only 'some' Cynics are said to be vegetarian abstainers from wine and willing to live in tubs rather than houses. And it is Aristo, Zeno's dissident pupil, to whom the 'indifference' doctrine is attributed. As we are told in Diogenes' Life of Aristo (7.160), it was he, rather than Zeno, who went the whole way with the Cynics.

That difference, however, as one starts to read the Life of Zeno in its Cynic context is not a matter of any great emphasis. We can expect to hear about Zeno's tutelage under Crates, as indeed we will hear of it, in quite some detail. Let us now ask how, if we were conservative Romans of elite status like Cicero, we would respond to a Stoic philosophy that not only advocated contempt for wealth, fame, and noble birth, which are unimpeachable Roman marks of status, but also espoused the scandalous doctrines that Zeno had put forth in his *Politeia*, the impetus to which had presumably reached him from Crates and more remotely from the Cynic Diogenes. Cicero dismisses the Cynics or 'some Stoics who are virtually Cynics' with scorn and unmistakable disgust (*De officiis* 1.128). He was not alone in his responses. Some Stoics had already become so embarrassed by Zeno's *Politeia* that one of them, as Diogenes tells us in his appendix (section O), a librarian at Pergamum, actually deleted the offending passages from Zeno's works.[29]

[28] Caizzi (1993) makes a convincing case for the view that Cynicism was a major part of the image that Zeno sought to convey.

[29] See Mansfeld (1986) 390–1 and Schofield (1991) 9–21.

In and out of the Stoa: Diogenes Laertius on Zeno

We are now in a position to return to the general drift of Apollonius' *Life of Zeno*, as we can conjecture it to have been. On the authority of Apollonius, Diogenes records an exchange of letters between Zeno and King Antigonus Gonatus of Macedonia (section F). The king congratulates Zeno on his perfect happiness and invites him to come to Macedonia as guide to the virtue of the populace. Zeno unctuously declines the invitation on grounds of old age. He assures the king, however, that he and his people, by cultivating philosophy, avoiding sexual pleasure, and associating with Zeno's students, will easily attain supreme happiness.

Hellenistic kings liked to have a famous philosopher in their courts, so we can believe that Antigonus did actually court Zeno. But the correspondence in this form must be fabricated. Nothing could be further from Cynic frankness than Zeno's courtly tone and the promise of an easy route to happiness. Apollonius has transmitted (or invented) a conventionally polished Zeno that counteracts Zeno's brusquely Cynic demeanour in many of Diogenes' anecdotes.[30]

Similar suspicion attaches to Zeno's extraordinary Athenian honours – a golden crown voted by public decree, a tomb in the Ceramaicus, public officials to implement these awards, and pillars inscribing the decree in the rival schools of the Academy and Lyceum, all at the city's expense. Even Apollonius, from whom Diogenes got this information, reported that it was the Macedonian king's agent at Athens who moved the decree proposing the awards (7.12, 15); it was not an outpouring of democratic enthusiasm for Zeno's contributions to civic life. Moreover, at the time of Zeno's death (261–2) Athens had just lost the Chremonidean war that it fought against Antigonus, making it unlikely that the city would be eager to give supreme honours to a man known to be the king's favourite.

It would be naïve to think that philosophy at Athens was immune to influence from political power brokers, but one

---

[30] In Zeno's letter to King Antigonus he describes himself as eighty years old. To give a semblance of authenticity, Apollonius greatly boosted Zeno's age at death, as we have seen (DL 7.28). Arcesilaus, in contrast to Zeno, is said to have shunned all contact with Antigonus (DL 4.39).

wonders what King Antigonus had to gain from getting the city to shell out so much cash and prestige on behalf of the seemingly reclusive Zeno. While parts of the decree are probably authentic, the text has almost certainly been tampered with.[31] Doctoring looks especially likely in the requirement for Zeno's awards to be publicized in the Academy and Lyceum. That clause reads as an attempt long after the fact to promote Stoicism by publicly honouring its founder in the locations of the school's leading rivals, the schools established by Plato and Aristotle. All in all, the terms of the decree and the cozy friendship between Zeno and the king boost Zeno's respectability, but at the cost of diluting his philosophical acumen and persona as an erstwhile Cynic. The material was transmitted, if not composed, by the prudent Stoic promoter Apollonius at a time when the historical Zeno was up for grabs, so to speak, and so found its way into Diogenes' uncritical hands.

Evidence both to acknowledge and to play down the influence of Crates comes from the sections I have marked B (7.2), I (7.25–6), C (7.3–5), and N (7.31–2) in my analytical summary. This material, as I mentioned above, raises two large and overlapping questions: Who were Zeno's philosophical teachers and how did Zeno come to be interested in philosophy?

Diogenes starts the biography proper (section B) by reminding his readers that he has already told them that Zeno was a student of Crates. He continues, with an evasive 'they say', to report that Zeno studied with the Megarian Stilpo and the Academic Xenocrates for ten years, according to Timotheus in his *Dion,* and with the Academic Polemo as well.[32] Two paragraphs later (section C), after describing how Zeno first encountered Crates and composed his *Politeia* under Crates' influence, Diogenes writes: 'He finally left Crates and studied with the abovementioned men for twenty years.'

---

[31] See Haake (2004) and (2013). Most scholars have accepted all the words of the decree at face value, cf. Tarn (1951) 330, who credits Zeno with a personality that 'long before his death had conquered Athens'.

[32] Timotheus was an Athenian author of *Lives* (DL 7.1). Stilpo (DL 2.113–20) is represented by Diogenes as very close to Crates. For Zeno's close associations with Megarian philosophers, including not only Stilpo and Diodorus but also Alexinus, see DL 2.109–10.

In and out of the Stoa: Diogenes Laertius on Zeno

Did the pupillage last ten or twenty years? The discrepancy does not inspire confidence in Diogenes' authorial control. Moreover, chronology excludes the possibility that Zeno had actual contact with the Platonist Xenocrates as well as his successor Polemo.

Crates, Stilpo, and Polemo would have given Zeno as broad an education as any budding ancient philosopher could want. But, near the end of the Life, Diogenes reports (section I), on the authority of Hippobotus (one of the earliest sources), that Zeno studied dialectic with Diodorus Cronus (7.25), and only after that training, as if it were a final necessary qualification, proceeded to Polemo. All of this, apart from the misinformation about Xenocrates, could be true. What we know, or think we know, of Zeno's philosophy from elsewhere could seem to authenticate it. Unfortunately, Diogenes himself says little to corroborate the details beyond the close and initial association with Crates, supplemented by Zeno's interest in dialectical disputes and sophisms (7.16, 7.25). Apart from his detailed appendix on Zeno's *Politeia*, which confirms the Cynic connection so pointedly, Diogenes says virtually nothing about Zeno's specific contributions to Stoic doctrine.

How did Zeno come to be interested in philosophy in the first place? On this theme the Life is even more uncertain. Sections B, C, and N give three distinct accounts.

(1) On the authority of the contemporaneous Hecato and Apollonius, roughly of Cicero's age, we are told (section B):

When Zeno consulted an oracle about what he should do to live the best life, the god replied that he should assume the complexion of the dead. Grasping the oracle's meaning, he studied the works of ancient authors.

What were the chronology and location of Zeno's oracular consultation? We are left to guess whether it occurred when Zeno was a youth in Cyprus or after he reached mainland Greece. Mysterious though the passage is, there can be little doubt about its implicit meaning: Zeno is represented, just like Socrates in Plato's *Apology*, as someone whose life-changing moment was an oracular response. In addition, we are to

257

understand that Zeno interpreted the oracle as an injunction to study works that could tell him about Socrates.

The Socratic connection is made definite in Diogenes' next paragraph (section C). There, however, instead of giving an elucidation of the oracle, Diogenes writes:

(2) He [Zeno] became a student of Crates under the following circumstances. Transporting a cargo of purple from Phoenicia to the Piraeus, he was shipwrecked. On reaching Athens (he was then a man of thirty), he sat down in a bookseller's shop. The bookseller was reading the second book of Xenophon's *Memorabilia,* and Zeno was so pleased that he asked where such men were to be found. At that very moment, fortunately, Crates happened to be walking past. Pointing him out, the bookseller said, "Follow *him.*" From then on he studied with Crates, proving in other respects well suited for philosophy, though he was bashful about adopting Cynic shamelessness. Hence Crates, who wanted to cure him of this, gave him a pot of lentil soup to carry through the Ceramicus. And when he saw that Zeno was ashamed and tried to keep it hidden, he struck the pot with his cane and broke it. As Zeno was running away, the soup streaming down his legs, Crates said, 'Why run away, my little Phoenician? Nothing terrible has happened to you.'

Xenophon's *Memorabilia,* on this second account, gave Zeno a fortuitous literary introduction to Socrates at a time when he was already a travelling salesman. The main point of this nicely embellished story is not to connect Zeno with Socrates but to explain how he became Crates' student. We should notice, though, that while the account is generally positive about Zeno's association with Crates, it is careful to exempt Zeno from Cynic shamelessness (*anadeia*).

We should now jump ahead to the third account, in section N, noting its curious position after the epigrams on Zeno's death:

(3) Demetrius of Magnesia [mid-first century BCE] in *Men of the Same Name,* says that Zeno's father, Mnaseas, being a trader, came often to Athens and brought home many books about Socrates for Zeno, who was still a boy. Thus even in his native place he got good training; and then, on reaching Athens, he attached himself to Crates. And it seems, he adds, that when the rest were in doubt about their views, Zeno defined the goal of human life. They say he used to swear 'by capers' just as Socrates did 'by the dog'.

This third story of Zeno's conversion to philosophy neatly reconciles the two earlier accounts. We now learn that Zeno

In and out of the Stoa: Diogenes Laertius on Zeno

was in fact devoted to Socrates long before he reached Athens. Hence his encounter with Crates was not fortuitous but deliberate. As the second account also proposes, Zeno attached himself to Crates as a means to gain insight into Socrates. To emphasize the figure of Socrates as Zeno's primary allegiance, this third account tells us that Zeno aped Socrates by adopting a special oath as his own trademark.

These three accounts are consistent, more or less, but their emphases differ strikingly. The first account, the oracular story, hints strongly at Socrates and omits Crates altogether. The second and third accounts connect Zeno with both Crates and with Socrates, but with differences of emphasis. The second account gives us a lively and largely positive portrait of Zeno's encounters with Crates.[33] The third account, focusing more strongly on Zeno's Socratic connections, is entirely factual and dispassionate.

No source for the second account is mentioned, but I think we can be fairly sure that Diogenes did not get it from Hecato and Apollonius, who were his sources for the oracular account. We can be sure that both these authors, writing at around the time of Cicero, were eager to play up Zeno's Socratic connections and play down his early Cynic phase, which had become a target for Epicurean critics to turn against the Stoa.[34] Cynicism, of course, was a Socratic movement in some of its ideas and prescriptions. In the Roman Empire, as we know from Seneca and Epictetus, Stoic philosophers were happy to acknowledge Cynic aspects of Stoicism. That phase of philosophical history, however, long postdates Diogenes' sources.

The second account is not only the fullest, it is also probably the earliest.[35] Which is not to say that it is historically exact. Was Zeno really, as this account claims, a Cypriot dye merchant, who suffered shipwreck? We are left guessing about

---

[33] As if to emphasize the decisive influence of Crates, Diogenes inserts his list of Zeno's writings (7.4), starting with the *Politeia* and concluding with *Recollections of Crates*, at the point when Zeno is about to leave Crates for the other teachers.

[34] See Philodemus, *De Stoicis* with discussion by Mansfeld (1986) 394–7.

[35] I conjecture that it derives ultimately from Antigonus of Carystus, basing this suggestion on the circumstantial detail that is that author's trademark.

the exact sequence of events. For after digressing to Zeno's publications, Diogenes returns to the shipwreck:

> He [Zeno] finally left Crates and studied with the above-mentioned men [i.e. Stilpo, Xenocrates, and Polemo for twenty years]. Hence he is reported to have said, 'I had a good voyage when I was shipwrecked'. Others, however, claim that Zeno said this in reference to Crates. Some say that he was spending time in Athens when he heard that his ship was wrecked, and he said, 'Fortune does well to drive me to philosophy.' But others say that it was after he had disposed of his wares in Athens that he turned his attention to philosophy.

The chronology is again wildly inaccurate, making Zeno more than fifty years old when he finished studying with other philosophers. As to the discrepant accounts of Zeno's turn to philosophy after shipwreck, what lies behind them is probably a Hellenistic liking for romantic stories about the conversion of a worldly figure to an ascetic lifestyle rather than anything genuinely historical.

The mercantile and shipwreck stories are completely absent from section N, the third account. Now it is not Zeno but his father who is the merchant. This account, the authority for which is the first-century BCE source Demetrius of Magnesia, reads like a further attempt to play down both the Cynic and the salesman connections in favour of Zeno as earnest schoolboy, dedicated to Socrates from his early days. This bland story, like the first one, was probably popular some 200 years after Zeno's death.

Attempts to detach the mature Zeno from his Cynic origins mark Diogenes' Life intermittently throughout, but in the end they fail to dislodge the impression that Zeno's encounter with Crates was the most decisive moment in his life. Much of the anecdotal material and many of Zeno's apothegms would be completely at home in Diogenes' biographies of the Cynics. Zeno has the Cynic Diogenes' gift for repartee, the cutting rejoinder, and the mockery of pomp and circumstance, and he too, though less drastically, practised poverty. The chief difference between Diogenes and Zeno, in Diogenes' two Lives, is stylistic and professional. Diogenes was a showman, using shock tactics as his teaching method and flourishing in the limelight. Zeno, temperamentally scholastic and retiring, became the professor who

In and out of the Stoa: Diogenes Laertius on Zeno

grafted Cynic challenges to conventional values onto a comprehensive philosophy of universal and human nature.

Crates/Socrates and Socrates/Crates. These names, and the relative influence of their bearers on Zeno's philosophy, predominate and alternate at the beginning and at the end of Diogenes' Life (sections C, D, and N). Once Diogenes has launched Zeno's career, we observe the Stoic founder engaging in caustic Cynic conversation and contempt for social nicety (which rings true), but we also see him represented as a pillar of the Athenian Macedonian establishment in his friendship and mentoring of King Antigonus. During these successive vignettes Zeno does nothing to show why his life made such a great splash at Athens and what was so special about his philosophical teaching and presence – until near the end, where Diogenes remarks (section J):

His extreme endurance (*karterikotatos*) and his frugality were unequalled; the food he ate was uncooked, and the cloak he wore was thin. Hence it was said of him:

Daunted not by winter's cold, by endless rain, by the heat of the sun, by sickness dire, he forgoes public festivals, cleaving to his studies ceaselessly day and night.

So Zeno's claim to fame according to Diogenes was his extreme asceticism combined with superb scholarly concentration. Who does that recall? Crates? No, Socrates rather, for Diogenes virtually quotes the following description of Socrates from Xenophon's *Memorabilia* 1.2:

Socrates was of all men the most self-controlled (*enkratestatos*) in regard to sex and the belly, and the most enduring (*karterikotatos* again) in facing winter and summer and all pains, and had trained himself to be so moderate in his needs that he was very easily satisfied with very little.

Xenophon's purpose was to refute the charge that Socrates corrupted the youth of Athens. Diogenes' sources have adapted this context to fit their final verdict on Zeno as paragon of moral and mental distinction. Does their much enduring and Socratic Zeno leave us satisfied that we now know what Zeno was really like? Hardly, I fear; for unlike Socrates, Zeno (if we believe Diogenes) never got into trouble, and ended up as the most celebrated of all its residents while never accepting the citizenship he was offered. He was or once had been a wealthy man who chose to forego ordinary comforts and indulgences. You hardly become the talk of the town that way. To know what Zeno was like, and to know what motivated his followers, we need the doctrines that made him a philosophical visionary– a radically classless and non-materialistic society, a cosmology grounded in a pantheistic and providential divinity, a rigorously empiricist philosophy of mind, and much more.

Diogenes' Life of Zeno, the biography proper, is an amalgam of fact, hearsay, and encomium. Which of these predominates? Fact, in my opinion, is to the fore in Zeno's formative encounter with Crates (however it came about), in the influence of Socrates (through oral and written accounts) and of Stilpo and Diodorus, in acquaintance with the Academic Polemo, and in the final testimony concerning Zeno's *Politeia*. Encomium emerges in the passages derived from Apollonius, where Zeno loses his Cynic pedigree and becomes rather pompous and complacent. As for the anecdotes and apophthegms, so typical of Diogenes' predilections, while some no doubt derive from reminiscences of Zeno recorded by his contemporary followers, many of them are interchangeable with other figures from other lives. The latter are only the stuff of a *Reader's Digest* Zeno, a Stoic without the qualities to inspire the real Stoa.

Zeno must have been a lot more interesting and brilliant than Diogenes makes him out to be. He was perhaps neither charismatic like Epicurus nor a model of imperturbability like Pyrrho, but challenging, witty, and iconic in his extreme indifference to creature comforts. Some of his impact was personal, but unlike Socrates Zeno spent much of his life as a reclusive scholar, authoring a set of five books on Homer and on many other topics. His writings have left only scanty marks on Diogenes' account of his life, but the biographer has given us our best record of Zeno's *Politeia*. In relegating it to an appendix, Diogenes reflects the prudish worries of later Stoics about their founder's respectability, but he did not suppress it, and for that we can be especially grateful.

CHAPTER 13

THE EMERGENCE OF PLATONIC AND ARISTOTELIAN AUTHORITY IN THE FIRST CENTURY BCE

GEORGIA TSOUNI*

In his 1997 article 'Plato's *auctoritas* and the rebirth of the commentary tradition', David Sedley discusses the way Plato became invested with authority (or its precedent, the Latin *auctoritas*, a word which uniquely combines the notions of authorship and authority)[1] among the first generation of scholars, who attempted to interpret his dialogues in the form of a philosophical commentary. Here, I wish to pay more close attention to the emergence of philosophical *auctoritas* and its earliest connection with Plato and Aristotle. Arguably, Antiochus through Cicero,[2] must be recognised as the first philosopher to present *auctoritas* as a positive quality of Plato and Aristotle, and as a marker of the truth and reliability of their views. In the first part of the chapter, I examine the way *auctoritas* is invoked in Antiochean passages in Cicero. In the second part, I examine the philosophical qualities that Antiochus connected with the claim of ancient *auctoritas*, focusing on the notion of a philosophical system and of

---

* I owe my thoughts on this topic largely to my collaboration as a PhD researcher in the Project 'Greco-Roman Philosophy in the First Century BCE' at the Cambridge Faculty of Classics during the period 2006–10, which David Sedley directed together with Malcolm Schofield. I owe gratitude to David for his supervision during this period, and, not least, for teaching me the merits of anti-authoritarianism.
[1] There is no exact Greek equivalent for the Latin term; see Sedley (1997) 111 and Wardy in this volume.
[2] Since no original work of Antiochus survives in Greek, we rely for the reconstruction of his philosophical views mostly on Cicero, and especially on his dialogues *On Ends* and *Academic Books*, which contain explicit references to an Antiochean pedigree. For a collection of Antiochean testimonia and fragments, see Mette (1986), and more recently Sedley (2012b). The epistemological doxography in Sextus Empiricus' *M* 7.141–260 may well have an Antiochean pedigree as well; see Tarrant (1985) and Sedley (1992b).

263

Georgia Tsouni

doctrinal consistency. In the third part, I will juxtapose the earliest appearance of Platonic and Aristotelian authority in Antiochus with the way later philosophers invoked the authority of Plato and Aristotle.

I

According to Antiochus, ancient philosophers (collectively referred to as the 'Old Academy') possess wisdom which is universally recognised and worthy of approval. This is crucially connected with the belief that the old *auctores* of the Academic tradition, contrary to the Academic sceptics, put forward a dogmatic epistemology which endorsed the possibility of knowledge and thus defended propositions with claims to truth. This signified a major departure from a centuries-long tradition initiated by Arcesilaus, according to which the true Platonic spirit is to be found in Socratic 'aporetic' inquiry. The aim of Platonic philosophy, according to this interpretation, is not to reach ultimate truths but to question the assumptions put forward by someone else, without reaching a definite conclusion about truth claims. To this effect, 'New Academics' (and Cicero as their proponent) encourage the use of one's judgement [*iudicium*] as a protection against the danger of succumbing to dogmatic truth, including blind adherence to the views of a founder of a school. In a suggestive passage from *On the Nature of Gods*, Cicero asserts that one should not attempt to find in his dialogues his own 'dogmatic' opinion on matters. For one, he adds, 'should not seek in debate so much the weight of authority as that of reason':[3]

Those, on the other hand, who ask what we ourselves feel about each topic are being more inquisitive than the case demands. For in debate it is not so much the weight of authority that should be sought as that of reason. In fact, for those who want to learn, the authority of those who profess to teach is usually a hindrance: they give up applying their own judgement, and take as sanctioned whatever they see to have been the judgement of the person they endorse. (Cic. *On the Nature of the Gods* 1.10[4] (Trans. Sedley (1997) 119.))

---

[3] For the opposition between *auctoritas* and *ratio*, see also Cic. *Acad.* 2.60.
[4] *Qui autem requirunt quid quaque de re ipsi sentiamus, curiosius id faciunt quam necesse est; non enim tam auctoritatis in disputando quam rationis momenta quaerenda sunt.*

Emergence of Platonic and Aristotelian Authority

Here, Cicero reveals his 'New Academic' credentials: unlike the devotees of particular masters, the 'New Academic' retains his power of judgement intact and experiences the freedom which results from not committing to a particular authority.

On the other hand, the word *auctoritas* also bears in Cicero particularly Roman connotations of dignity and (especially in a legal context) trustworthy testimony, which must have resonated with Cicero's audience.[5] Traditional political institutions like the Senate and the example of the *mos maiorum* offered in Roman society reliable guidance for action, which could be trusted without the need to be critically scrutinised.[6] In the Ciceronian dialogues, we may trace the equivalent of trustworthy testimony in the philosophical domain, attributed to figures who possess a great reputation, not least by virtue of their ancestry;[7] Pythagoras is the example *par excellence*. He is shown to represent in Cicero a kind of authority which is grounded primarily in personal merits.[8] According to this, X is true if Pythagoras said so (a stance encapsulated in the formula 'He [sc. Pythagoras] said', Lat. *ipse dixit*).[9] As Cicero notes, this seems to be a case of 'authority having validity without the aid of reason' (*sine ratione ualeret auctoritas*).[10]

The Antiochean reconstruction of the teaching of the 'ancients' in Cicero is also recommended through the invocation of *auctoritas*. For example, at *Fin.* 4.61 Cato is asked to change his allegiance from the Stoics to the school of Plato

---

Quin etiam obest plerumque iis qui discere uolunt auctoritas eorum qui se docere profitentur; desinunt enim suum iudicium adhibere, id habent ratum quod ab eo quem probant iudicatum uident.

[5] See e.g. Cic. *Or.* 3.68 and *Top.* 73.

[6] See e.g. Cic. *Inu.* 1.101.

[7] For the association of philosophical authority with ancestry, see especially *Tusc.* 1.26.

[8] See Cic. *Tusc.* 1.38.

[9] Such arguments *ex auctoritate* are referred to in Cic. *Top.* 24.

[10] Cic. *ND.* 1.10: *nec uero probare soleo id quod de Pythagoreis accepimus, quos ferunt, si quid adfirmarent in disputando, cum ex iis quaereretur quare ita esset, respondere solitos 'ipse dixit'; ipse autem erat Pythagoras: tantum opinio praeiudicata poterat, ut etiam sine ratione ualeret auctoritas.*

and his pupils, provided that the criterion of decision is the 'authority' associated with those thinkers.[11] However, the Antiochean is a kind of *auctoritas* with pretensions to truth that is not hostile to *ratio* and is not based solely on personal merit or 'faith'. It is invested with respect for ancestry and the reputation of erudition, but also with the possession of intellectual merits, which have to be demonstrated through dialectical confrontation and argumentative methods.

II

Antiochus' turn to the authority of the 'ancients' took place in a transitional period following Sulla's sack of Athens in 86 BCE, an event which coincided with the interruption of the centuries-long tradition of philosophical schools in this city.[12] Antiochus' answer to the challenges of his day was to reconstruct the identity of the Academy on a new basis, disconnected from the 'official' line of institutional continuity. Rejecting the sceptical orientation of the 'New Academics' but also the philosophical style of his contemporary Peripatetics, Antiochus founded a new 'school' based on the dogmatic reading of the texts of both Plato and Aristotle. To this end he employed a model that was familiar to him, that of the major contemporary Hellenistic schools of Stoicism and Epicureanism.

In line with this model, Plato is the founder of the 'Old Academic' 'school', whereas his followers diligently preserve (but also elaborate on) his teaching.[13] According to Antiochus' reading, Plato and his successors down to Crantor, as well as Plato's pupil Aristotle and Aristotle's pupil Theophrastus, agree on all the major philosophical points. The position rested

---

[11] *sin te auctoritas commouebat, nobisne omnibus et Platoni ipsi nescio quem illum anteponebas?*

[12] This led to the decentralisation of philosophical activity, a phenomenon which Sedley identified as 'the most significant change to occur in the entire history of ancient philosophy' (Sedley 2003) 31.

[13] For the connection of *auctoritas* with an originator or *inuentor*, see Cic. *Or.* 3.148. The founder of a philosophical school is called an *auctor* at *Fin.* 1.29 (with reference to Epicurus): *Primum igitur' inquit 'sic agam ut ipsi auctori huius disciplinae placet.*

Emergence of Platonic and Aristotelian Authority

crucially on a *genealogical* argument, i.e. on the successions of master–pupil relationships, according to which doctrines are inherited and preserved from one generation to the next via channels of transmission and trust.[14] Such relationships serve Antiochus' inclusive picture of the Academic tradition; even though, both Aristotle and Zeno founded their own schools in different locations in Athens, they are still presented as members of a single Academic tradition.

Auctoritas in Antiochus is further linked to direct access to the writings of the 'ancients'. In particular, the Aristotelian school-treatises which were rediscovered around that time and were transferred as booty from Athens to Rome served as a basis for Antiochus' construction of an Academic philosophical system, especially in the domain of ethics.[15] It is suggestive that *Fin.* 3, which precedes the Antiochean account in the same work, plays out in the library of Lucullus (the patron of Antiochus) where Cicero goes to search for some Aristotelian 'treatises' [*commentarii*].[16] Piso begins his account at *Fin.* 5.9–11 with a catalogue of the most important Aristotelian and Theophrastean treatises, according to the threefold division of physics, ethics and dialectic.[17] The way the Antiochean account in *On Ends* 5 is framed by introductions which underline the direct access to philosophical writings points to the importance of authoritative texts as the basis of philosophical activity.

An important claim connected with the *auctoritas* of the 'ancients' in Antiochus is that the texts of the members of the

---

[14] Sedley (2003) 36 identifies chronicling the history of philosophy as another characteristic of the transitional period of the first century BCE.

[15] The official story based on the evidence of both Strabo and Plutarch suggests that after the conquest of Athens Sulla took possession of Appellicon's library, which contained the school treatises of both Aristotle and Theophrastus, and brought it as booty to Rome. See Strabo *Geography* 13.54 and Plutarch, *Life of Sulla* 26. The importance of the availability of the texts of the founders for the cohesion of a philosophical school is discussed in Sedley (1989) 100.

[16] Cic. *Fin.* 3.10: *Commentarios quosdam inquam Aristotelios, quos hic sciebam esse, ueni ut auferrem, quos legerem dum essem otiosus.*

[17] At *Fin.* 5.9–11, the Antiochean spokesperson alludes to the Aristotelian *On Heavens*, to the Aristotelian biological treatises on animals and to the Theophrastan treatises on plants, to the *Topics*, to a collection of some lost political Aristotelian and Theophrastan treatises on constitutions and laws, as also to a treatise on the defence of the contemplative life.

Georgia Tsouni

school convey a systematic and consistent body of doctrines.[18] In a passage from Varro's speech in Cicero's *Academic Books*, we find the idea that Plato was the 'originator' of a single school, which includes both Academics and Peripatetics, coupled with the view that this 'school' conveys a uniform and consistent system (*una et consentiens ... philosophiae forma*)[19]:

> Originating with Plato, a thinker of manifold variety and fertility, there was established a philosophy that, though it had two appellations, was really a single and uniform system, that of the Academic and the Peripatetic schools, which while agreeing in doctrine differed in terminology. (Cic. *Acad.* 1.17)[20]

It is a peculiar feature of Antiochus' stance that he takes the founders of the Academy and the Peripatos, i.e. Plato and Aristotle, respectively, to possess *equal* authority. This is indicated by the fact that, when Piso turns to expounding on the 'Old Academic' views on ethics, he turns wholly Peripatetic, assuming that this is not a problematic move.[21] There are also some further assumptions about *auctoritas* which emerge from the above-mentioned text. First, that it is transferable, since it is transferred through the succession of master–pupil relationships from Plato to his followers, the Academics, but also to the Peripatetics by whom Antiochus meant only two, namely Aristotle and Theophrastus (I will return later to this restriction).[22] The fallacy inherent in this idea consists in assuming that institutional continuity is necessarily accompanied by doctrinal or methodological continuity. It is suggestive that Antiochus seems to ignore the differences between the views of different leaders of the post-Platonic Academy, attested in other sources. Even the Stoics are included in the

---

[18] For a link between written sources and *auctores*, see e.g. Cic. *Or.* 1.240 (from the context of legal interpretation).

[19] The 'Old Academic' system is described by the Antiochean Varro in Cicero's *Acad.* 1.17 with the expressions *certam quandam disciplinae formulam*; *ars philosophiae*; *rerum ordo et descriptio disciplinae* – all alluding to the clear delineation of the philosophical material into branches and defined topics of inquiry.

[20] *Platonis autem auctoritate, qui uarius et multiplex et copiosus fuit, una et consentiens duobus uocabulis philosophiae forma instituta est Academicorum et Peripateticorum qui rebus congruentes nominibus differebant.*

[21] See Cic. *Fin.* 5.9.

[22] See *Acad.* 1.34–5: *primi Platonis rationem auctoritatemque susceperant.*

268

Emergence of Platonic and Aristotelian Authority

same lineage through an argument from succession based on the fact that Zeno, the founder of the Stoa, was a pupil of Polemo.[23]

A second related aspect of *auctoritas*, which emerges from the Antiochean texts, is that it is dynamic and allowing for progress within the 'authoritative' tradition. Although for Antiochus Plato's dialogues contain the starting points of all subsequent philosophical developments, contrary to later Platonists, Plato alone (or his text) does not claim here infallible access to truth but can, or in fact should, be read *through* his followers.[24] Plato is thus acknowledged as the authoritarian source of the tradition, but his doctrines are taken to have been legitimately elaborated upon by his followers. Antiochus' reading was further facilitated by the idea that different terminology does not suggest difference in philosophical doctrine.[25] In a text in Sextus, which precedes the epistemological doxography in *Against the Professors* 7, a similar defence of *auctoritas* on the part of the 'Old Academy' is made.

These thinkers (sc. Xenophanes and Archelaus), however, seem to have handled the question incompletely, and, in comparison with them, the view of those who divide philosophy into physics, ethics, and logic is more developed. Of these Plato is potentially [δυνάμει] the originator, as he discussed many problems of physics and of ethics, and not a few of logic; but those who most explicitly [ῥητότατα] adopt this division are Xenocrates and the Peripatetics, and also the Stoics. (Sextus Empiricus *Against the Professors* 7.16 = Fr. 82 Isnardi Parente (Xenocrates))[26]

In this testimony, it is stated that Plato was potentially the originator of the division of philosophy into three branches, since he discussed many issues pertaining to physics, ethics and dialectic. However, the source adds that the division was 'in the

---

[23] See e.g. Cic. *Acad.* 1.35, *Fin.* 4.51 and ibid. 4.61.

[24] This emerges also from Antiochus' discussion of Plato's epistemological views in Sextus' *M* 7.141–4; see Sedley (2012a) 97.

[25] See e.g. *Fin.* 4.5, where again Cicero represents the Antiochean view: *qui sit enim finis bonorum, mox; hoc loco tantum dico a ueteribus Peripateticis Academicisque, qui re consentientes uocabulis differebant.*

[26] πλὴν οὗτοι μὲν ἐλλιπῶς ἀνεστράφθαι δοκοῦσιν, ἐντελέστερον δὲ παρὰ τούτους οἱ εἰπόντες τῆς φιλοσοφίας τὸ μέν τι εἶναι φυσικὸν τὸ δὲ ἠθικὸν τὸ δὲ λογικόν· ὧν δυνάμει μὲν Πλάτων ἐστὶν ἀρχηγός, περὶ πολλῶν μὲν φυσικῶν, [περὶ] πολλῶν δὲ ἠθικῶν, οὐκ ὀλίγων δὲ λογικῶν διαλεχθείς· ῥητότατα δὲ οἱ περὶ τὸν Ξενοκράτη καὶ οἱ ἀπὸ τοῦ Περιπάτου, ἔτι δὲ οἱ ἀπὸ τῆς Στοᾶς ἔχονται τῆσδε τῆς διαιρέσεως.

269

most explicit way' made by the followers of Xenocrates and of the Peripatos, whereas the members of the Stoa are also added as those who followed the two groups in making the same division. The inclusion of both Academics and Peripatetics alongside Plato as precursors of an idea found in the Stoics points directly to Antiochus as a source of the text in Sextus. It is suggestive that the Stoics, who are credited in Diogenes Laertius with the creation of a division of philosophy into physics, ethics and logic,[27] are presented not as the originators of the threefold division but as the developers of it, in a way that preserves the *auctoritas* of the ancients.[28]

Crediting the *auctores* with a Stoic idea suggests that Antiochus was reading the 'ancients', as it were, backwards with a contemporary lens and with a view to establishing their originality, and consequently their *auctoritas*, in relation to the most important Hellenistic philosophical developments (at least of Stoic provenance). This does not mean that Antiochus is clear about his hermeneutical assumptions. Although, it is conceded, as in the passage in Sextus above, that some ideas were only implicit in the texts of Plato, the more explicit statements of the threefold division of philosophy into distinct areas of study are attributed to the followers of Plato and the Peripatetics, rather than exclusively to the Stoics. Nowhere is the philosophical contribution of the Stoics themselves recognised. By contrast, in the Antiochean passages it is (polemically) argued that, although the Stoics formed part of the Academic tradition, they expressed ideas derivative from the *auctores* and lacking in substantive originality.[29] The ambivalence of Antiochus towards the Stoics is captured by

---

[27] For the ascription of the tripartition of the philosophical *logos* to Zeno, see Diogenes Laertius 7.39. At *Fin.* 4.5, by contrast, Cicero states that Zeno retained the tripartite division that he inherited from the 'old Academics': *totam philosophiam tris in partis diuiserunt, quam partitionem a Zenone esse retentam uidemus.*

[28] Cf. Cic. *Acad.* 1.19.

[29] In the anecdotal tradition transmitted via Diogenes Laertius this gave rise to the image of Zeno as the 'cunning' Phoenician who steals the doctrines of the Academy and changes their names in order to remain undetected. Stoics themselves vehemently opposed the Antiochean understanding of Stoicism; see e.g. Balbus at *ND.* 1.16 (with regard to the topic of the nature of the 'good').

Emergence of Platonic and Aristotelian Authority

the use of the word *correctio* to characterise Stoic activity; the word equivocates between genuine philosophical progress on the one hand and mere substitution of names on the other.[30] This ambiguity is reflected in the way Antiochus both makes ample use of Stoic terminology for the presentation of 'Old Academic' views[31] and reduces such terminology to a repetition of ancient ideas.

Another aspect of the consistent philosophical system that Antiochus associated with the 'ancients' was the identification of a particular set of doctrines, consistent with each other, in all areas of philosophy. This imposed a strategy of exclusion of members of the tradition, which could not fit into the homogeneous system that Antiochus wished to ascribe to the 'ancients'. The Academics after Arcesilaus were *de facto* excluded by virtue of their sceptical orientation. Furthermore, all Peripatetics after Theophrastus are attacked and accused in the Antiochean presentation of 'Old Academic' ethics as 'heterodox' both on grounds of presentation style and philosophical doctrine. Hieronymus of Tyre, for example, is accused for identifying the *telos* with absence from pain,[32] something utterly incompatible with Antiochus' identification of the 'Old Academic' *telos* with 'a life according to virtue in the presence of bodily and external goods'. A more subtle critique is that against Critolaus: Antiochus on the one hand praises his style but again accuses him of breaking from the *auctoritas* of the ancients on philosophical grounds.[33] Critolaus is criticised also in Didymus' *Outline of Peripatetic ethics*, a source

---

[30] For the use of the word in relation to Stoic theory, see e.g. *Acad.* 1.35. As David Sedley remarked in private conversation, a Greek equivalent of the word *correctio* would be ἐπανόρθωσις, a term from rhetorical theory meaning the recalling of a word in order to use a stronger one in its place; see LSJ s.v.

[31] For example, in ethics he adopts the formula of a 'life according to nature', which was in all probability first introduced by Zeno. See Diogenes Laertius 7.4. This is interpreted by Antiochus along Peripatetic lines as a life whereby all human faculties are fulfilled and 'nothing valuable is missing'.

[32] Cic. *Fin.* 5.14: *Hieronymum, quem iam cur Peripateticum appellem nescio. summum enim bonum exposuit uacuitatem doloris; qui autem de summo bono dissentit de tota philosophiae ratione dissentit.*

[33] Ibid.: *Critolaus imitari uoluit antiquos, et quidem est grauitate proximus, et redundat oratio, ac tamen <ne> is quidem in patriis institutis manet.*

Georgia Tsouni

almost contemporary with Antiochus, which may as well bear Antiochean influence.[34] Critolaus is among the 'younger Peripatetics' (alluded to in the first part of the doxography) who suggested that the *telos* is a form of 'joint completion' [*sumplērōma*] of all three different categories of goods.[35] This however, according to Didymus, fails to do justice to the Aristotelian understanding of happiness as 'action' or most generally (virtuous) 'activity', which cannot be put on a par with the bodily and external goods.

Antiochus' critique of the Hellenistic Peripatos is suggestive of a new orientation of philosophical activity; whereas, both the Academy and the Peripatos in their post-Platonic and post-Aristotelian eras encouraged competition, innovation and disagreement with the tradition for the sake of the production of new knowledge, from Antiochus onwards the focus lies on the reconstruction and transmission of an authoritative teaching.[36]

Even some of the views of the 'founders' themselves become criticised for the sake of an authority based on consistency; thus, both Theophrastus' views on the happy life, as also Aristotle's critique of Platonic ideas is shown to lack *auctoritas*.[37] On the other hand, both Plato and Aristotle are shown to agree on the doctrine that virtue guarantees happiness. Even though, both admit of a plurality of goods alongside virtue, Antiochus argued that they both recognise the supreme contribution of virtue towards happiness, and grant a far lesser role to the other kinds of 'goods' (something that the Peripatetic Critolaus allegedly failed to acknowledge). Antiochus formulated the views of the 'ancients' on the matter by making use of the distinction between a 'happy life' [*uita beata*] and a 'supremely

---

[34] The authorship and relative date of this text is discussed in Tsouni 2016.

[35] Didymus *apud* Stobaeus 46.1.10–13 Wachsmuth: Ὑπὸ δὲ τῶν νεωτέρων Περιπατητικῶν τῶν ἀπὸ Κριτολάου "τὸ ἐκ πάντων τῶν ἀγαθῶν συμπεπληρωμένον" (τοῦτο δὲ ἦν "τὸ ἐκ τῶν τριῶν γενῶν"), οὐκ ὀρθῶς. Οὐ γὰρ πάντα τἀγαθὰ μέρη γίνεται τοῦ τέλους· οὔτε γὰρ τὰ σωματικὰ, οὔτε τὰ ἀπὸ τῶν ἐκτός, τὰ δὲ τῆς ψυχικῆς ἀρετῆς ἐνεργήματα μόνης.

[36] Cf. Sedley (2003) 37: 'With the demise of Athens as a philosophical centre, the actual history of philosophy reaches its *de facto* end, and is replaced by the scholarly task of recording and understanding it'.

[37] See *Fin.* 5.12 and *Acad.* 1.33.

272

Emergence of Platonic and Aristotelian Authority

happy life' [*uita beatissima*]; whereas for the former, virtue is sufficient, the latter requires an add on of bodily and external goods as well.[38] In this way, the 'ancients' could be credited with the view that virtue is sufficient for happiness while a certain value was attributed to non-psychic goods as well.[39]

The treatises of both Plato and Aristotle are, accordingly, read in a way that shows the 'harmony' of their views. Consider, for example, the way Antiochus traces the view of the sufficiency of virtue for a happy life in the (newly discovered) *Nicomachean Ethics*.[40] In some passages, Aristotle may seem to point to two degrees of happiness, a 'happy' and a 'blessed' state; for the former the possession of virtue is both necessary and sufficient, while for the latter only necessary but not sufficient, since it may be influenced by luck. Thus, in a passage from *Nicomachean Ethics* Book 1, we read that 'the happy person can never become miserable – though he or she will not reach blessedness, if met with fortunes like those of Priam'.[41] One may read the two terms denoting happiness as not synonymous, in the way Antiochus does. But this is not supported by the immediate context of the passage: only a few lines before we find *makarios* used as a synonym for *eudaimon*, and a few lines later we find the idea that *eudaimonia* itself requires a 'sufficient' amount of external goods.[42] If we assume

---

[38] See e.g. Cic. *Fin.* 5.71: *Illa enim quae sunt a nobis bona corporis numerata complent ea quidem beatissimam uitam, sed ita, ut sine illis possit beata uita existere.*

[39] Notice the polemical text from Cic. *Tusc.* 5.34, where the thesis that virtue is sufficient for happiness is referred back to the *auctoritas* of Plato, rather than to Zeno himself: *Et, si Zeno Citieus, aduena quidam et ignobilis uerborum opifex, insinuasse se in antiquam philosophiam uidetur, huius sententiae grauitas a Platonis auctoritate repetatur apud quem saepe haec oratio usurpata est, ut nihil praeter uirtutem diceretur bonum.*

[40] Cic. *Fin.* 5.12: *Quare teneamus Aristotelem et eius filium Nicomachum, cuius accurate scripti de moribus libri dicuntur illi quidem esse Aristoteli, sed non uideo, cur non potuerit patri similis esse filius. Theophrastum tamen adhibeamus ad pleraque, dum modo plus in uirtute teneamus, quam ille tenuit, firmitatis et roboris.* The remark on the dubious authorship of the text might suggest that it predates the editorial activity of Andronicus, which most probably took place later in the course of the first century BCE.

[41] Arist. *NE* 1.10 1101a6–8: εἰ δ' οὕτως, ἄθλιος μὲν οὐδέποτε γένοιτ' ἂν ὁ εὐδαίμων, οὐ μὴν μακάριός γε, ἂν Πριαμικαῖς τύχαις περιπέσῃ.

[42] Ibid. 1101a14–16: τί οὖν κωλύει λέγειν εὐδαίμονα τὸν κατ' ἀρετὴν τελείαν ἐνεργοῦντα καὶ τοῖς ἐκτὸς ἀγαθοῖς ἱκανῶς κεχορηγημένον μὴ τὸν τυχόντα χρόνον ἀλλὰ τέλειον βίον;

that the Antiochean distinction between *uita beata* and *uita beatissima* reflects the two adjectives of *eudaimon* and *makarios* in Aristotle's text, then this may suggest that Antiochus felt free to read passages in isolation from their context with a view to establishing what he saw as a standard of consistency.

In the domain of epistemology as well, the creation of consistency in the opinions of the *auctores* is attempted by criticising Aristotle's attack on Platonic Forms:[43]

Aristotle was the first to undermine the 'ideas' of which I spoke a little while before and which Plato cherished in such a miraculous way that he said that they contain something divine. (Cic. *Acad.* 1.33)[44]

The reading of Antiochus reveals an interest in defending the existence of Platonic ideas (*pace* Aristotle), but in so doing he follows a Stoicising reading according to which 'ideas' are merely thoughts in one's mind and do not have independent metaphysical existence.[45] In line with this, there is in Antiochean passages not a clear differentiation between mental concepts of universals, ἔννοιαι or *notiones*, and the 'ideas' found in Platonic texts.[46] This seems to suggest that Antiochus saw in the Platonic Forms an answer to contemporary epistemological debates for which little could be found in the resurrected Aristotelian treatises. Concept formation and the discussion of ἐννοήματα had become topical in Hellenistic philosophy, and Antiochus might have found in the identification of Platonic 'ideas' with Stoic concepts[47] a confirmation of his thesis that the Stoic

[43] Passages in which Aristotle advances a critique of self-subsistent Platonic Forms include *Met.* Z.6 1031a28ff; *NE* 1.6.1096a11ff.; *APo* 1.22 83a28.

[44] *Aristoteles igitur primus species quas paulo ante dixi labefactauit, quas mirifice Plato erat amplexatus, ut in iis quiddam diuinum esse diceret.*

[45] See Cic. *Acad.* 1.30–2. The lack of reference to the metaphysical status of 'ideas' and the focus on their epistemological aspects may also be due to the fact that Antiochus had the (Stoic) division of ethics, dialectic and physics in his mind as a model for the presentation of the views of the 'ancients'.

[46] Accordingly, Varro moves from a reference to Platonic 'ideas' in *Acad.* 1.30 to a reference to 'concepts of the soul' (*animi notionibus*) in ibid. 1.32. However, 'ideas' are discussed in the *Phaedo* as well as concepts (ἔννοιαι), i.e. as contents in one's soul or mind, and not as independently existing entities: Plato *Phaedo* 73c–d: ἆρα οὐχὶ τοῦτο δικαίως λέγομεν ὅτι ἀνεμνήσθη, οὗ τὴν ἔννοιαν ἔλαβεν;

[47] Such an identification of 'ideas' (ascribed to the 'ancients') with concepts may be traced in a doxographical fragment on Stoic epistemology which survives in the first

Emergence of Platonic and Aristotelian Authority

doctrines are prefigured in the writings of the 'ancients'. Further, one might want to see in this attack on Aristotle an attempt on the part of Antiochus to defend the innate basis of concept formation in opposition to the Aristotelian model of induction and abstraction (as briefly discussed in *Posterior Analytics* 2.19). Such a nativist stance is advocated at *Fin.* 5.59 by the Antiochean spokesperson Piso, who states that nature 'implanted in human beings rudimentary ideas of the most important things':

> Although (nature) bestowed upon us a mind capable of grasping all virtue and, apart from any teaching, implanted in us rudimentary ideas of the most important things, and began so to speak our education and included among our constitutional endowments the ground-work, as we may call it, of the virtues, yet virtue itself she merely sketched in outline, nothing more.[48] (Cic. *Fin.* 5.59)

III

The defence of ancient *auctoritas* in the subsequent centuries assumed new forms, although crucially it remained faithful to a dogmatic reading of Plato. Subsequent thinkers ceased to defend the *auctoritas* of the whole Academic tradition, and concentrated on the exclusive authority of either Plato or Aristotle. The development of an exclusive Aristotelian authority on the basis of the (established) authorship of a particular body of texts is a creation of the Imperial period and went hand in hand with the parallel creation of a proper Platonist identity.[49] Both movements of Aristotelianism and

---

book of Stobaeus 1.136.21 Wasmuth = *SVF* 1.65 (possibly originating from the epistemological part of Didymus' summary): Ζήνωνος καὶ τῶν ἀπ' αὐτοῦ. Τὰ ἐννοήματά φασι μήτε τινὰ εἶναι μήτε ποιά, ὡσανεὶ δέ τινα καὶ ὡσανεὶ ποιὰ φαντάσματα ψυχῆς· ταῦτα δὲ ὑπὸ τῶν ἀρχαίων ἰδέας προσαγορεύεσθαι.

[48] *etsi dedit talem mentem quae omnem uirtutem accipere posset ingenuitque sine doctrina notitias paruas rerum maximarum et quasi instituit docere et induxit in ea quae inerrant, tamquam elementa uirtutis sed uirtutem ipsam inchoauit, nihil amplius.*

[49] Note also how the term 'Academic' is favoured by Antiochus over the term 'Platonist', which occurs as a self-conscious characterisation of philosophical identity only after Antiochus in the second century AD. For a sketch of this development, see Glucker (1978) 206–25. There is little evidence to support Theiler's claim (1930) 51 that Antiochus was the 'founder of Platonism in the Imperial period', or Dillon's, who ranks him as the first among the 'Middle Platonists' (1996) 433. For a similar claim more recently, see Karamanolis (2006) 45.

Platonism focused more on the differences rather than the similarities between Plato and Aristotle. Following this trend, we find in the subsequent centuries the appearance of critical voices, such as Atticus (belonging to the co-called 'Middle Platonists'), who explicitly opposed the attempt to read Plato through a Peripatetic lens.[50] Furthermore, Plato became for later Platonists the source of infallible truth with almost divine attributes.[51] In line with this, one of the hallmarks of Platonists became a strong claim of the infallibility of Plato's words *in their own right*, against a lesser authority of Aristotle and subsequent philosophers.[52] This claim of infallibility but also the thesis of the exclusivity of Platonic authority is missing in Antiochus who believes that Platonic views can and should be supplemented by Academic, Aristotelian and, in some cases, even Stoic ideas, in order to meet contemporary, systematic standards of philosophical debate.[53]

A significant shift in philosophical focus is attested in writers drawing on Plato's authority after Antiochus, as well: whereas metaphysics and the independent ontological status of Platonic Forms is not explicitly discussed in Antiochean passages, much of the identity of a Platonist in the subsequent centuries is connected with a quest for intelligible principles. Forms acquire central importance and feature in the scheme of Middle-Platonic 'first principles', alongside god and matter.[54] In the domain of ethics, 'assimilation to god', a formulation which does not yet have special importance in Cicero, becomes identified for later Platonists with the Platonic *telos*.[55]

[50] See Atticus' fragments 1–9 des Places from *Against Those Who Undertake to Interpret Plato's Doctrines through Those of Aristotle* (Πρὸς τοὺς διὰ τῶν Ἀριστοτέλους τὰ Πλάτωνος ὑπισχνουμένους). A discussion of Atticus' views can be found in Karamanolis (2006).

[51] Cf. Atticus *ap.* Eusebius, *PE* 11.2.4.

[52] Cf. Boys-Stones (2001) 103: 'Platonists were able to commit themselves to the truth of a proposition *on the grounds that* Plato had said it, and, it might be, even before they themselves understood *why* it was true.' Plotinus and Simplicius co-opt Aristotle but only in so far as it serves the understanding of the 'divine' Plato.

[53] See Sedley (2012a) 81. As Boys-Stones (2001) 143 notes, Antiochus' is 'an argument *from* the consensus established by Plato, not *to* the authority of Plato'.

[54] See e.g. Alcinous' theological chapters in his *Did.* 8–10.

[55] The formula appears, perhaps for the first time, in the anonymous commentary to Plato's *Theaetetus*; see Sedley (1997) 127. Other early occurrences include a passage

Emergence of Platonic and Aristotelian Authority

Finally, Platonists and Aristotelians developed new, more rigorous, hermeneutical strategies for the reading of the authoritative corpus. Although it relies on 'authoritative' texts, Antiochus' use of Platonic and Peripatetic writings is not strictly speaking exegetical; there is no evidence that he wrote a commentary and the exact *lexis* of Plato, Aristotle or Theophrastus is not of primary importance in Antiochean passages.[56] Antiochus' preoccupation with ancient texts serves rather the succinct presentation of doctrines in a framework which is still largely Hellenistic in its philosophical method. Thus, an important post-Antiochean development is the dissociation of authorities from extraneous standards of interpretation. For example, the anonymous commentator to Plato's *Theaetetus* focuses on the *ipsissima uerba* of Plato's text,[57] whereas Plutarch applies in his Platonic treatises the principle of reading 'Plato from within Plato' [*Platonem ex Platone*], a hermeneutical rule borrowed from Homeric scholarship.

Despite such developments, it remains a most significant fact for the history of ancient philosophy that Platonic and Aristotelian authority, as the proper starting point of philosophising, was never seriously questioned from the time of Antiochus' onwards.

---

in the first part of Didymus' doxography in Stobaeus 49.8–50.10 Wachsmuth and in Alcinous *Did.* 28.1.

[56] There is a clear difference in this respect between the method of Antiochus and that of the Peripatetics Boethus and Xenarchus, who lived in the second half of the first century BCE; the latter supported their tenets explicitly through evidence from the Aristotelian texts, see e.g. Alexander of Aphrodisias *Mantissa* 151.1–13b (discussing views from Aristotle 'on the first object of appropriation'). For Xenarchus, see Falcon (2012).

[57] See Sedley (1997).

CHAPTER 14

CICERO ON *AUCTORITAS*

MALCOLM SCHOFIELD*

This paper explores the way appeal to *auctoritas* is made or viewed by Cicero in the two spheres of politics and philosophy. A first impression might be that whereas in politics the role of *auctoritas* is of huge importance for him and indeed for the Roman elite generally, in philosophy the Academic scepticism to which Cicero affirms allegiance rejects the validity of any appeal to *auctoritas* whatever, in the interests of the freedom to exercise one's own judgement: in short, that for him politics and (inextricably bound to politics) religion were rightly conceived as the domain of *auctoritas*, whereas in philosophy it was *ratio* alone that should count. That impression would not be altogether wrong. But I try to show by way of a few examples that unsurprisingly the negotiations he conducts between *auctoritas* and *ratio* in both domains were in fact rather more complex. Evidence for this is culled principally from the philosophical dialogues of both the late 50s and 45–44 BC, with particular attention paid to *De Senectute* and *De Amicitia*, works not much considered in current work on Cicero by scholars of ancient philosophy, while among the speeches I focus particularly on *De Haruspicum Responso*.

Auctoritas in Public Life, *Ratio* in Philosophy

In mid-December 44 BC we find Cicero delivering a powerful attack on Mark Antony to a popular assembly (*contio*) in the fourth of his so-called *Philippics*. After a somewhat

---

* David Sedley has been my closest colleague and friend in our subject for decades, and with the dedication of this paper in his honour I take the opportunity to thank him and Bev for all their support through good times and bad.

278

Cicero on *Auctoritas*

disingenuous announcement that the senate has declared Mark Antony – 'in reality if not in word' – public enemy No.1 (*Phil.* 4.1–2), Octavian is at once praised for his defence of the *res publica* and 'your liberty' (ibid. 4.2–4). Then Cicero turns to congratulate the Martian legion, originally levied by Julius Caesar for his campaigns in Gaul. What he celebrates is their action in rallying to support the '*auctoritas* of the senate, your liberty, the *res publica* as a whole' (ibid. 4.5–6).

That twinning of the *auctoritas* of the senate and the *libertas* of the Roman people was a trope to which Cicero often resorted and – provided he had sufficiently emphasized popular liberty – was one he expected to meet with a favourable reception at a *contio* as well as in the senate. The *auctoritas* of the senate constituted the central theme of his conception of how the *res publica* functioned and needed to function if it was to be and remain a true *res publica*. The theme had nowhere been more clearly articulated than in a passage in the political manifesto staked out in his speech *Pro Sestio* of 56 BC. Here is the account he presented there of the development of the Roman constitution (*Sest.* 137):

> Since they ceased to find the power (*potestas*) of kings tolerable, they created annual magistracies. Their idea was to set the *consilium* of the senate to preside over the *res publica* for ever, but to have them chosen for that *consilium* by the people as a whole, and to make admission to the highest order open to the industry and virtue of all the citizens. They set up the senate as guardian, president, and champion of the *res publica*. They wanted the magistrates to avail themselves of the *auctoritas* of this order, and to act as though they were servants of its *consilium*. But they also wanted the senate itself to be strengthened by the prestige of the orders closest to it, and to protect and enlarge the liberty and advantages of the mass of ordinary people.

This same conception of the key role of the *auctoritas* that needs to be exercised by the *consilium* of the *principes*, the leading citizens, was encapsulated in the theory of the well-balanced constitution that he would then work out in *De Republica* (55–52 BC: *Rep.* 1.69, 2.57), and would duly find exemplified once again in the development of the Roman *res publica* (e.g. *Rep.* 2.55–6).

The *auctoritas* he talks of there belonged to the senate or the *principes* as a corporate body. But a leading citizen could

Malcolm Schofield

expect to exercise *auctoritas* on his own account, by virtue of the mutually reinforcing effects of high birth, political or military achievement, and personal attributes, together with the respect and influence they earned him. In writings of every kind Cicero constantly refers to the *auctoritas* such figures command. References to *consilium et auctoritas*, his own of course included, are particularly frequent.[1] At one particularly low moment – in exile in Thessalonika in June 58 – he claims in a letter to his brother Quintus that he was once 'the equal of any man who ever lived in prestige (*dignitas*), moral standing (*auctoritas*), reputation (*existimatio*), influence (*gratia*)' (*Ad Q. Fr.* 1.3.6, in Shackleton Bailey's translation).

In philosophy *auctoritas* appears to be viewed very differently, at any rate as practised by someone with an Academic allegiance. The exposition of Antiochus' Stoicizing theory of knowledge in the *Lucullus* ends with words defending *auctoritas* against the Academics' insistence that those who listen to a philosophical discussion should be guided by *ratio* rather than *auctoritas* (*Lucullus* 60). That Academic viewpoint is often voiced in Cicero's philosophical dialogues. The preface to *De Natura Deorum* expresses his disapproval of the Pythagorean resort to the formula *ipse dixit*. It had the effect of making *auctoritas* prevail even without any *ratio* at all being supplied: whereas in philosophical discussion it is to the weight of *ratio*, rather than of *auctoritas*, that we must look (*ND* 1.10). At the end of *De Diuinatione*, in summing up Academic method, Cicero writes (*Div.* 2.150):

> What distinguishes the Academy is that it does not introduce its own verdict. It gives approval to what appears to get closest to the truth. It compares the cases put on either side, and it draws out what can be said for any point of view; and without asserting its own authority it leaves the judgment of those who are listening intact and free.

The emphasis on freedom in contrast to subservience to authority is encountered elsewhere in such contexts. 'We are freer and more untrammeled', says Cicero at the beginning of

---

[1] See those collected in Hellegouarc'h (1972) 255 n. 12. Particularly striking is *Phil.* 1.1, where Cicero announces his return to participation in public affairs.

Cicero on *Auctoritas*

the *Lucullus*, 'because our power to judge is intact' (*Lucullus* 8); 'we alone are free', he insists in the fifth book of the *Tusculans* (*Tusc.* 5.33) – the implicit contrast is with other philosophical schools, notably the Stoics and the Epicureans, which are regarded as committed to a body of doctrine associated with a founding figure.[2] Someone who philosophizes in the mode advocated and practiced by the Academy, therefore, neither attempts to impose his own authority nor submits to the constraints of any others'.

Does Cicero anywhere give any sign of recognizing what at least at first sight looks like a stark opposition between his attitudes to *auctoritas* in these two different spheres, or of registering concern on this count? Here we might note a passage in the *Lucullus* shortly after the reference to the Academics' stress on the need to follow *ratio* rather than *auctoritas*. Lucullus – significantly in the very last words of his entire speech – is made to taunt Cicero with what he represents as some sort of contradiction or incongruity (*Lucullus* 62). Cicero had notoriously claimed on oath when consul in 63 BC that he had 'obtained information' (*comperisse*) that the Catilinarians had devised a secret plot: something he can therefore be described as having brought to light. How can he now assert that nothing whatever can be known or grasped? Is not he himself in danger of diminishing the *auctoritas* of a glorious political achievement? Or (as we might recast the point) is not his sceptical deployment of *ratio* in philosophy threatening his *auctoritas* in public life?

The sequel to this final sally by Lucullus does not suggest that Cicero is rattled by it. Indeed, it comes to look more like a piece of self-conscious authorial wit. What happens next is that Catulus – who was the spokesman for the Academy in the preceding companion dialogue – advises Cicero that if on the strength of Lucullus' arguments he has changed his view because things now look that way to him, far be it from Catulus to stand in his way. But what should not shift him is

---

[2] See especially Sedley (1989), a seminal article like so much else in his oeuvre; cf. also Sedley (1997) 118–19.

Lucullus' *auctoritas.* Lucullus' final point – as he himself more or less admitted – was the sort of debating point an unscrupulous tribune might try to exploit at a *contio* (*Acad.* 2.63). Cicero then responds by turning this brief intervention by Catulus into an opportunity to hand out compliments to him and Lucullus alike: Lucullus' great *auctoritas* was unquestionably having an effect on him – had not Catulus opposed to it an *auctoritas* no less impressive (*Acad.* 2.64). So he ends up – so far as *auctoritas* goes – suspending judgement, in true Academic style (thus on whatever basis remaining to the Academic practitioner of *ratio* that he is), and in true Ciceronian manner effectively converting the whole brief episode into something self-congratulatory.

The Waters Muddied: *Ratio* and *Auctoritas* in Religion

Rather more intriguing theoretically is the opening of Book 3 of *De Natura Deorum.*[3] Book 3 of the dialogue is taken up with the reply by the Academic sceptic Cotta to the case for Stoic rational theology presented by Balbus in Book 2. Cotta will offer a whole battery of sceptical arguments exhibiting flaws or implausibility or non-conclusiveness of one sort or another in Balbus' attempt to prove that the universe itself is an incomparably beautiful and intelligent animate rational being, exercising providential care over its order and in the construction of animal creation, above all that of the human race. But before getting down to the job in earnest, he makes some prefatory remarks of a different kind. Balbus has rounded off his exposition of Stoic theology with a reminder that Cotta is a leading citizen (*principem ciuem*) and a *pontifex*, a member of the priestly order charged with a wide range of responsibilities relating to state cults and the interpretation of religious law. He needs to consider whether arguing against the gods is really something someone with those duties should be doing. Should he not be deploying the resources of rhetorical

---

[3] For the treatment of Book 3 of *De Natura Deorum* and of *De Diuinatione* that now follows, see for comparison Görler (1974) 157–61.

Cicero on *Auctoritas*

persuasion that the Academy fosters to the opposite effect (*ND* 2.168)?

Cotta offers a reply to this reminder that he is 'a Cotta and a pontiff'. He says he is quite shaken (*non mediocriter moueor*) by Balbus' *auctoritas*, and by what Balbus has said about his public role. But he insists that no rhetoric will ever persuade him out of his opinion that the cult of the immortal gods and the practices of Roman religion are sound, and constitute the very foundation of the Roman state. That is the position he will always defend, and which as a Cotta and a pontiff he ought to be prepared to accept *etiam nulla ratione*, 'even if no reasons are given or available', from *maiores nostri*, 'our forefathers' – in other words from tradition. After reviewing the main heads of Balbus' argument, he goes on to insist that he cannot be shaken from his acceptance that there are gods, as all who have any respect for religion agree (*omnes nisi admodum impios*). But it is something he is persuaded of by the *auctoritas maiorum*, not by philosophical reasoning as to why there should be gods: which is what Balbus undertakes but fails to show (*ND* 3.5–6).

There is quite a lot going on in this passage. For our purposes the main thing to register is the implication in Cotta's stance that there is or need be no contradiction or even tension between demolishing arguments for the existence and providence of gods, on the one hand, and accepting that there are gods who take an interest in human affairs and maintaining appropriate cultic practices accordingly, on the other. Arguments are the province of philosophy, where the weight of *ratio* must be what counts. Public cult, and the basic commonly accepted tenets of religion that it presupposes, is a matter for the state and the institutions it has ordained for the oversight of public cult. Here what must carry weight is the *auctoritas* of tradition, and particularly the *auctoritas* of celebrated chief pontiffs of previous eras.[4]

One might think that the postulation of two domains that can remain insulated from each other would be vulnerable to

---

[4] On Cotta's stance, see now the full discussion in Wynne (2014).

the objection (for example) that if the weight of philosophical *ratio* dictated the conclusion that there are no gods, its findings would directly contradict the presuppositions about the gods implicit in traditional religious practice. But what the Academic argumentation that Cotta supplies will offer is something different: demonstration that none of Balbus' Stoic arguments to prove that gods exist and have certain specific attributes and powers is successful; in other words, demolition of Stoic *ratio*, not of the theses that *ratio* was attempting to establish in and of themselves. This makes it look as if the potential of *ratio* to undermine *auctoritas* is non-proven to the extent that *ratio* attacks just *ratio* itself. If it were to pronounce directly on precisely those same matters on which *auctoritas* pronounces, we would have as yet no reason to think that it could not undermine it.

For Cicero's stance on that issue, the *De Divinatione* – sequel to *De Natura Deorum* – furnishes interesting material. In this dialogue his brother Quintus is given the job of arguing in Book 1 for the validity of divination as a means of predicting the future on the basis of what are interpreted as divine messages or signs of one sort or another, with Cicero himself in Book 2 acting as the proponent of the sceptical case against. Here *ratio* demolishes not only the *ratio* – broadly Stoic in cast insofar as philosophical resources are deployed – that is developed in Book 1, but the very existence of such a method of predicting the future. *Diuinationem nego*, says Cicero (*Diu.* 2.8, 45, 74), even if he tells us at the outset that this is to be taken not as a claim to certain knowledge, but as an expression of doubt on the question (*Diu.* 2.8), a tone not consistently sustained in what follows.[5]

Cicero's representation of what his argument in Book 2 is designed to achieve is likewise not consistent. Sometimes he represents belief in divination as the superstition of weak minds unable to discern the truth (*Diu.* 2.81–7). This is the vein in which he writes his peroration, where he repeats the point

---

[5] For more on the issues relating to *De Diuinatione* that I discuss here, see Schofield 1986: 59–60, some of which I recapitulate in the paragraphs that follow.

Cicero on *Auctoritas*

(already made, he says, in *De Natura Deorum*), and proposes with almost Lucretian fervour, that while true religion is to be fostered, 'all the roots of superstition are to be weeded out', adding that he felt it would be an important service to his country if he had been able to achieve that (*Diu.* 2.148–9; *eam funditus sustulissemus*: note the past counterfactual mood). But that is not the note he ends up wanting us to hear as the one predominantly struck. The expression of philosophical doubt at the outset (*Diu.* 2.8) is matched by the conclusion to the book as a whole, where Cicero says his argument has been almost entirely a dispute with other philosophers (i.e. of *ratio* with *ratio*): he has simply been putting the case against their views (*Diu.* 2.150). And when earlier (*Diu.* 2.28) he began his discussion of the various different methods of divination, in programmatic vein once again he stated the view that *haruspicina* – divination from inspection of animal entrails – is to be practised 'for the sake of the *res publica* and common religious sentiment' (elsewhere he says that taking the auspices is something to be done 'out of regard for popular opinion and for their great utility for the *res publica*': *Diu.* 2.70).

These Ciceronian vacillations are instructive in a variety of ways. The stance into which he settles at the very end of *De Diuinatione* (*Diu.* 2.150), and articulates in his more programmatic remarks at earlier points in Book 2, is highly characteristic both of his general political mindset and of his general style of philosophizing in the Academic dialogues of 45–44 BC. It returns him essentially to Cotta's posture in *De Natura Deorum*. That is to say, the need for respect for *auctoritas* to be the keynote of the conduct of public affairs is reaffirmed (*Diu.* 2.28, 70), and *ratio*'s business is once more treated largely as engagement with *ratio* itself (*Diu.* 2.150), presenting no threat to *auctoritas*, and in fact something for private exploration: 'we are alone', he says to Quintus, adding that they may therefore conduct their enquiry without provoking ill-will, especially since on most matters he remains in doubt (*Diu.* 2.28). *Religio* must be supposed to be conceived principally as orthopraxy, with questions of belief more or less bracketed, and the praxis in question taken to include the divinatory

Malcolm Schofield

practices sanctioned by *auctoritas*. On such a conception *superstitio* would presumably be a matter of excessive personal preoccupation with divinatory precautions, far over and above what public cult requires.

But in the peroration to the main case developed in Book 2 (*Diu.* 2.148–9), and in much of its detailed argumentation earlier, we see larger ambitions for *ratio*. Order in the heavens and the beauty of the universe compel Cicero (he says here) to the view to which he was inclining at the end of *De Natura Deorum* (*ND* 3.95: the Stoic argument 'seemed to me to approach closer to a semblance of the truth'), viz. that there is a supreme eternal being responsible for that order and that beauty. *Religio* is now conceived as something involving knowledge of nature (not just a matter of orthopraxy and respect for the *auctoritas* of tradition), and needs to be promoted as such. By the same token the roots of beliefs such as those that divinatory practices are liable to impress on weak human minds are to be eradicated. *Ratio* no longer engages only or mostly with other philosophical *ratio*. It aims to establish or at any rate give grounds for believing some things and disbelieving others. And it has a public agenda.

That public agenda does indeed threaten to undermine the *auctoritas* of the *maiores* and of tradition and custom. It is true that Cicero claims that the wise person will 'preserve the institutions of the *maiores* by retaining their rites and ceremonies' (*Diu.* 2.148). But when he goes on to talk of weeding out the roots of superstition, he lists the things that 'press and urge and follow' people at every turn as precisely the different divinatory practices he has been discussing throughout Book 2. No doubt individuals liable to find a worrying omen in a broken shoestring or a sneeze (*Diu.* 2.84) may be the sort of thing he mostly has in mind here. But the study of omens was central to the conduct of the business of the *res publica*. Interestingly there is no mention at *Diu.* 2.148–9 of the need to respect popular opinion. The focus lies elsewhere: the passage ends, very much as Lucretius might have ended it, with a comment on the incompatibility between superstitious belief and mental tranquillity.

Cicero on *Auctoritas*

This is by no means the only place in Cicero's writings where *ratio* figures within a public agenda. A particularly notable example of an altogether different stamp is a passage in the highly political *De Haruspicum Responso* (56 BC), one episode in his bitter and protracted struggle with Publius Clodius. Here he offers what Ingo Gildenhard describes as 'some programmatic reflections on his attitude to religion'.[6] His primary 'authorities (*auctores*) and teachers' are the *maiores*, and the wisdom of their endorsement of the pontifical order, the augurs, and reliance on books of prophecy and soothsayers as securing proper religious observance. But he then mentions learned theological writings (which read, he says, as though they reflect the teaching of the *maiores*). And the high point is reached when he appeals simply (without mentioning philosophy or Stoicism) to the basic elements of the Stoic argument for the existence and providence of the gods from the order of the heavens and the way the universe is organized – and finally to realization that the Roman empire itself was created, has grown, and is maintained through divine will and power (*Har.* 18–19).

Someone who had just read the peroration to Book 2 of *De Diuinatione* might be surprised to find the same reasoned appeal to the existence and providence of the gods being treated as entirely compatible with (and indeed taken to be supportive of) belief in divination. But here we may note a parallel in another work on the role of religion in the public domain. In Book 2 of *De Legibus* (probably 52–50 BC), when the question is raised whether there really is such a thing as divination or whether it has simply been invented for its usefulness to the *res publica*, Cicero answers with a brief resume of the Stoic argument for providence, and draws the inference that providence may include giving signs of what will happen in the future (*Leg.* 2.32–3). Whether or not we should postulate a shift in Cicero's philosophical stance on the Stoic position on divination from the 50s BC to the later 40s, the main point for present purposes is that *ratio* and the *auctoritas*

---

[6] Gildenhard (2011) 330.

Malcolm Schofield

of tradition are in *De Haruspicum Responso* presented in a thoroughly public forum as supplying independently but jointly the more powerful bases for sound politics and religion.

Auctoritas in Cicero's Philosophizing

In some contexts, then, Cicero sees philosophical *ratio* as legitimately making its presence felt in the public domain, at any rate when it does not undermine *auctoritas*. But is the converse ever true? Is there room for *auctoritas* of any kind anywhere in philosophy? When Cicero endorses what he represents as Academic insistence that in that sphere *ratio*, not *auctoritas*, is what we should give most weight to, one might start to think that he regards any kind of appeal to *auctoritas* in the way philosophy is presented or debated as intrinsically unphilosophical – because inconsistent with reliance on *ratio*.

But things are not that clear cut. There is plenty of evidence complicating the picture. Consideration of the prefaces to *De Senectute* and *De Amicitia* will make the point immediately apparent. These two works come relatively late in the sequence of dialogues written in 46–44 BC, *De Senectute* probably late in 45, *De Amicitia* a few months later (*De Officiis*, completed near the end of 44, accordingly declares that to avoid duplication it will say nothing on the topic of acquiring friends: *Off.* 2.31). This is the period when Cicero is explicit about his allegiance to Academic scepticism, both in works which contain whole sequences of argumentation in a sceptic mode (such as *De Natura Deorum* and *De Diuinatione*, as well as the *Lucullus*) and in those which do not (such as *Tusculan Disputations* and *De Officiis*). Cato 'the censor' is the main speaker in *De Senectute*, Laelius in *De Amicitia*: two Roman statesmen of the previous century. Cicero explains that scarcely anyone in Cato's day surpassed him either in the great age he attained or in wisdom, while the friendship between Laelius – also reputed for his wisdom – and Scipio was legendary (*Amic.* 4–5). But in each case, Cicero tells his friend Atticus, dedicatee of both dialogues, the rationale for choosing them as speakers is

288

Cicero on *Auctoritas*

constituted partly by the greater *grauitas* (weight, impressiveness) this sort of discourse seems to acquire if ascribed to the *auctoritas* of the men of old (ibid.; cf. *Sen.* 3).

This remark of Cicero's about *auctoritas* resonates with those he had made about the composition of *De Republica* in a letter written to his brother Quintus late in 54 BC, almost ten years earlier. Having described the plan of the work, and having listed the cast of characters he is imagining as participants in the dialogue, with Scipio and Laelius prominent among them, he continues (*Ad Q. Fr.* 3.5.1):

> The composition of the work was going forward very nicely, and the high rank (*dignitas*) of the participants lent weight (*pondus*) to their words. But when the two books [i.e. the two he had already drafted out of a projected nine] were read to me at Tusculum in Sallustius' hearing, he pointed out that these matters could be treated with much more authority (*auctoritas*) if I spoke of the commonwealth (*res publica*) in my own person. After all, he said, I was no Heraclides of Pontus [a prolific writer of dialogues in the generation after Plato] but a Consular, one who had been involved in most important state affairs (*res publica*). Speeches attributed to speakers so remote in time would appear fictitious. In my earlier work on the theory of oratory, he said, I had tactfully separated the conversation of the orators from myself, but I had put it into the mouths of men I had personally seen. Finally, Aristotle's writings on the state (*res publica*) and the preeminent individual are in his own person. (Trans. D. R. Shackleton Bailey)

Cicero tells Quintus that this intervention by Sallustius (a friend of long standing) had shaken him, the more so because his decision about the interlocutors had prevented him from touching on contemporary political upheavals (even though it had the advantage of avoiding offence to any of his readers). He says he will now rewrite the dialogue as a conversation between himself and Quintus – which in fact he never did.

The importance of selecting speakers with the *dignitas* that will lend weight to what they say is something in effect amplified in *De Re Publica* itself, as we now have it, conceivably in an attempt to forestall criticism such as that voiced by Sallustius. Here we can point particularly to the passage in Book I where Laelius presses Scipio to give his views on the best form of *res publica*. Scipio in his response is made first to refer to his

289

own experience in politics (as the family profession), already mentioned by Laelius, and then to stress on the one hand that he has read the Greek philosophers on the subject, and on the other hand that he owes more to his Roman upbringing than to books. Lucius Furius Philus, another of those present, then completes the endorsement with comments on Scipio's ability, experience of politics at the highest level, study of the theory of government in particular, and finally his eloquence (*Rep.* 1.34–7). As for the choice of figures from the past to populate a dialogue on this theme, Cicero in his preface has rounded off comments on the *auctoritas* required to handle it with a reference to his own similar credentials, followed by the assertion that the *ratio* he will expound is nothing new, but recalls a discussion between those who were in their time the most eminent and wisest men in the republic (*ciuitas*) (*Rep.* 1.12–13).

Now Sallustius was presumably right in taking the line that this was no recollection but a fiction. But on reflection Cicero must have concluded that he had developed in the work ideas and arguments sufficiently similar to the thinking of figures contemporary with Scipio and Laelius – Polybius and Panaetius, with whom as Cicero's Laelius points out Scipio had associated (*Rep.* 1.34), and again Carneades (*Rep.* 3.8) – for the fiction to be a plausible one. In 45–44 BC he was certainly ready to make Scipio and Laelius (and in addition Cato) protagonists once more in further dialogues. Here he was to tackle the issue of plausibility explicitly in the preface to *De Senectute*, where he differentiates his choice of Cato as speaker – with no pretence that he is to expound anything other than Cicero's own views on old age – from the Peripatetic Aristo of Ceos' decision to make the purely mythical figure of Tithonus the main speaker in his work on the subject: 'There is too little *auctoritas* in a story (*fabula*)'. Against the possible charge that his Cato is more erudite than the author of works by the real Cato, Cicero is careful to explain that the old man had read a lot of Greek literature late in life (*Sen.* 3). In *De Amicitia*, by contrast, he is at pains to represent to the reader that the entire dialogue is a phenomenal feat of memorization, on the part first of Quintus Mucius Scaevola and then of Cicero himself (*Amic.* 1–5; one is

Cicero on *Auctoritas*

reminded of the similar mise-en-scène in the preface to Plato's *Parmenides*).[7]

Making only the dead, not the living, the main players in a philosophical dialogue is represented by Cicero in a letter of July 45 as having been for a while a determined policy of his. The principal motive he suggests is that of averting jealousy – presumably on the part of those who might think they had a better claim on a role as a Ciceronian protagonist than those of their contemporaries that might in the event have been chosen. However, the policy could work properly only if the *dramatis personae* met the *auctoritas* criteria indicated in the three dialogues discussed above. With the *Academica*, revised shortly before that letter was composed, Cicero had been unable to think of suitably distinguished deceased members of the Roman elite who had been appropriately experienced in relevant philosophical discussion, and had therefore abandoned implementation of the policy in that case. He had ended up – not without some anxiety – giving the Antiochean side of the argument (articulating a fundamentally Stoic stance in epistemology) to the hugely learned Varro, who had been intimating to Atticus that he wanted a part in one of Cicero's dialogues and as it happened was an Antiochean in philosophy, and making the sceptic counterargument himself: something he associates with Aristotle's practice of taking the lead role himself, although he was careful (he says) to make sure he did not make the case he took on look stronger. But in *De Finibus*, currently being composed (it appears), he has reverted by and large to the old policy, with recently deceased speakers suitably qualified, although taking a prominent role himself also (*Att.* 13.19.3–5).

De Senectute is in fact the first dialogue in the later sequence, however, that presents the reader with protagonists not only not still living but from a previous era: in fact from the same period and the same milieu as Cicero had invoked in *De Republica*. It is not hard to conjecture the main reasons for

---

[7] See further on Cicero's choice of speakers Blom (2010) 124–8, 168–74, 243–51; also Baraz (2012) 184–5.

291

reversion to an earlier model. *De Senectute* represents a notable shift in authorial stance from the philosophical dialogues that immediately preceded it. Most of those dialogues (as well as *De Diuinatione*, which followed it) were written (as *De Fato* puts it) in the form of *perpetua oratio in utramque partem*, in such a way as to leave *iudicium* as to which case seems most deserving of acceptance to the individual reader (*Fat.* 1) in the Academic sceptic style. *Tusculan Disputations* and *De Fato* itself followed a different pattern of Academic dialogue, but neither are works in which Cicero is recommending his own viewpoint as such, without presentation of any opposing viewpoint, as he is in *De Senectute* (*nostrum omnem de senectute sententiam: Sen.* 3), and somewhat less explicitly in *De Amicitia.* Old age and friendship were in different ways topics evidently close to Cicero's heart and mind, on which he wanted to give a personal view, and in these respects resembling the questions about the orator and the *res publica* he had explored in *De Oratore* and *De Republica* ten years before, rather more than the subject matter he had more recently been dealing with in the philosophical encyclopaedia that began with *Hortensius* and ended with *De Fato.* The obvious inference is that it was to give his treatment of these topics maximum *auctoritas* that he reverted to the same style and setting as he had adopted in *De Republica*, placing it on the lips of the great men of old.

In philosophy, in the writing of philosophy at any rate, it was from the beginning and remained to the end important for Cicero that speakers in his dialogues should command *auctoritas* if the views he had them express were to carry the appropriate weight. Moreover from *De Republica*, *De Senectute*, and *De Amicitia* alike we get a fairly clear sense of what criteria such a claim to *auctoritas* might need to satisfy, at any rate on topics like the ones explored in these works: experience and notable achievement in the relevant area (politics, old age, friendship); appropriate learning, especially in studying what the Greeks had to say; wisdom and eloquence; and with the *auctoritas* these qualifications bestow enhanced if they are possessed by one of the great men of a previous generation.

Cicero on *Auctoritas*

The view that there is a need for such *auctoritas* is not formally speaking inconsistent with the principle that in philosophy it is weight of *ratio*, rather than *auctoritas*, that should guide us. We may want to ask, however, how in that case the weight of *auctoritas* can legitimately be made to count at all. One answer might be that the proper function of a speaker's *auctoritas* is to predispose us to take the argument he presents more seriously than we might otherwise do. Given the concerns Cicero expresses in his prefaces about the prejudices he needs to confront – most relevantly for this issue, distaste for the whole enterprise of philosophizing, or for any more than a passing interest in it, or for reading philosophy in Latin (*Fin.* 1.1–12) – there was obvious reason for him to represent the philosophizing in Latin he presents in his dialogues as something engaged in by Romans of great distinction in fields other than philosophy, who can nonetheless be credibly portrayed as expert in it and energetic in its pursuit.

But it seems unlikely that that could exhaust the benefit Cicero hoped to extract from the appeal to *auctoritas* in works like *De Republica*, *De Senectute*, and *De Amicitia*. Here we need to recall the emphasis on the relevant practical experience that the principal speakers in these dialogues have amassed, and the wisdom they have acquired in the process. Scipio's upbringing and his signal achievements in statesmanship, Cato's very great age after a lifetime devoted to shrewd interventions in the politics of his day (*Amic.* 6), and the 'exceptional glory of the friendship' (*Amic.* 5) Laelius had with Scipio in each case make them particularly well equipped to discuss the topic to be addressed. These are all matters on which pure reason and highly abstract reflection cannot adequately pronounce. All concern the practicalities of the human sphere, where experience of life is needed to arrive at a valid theoretical treatment of the issues, as for example is reflected in Scipio's decision (applauded by Laelius) to take Rome's historical development as the right way to approach the question of 'the best condition of the *res publica*', not Plato's invention of an ideal state 'totally alien to human life and customs' (*Rep.* 2.21–2). Here, in contrast to Cotta's view of the theological domain explored in *De Natura Deorum, ratio* and *auctoritas* need to be seen not as alternatives but as mutually implicated. Without an appropriate basis in experience as interpreted by a wise statesman with an *auctoritas* deriving in part from that experience, *ratio* will be unable to develop an appropriate theory, but the experience could never have been interpreted with the requisite *auctoritas* without the *ratio* inherent in *prudentia*, practical wisdom (cf. *Rep.* 2.45, 51, 67).

In the practical sphere there is also arguably a need for something like role models: paradigmatic exemplifications of human accomplishments such as statesmanship or friendship, which may then be represented as authoritative. By locating such paradigms in the past, Cicero was clearly wanting to capitalize on Roman reverence for tradition, and on the sense evidently widely shared that a sounder polity had existed and sounder values had prevailed in the years before the cycle of violence set in that marked Roman politics from the time of the ascendancy of the Gracchi on into the present. Of course, it would only be reasonable to attach weight to words spoken by role models of previous and better times, just on account of their status as such, if it was credible that words something like those attributed to them by Cicero really did represent what they would have been likely to say on the topics they are made to address. That is presumably why he invests the efforts we have noted in the relevant dialogues to assure the reader of their historical plausibility.

Conclusion

So is it that *auctoritas* calls the tune in politics and religion, *ratio* in philosophy? I have sought to endorse but also to complicate that picture. I have made the argument by focusing on relevant passages in which Cicero introduces the actual notions of *ratio* and (especially) *auctoritas*, or at any rate makes it clear that *ratio* and *auctoritas* are what he has in mind; and which indicate that he can allow *ratio* in spheres where he will insist that *auctoritas* should prevail, and *auctoritas* an importance in philosophical argument, whether bringing something intrinsically relevant to proper *ratio* or more modestly predisposing the reader to attend to *ratio* seriously. There is much more evidence that could be brought to bear on the topic.[8] For example, Cicero's entire project of philosophical writing might be seen as an attempt to reshape Roman culture by *ratio* and equip it with a new conception of education, particularly moral and oratorical education, continuous with traditional norms at least in the ethical field, but reshaping them.[9] Or one might look at the way appeal to the *auctoritas* of Greek philosophers of the past – something I have not touched upon – works in the actual philosophical argumentation of the dialogues. For the present I hope simply to have opened a window on some of the issues at stake.

---

[8] See Görler (1974) 54–71 for a rich assembly and discussion of material pertaining to it, focused particularly on *auctoritas*.

[9] See now Moatti (2015).

CHAPTER 15

AUTHORS AND AUTHORITIES IN ANCIENT CHINA: SOME COMPARATIVE OBSERVATIONS

G. E. R. LLOYD

There was no ancient Chinese category that corresponds to *philosophia* in ancient Greek or Latin, or to the terms in European languages that derive from that, though it is certainly not the case that 'philosophy', 'philosophie', 'Philosophie', 'filosofia' and so on are understood in exactly the same way in the English-speaking world, in France, in Germany and in Italy, for example (cf. Lloyd 2009: ch. 1). So it might look as if nothing useful is to be learned from considering the Chinese experience in relation to the principal questions that are central to this volume, the notions of authorship and authority in Greco-Roman philosophy, the development of philosophical schools, the treatment of anonymous texts and the rest.[1]

However, that negative conclusion is premature. Although the Chinese had no 'philosophers' as such, many of those who called themselves 'wandering persuaders' (*you shui*), 'men of broad learning' (*bo shi*) or just simply 'knights' *(shi)* or members of the literate elite (*ru*)[2] wrote on recognisably moral, ethical, and political subjects, discussed the conditions of change, and speculated about the origins of the world. We can certainly explore how those who wrote such texts organised themselves, the notions of authorship they entertained and the modes of debate they cultivated[3]. As always, we have to

---

[1] Note on Chinese texts: I cite texts from the dynastic histories from the standard Zhonghua shuju editions and the *Zhuangzi* from the Harvard- Yenching Sinological Index series, Supplement 20, Beijing (1947).
[2] This is conventionally translated as 'Confucian' though that is quite misleading since the individuals concerned often expressed no allegiance to the teachings of Kong Fuzi.
[3] It would of course be possible to pursue similar issues also in relation to ancient Mesopotamia, Egypt and India, but quite apart from the matter of my competence to do so, that would far exceed what can sensibly be discussed in a single chapter.

Authors and Authorities in Ancient China

be wary of imposing our Western categories on Chinese materials. As always, we have to be cautious about the viability of generalisations across heterogeneous data subject to considerable variations over time. But the very diversity of the experience of China in these matters, compared with that of Greco-Roman philosophy, can be turned to advantage, for we can investigate what is distinctive in either case and even attempt to pin down why some such differences emerged.

But how can we set about accounting for any of the relevant similarities or differences we encounter when we compare these two ancient civilisations? In the background lie fundamental, even if extraordinarily difficult issues. Do the resemblances reflect universal features that we should expect to find in any society that produces a self-conscious literate elite? Is 'philosophy', when broadly construed, a universal human concern? But if on the other hand we find differences, we have to ask why they occur and what they tell us about, among other things, the formation of such elites, their differing self-representations and their relationships with their audiences and readerships? In the first part of this study I shall concentrate on locating those Chinese 'wandering persuaders' in relation to other claimants to prestige and knowledge, before I turn at the end to the more difficult question of how far explanations or at least correlations seem possible.

In China, as in the Greco-Roman world, the concept of 'author' in play in relation to (broadly) philosophical texts must be understood against a background of the growth of notions of 'authorship' and 'authenticity' more generally. In Greece the first author to lay claim to his own work is Hesiod[4], but it was of course in the courts of the Ptolemies at Alexandria that philology and literary scholarship attained a position of pre-eminent prestige. The Homeric epics were subjected to minute scrutiny, suspect passages were obelised, sometimes on the grounds of inconsistency, sometimes on the basis of assumptions about what was or was not thought worthy of their presumed author, where the grounds might

---

[4] Some early Homeric scholarship was criticised by Aristotle for remarking on trivial similarities while ignoring major ones (*Metaphysics* 1093a26ff.).

be aesthetic or indeed moral[5]. But similar questions were also raised of course in relation to prose works, including technical treatises. It is assumed that the body of medical texts we know as the Hippocratic Corpus was assembled, edited and commented on by Alexandrian scholars who here too were sensitive to problems of authorship and authenticity[6]. Among the by-products of this work were lexica glossing rare or problematic terms.

Two immediate points of similarity can be suggested with ancient China, one concerning the specific issue of the production of lexica, the other the more general question of the development of philological scholarship. On the first question, the encyclopaedic compilation of the explanation of terms that we know as the *Erya* was put together probably in the third century BCE. It contained glosses on or elucidations of difficult terms that appeared in ancient texts, but as Nylan (2018) has shown, it was often appealed to in order to justify the emendation of those texts.

More generally, in China too, as in Ptolemaic Alexandria, the task of assembling and classifying the books in the Han imperial library generated a considerable body of scholarship, the work not just of Liu Xiang, his son Liu Xin and the polymath Yang Xiong around the turn of the millennium, but also that of many others. Of course the Han historians, first and foremost Sima Tan and Sima Qian, the authors of the first great Chinese universal history, the *Shiji* at the start of the first century BCE, described the first emperor, Qin Shi Huang Di, as implementing a policy of burning the books of which he disapproved, a legend that was repeated and amplified down the centuries.[7] However, we should be clear first that texts on technical subjects, such as medicine, divination and agriculture, were spared, and secondly that the books in question

---

[5] On Homeric scholarship in Alexandria, see most recently Hatzimichali (2013a).

[6] See Nutton (2004) ch. 4.

[7] The story comes in different, not altogether consistent, versions in the *Shiji*, at 6: 255.6ff., 15: 686 and 87: 2546.11ff. The policy is ascribed to Li Si who was Qin Shi Huang Di's Chief Minister but who had been a pupil of the notable third-century BCE philosopher Xunzi.

were those in private hands. Those in the imperial library were not affected, though it, like the library at Alexandria, suffered from periodic catastrophic losses from fire or depredation. By the time Liu Xiang set to work, the task of cataloguing all the texts that library contained was formidable. One source (cf. Nylan 2018) reports that he had to deal with 13,296 scrolls.

His classification, preserved in the second great universal dynastic history, the *Han Shu* 30, contains some surprises. In some cases, his categories appear to correspond very roughly to those we are used to, writings concerned with military matters, or with medicine, for instance. But any attempt to match his classes exactly with ours soon breaks down, nor should we expect a close correspondence between them.

Take one of his main categories which was labelled *shu shu* (roughly 'calculations and methods'). It was subdivided into six. While these all involved *some* calculation and *some* method, the subjects to which, and the ways in which, they were applied, were quite diverse. Thus *tian wen,* the 'patterns in the heavens', included descriptions of the heavens (both cosmography and cosmology) and prognostications on their basis. Next, *li pu* ('calendars and chronologies') dealt with, as its name suggests, calendrical astronomy, genealogies and chronologies. The third group, labelled *wu xing* 'five phases', contained works that discuss the interactions of those five (Fire, Earth, Metal, Water, Wood) which provided a general schema for accounting for change, whether among physical phenomena or in the political domain[8]. Milfoil and turtle divination formed a separate fourth group, *shi gui,* and the last two *za zhan* and *xing fa* dealt with 'mixed prognostications' and 'the way of forms', namely physiognomy. We might assume that the Book of Changes, the *Yi jing*, would also be included among works to do with divination. But that does not appear under *shu shu* but in the section of the catalogue dealing with canonical texts (*jing*).

---

[8] The five phases have often been represented as 'elements' in Western scholarship, though they are more correctly understood as interacting processes – which are not limited to physical phenomena but can include, for example, dynastic changes. The complex story of the gradual development and multiple applications of five-phase doctrine is set out in Lloyd and Sivin (2002) ch. 5 and Appendix.

Indeed by the time Liu Xiang was at work there had been a certain stabilisation in what were considered the principal canonical texts, a process that his own editorial work undoubtedly accelerated, for he drastically reorganised such texts as the *Liezi*, the *Zhuangzi* and even the *Xunzi*, to the point where it is difficult to reconstruct the state of those texts before his interventions (cf. Loewe 1993, Nylan and Loewe 2010, Nylan 2018). Already in 136 BCE the Han Emperor, Wu Di, selected five of the main canons, not just the *Changes* (*Yi*), but also the *Odes* (*Shi*), *Documents* (*Shu*), *Rites* (*Li*) and *Spring and Autumn Annals* (*Chun qiu*), to form the basic curriculum of the Imperial Academy that he founded.

Furthermore, he assigned teachers, men of broad learning (*boshi*) or Academicians, to give instruction in each of them. While this provided the basis for what we might call 'higher education' in China, we must be clear that, unlike Plato's Academy or other Greek philosophical schools, which were all private foundations, the Chinese Imperial Academy was an official state institution. It aimed not just to educate its students but to train them for public service, for most of them would be expected, on graduation, to take their places in the Imperial Civil Service. The Chinese canonical texts could be mined for lessons relevant to morality, good behaviour, good governance, but the prime duty of students was to commit those lessons to memory, not to use them as a springboard for further reflection and debate. For their part, the Academicians made their reputation by their mastery of the canons, rather than through any originality or ability to go beyond them, though in practice we can see that they sometimes did so[9].

The question of the authorship of these canons takes us to a central problem, and the first aspect of that relates to the extent to which Confucius himself was involved either in writing or in editing them. He was, for example, held to have

---

[9] A notable case of a Chinese commentator who represents himself as essentially preserving the teaching in the canonical *Book of Changes*, but who certainly elaborates its doctrines and goes far beyond them, is the polymath Yang Xiong, active around the turn of the millennium (see Nylan and Sivin (1995)).

edited the *Odes* and to have written the *Springs and Autumns.* There is no reason to suppose that he was an entirely legendary figure (as is probably the case with Laozi the reputed author of the *Daodejing*[10]). His traditional dates were put at 551 to 479 BCE and we have a good deal of information about his life, his origin in the state of Lu and his travels in search of a ruler who would be worthy to receive his advice, an ambition that was never fulfilled. Yet modern scholars nowadays discount the stories of his editing let alone authoring various of the five texts that got to be labelled the Five 'Confucian' Classics (see Nylan 2001 for a comprehensive analysis). Even the further work that is still more often ascribed to him, the *Lunyu* or *Analects* – which was not included in Han Wu Di's chosen group of five canons – is nowadays understood to be a composite work assembled over several decades by his pupils (Brooks and Brooks 1998).

We can clearly see at work the desire to attach an individual name, especially one with the aura of antiquity or of a reputation for wisdom, to what were considered the more important texts. Indeed, this applies not just to the principal 'canons' but also to technical treatises, which were also sometimes called *jing*. The three recensions of what we know as the *Huangdi neijing* or *Inner Canon of the Yellow Emperor* became the chief texts from which medicine was taught – and they still figure today in modified versions in schools of 'Traditional Chinese Medicine' (see Sivin 1987). We hear also of an *Outer Canon* (*waijing*) though that has not survived. The texts of the *Inner Canon* represent the Yellow Emperor in dialogue with various advisers. But there was sometimes an implicit claim, even among those who appreciated that that august figure antedated historical records by several centuries, that he had sanctioned the whole work, even that he may have written it himself.

[10] Graham (1989) 217 speculates that Daoists took over the idea that Laozi ('Old Dan') taught Confucius from Confucian texts. But that depends on a questionable assumption that we are in a good position to identify purely Daoist, and purely Confucian, writings. But neither of those two categories is firm. While the *Zhuangzi* is regularly used to exemplify the former, that may be to underestimate its hybrid character, and I discuss the problem of 'Confucian' writings in my text.

G. E. R. Lloyd

For us the way in which these various works were originally composed is less important than the manner in which they were used. The scholars, known as *ru*, who preserved and transmitted the principal canons, formed what, by Eastern Han times, were called *jia*, lineages, more literally families. (I shall be coming back shortly to the question of the extent to which they formed well defined sects or schools.) But different versions of the same text often existed and would be taught by different teachers. The *Huangdi neijing* comes down to us, as noted, in three different recensions, the *lingshu* ('Divine Pivot') *suwen* ('Basic questions') and *taisu* ('Grand Basis'). More strikingly still, the work associated with Laozi, the *Daodejing*, exists in different editions, not just the one that was more usually transmitted, but also in another version, in which the section dealing with the 'Way' (*Dao*) comes after that dealing with *De* ('virtue', 'potentiality'[11]) forming not a *Daodejing* but a *Dedaojing*. A copy of such a *Dedaojing* came to light in a Han tomb at Mawangdui that was sealed in 168 BCE.[12]

So on the one hand we can detect in China, as in Hellenistic Greece, the urge to identify a prestigious author for important texts even when the texts themselves, strictly speaking, are anonymous in that they do not themselves openly announce who wrote them. On the other hand, there is less of a preoccupation, in China, with the idea of establishing a single, original, Ur-text, even though scholars were concerned to improve the versions they transmitted by editing and reorganising them.[13] Conversely there is, down to the end of the Han, less of a concern with exposing spurious works as such, though for later scholarship, and not just in modernity, that certainly was to prove an important issue.

---

[11] *De* tends to be rendered 'virtue', but it is wider than that translation intimates. In certain contexts, it comes close to 'power' or 'potentiality' or what the term *dunamis* suggests. See Gassmann (2011).

[12] On the multiple versions of this text, including those excavated at Mawangdui in 1973, see Boltz (1993).

[13] One may compare and contrast the ambition of various followers of Socrates, authors of 'Socratic discourses', to create an image of his teaching and persona. The similarity would be the ambition to invoke the authority of an acknowledged sage, but the point of contrast is that, given it was well known that Socrates left nothing in writing, none of these *logoi* could claim to be by him.

Authors and Authorities in Ancient China

There were, however, disputes, as between different lineages, as to what the key texts and iconic figures stood for. One example of this relates to 'Mohists', or followers of Mo Di, though admittedly our evidence comes from hostile sources. Thus both the *Hanfeizi* (ch. 50) and the *tian xia* chapter (33) of the *Zhuangzi* compilation refer to different groups who proposed very divergent views of Mo Di's teaching and accused one another of drastically misrepresenting it. Those reports of controversy within the school were used to throw doubt on the reliability of *any* interpretation of what Mo Di himself taught. Yet we should be wary of using any Western concepts of orthodoxy and heterodoxy ('heresy') in the Chinese situation[14]. There were certainly no sanctions that could be applied to those who were criticised for deviant philosophical interpretations. Of course disputes over what Plato or Socrates or Zeno really stood for were common in the Greco-Roman world, but it was only in a religious context, and after the rise of Christianity to a position of dominance, that the phenomenon of sanctions taken against those criticised for deviant positions took on an altogether new dimension in the West.

The Mohists are one of six *jia* identified in Sima Tan's account of earlier philosophy included in the final chapter (130) of the *Shiji*. He refers also to the *ru*, but otherwise his groups are labelled by their doctrines or theories, *yin yang*, the law *jia* *(fa jia),* the school of Names (*ming jia*) and finally the view that Sima Tan himself favoured, named after the *Dao* itself. Although Sima Tan sees some merit in the teachings of all six groups, his agenda is clearly to proclaim the superiority of the *Dao*. We should certainly not straightforwardly accept that the six in question all formed well-defined schools or sects despite Sima Tan's story. Indeed, it would be more accurate to say

---

[14] Indeed, the Greek term *hairesis* has, as its primary meaning, 'choice'. When Diogenes Laertius (7.167) reports the dispute between Chrysippus and Ariston on Zeno's teaching, he uses the same term ('differed') when describing Chrysippus' disagreements with Zeno as he does when identifying the deviant views of Ariston, Herillus and Dionysius. In this Greek context, too, then, the terms 'heterodoxy' and 'heresy' have to be used with caution, for the 'orthodoxy' they are contrasted with is far from the definitive set of dogmata that were given that label in some Christian contexts.

303

that none did. Even the Mohists, who are the best candidates, disagreed among themselves, as we have seen, about the teaching of Mo Di. As for the *dao*, embodying that is an ideal for just about every teacher in question. Although the two teachers who are regularly identified as representatives of the School of Names, namely Hui Shi in the fourth century BCE and Gongsun Long in the next, share with Greek sophists a love of paradox, they were certainly quite unlike those sophists in other respects (*pace* Reding 1985), notably in that there was no suggestion that they offered their teaching to anyone who was prepared to pay for it.

The model that is more appropriate to understand these groupings is the one we have identified before, of particular teachers seeing as their duty the preservation, transmission and interpretation of particular writings. As it is, several of the most prominent texts of the Warring States and Qin Han periods use and endorse ideas that can be found in a variety of earlier lineages. This applies particularly, in my view, to two of the most important compendia, put together by Lü Buwei and by Liu An, the king of Huainan, that purport to set out all the useful knowledge that the ruler will need, namely the *Lüshi chunqiu*, around 239 BCE, and the *Huainanzi* about 100 years later. Instead of either labelling these texts (merely) 'eclectic' or trying to pin down their allegiance to a particular point of view, it would be more accurate to allow that their authors or compilers were not particularly constrained to adhere to what in later times came to be thought of as the teachings of individual schools. Both compilers would appear to have taken over what they considered useful ideas wherever they could find them, all with the aim of producing a compendium of the knowledge the ruler will need for good government. But although that makes them 'eclectic' in one sense, we should not underestimate the originality of the syntheses they created.

This is not to dismiss the evidence concerning *jia* in *Shiji* 130 entirely; merely to notice that each of Sima Tan's groups is, to a greater or less extent, his construct, serving, as noted, his own particular polemical agenda. It is notable, however, that

Authors and Authorities in Ancient China

his line is not that other views have nothing in their favour, but rather that none of them captured the whole *dao*[15].

That takes us to the crucial topic of the nature of the debates held on different topics between different members of the literate elite in different contexts from Warring States through to the end of the Han. Even earlier, in the *Springs and Autumns* period, discussions of policy are frequently reported in such texts as *Zhanguoce*. China had plenty of autocratic rulers even before the unification, but they were usually canny enough to take advice from ministers and courtiers. Those advisers, for their part, devoted considerable efforts to gaining and keeping the confidence of those rulers. We have plenty of evidence relating to debates at court, and there is even a particular genre of writing, rather distinctive of ancient China, namely the memorial, known as *zou*, a written text sent up to the ruler for his consideration. We know of some cases where the text never arrived, but was intercepted by a minister or courtier. This happened to the memorials prepared by Li Si in defence of his conduct, after he had himself been replaced as chief minister of Qin Shi Huang Di by one of his rivals[16]. The crucial point about the great majority of the controversies recorded, whether in the written or the oral mode, is that the ultimate decision remained in the hands of the ruler himself, or of those who could claim with greater or less legitimacy that they represented him.

This is relevant to some of the debates we know were held on technical issues. We have good evidence of several that related to astronomical or calendrical problems in the Eastern Han

---

[15] The *tian xia* chapter (33) in the *Zhuangzi* similarly finds that the teachers it criticises all captured some aspects of the way, though none did so entirely. It even includes Zhuang Zhou, that is Zhuangzi himself, among those criticised, which throws further light on the composite nature of this text. Both *Shiji* 130 and *Zhuangzi* 33 seek to accommodate other points of view to those their authors favoured, at least to some extent, rather than dismissing their rivals outright.

[16] The evidence comes from the biography of Li Si in the *Shiji* 87. Quite how Sima Tan or Sima Qian had access to the contents of Li Si's memorials (which they claim to cite verbatim) remains something of a mystery, though that by itself does not cast doubt on the general point that Li Si's rival, Zhao Gao, blocked his access to the emperor.

G. E. R. Lloyd

(in 175 CE). One recorded in the *Hou Han Shu zhi* 2: 2037–8 goes into detail on the scene at court (cf. Cullen 2007). The Three Excellencies sat facing south (showing that they represented the emperor himself). The 'Palace attendants, Leader of the Court Gentlemen, Grand Masters and those with emoluments of 1000 and 600 piculs' sat in serried ranks facing north. The east side was occupied by 'court gentlemen for consultation and erudits', and the west by 'all the [rest of] the officials'. A clerk read out the imperial edict, summoning the debate to discuss a proposal that the date of the epoch from which the calendar was calculated needed reform. One might have thought this a purely technical question. Yet more was at stake than we might imagine. Given that the regulation of the calendar was of crucial importance for good order in the state, and thus a matter for which the emperor himself was ultimately responsible, he was bound to be implicated in the debate. We are told that Cai Yong and those who had suggested the need for reform (called Huang and Guang) raised problems and questions with one another. But the outcome was that the authorities considered that the reformers were not just wrong, but guilty of high treason. They were indeed sentenced to death, although the emperor stepped in to commute the penalty. The crucial point here is that the authorities who adjudicated such debates wielded political power to back up their intellectual judgement.

Another earlier episode from Chinese astronomical debate, reported again in the *Hou Han Shu zhi* 2: 3030, illustrates a further complicating factor. In 103 CE an astronomer called Jia Kui attempted to push through a proposal that the longitudinal movements of the sun and moon should be measured along the ecliptic rather than the equator. He even introduced a new bronze armillary with an ecliptic ring to support his view that that was the more accurate method. It seems that he won the debate, only to have his proposal ignored in practice. The Clerks in the Astronomical Bureau objected that the new armillary was too complicated and simply refused to use it. It is clear that in this case the reform was blocked by Jia Kui's colleagues and rivals, rather than by ministers who claimed

Authors and Authorities in Ancient China

to represent the emperor. So in such a case we have disputes between competing technical experts, though some of these were clearly better placed to have their way than others.

Our sources show that on occasion viva voce debates were held in formal, public, settings. Nevertheless, in the disciplines that approximate only very roughly, as we have said, to what we might include as 'philosophy', or 'mathematics', or 'medicine', the more usual pattern was for the more hard-hitting polemics to be conducted in writing and often not with living opponents but those who were safely dead and could not answer back. Let me give one example from 'mathematics' before turning to a couple from 'philosophy', in this context the discussion of questions of behaviour and of morality.

In mathematics the commentary tradition is often the locus of criticism of earlier writers. Our earliest extant Chinese mathematical text is the *Suanshushu* ('Writings on Reckoning') excavated from a tomb sealed in 186 BCE. But we have a far more systematic collection of discussions of mathematical puzzles in the *Jiuzhang suanshu* (*Nine Chapters on Mathematical Procedures*) compiled some time around the turn of the millennium, and it was this text that was the subject of a whole series of commentaries. Our first extant one was by Liu Hui in the third century CE, who takes issue with the *Nine Chapters* on several occasions, only to be criticised in his turn by later commentators, especially Li Chunfeng and his associates in the mid-seventh century CE. Although the contributions of different scholars are often difficult to disentangle, there is a clear sense of a dialogue conducted over several hundred years by those for whom the *Nine Chapters* was the chief source of mathematical learning.

Then a first philosophical example of similar criticism and debates comes in Xunzi's chapter 6 'Against the Twelve', an attack on twelve earlier philosophers. These included even Mencius, generally considered to have been Confucius' chief successor in the generation preceding Xunzi, but now of course no longer a living rival. It is notable too that Xunzi criticises not just the opinions of those philosophers but also their behaviour and that of their followers, that is those who, in his

307

own day, claimed to be their disciples. Some of those are taken to task for their sloppy dress and conceited manner, their misbehaviour at official banquets and in performing ritual ceremonies. We have to remember that such matters were subject to strict state regulations. It was how you and your followers acted, as much as, or more than, what you and they believed, by which you would be judged.

Xunzi was also involved in another controversy over whether humans are, by nature, inherently good, bad or indifferent, and again he attacks Mencius. He had taken the view that humans are good, and had criticised a contemporary of his, named Gaozi, for suggesting that humans were neither good nor bad in their nature. Xunzi's position diverged from both of theirs. In his chapter 23, *xing e* ([human] nature is bad), he countered the arguments that both his predecessors had used and insisted that, left to themselves, humans are evil. What they needed, to remedy the situation, and to become proper 'gentlemen', *junzi*, was, of course, to have a teacher such as Xunzi himself. The issue was, in fact, about who to trust for advice, in this case, on the matter of proper education itself.

Let me now attempt to sum up the major points of similarity and divergence in the practices and modalities of debating between the Greco-Roman world and ancient China. In both ancient civilisations we have evidence for both oral debates and those conducted mainly in writing. In China oral debates were certainly frequent on affairs of state, but in other contexts much of the controversy was conducted by way of written argument. Some of the Chinese discussions were certainly between groups of 'philosophers', doctors, mathematicians or individuals who treated their opponents as their peers or colleagues. But on state matters and even on many technical issues the ultimate decision, in China, rested with the state authorities, even the ruler or emperor in person. There is thus no parallel in China for the styles of debate with which many Greeks were familiar, whether in the context of political assemblies or lawcourts, or in that of sophistic exhibition lectures (*epideixeis*), where it was the audience, the citizens in assembly, the dicasts, or those present at sophistic debates, who decided who had

Authors and Authorities in Ancient China

won. The issues in Greece were sometimes decided by acclaim, but in the Athenian law-courts by secret ballot. There is no evidence for that in ancient China.

This takes me now to the typical career patterns and ambitions of the writers with whom we are concerned. Most of them aspired to political office. Confucius, as noted, looked for a ruler to advise, as did Mozi, Mencius, Xunzi and Hanfeizi, all with varying degrees of success. The compilers of the two major compendia I mentioned were, in the case of the *Lüshi chunqiu,* a prominent statesman, prime minister to the man who was to unify China, and in the case of the *Huainanzi,* a king – and uncle of Han Wu Di. It is true that there are important exceptions. Zhuang Zhou, the purported author of the *Zhuangzi,* is reported as rejecting an offer made to him to take over the government of a state[17]. The text contains some delicious satires of the pretensions of Confucius. Yet it also records Zhuang Zhou in dialogue with one of his favourite interlocutors, Hui Shi, and Hui Shi, we know, was one who held ministerial office. In the case of another recluse, Wang Chong, he retired from public life in the first century CE, largely out of his disappointment at his own failure to secure anything more than a very humble official position. Even so, his being a recluse did not stop him trying to exert his influence on his contemporaries by composing a lengthy polemical treatise, the *Lun Heng,* or 'Discourses weighed on the balance', attacking all sorts of widely held beliefs and practices.

Of course many Greek and Roman intellectuals, Plato, Isocrates, Aristotle among them, had an ambition to offer advice to rulers. But in China this is far more frequent; it was the norm[18]. Indeed, we saw that one of the terms the ancient

---

[17] In one exchange, some courtiers are represented as trying to persuade Zhuang Zhou (that is Zhuangzi) to accept a position as chief minister. Zhuang Zhou refers to a dead turtle kept in a box in an ancestral shrine. Would it prefer to be dead, to be so honoured, or rather to be alive 'dragging its tail in the mud'? Obviously the answer is to be alive: so Zhuangzi dismisses the courtiers and says he will drag his tail in the mud. (*Zhuangzi* 17: 81–4, Graham (1989) 174).

[18] Although Sima Tan and Sima Qian, the authors of the first universal history, composed their works as private individuals, not on the orders of the emperor,

Chinese themselves use for those whom we call 'philosophers' was *you shui*, literally 'wandering persuaders'. Given the fickleness of the rulers they were trying to persuade, this could be a dangerous job. Yet it was accepted that it was the duty of an adviser to remonstrate with rulers and those in authority, even though we hear of many instances where that led to the adviser falling from favour, being punished or even paying for unpopular advice with his life (Lloyd 2010). We have noted that technical issues in what we call astronomy could have implications of state importance. It is striking that in the medical classic, the *Huangdi neijing*, the dialogues between medical experts such as Qi Bo and the Yellow Emperor follow the pattern of discussions of affairs of state, with Qi Bo making much of the parallelism of health in the body with good order in the state. Implicitly the text makes a claim that knowledge about health and disease could be useful for rulers. Doctors, too, then, sometimes cast themselves in the role of political advisers of a sort.

On the one hand, then, we can identify certain important differences in some of the contexts in which ideas were exchanged and debated, as between the Greco-Roman world and China. On the other hand, there are also essential similarities where in either society state policy decisions were in the hands of autocrats. Clearly it would be extravagant to claim that the contexts *determined* the styles of argument and indeed the styles of writing cultivated in each ancient civilisation. But different models, of the paradigmatic persuasion situation, do exercise an influence on how authors represent themselves. To generalise rather drastically, the importance of the peer group who have to be persuaded in oral debate is greater in the Greco-Roman world than in China, where the ultimate target

---

they both held the office of *Tai Shi* or chief scribe, at least until Sima Qian fell out of favour with Han Wu Di. But reference is made, in the *Shiji*, to their hope that the work will prove useful to later generations (18: 878.4ff, cf. 6: 278.9ff.). From the *Hanshu* onwards most of the dynastic histories were commissioned directly by the emperor. The obvious similarities to and differences from Greco-Roman historiography are discussed in Lloyd (2009) ch. 3.

Authors and Authorities in Ancient China

of persuaders is more generally the political authorities, when not the emperor in person.

Let me now come back, in conclusion, to the questions I posed at the beginning, and first to the question of authorship. The ascription of many of our extant Chinese texts to named authors, ancient or distinguished ones especially, is often, even generally, apocryphal. Texts that are strong unities attributable to identifiable individuals may even be a minority among those extant from the period down to the end of the Han. Many members of the Chinese literate elite belonged to lineages, *jia*, and saw their chief responsibility to be the preservation and transmission of the texts entrusted to them, some of which came to form the core curriculum of the Imperial Academy. The sense that what should unite them is a set of *doctrines* is less highly developed in those Chinese lineages than it is in Greek or Roman philosophical or medical *haireseis*.

Nevertheless, many of those involved saw their role not just as teachers but also as persuaders. This is true particularly of those who endeavoured to influence rulers, and who in the process engage in discussion of what we – and the ancient Greeks – would have labelled ethical, political, physical and cosmological issues. Even so that did not suffice to mark out their brand of learning as 'philosophical', let alone lead them to claim, as some Greek writers did, that their activity, 'philosophy', was the supreme intellectual discipline. Rather their goal or ideal was, as I noted, to attain the Dao, and that was a matter of embodying it, not one of some purely intellectual achievement.

Where styles of debate are concerned, it seems possible to detect the contrasting influences of the prototypical or paradigmatic contexts of communicative exchange in either civilisation. The real or imagined situation in China is often that of the presentation of advice to the king or to those in authority. In the Greco-Roman world, especially though not exclusively in classical Greece, the influence of the model set by the political assemblies and law-courts spreads into other domains of inquiry. This is so even when criticisms of that model are expressed, as by Plato and Aristotle, who

311

condemned the merely persuasive arguments that could convince the crowd and contrasted them with the ideal of objective demonstrations that they proposed – a theme I have developed on other occasions (e.g. Lloyd 2014a: ch. 1). Yet while those Greek intellectuals were shocked by the notion that any matter of importance should be decided by majority vote, they nevertheless still signed up to the ideal that anyone in a position of authority or influence should be prepared to give a rational account of themselves, their ideas and their practices. The Greek ideal was that the ultimate judge was the truth, difficult as that was to attain. The Chinese by contrast imagined the very different ideal, of a sage ruler who embodied the Dao.

The further more fundamental question I broached related to the extent to which our examination of these issues suggests we are dealing with human cross-cultural universals, or with distinct cultural specificities. The reflections which our Greek–Chinese comparison prompts are the following. Some concern with justice and injustice, right and wrong, good and evil would indeed seem to be a feature of every human society. Yet that does not commit us to some notion of a *philosophia perennis* for we have also seen the impact that different social organisations and institutions may have. Ancient China developed its styles of persuasion and debate, creating distinct niches for advisers and teachers in different areas of learning, where that was encapsulated in texts, transmitted and commented on across generations. The self-representation of those involved differed appreciably from that of Greek or Roman self-conscious philosophers. What the comparison and contrast of these two ancient civilisations thus bring to light is just how closely the image of the authority cultivated reflects the social and political circumstances of its practice. That is not to deny the purely intellectual effort that went into the analysis of argument, the development of formal logic, the creation of an ideal of strict demonstration, and many other well-known achievements of Greek philosophy. But it is to draw attention to what they owe to the particular circumstances in which the philosophers in question operated.

CHAPTER 16

ANTIQUE AUTHORITY?

ROBERT WARDY

Much of the emphasis of my ruminations falls on the question mark in the title: what I have to say about philosophical authors and authorities comes under a sign of interrogation, in a quizzical mode. By default, I inhabit a frame of mind whence the very concept of *intellectual* authority seems off limits to philosophers – and vesting it in antiquarian texts only makes the offence more flagrant. But what, here, is the sense of 'intellectual'? For since one should not brush aside the possibility that philosophers might, or even should, derive inspiration from paradigms of generic intellectual virtue, I must clarify the force of my prohibition. That is, thinkers in diverse fields of intellectual endeavour are called on to display such admirable qualities as disciplined industry, scrupulous attention, honesty, and, perhaps, courage in discharging their tasks. This illustrative list is, of course, open-ended: other virtues – moderation, for example – might well have their place; success on the part of different workers diversely situated is likely enough not to require just the same equipment; finally, how to divide off virtues of character from their strictly intellectual cousins would be a nice operation. But any which way, I perceive nothing intrinsically wrong in the prospect of some philosopher drawing encouragement from the pertinacity of a Louis Pasteur – or, for that matter, of an Abraham Lincoln.[1]

---

[1] Which obvious acknowledgement does not preclude mistaken humility in the face of *e.g.* the 'authoritative' deliverances of neurophysiology when some scientist philosophers are pursuing the philosophy of mind, *vel sim.* (I owe this shrewd observation to Michael Withey).

Robert Wardy

So, granted that such ethical models are freely available to agents regardless of the specifics of their intellectual efforts, what distinction marks off the philosophical endeavour as allergic to exemplary guidance from within, as it were? The answer can be located in two of its fundamental sources. At the fountainhead of the philosophical enterprise we find Heraclitus' emphatic repudiation of learned expertise: 'Scholarship doesn't impart intelligence; otherwise it would have smartened Pythagoras, and again Xenophanes and Hecataeus.'[2] He is not saying either that his celebrities' reputation for wide-ranging knowledge is fraudulent, or, indeed, that such knowledge lacks value – for purposes other than his own, which he has made ours. And the most deeply and perennially paradoxical aspect of the denial is Heraclitus' refusal to substitute credence in Heraclitus for reliance on irrelevant scholarship: 'listening not to *me* but to the *logos* it is wise to agree with *it*';[3] where proper attention to the *logos* apparently justifies 'I investigated myself',[4] the 'I' token-reflexively denoting the glorious anonymity of any genuine instance of philosophical rationality. Pair Heraclitus' deflective injunction with Parmenides' imperious invitation: 'judge by *logos* the much-contested disproof declared by me'.[5] Recourse to critical judgement is what will isolate Parmenides from, and above, the undiscerning common run of folk (ἄκριτα φῦλα, fr. 6). How then, is he not himself the daunting, authoritative exception? And since, in his revelation, the behest is put in the mouth of a goddess confronting her *initiand kouros*, does Parmenides not, in fact, extol privileged enlightenment preserved for the select? Not if the judgement enjoined can be executed without divine trappings, in the sobriety of our studies, rather than just beyond the gates of night and day. What conditions access to *logos*? Who speaks for or from it? The challenge of reconciling the experience of

---

[2] πολυμαθίη νόον ἔχειν οὐ διδάσκει· Ἡσίοδον γὰρ ἂν ἐδίδαξε καὶ Πυθαγόρην αὖτίς τε Ξενοφάνεά τε καὶ Ἑκαταῖον (Heraclitus B40).

[3] οὐκ ἐμοῦ, ἀλλὰ τοῦ λόγου ἀκούσαντας ὁμολογεῖν σοφόν ἐστιν ἓν πάντα εἶναι ... (Heraclitus B50).

[4] ἐδιζησάμην ἐμεωυτόν (Heraclitus B101).

[5] κρῖναι δὲ λόγωι πολύδηριν ἔλεγχον ἐξ ἐμέθεν ῥηθέντα (Parmenides B7).

314

Antique Authority?

rational autonomy with the respect reason commands from its adherents is already inscribed in philosophy's primal scene, the *kouros* obedient to the instruction to think himself through the incredible.

I must tread somewhat warily, so as to avoid the pratfall of paying august names inconsistent respect in the midst of cocking a snook at the idea of deference on the part of philosophers: for why am I conjuring with these Presocratics, if not because they are towering presences in the history of philosophy – which seems tantamount to an admission that they exert considerable authority over it? The way out lies in the realisation that while the likes of Heraclitus and Parmenides do indeed partially define the activity of philosophising, and accordingly set down what could count as doing well at philosophy, their constitutive definition remains very largely formal. To imitate their rational example is no more – or less – than to pledge one's allegiance to *logos*; without any further commitment to its deployment in their manner, let alone to substantive Heraclitean or Parmenidean doctrines, this emulation is not following in the tracks of seniority.

Not but that a would-be exclusive concentration on the rigorous discipline of impersonal *logos* is not subject to conspicuous lapses. Just consider some of the most prominent philosophical saints and sinners. Bristlingly ostentatious avoidance of the name 'Democritus' seems to bespeak a degree of theoretical repugnance which has spilled over into contemptuous hostility *ad hominem*: Plato gets quite personal over materialistic atomism. The unbeatable convenience of Democritus' angelic opposite number resides in the enigmatic character of the Socratic mission, whose plasticity, however, hardens all too easily into the static casts representative of the incompatible versions of the master espoused by the warring schools of his disciples, as witnessed, perhaps, by Aristippus' rebuke to the intolerant Plato, 'anyway our companion [Socrates] never expressed himself in that manner'. This report in Aristotle's *Rhetoric* (1398b30–3) is worth pausing over briefly. The anecdote features as an example of how one might discomfit an opponent through citation of a

Robert Wardy

prior judgement to flout which would be an embarrassment, on account of the precedent's authority: so Plato is chastised for his presumption of authority, in unpleasant contrast to 'our companion', who set the authoritative example – of unassuming modesty. The text runs 'as Aristippus reacted to Plato, who – as he imagined – had said something too professorially'; thus Aristotle, who elsewhere proclaims *amicus Plato, sed magis amica ueritas* – or words to that effect – is here careful not himself to endorse the criticism of Plato as overbearing.[6] The nasty problem with charismatics, philosophical or otherwise, is the innocent occasion they provide for the formation of noxiously repressive personality cults, whether among bickering Socratics or holier-than-thou Wittgensteinians. On the whole easier for working philosophers to accommodate are strawmen to jostle about dialectically ('Cartesian dualists' are the other, benighted lot), or streamlined figureheads handier for thinking with than unwieldy historical figures (for instance, the creative misprision which spawned Kripkenstein).

That philosophy and authority make awkward bedfellows is demonstrated most tellingly by a speaking silence. Research easily yields voluminous materials on the philosophical theme of political authority, but one looks in vain for the self-reflexive move: philosophers asking themselves what, if anything, would constitute authority within the philosophical sphere itself.[7] If Kantians have a positive fetish for invoking the tribunal of reason, its status as supreme arbiter would seem to originate, at least in part, from the conviction that rationality and impersonality go hand in hand. It is as if philosophers silently anticipate, in their own special case, the inevitable semantic

---

[6] ὥσπερ Ἀρίστιππος πρὸς Πλάτωνα ἐπαγγελτικώτερόν τι εἰπόντα, ὡς ᾤετο· "ἀλλὰ μὴν ὅ γ᾽ ἑταῖρος ἡμῶν", ἔφη, "οὐθὲν τοιοῦτον", λέγων τὸν Σωκράτη (*Rhetoric* 1398b30–3). Cf. τὴν παιδείαν οὐχ οἵαν τινὲς ἐπαγγελλόμενοί φασιν εἶναι τοιαύτην καὶ εἶναι (*Republic* 518b7–8): Plato hoist with his own petard?

[7] Some subtle discussion in the Christian tradition of the interplay between faith and reason furnishes an exception to this generalisation: see Augustine, *De utilitate credendi* 11.25, Aquinas, *Summa theologiae pars prima* q1 a8. As we shall see, a most interesting exception unalloyed by non-philosophical matter will come from an unanticipated quarter: Seneca.

Antique Authority?

degeneration of 'authoritative' into 'authoritarian', that they could only be bending the knee to a tyrant of the mind; as if on their own ground, they all should find this ringing declaration from Emma Goldman immensely congenial: 'anarchism urges man to think, to investigate, to analyse every proposition'.[8] Now one might have thought that, from the perspective of anarchist philosophy – that is, from what looks to be plain philosophy's point of view – nothing could appear more abhorrent than the reduction of its history to annotations embroidering a magisterial, antique theory. If that is surely how it looks, inspection of what he actually meant surprisingly shows that Whitehead was not at loggerheads with Goldman. Here is the actual, always unread context of that famous, or notorious, consignment of subsequent philosophical speculation to the bottom of the Platonic page: 'the scheme of interpretation here adopted can claim for each of its main positions the express authority of one, or the other, of some supreme master of thought ... But ultimately nothing rests on authority; the final court of appeal is intrinsic reasonableness. The safest general characterisation of the European philosophical tradition is that it consists of a series of footnotes to Plato. I do not mean the systematic scheme of thought which scholars have doubtfully extracted from his writings. I allude to the wealth of general ideas scattered through them.'[9] Hence, contrary to what one might well have predicted, subscription to the 'footnotes' picture does not entail subordination of one's own work to a master text for glossing: 'in one sense by stating my belief that the train of thought in these lectures is Platonic, I am doing no more than expressing the hope that it falls within the European tradition'.[10] Whitehead confesses no

---

[8] Goldman (2005) 56.

[9] Whitehead (1978) 39.

[10] Ibid. Cf. Frede, this volume, p.82 on Plato's school: 'that several other "superannuated" students [in addition to Aristotle] continued to work as members of the Academy, once their apprentice years were over and they developed philosophical ideas of their own that diverged from Plato's and sometimes were openly critical of them, is a strong witness not only to Plato's and his school's reputation, but also to the liberal spirit in which the school must have been organized and to the high level of discussion and research that prevailed within the institution'.

Robert Wardy

crippling inhibitions for even a rampant, totally uninhibited anarchist to disparage.

If we are willing to regard Whitehead as a revealing test case for philosophy's pronounced disinclination to brook authority, we might further be tempted to speculate that when Cassius Dio informs us that the Greek for 'auctoritas' is the transliterated 'αὐκτώριτας', he inadvertently teaches the particular lesson that anything like that Roman concept is quite alien to the mindset of anarchic Greek philosophy.[11] Contrariwise, Diogenes Laërtius the Greek triumphalist, insists that *all* non-Greeks cannot even manage a calque, but are obliged to transliterate φιλοσοφία (1.4)[12] – which is not to say, *pace* Diogenes, that one cannot inventively Romanise anarchism within reputable bounds, as Seneca testifies in his manifesto of intellectual liberty from the trammels of school precedent. According to his elegant political trope, in the first instance he would cleave to *exempla* rather than *praecepta*, showing himself to be an independent senator, rather than some biddable sectarian.[13] My response to Dio will be the seemingly wayward gambit of digging us in all the deeper, by conducting a brief excursion into some relatively contemporary epistemological theorising. The idea is to raise hopes of rendering a viable conception of philosophical authority more palatable, only to dash them. Now why would that manoeuvre be anything but a uselessly perverse exacerbation of the fix I am claiming we find ourselves

---

[11] ἑλληνίσαι γὰρ αὐτὸ καθάπαξ ἀδύνατόν ἐστι: *Roman History* 55.3. 'As the Greeks themselves admitted, *auctoritas* was a concept *inexpressible* in their own language'; then 'just because the Greek language *could not* express the notion of *auctoritas*, it does not follow that the phenomenon which it describes was absent from Greek philosophical schools' (Sedley (1997) 111, emphases added). Local ineffability is not in the frame: *pace* Sedley, 'the phenomenon which it describes' was not to be found in Greek philosophical schools before their decadence.

[12] Warren is properly sceptical ('the *purported* fact' (Warren (2014a)) 140, emphasis added).

[13] *De Otio* 2.1; then 'hoc Stoicis quoque placere ostendam, non quia mihi legem dixerim nihil contra dictum Zenonis Chrysippiue committere, sed quia res ipsa patitur me ire in illorum sententiam, quoniam si quis semper unius sequitur, non in curia sed in factione est' (3.1; and cf. *Epistulae Morales* 21.9 and 113.23). Horace had already phrased the bold generalisation, 'nullius addictus iurare in uerba magistri' (*Epistle* 1.1.14). These unbending Roman protestations to be pondered in conjunction with 'epistemology will not be truly socialised until it has been appropriately politicised' (Fricker (1998) 174).

Antique Authority?

in already? I am wanting to illuminate as vividly as I possibly can the extreme, pure asymmetry between philosophy's theoretical situation – maybe, indeed, its predicament – and how the land lies in a host of other pursuits of the mind – maybe, to chance my hand, in them all. I hope to evade the charge of time-wasting perversity on condition that I might achieve greater clarity on how, if at all, authentic philosophy might tolerate some curbing of its freest play.

Let us probe the potential implications of 'social epistemology', so-called. This ramified, well-entrenched movement credibly enough constructs a historical pedigree for itself with a remote starting point in the venerably Socratic task of scrutinising titles to τέχνη, but it really gained momentum during the latter decades of the twentieth century; remark the piquant title of an essay Anthony Quinton originally published in 1971: 'Authority and autonomy in knowledge'.[14] Essentially, social epistemology is a philosophical protest front which deprecates what it perceives as the unrealistic, overweening pretensions of the aspirant knower determined to go it alone; reform is initiated by the realistically modest recognition that people are actually embedded in supportive communities pooling epistemological resources. Replace Descartes meditating before the fire in arrogant isolation with Hume healthily out of his writing closet and chatting urbanely with the denizens of a coffee shop.

Here is the key move: the main channel for the circulation of intellectual commodities throughout a society is testimony, and its credentials are to be firmly validated. Publication of the landmark text by Coady[15] was described by Myles Burnyeat as 'an important event in philosophy'.[16] Testimony, so far from being the debased currency of weakly credulous believers, functions as the irreplaceable conduit for the stream of vital information between us who strive to know. There is indeed cheap hearsay, lapsing into the dregs of idle rumour and paltry

---

[14] Quinton (1982).
[15] Coady (1992)
[16] On the book's dust jacket.

319

Robert Wardy

gossip for the delectation of the gullibly curious mob – ἄκριτα φῦλα with a vengeance! But, by the same token, we all of us rightfully assume that our better informants are, by and large, trustworthy. The crucial claim so far as the prospects for reconciling philosophy's demand for cognitive autonomy with tolerance of a proper authority internal to it is that the 'all of us' dependent on what we are told includes not only children schooled by adults or the uneducated adult laity, but also true experts reliant on input from their colleagues in other departments for material the value of which they are obliged to trust in order to pursue their own researches. In a pair of justifiably celebrated, much-discussed articles,[17] John Hardwig drives the point home as forcibly as possible. To cut to the quick: 'scientists, researchers, and scholars are, sometimes at least, knowers, and all of these knowers stand on each other's shoulders in the way expressed by the formula: B knows that A knows that p'; and '... we can see how dependence on other experts pervades *any* complex field of research when we recognise that most footnotes that cite references are appeals to *authority*. And when these footnotes are used to establish premises for the study, they involve the author in layman–expert relationships even within his own pursuit of knowledge.'[18]

The conclusion that 'scientists, researchers, and scholars' are good company to keep comes easily: whyever presume that philosophers are the oddly independent thinkers exempt from the reassuring duty to trust their fellows quite liberally – and, at the ideal limit, to have succeeded in happily reposing their confidence in legitimate philosophical authority? But, as it happens, the dismissive presumption is perfectly well grounded. Hardwig makes use of two kinds of striking example, drawn from 'big science' and mathematics. In both, the research is necessarily corporate: because the sheer quantity of the data to be assimilated is beyond any single individual's capability; or because numerous recondite specialisms are in cooperative play, and control of this formidable multiplicity must be parcelled

[17] Hardwig (1985) and (1991).
[18] Hardwig (1985) 345 and 348, emphases added.

Antique Authority?

out; or for both kinds of reason. Therefore '... we must also say that someone can know "vicariously" – *i.e.* without possessing the evidence for the truth of what he knows, *perhaps without even fully understanding what he knows*'.[19] Lack of understanding is the nub of the matter: the contentedly interdependent co-workers of the relatively new theory of knowledge might well have little or no real insight into the meaning of what comes together with their own contribution from other nodes within the distributed network of acquired knowledge and ongoing discovery. After his cautious denial that full understanding is a common possession, Hardwig offers this alternative: 'if the conclusion is unpalatable, another is possible. Perhaps that *p* is known, not by any one person, but by the *community* ... The community is not reducible to a class of individuals, for no one individual and no one individually knows that *p*.'[20] However, it is revealing that he phrases this option in terms of something like a group mind which houses pooled knowledge, not full-blown understanding. Alvin Goldman, the doyen of social epistemology, is resistant to the radical tenor of Hardwig's proposal: 'the critical point Hardwig ignores is the possibility of knowing *that* a specialist is an expert without knowing *how* or *why* he is an expert ...'.[21] One knows very well what to make of the pertinent, expanded adaptation of this riposte: 'do not overlook one philosopher's capacity for understanding that another might serve as an expert on some question, despite incomprehension of the grounds on which that fellow philosopher deserves to be invested with authority'.[22] Nothing here to ignore.

[19] Hardwig (1985) 348, emphasis added.

[20] Hardwig (1985) 349.

[21] Goldman (1999) 270; and cf. his use of the tactic of 'indirect argumentative justification' (Goldman (2001)).

[22] At first blush John Rawls might seem to be just such a philosopher: '... I have learnt from Burton Dreben, who made W. V. Quine's view clear to me and persuaded me that the notions of meaning and analyticity play no essential role in moral theory as I conceive of it' (Rawls (1971) xi). Does Rawls not instantiate Hardwig's model, since the expert within the sealed space of ethical theory takes on trust the word of the semanticist that the Quinean theory (so much Greek to the ethicist) luckily has no bearing on his own technical concerns? No: that would be a travesty of the Rawls–Dreben relationship. I presume that the latter *persuaded* the former through argument which Rawls could follow and verify, despite his specialising in ethics

Robert Wardy

Here is Goldman's 'rough' definition: 'person A is an authority in subject S if and only if A knows more propositions in S, or has a higher degree of knowledge of propositions in S, than almost anyone else'.[23] This seems an unexceptionable shot at the concept; but the notion that it might be applicable to philosophy is simply grotesque. The superior philosopher is not one who knows more philosophical propositions – for starters, there is no agreed criterion for their very identification, so *a fortiori* no consensus on what philosophy there is to be known (even if we allow the idea of '*knowing* philosophy' to pass muster just for now). Goldman's second disjunct is more to the point, if we might equate 'has a higher degree of knowledge of propositions in philosophy' with something along the lines of 'possesses a more fecund understanding of philosophical propositions'; but since, as I have already said, which assertions should be admitted as philosophical and eligible for our evaluation is itself an abiding puzzle, the claim that A is a philosophical 'authority' always remains vacuously presumptuous. Since I fail to see that any other acceptable analysis would scotch these fatal difficulties, I propose that we should consequently not hesitate to resolve that there are *no* philosophical authorities or experts, full stop:[24] philosophy is nothing whatsoever like a knowledge-bank, accounts wherein are richer or poorer. Correlatively, since '... to teach *authoritatively* is primarily to declare the things one is teaching,

---

rather than logic. Philosophers incompetent to do likewise beyond the borders of their specialisms (if they have any) are just that: incompetent philosophers. (With thanks to Chris Bobonich).

[23] Goldman (1999) 268.

[24] At any rate the *Platonic* Socrates might beg to differ: '... when someone *lacking expertise about arguments* is confident that some argument is *sound* ...' (... ἐπειδάν τις πιστεύσῃ λόγῳ τινὶ ἀληθῆ εἶναι ἄνευ τῆς περὶ τοὺς λόγους τέχνης ... *Phaedo* 90b6–7). Since the context is Socrates inveighing against the temptation to give in to misology, maybe one could translate 'valid' rather than 'sound' and tone the implication down to there being skill at pure logic, rather than philosophical authority as such. However, since hapless arguers degenerate into misologists as a consequence of the repeated discovery that what they had incorrectly taken for good arguments are actually bad ones, the weaker construal seems less plausible: presumably exposure to the *facts* is what brings the error of these vulnerably inexpert people to light, and that is easier to understand as the way things really are giving the lie to an immaculately derived conclusion, rather than laying bare some inferential defect. If that is right, so much the worse for this version of Socrates.

Antique Authority?

demanding attention and mastery of what one says from one's pupil',[25] we had best proceed with great circumspection, as we philosophers attempt to train our charges. The irony might just be that a social epistemology tailored more neatly than its antecedents to the shapes of non-philosophical thinking, both lay and expert, does not begin to fit philosophy itself. After all, Hume did spend much time all on his own in that writing closet, staring at the quires of notes on his desk. If I seem to be suggesting that interchange on the topic 'authors and authorities in ancient philosophy' might not prove very fruitful, at least draw immediate comfort from the proud comparative hypothesis one might well propound: that no cognitive playing field is more level than philosophy's arena; and I promise to finish up with a much more robustly optimistic suggestion.

What is the genesis of the deformative, pathological delusion that philosophy admits authorities to whose rulings we lesser folk must submit? I catch the scent of an alliance probably less than holy, if surely not a downright conspiracy, between paraphilosophical movements such as Pythagoreanism first and foremost, and those eager to compose a history for philosophy.[26] On the one hand, there are the pseudo-rational, mathematical cultists chiming *ipse dixit*, indignantly snatching up prestigious intellectual goods from philosophical upstarts for attribution to their guru. This is the original incarnation of the sinister tendency to indulge in authoritarian mystification which has accompanied philosophy from its inception – whether as a matter of unfortunate, brute historical contingency, or in consequence of an innate malaise prompting us to relinquish our autonomy, I cannot say. On the other hand, there are those keen on composition of an explanatory narrative: that their story of how philosophy came to be is strung along lines of supposed influence imposed by leader on followers who themselves grow into leadership to spawn their own followers, and so forth, is well-nigh unavoidable. Persistent continuities are very

---

[25] Anscombe (1981) 44, emphasis added.
[26] Warren (2014a) 133: 'Philosophy, a notoriously difficult practice to define, attracts organisers and history-writers.'

much to the taste of such intellectual historians.[27] Compound these redoubtable inclinations, and philosophy will look like an authoritative system, or perhaps a collection of competitive systems vying for victory in the contest over conclusive legitimation. My guarded hope is that the makings for an antidote to this compound toxin might prove accessible in our Platonic–Whiteheadian heritage. First, take note of Plato's way with the Pythagoreans. If their invocation in the dialogues is never less than respectful, and sometimes reverent,[28] Plato's borrowings from them are, I think, always underpinned by his own, transformative argumentation, such as to dissipate any impression that he is in thrall to Pythagoras. Second, what are his fulminations against sophistry, if not, in large part, a vehement warning not to be beguiled by counterfeit expertise? But third, some of the rationale for both resorting to the dialogue form and postulating a transcendental reality is plausibly enough to be found in the firmest dedication to the detachment of authority from any personal connotations. Aristotle, fierce friend of the implacable truth, in arguing against what might smack of his teacher's mistaken authority keeps faith with ideal Platonism.

There are times and places at which any effort to eliminate authority would prove at best futile, at worst crazily reckless. It should be blindingly obvious that Anscombe's description of authoritatively declarative pedagogy applies unqualifiedly to how we raise our children – that is, our very young children, endowed with an only embryonic rational faculty. But even here, where the imposition of authority is welcome, qualifications soon set in: for the good parental teacher is always on the lookout to exploit opportunities as they arise for promoting an internalised understanding of the information we seek to convey. It is a dull child that does not hunger after the reason why; philosophers are the neotenous questioners of

---

[27] A. A. Long, this volume, p.243: 'By calling them [Aristo, Herillus and Dionysius] "the dissidents", Diogenes again underlines Zeno's authority for the Stoic apostolic tradition.'

[28] Unless, that is, they do not emerge unscathed from the blistering assault on harmonic theorists in *Republic* 7 (530dff.).

Antique Authority?

others and themselves permanently discontent with the deadly conversation stopper, 'because I told you so'. My recalcitrance sits altogether comfortably with the assurance that plenty of fine philosophy has been done within the constraints of non-philosophical dogma taken as gospel, or otherwise felt to be authoritative – 'authoritative', that is, from an outlook not philosophy's own. Analogously, nothing prevents plenty of wonderful Hellenistic school philosophy from keeping within the doctrinal limits dictated by how the perceived theoretical commitments of the school's founder manifest themselves (put aside the obnoxious imputation that Epicureans slavishly idolise a swindling anti-god). But I intend no more than a careful analogy: this concession does not further concede that e.g. a Stoic who has signed up to Zeno's theories precisely insofar as he is persuaded of their soundness bows to Zeno's 'authority', in the proper sense of the word.[29] Stoics strenuously cultivate λόγος, and the λόγος is ownerless.[30] Here is an opportunity to factor in Cicero's finely judged Academic *non*-commitment, his unfettered picking and choosing between heterogeneous theses on the basis of how he assesses them now.[31] Vibrant philosophy is healthily stimulated by the concoction of splendid ingenuities. Nothing more instructive than the plain nonsense of trying to elevate Diodorus Cronus into a philosophical authority – he's far too good for such shabby treatment!

To recur briefly to Aristotle's evocative anecdote: does the professorial Plato show us nothing more uplifting than how

---

[29] Baltzly (2014) 794 is spot on: 'members of the Stoa might argue that the views that they advocated were consistent with those of Zeno, but quoting Zeno was not an argument for the *truth* of a view – only its right to be called a *Stoic* view'. And *pace* Boys-Stones, this volume, p.184: '... every one of the Hellenistic schools subscribed, ostensibly at least, to the authority of their founder. No Stoic, for example, is ever caught suggesting that the founder of Stoicism, Zeno, was *wrong* about something: on the contrary, a Stoic might go to some lengths to show how their own view was consistent with that of Zeno'.

[30] Or reversed, but to the same effect: *quod uerum est, meum est*; with *non sumus sub rege*; *sibi quisque se uindicat* (Seneca, *Epistulae Morales* 22.11 and 33.4; and cf. *De uita beata* 3.2.3).

[31] This is a simplification. Schofield's sophisticated chapter in this volume convincingly argues that in some Ciceronian texts '... *ratio* and *auctoritas* need to be seen not as alternatives but as mutually implicated' (p.294).

we are bound to fail Socrates, failing to be Socrates? In some bleak moods I find myself minded to suspect that the sorry affair of philosophy is diminished to not even so much as servile notes to a Platonic master text, but rather abased to self-stultifying mimicry of that inimitable Socratic voice, muffled, if not quite stifled, in the inimical antiquarian environment of the Roman empire, under which decadent Platonists were second to none in masking the real ingenuity they should, by rights, have gladly flaunted, as neutral exposition of invaluable truths brought to light in canonical texts. A destructive lust for inherited authority centrally motivates the whole commentarial movement, both Platonic and Aristotelian, whose goal is the construction, *not* the discovery, of coherent corpora from what, in its heyday, was magnificently contingent enquiry. These are thinkers on the verge of succumbing to the dead hand of what they imagine the motionless philosophical past to have been.[32]

Darkest before the dawn: high time to puncture what one would fervently hope to be the *reductio ad absurdum* that philosophy effectively *ended* its brief career with that fellow Socrates![33] We shall arrive at my upbeat, if inconclusive, conclusion by getting to grips with the evidently pressing question: how are we to square the glaring absence from philosophy of the expertise dominant elsewhere with the reliable presence of decent, well-distributed competence, and the exceptional efflorescence of true philosophical greatness? An answer to that would also bring in its train a solution to the problem of how the powerfully old might serve as our

---

[32] Or all the way there: 'Simplicius ... allows that a Platonist like himself will, of course, treat Plato as completely infallible' (Sedley (1999) 110); with 'we know that its [the authority of Platonic dialogues] apotheosis – or apocolocyntosis, depending on your taste for Neoplatonism – is at hand when Proclus says at the beginning of the *Platonic Theology* that Plato's philosophy was revealed by beneficent higher beings' (Baltzly (2014) 793).

[33] This hits the nail on the head: 'if Socrates belongs in a volume on Authors and Authorities, that is because, in line with the old slogan that "for any one pair of opposites, there is a single branch of knowledge", he can illuminate philosophical authorship and philosophical authority by being so distant from them both' (Denyer, this volume, p.41).

326

Antique Authority?

venerable touchstones for excellence, rather than collapsing into outmoded rubbish.

Philosophical heroes are intellectually provocative: not in the superficial way of some strutting sophist, but profoundly so, in their instigation to think dialectically.[34] The best of us are gadflies who sting the remainder into adopting the true Socratic stance despite its vertiginous discomfort – and on occasion we switch and swap about.[35] Positioned so precariously, we revel in an exhilarated intellectual openness, a plasticity which bestows probationary investigative authority on what is our favourite tack – for the time being, since we are not only always disposed to correct it, but also do indeed change course, and often.[36] Even Lorraine Code, the most ardent advocate of a modestly provisional, communitarian epistemology with whom I am acquainted, permits herself this uncharacteristic flight: 'rare individuals have the insight, understanding, and courage to resist the stronghold of tradition: such were the philosophers who were able to bear the pain and loneliness of turning their back on the images in Plato's cave and facing the light, however unbearable. These individuals can urge others to follow; hence the normative value of the ideal *character*, the genuine exemplar of intellectual virtue.'[37] If I achieve anything, it will be to have heightened our awareness of the complexities of

---

[34] Code (1987) 249: 'Often one consults authorities intending to believe them, but often, too, one wants to know what another person thinks in order to know what one does not want to think. The role of experts sometimes is to be agents of articulation, expressers of points of view that they can make clearer. Whether one is inclined to agree or not is sometimes beside the point.' This is intriguing, because it is also, and often, the role of philosophers to serve as non-expert, contrarian 'agents of articulation'. (A. G. Long, this volume, p.58: 'Socrates did not put his philosophy into writing, and he is not straightforwardly an authority, at least if authorities are thought to possess knowledge or expertise'). Code's thesis possibly gestures at the whereabouts of the closest point of approach between expertise and philosophy – and revealingly demonstrates how far they nevertheless remain from intersection.

[35] I am persuaded by Denyer that knowledge of an interlocutor's revealed ignorance pooled by dialectical partners in a Socratic conversation permits us to '... revere him for his philosophical expertise in bringing about such demonstration. But if this is his sole philosophical expertise, we cannot revere him as a philosophical authority' (Denyer, this volume, p.57).

[36] Robinson (1953) 70: '... the word "dialectic" had a strong tendency in Plato to mean "the ideal method, whatever that may be"'.

[37] Code (1987) 251.

327

Robert Wardy

what might be involved in 'following' the example of a break-away philosophical hero, some Moses, as it were.[38]

I conclude with a last crack at what is intended as helpful articulation, to propel us some distance beyond the sentimentalism of grand intellectual exploits I have just now been peddling. I conjecture that while it has no space for authority as such, philosophy does experience a crying need for an intellectual counterpart to the excellent conduct of Aristotelian φρόνιμοι in human affairs. I introduced this chapter with some discussion of paradigms of *generic* intellectual virtue: so what about specifically *philosophical* virtue? Most sketchily, being really good at philosophy entails the exercise of refined constructive and destructive talents: the superb practitioner both generates a profusion of unexpected, novel arguments which disclose new vistas, and has an uncommon ability to dissect arguments already in the philosophical domain with a view to detecting where fallacy lurks.[39] Since philosophy is no knowledge bank, it does not make readily evident cumulative progress; I suspend judgement on whether it makes real advances on any major front. Overarching philosophical questions define its epochs; the defining philosophers are those who, in addressing the questions of their time and place, bear witness to rationality.[40] Much too vague to prove helpful? Recollect two relevant claims Aristotle makes for φρόνιμοι: they grasp how things are and should be by means of enhanced perception, not amenable to stipulative prescription; and we others improve by dint of imaginatively projecting ourselves into our best approximation of wisdom.[41] Such projection might well

---

[38] *Qui alium sequitur, nihil inuenit, immo nec quaerit*; and *Non ergo sequor priores? Facio, sed permitto mihi et inuenire aliquid et mutare et relinquere. Non seruio illis, sed adsentior* (Seneca *Epistulae Morales* 33.11 and 80.1).

[39] I am looking to adumbrate a high-powered variant of what Aristotle calls σύνεσις.

[40] Plato once more: he '… was, then, treated as an authority in his life and beyond his life, an authority one could haggle with, but nevertheless an important, if not *the* most important authority' (Frede, this volume, p.89); and 'a critical discussion of Platonic views was not the exception but rather the rule in the Academy' (ibid. p.98).

[41] Might there be some sort of poetic parallel? Poets of genius (those whom Harold Bloom in *The Anxiety of Influence* (authoritatively?) denominated the 'strong(est)') cast a spell over their peers, and their legacy is a defining *way* to compose verse. Furthermore, their influence is perhaps felt most keenly within the realm of

Antique Authority?

be catalysed by the perusal of antique literary remains through which philosophical ghosts retain some measure of their unsettling eloquence. Thus my last suggestion: the most we can say is that accomplished philosophers are equipped with acute mental vision enabling them to see logical contours to which others, left to their own devices, remain blind, and hypersensitive noses for argumentative rot. All manner of benefit flows from these inexpertly virtuous non-authorities to the philosophical community; to pursue the philosophical life in such exceptional company is the greatest of fortunes.[42]

poetry as a metrical craft (think of Virgil): is this an analogue of the sure-footed dialectician's navigation through the technicalities of complex argumentation? If so, the analogue may be only partial: ambitious Bloomian poets who themselves ascend to the pantheon do so through rebellious 'misprision' of their magnetic forbears, while it would be awfully foolish of philosophers to re-embrace an unmasked fallacy. Another possible, negative parallel might be between baneful 'school' philosophy and the dismal products of creative writing workshops. (With thanks to Rachel Briggs.)

[42] With warm thanks to Marina Frasca-Spada, Brian Fuchs, Stephen Menn, James Warren and, especially, Brad Inwood. The audiences at the original *Sedfest* conference and the philosophy colloquium of Stanford University helped me to sharpen my ideas. I have never encountered a Stoic Sage; but I have been so fortunate as to live in a fellowship in the habit of talking with the great dead, and which boasts a paragon at once ethical and dialectical, whose name is David Sedley. This chapter was written in the trying circumstances of my father's death, and is dedicated to him. His judgement on David Sedley was that he enjoyed remarkable tranquillity, which I should do my best to emulate. If that is not me, I have nevertheless gleaned as much as I could from both their examples.

REFERENCES

Ackrill, J. L. (1963) *Aristotle's Categories and De Interpretatione*, Oxford

Algra, K. (2000) 'The treatise of Cleomedes and its critique of Epicurean cosmology', in M. Erler (ed.) *Epikureismus in der späten Republik under der Kaiserzeit. Akten der 2. Tagung der Karl-und-Gertrud-Abel-Stiftung vom 30. September–3. Oktober 1998 in Würzburg*, Stuttgart: 164–89

(2002) 'Zeno of Citium and Stoic cosmology', in T. Scaltsas and A. Mason (eds.) *The Philosophy of Zeno*, Larnaka: 155–85

(2016) 'The Academic origins of Stoic cosmo-theology and the physics of Antiochus of Ascalon - some notes on the evidence', in Y. Liebersohn, I. Ludlam, and A. Edelheit (eds.) *For a Skeptical Peripatetic. Festschrift in Honour of John Glucker*, Sankt Augustin: 158–76

Annas, J. (1976) *Aristotle Metaphysics, Books M and N*, Oxford

(1988) *Arisotle's Metaphysics, Books M and N*, Oxford

Annas, J. and Rowe, C. (eds.) (2002) *New Perspectives on Plato*, Cambridge, MA

Anscombe, G. E. M. (1981: originally published 1962) 'Authority in morals', in Anscombe G. E. M. (ed.) *Ethics, Religion and Politics, Collected Philosophical Papers*, vol. III, Oxford: 43–50

Arrighetti, G. (1970) *Epicuro: Opere* (2nd edn), Florence

Asmis, E. (1984) *Epicurus' Scientific Method*, Ithaca

Babut, D. (2005) 'Sur les *dieux* d'Épicure', *Elenchos* 26: 79–110

Bailey, C. (1947) *Titi Lucreti Cari De Rerum Natura Libri Sex*, Oxford

Bailey, D. (2005) 'Logic and music in Plato's *Phaedo*', *Phronesis* 50: 95–115

Balsdon, J. P. V. D. (1960) 'Auctoritas, dignitas, otium', *The Classical Quarterly* 10: 43–50

Baltes, M. (1999) 'Plato's school, the Academy', *Hermathena* 155: 7–28, 1993, repr. in *Dianoêmata – Kleine Schriften zu Platon und zum Platonismus*, Stuttgart: 249–74

Baltussen, H. (2000) *Theophrastus Against the Presocratics and Plato: Peripatetic Dialectic in the De Sensibus*, Leiden

(2008) *Philosophy and Exegesis in Simplicius. The Methodology of a Commentator*, London

(2015) 'Ancient philosophers on the sense of smell', in M. Bradley (ed.) *Smell and the Ancient Senses*, London: 30–45

Baltzly, D. (2014) 'Plato's authority and the formation of textual communities', *Classical Quarterly* 64: 793–807

References

Baraz, Y. (2012) *A Written Republic. Cicero's Philosophical Politics*, Princeton

Barnes, J. (1982) *The Presocratic Philosophers*, London and New York

    ed. (1984) *Complete Works of Aristotle. The Revised Oxford Translation* (2 vols.), Princeton

    (1988) 'Scepticism and relativity', *Philosophical Studies* 32: 1–31

    (1989) 'Antiochus of Ascalon', in J. Barnes and M. Griffin (eds.), *Philosophia Togata I*, Oxford: 51–96

Bees, R. (2011) *Zenons Politeia*, Leiden

Blanchard, B. (1939) *The Nature of Thought*, London

Blom, H. van der (2010) *Cicero's Role Models. The Political Strategies of a Newcomer*, Oxford

Bloom, H. (1973) *The Anxiety of Influence: A Theory of Poetry*, Oxford

Bodéüs, R. (2001) *Aristote: Les Catégories. Traduction et notes*, Paris

Bollack, M. (1975) *La raison de Lucrèce*, Paris

Boltz, W. G. (1993) 'Lao tzu: Tao te ching', in M. Loewe (ed.): 269–92

Bonazzi, M. (2013a) 'Pythagoreanizing Aristotle: Eudorus and the systematization of Platonism', in M. Schofield (ed.): 160–86

    (2013b) 'Eudorus of Alexandria and the "Pythagorean" Pseudepigrapha', in G. Cornelli, R. McKirahan and C. Macris (eds.), *On Pythagoreanism*, Berlin: 385–404

Bosanquet, B. (1911) *Logic, or the Morphology of Knowledge*, vol. II, Oxford

Bowen, A. C. and Todd, R. B. (2004) *Cleomedes' Lectures on Astronomy. A Translation of The Heavens with an Introduction and Commentary*, Berkeley

Boys-Stones, G. R. (2001) *Post-Hellenistic Philosophy. A Study of Its Development from the Stoics to Origen*, Oxford

    (2004) 'Phaedo of Elis and Plato on the soul', *Phronesis* 49: 1–23

Bradley, F. H. (1897) *Appearance and Reality: A Metaphysical Essay*, Oxford

Brenk, F. E. (2005) 'Plutarch's Middle-Platonic God: about to enter (or remake) the Academy', in F. Graf, H. G. Kippenberg and L. E. Sullivan (eds.) *Religionsgeschichtliche Versuche und Vorarbeiten*, Berlin: 28–49

Brisson, L. (1997) 'Perception sensible et raison dans le *Timée*', in T. Calvo and L. Brisson (eds.) *Interpreting the Timaeus-Critias: Proceedings of the IV Symposium Platonicum*, Sankt Anton: 307–16

    (1999) 'Plato's theory of sense perception in the *Timaeus*: How it Works and What it Means', in J. J. Cleary and G. M. Gurtler (eds.) *Proceedings of the Boston Area Colloquium in Ancient Philosophy* 13, Leiden: 147–85

Brittain, C. F. (2001) *Philo of Larissa: The Last of the Academic Sceptics*, Oxford

    (2006) *Cicero: On Academic Scepticism*, Indianapolis

Broadie, S. and Rowe, C. (2002) *Aristotle: Nicomachean Ethics. Translation, Introduction, and Commentary*, Oxford

References

Broadie, S. (2003) 'Aristotelian piety', *Phronesis* 48: 54–70

(2012) *Nature and Divinity in Plato's Timaeus*, Cambridge

Brooks, E. B. and Brooks, A. T. (1998) *The Original Analects: Sayings of Confucius and His Successors*, New York

Brouwer, R. (2014) *The Stoic Sage*, Cambridge

Brown, E. (2012) 'The unity of the soul in Plato's *Republic*', in R. Barney, T. Brennan and C. Brittain (eds.), *Plato and the Divided Self*, Cambridge: 53–74

Brunschwig, J. (2002) 'Zeno between Kition and Athens', in T. Scaltsas and A. S. Mason (eds.) *The Philosophy of Zeno*, Larnaca: 11–28

Bryan, J. (2012) *Likeness and Likelihood in the Presocratics and Plato*, Cambridge

Burkert, W. (1972) *Lore and Science in Ancient Pythagoreanism*, Cambridge, MA

Burnet, J. (ed.) (1993) *Platonis Opera*, vol. IV, Oxford

Burnyeat, M. (1982) 'The origin of non-deductive inference', in J. Brunschwig, M. Burnyeat and M. Schofield (eds.) *Science and Speculation: Studies in Hellenistic Theory and Practice*, Cambridge: 193–238

Butterfield, D. J. (2008) 'Three Lucretian emendations', *AAntHung* 48: 351–64

(2013) *The Early Textual History of Lucretius' De rerum natura*, Cambridge

(2014) *'Lucretius auctus*? The question of interpolation in *De rerum natura'*, in J. Martínez (ed.) *Fakes and Forgers of Classical Literature: Ergo decipiatur!*, Leiden: 15–42

Caizzi, F. D. (1993) 'The porch and the garden: Early Hellenistic images of the philosophical life', in A. W. Bulloch, E. S. Gruen, A. A. Long and A. Stewart (eds.) *Images & Ideologies: Self-Definition in the Hellenistic World*, Berkeley and Los Angeles: 303–29

Case, T. (1910) 'Aristotle' *Encyclopaedia Britannica* 2: 501–22

(1925) 'The development of Aristotle', *Mind* 34: 80–6

Castañeda, H. (1972) 'Plato's *Phaedo* theory of relations', *Journal of Philosophical Logic* 1, 467–80

(1978) 'Plato's relations, not essences or accidents, at *Phaedo* 102b2–d2', *Canadian Journal of Philosophy*: 8: 39–53

(1982) 'Leibniz and Plato's Phaedo theory of relations and predication', in M. Hooker (ed.) *Leibniz Critical and Interpretative Essays*, Manchester: 124–59

Centrone, B. (2014) 'The pseudo-Pythagorean writings', in C. A. Huffman (ed.): 315–40

Cerri, G. (2011) 'The astronomical section in Parmenides' poem', in N. Cordero (ed.) *Parmenides Venerable and Awesome*, Las Vegas: 81–94

Cherniss, H. F. (1935) *Aristotle's Criticism of Presocratic Philosophy*, Baltimore, MD

(1945) *The Riddle of the Early Academy*, Berkeley

333

References

(1962) *Aristotle's Criticism of Plato and the Academy*, vol. I (2 vols.), reprint New York

Chiaradonna, R. (2009) 'Autour d'Eudore. Les débuts de l'exégèse des Catégories dans le moyen platonisme', in M. Bonazzi and J. Opsomer (eds.) *The Origins of the Platonic System. Platonisms of the Early Empire and Their Philosophical Contexts*, Leuven: 89–111

Clay, D. (1986) 'The cults of *Epicurus*', *Cronache Ercolanesi* 16: 12–28

Coady, C. A. J. (1992) *Testimony: A Philosophical Study*, Oxford

Code, L. (1987) *Epistemic Responsibility*, London

Coxon, A. D. (2009) *The Fragments of Parmenides: A Critical Text with Introduction and Translations, the Ancient Testimonia and a Commentary* (rev. and exp. edn, ed. R. D. McKirahan), Las Vegas

Crubellier, M. (2012) 'The doctrine of forms under critique – part II', in C. Steel (ed.) *Aristotle's Metaphysics Alpha*, Oxford: 297–334

Cullen, C. (2007) 'Actors, networks and "disturbing spectacles" in institutional science: 2nd century Chinese debates on astronomy', *Antiquorum Philosophia* 1: 237–67

Curd, P. (1998) *The Legacy of Parmenides*, Princeton

Davies, J. (1718) *M. Tullii Ciceronis De Natura Deorum Libri Tres*, Cambridge

De Vogel, C. J. (1965) 'Did Aristotle ever accept Plato's theory of transcendent ideas? Problems around a new edition of the *Protrepticus*', *Archiv für Geschichte der Philosophie* 47: 261–98

Deman, T. (1942) *Le Témoignage d'Aristote Sur Socrate*, Paris

Denyer, N. (2007) 'The *Phaedo*'s final argument', in D. Scott (ed.), *Maieusis: Essays in Ancient Philosophy in Honour of Myles Burnyeat*, Oxford: 87–96

des Places, É. (1973) (ed.), *Numénius. Fragments*, Paris

Diano, C. (1974) *Epicuri ethica et epistulae*, Florence

Diels, H. (1879) *Doxographi Graeci*, Berlin

(1917) *Philodemus über die Götter, Drittes Buch*, Abhandlungen der Königlich Preussischen Akademie der Wissenschaften 4, 6

Dillon, J. M. (1969) 'A date for the death of Nicomachus of Gerasa?', *Classical Quarterly* 19: 274–5

(1996) *The Middle Platonists. 80 B.C. to A.D. 220*, rev. edn with a new afterword, New York

(1997) 'Iamblichus' Νοερὰ Θεωρία of Aristotle's *Categories*', *Syllecta Classica* 8: 65–78

(2003a) *The Heirs of Plato: A Study of the Old Academy (347–274 BC)*, Oxford

(2003b) 'The Timaeus in the Old Academy', in G. Reydams-Schils (ed.) *Plato's Timaeus as a Cultural Icon*, Notre Dame, IN: 80–94

Dirlmeier, F. (1960) *Aristoteles, Nikomachische Ethik. Übersetzung und Erläuterungen*, Berlin

References

Dodds, E. R. (1960) 'Numenius and Ammonius', in *Les Sources de Plotin* = *Entretiens sur l'Antiquité classique* 5, Geneva: 1–32

Dorandi, T. (1991) *Filodemo. Storia dei filosofi. Platone e l'Academia*, Naples

Duncombe, M. (2012) 'Plato's absolute and relative categories at *Sophist* 255c14', *Ancient Philosophy* 32: 77–86

   (2013) 'The greatest difficulty at *Parmenides* 133c–134e and Plato's relative terms', *Oxford Studies in Ancient Philosophy* 45: 43–61

   (2015) 'Aristotle's two accounts of relatives in *Categories* 7', *Phronesis* 60: 436–61

Düring, I. (1961) *Aristotle in the Ancient Biographical Tradition*, Göteborg

   (1966) 'Did Aristotle ever accept Plato's theory of transcendent ideas?', *Archiv für Geschichte der Philosophie* 48: 312–26

Dyck, A. R. (2003) *Cicero, De Natura Deorum I*, Cambridge

Eichholz, D. E. (1965) *Theophrastus: De Lapidibus*, Oxford

Erler, M. (2001) 'Epicurus as *deus mortalis*: *homoiosis theôi* and Epicurean Self-Cultivation', in D. Frede and A. Laks (eds.) *Traditions of Theology: Studies in Hellenistic Theology, Its Background and Aftermath*, Leiden: 159–81

Erler, M. and Schofield, M. (1999) 'Epicurean ethics', in K. Algra, J. Barnes, J. Mansfeld, and M. Schofield (eds.) *The Cambridge History of Hellenistic philosophy*, Cambridge: 617–41

Erler, M., Schorn, S., and Döring, K. (eds.) (2005) *Pseudoplatonica: Akten des Kongresses zu den Pseudoplatonica vom 6.–9. Juli 2003 in Bamberg* (= *Philosophie der Antike*. Bd. 22), Stuttgart

Essler, H. (2011a) *Glückselig und unsterblich: epikureische Theologie bei Cicero und Philodem (mit einer Edition von Pherc. 152/157, Kol. 8–10)*, Basle

   (2011b) 'Cicero's use and abuse of Epicurean theology', in J. Fish and K. R. Saunders (eds.), *Epicurus and the Epicurean Tradition*, Cambridge: 129–51

Ewing, A. C. (1934) *Idealism: A critical survey*, London

Falcon, A. (2012) *Aristotelianism in the First Century BCE*, Cambridge

Fauth, W. (1973) '*Divus Epicurus*. Zur Problemgeschichte philosophischer Religiosität bei Lukrez', *ANRW* I.4: 205–22

Ferguson, J. (1990) 'Epicureanism under the Roman Empire', *ANRW* II.36.4: 2261–327

Ferrari, F. (1995) *Dio, idee e materia. La struttura del cosmos in Plutarco di Cheronea*, Naples

   (2012) 'L'esegesi medioplatonica del Timeo: metodi, finalità, risultati', in F. Celia and A. Ulacco (eds.) *Il Timeo. Esegi greche, arabe, latine*, Pisa: 81–131

Fine, G. (1993) *On Ideas. Aristotle's Criticism of Plato's Theory of Forms*, Oxford

   (ed.) (1999) *Plato 1: Metaphysics and Epistemology*, Oxford

References

(2008) 'Does Socrates claim to know that he knows nothing?', *Oxford Studies in Ancient Philosophy* 35: 49–88

Fitzgerald, W. (1850) *Selections from the Nicomachean Ethics of Aristotle*, Dublin

Flinterman, J.-J. (2014) 'Pythagoreans in Rome and Asia Minor around the turn of the common era', in C. A. Huffman (ed.): 341–59

Ford, A. (2011) *Aristotle as Poet: The Song for Hermias and Its Contexts*, New York and Oxford

Forrester, J. W. (1974) 'Arguments and (*sic*) able man colud (*sic*) refute: *Parmenides* 133b–134e', *Phronesis* 19: 233–7

Fortenbaugh, W. W., Huby, P. M., Sharples, R. W. and Gutas, D. (eds.) (1992) *Theophrastus of Eresus: Sources for his Life, Writings, Thought and Influence* (2 vols.), Leiden

Fraser, P. M. (1972) *Ptolemaic Alexandria* (3 vols.), Oxford

Frede, D. (2012) 'The Doctrine of Forms under critique – Part I', in C. Steel (ed.) *Aristotle's Metaphysics Alpha*, Oxford: 265–96

Frede, M. (1987a) 'Numenius', *ANRW* II.36.2: 1034–75

(1987b) 'The title, unity, and authenticity of the Aristotelian *Categories*', in M. Frede, (ed.) *Essays in Ancient Philosophy*, Oxford: 11–28

(1994) 'The Stoic notion of a *lekton*', in S. Everson (ed.), *Companions to Ancient Thought vol. III: Language*, Cambridge: 109–28

(1999) 'Epilogue', in K. Algra, J. Barnes, J. Mansfeld and M. Schofield (eds.), *The Cambridge History of Hellenistic Philosophy*, Cambridge: 771–97

Frege, G. (1893) *Grundgesetze der Arithmetik* (2 vols.), Jena

Fricker, M. (1998) 'Rational authority and social power: Towards a truly social epistemology', *Proceedings of the Aristotelian Society* N. S. 98: 159–77

Gaca, K. L. (2003) *The Making of Fornication. Eros, Ethics, and Political Reform in Greek Philosophy and Early Christianity*, Berkeley and Los Angeles

Gale, M. R. (1994) *Myth and Poetry in Lucretius*, Cambridge

Gallop, D. (1975) *Plato: Phaedo*, Oxford

Gaskell, E. (1853) *Cranford*, London

Gassendi, P. (1649) *Animadversiones in Decimum Librum Diogenis Laertii*, Lyons

Gassmann, R. H. (2011) 'Coming to terms with dé: the deconstruction of "virtue" and an exercise in scientific morality', in R. King and D. Schilling (eds.) *How should one live? Comparing Ethics in Ancient China and Greco-Roman Antiquity*, Berlin: 92–125

Gatzemeier, S. (2013) Ut *ait* Lucretius. *Die Lukrezrezeption in der lateinischen Prosa bis Laktanz*, Göttingen

Gauthier, R. A. and Jolif, J. Y. (1970) *Aristote. L'Éthique à Nicomaque*, 2nd edn, (2 vols.), Louvain and Paris

Gentzler, J. (1991) 'συμφωνεῖν in Plato's *Phaedo*', *Phronesis* 36: 265–76

References

Giannantoni, G. (1990) *Socratis et Socraticorum reliquiae* (SSR), (4 vols.), Naples

Gildenhard, I. (2011) *Creative Eloquence. The Construction of Reality in Cicero's Speeches*, Oxford

Gill, C. (2006) *The Structured Self in Hellenistic and Roman Thought*, Oxford

    (2013) '"Socratic" psychology in Plato's *Republic*', in G. R. Boys-Stones, D. El Murr and C. Gill (eds.), *The Platonic Art of Philosophy*, Cambridge: 110–21

Giussani, C. (1896–8) *T. Lucreti Cari De Rerum Natura Libri Sex*, Turin

Glucker, J. (1978) *Antiochus and the Late Academy* Hypomnemata 56, Göttingen

Goldman, A. I. (1999) *Knowledge in a Social World*, Oxford

    (2001) 'Which ones should you trust?', *Philosophy and Phenomenological Research* 63: 85–110

Goldman, E. (2005: originally published 1910) *Anarchism and Other Essays*, New York

Gordon, P. (2012) *The Invention and Gendering of Epicurus*, Ann Arbor

Görler, W. (1974) *Untersuchungen zu Ciceros Philosophie*, Heidelberg

Gottschalk, H. B. (1987) 'Aristotelian Philosophy in the Roman world from the time of Cicero to the end of the second century AD', in *Aufstieg und Niedergang der Römischen Welt* Bd. II.36.2: 1079–174

    (1998) 'Theophrastus and the Peripatos', in J. M. van Ophuijsen and M. van Raalte (eds.) *Theophrastus: Reappraising the Sources*, RUSCH VIII, New Brunswick, NJ: 281–98

Graham, A. C. (1989) *Disputers of the Tao*, La Salle, IL.

Graham, D. W. (2002) 'Heraclitus and Parmenides', in V. Caston and D. Graham (eds.) *Presocratic Philosophy*, Burlington VT: 27–44

    (2013) *Science before Socrates: Parmenides, Anaxagoras, and the New Astronomy*, Oxford

    (2014) 'Philolaus', in C. A. Huffman (ed.) *A History of Pythagoreanism*, Cambridge: 46–68

Granger, H. (2002) 'The cosmology of mortals', in V. Caston and D. Graham (eds.) *Presocratic Philosophy*, Burlington VT.: 101–16

Griffin, M. J. (2012) 'What has Aristotelian dialectic to offer a Neoplatonist? A possible sample of Iamblichus at Simplicius *on the Categories* 12,10–13,12', *The International Journal of the Platonic Tradition* 6: 173–85

    (2015) *Aristotle's Categories in the Early Roman Empire*, Oxford

Guthrie, W. K. C. (1939) *Aristotle on the Heavens*, Harvard, MA

    (1957) 'Aristotle as a historian of philosophy: Some preliminaries', *Journal of Hellenic Studies* 77: 35–41

    (1962) *A History of Greek Philosophy. Vol. 1: The Earlier Presocratics and the Pythagoreans*, Cambridge

    (1965) *A History of Greek Philosophy. Vol. 2: The Presocratic Tradition from Parmenides to Democritus*, Cambridge

References

Haake, M. (2004) 'Documentary evidence, literary forgery, or manipulation of historical documents', *Classical Quarterly* 54: 470–83

    (2013) 'Illustrating, documenting, making-believe: The use of *psephismata* in Hellenistic biographies of philosophers', in P. Liddel and P. Low (eds.) *Inscriptions and Their Uses in Greek and Latin Literature*, Oxford: 79–124

Hahm, D. (1978) 'Early Hellenistic theories of vision and the perception of color', in P. K. Machamer and R. G. Turnbull (eds.) *Studies in Perception: Interrelations in the History of Philosophy and Science*, Columbus, OH: 60–95

    (1992) 'Diogenes Laertius VII: On the Stoics', *Aufstieg und Niedergang der römischen Welt* II.36.6: 4076–182

    (2002) 'Zeno before and after Stoicism', in T. Scaltsas and A. S. Mason (eds.) *The Philosophy of Zeno*, Larnaca: 29–56

Harari, O. (2011) 'The unity of Aristotle's category of relatives', *The Classical Quarterly (New Series)* 61: 521–37

Hardwig, J. (1985) 'Epistemic dependence', *The Journal of Philosophy* 82: 335–49

    (1991) 'The role of trust in knowledge', *The Journal of Philosophy* 88: 693–708

Hatzimichali, M. (2012) 'Antiochus' biography', in D. Sedley (ed.) *The Philosophy of Antiochus*, Cambridge: 9–30

    (2013a) 'Encyclopaedism in the Alexandrian Library', in J. König and G. Woolf (eds.): 64–83

    (2013b) 'The texts of Plato and Aristotle in the first century BC', in M. Schofield (ed.): 1–27

Heidel, W. A. (1906) 'Qualitative change in Presocratic philosophy', *Archiv für Geschichte der Philosophie* 19: 333–79

Heinze, R. (1925) 'Auctoritas', *Hermes* 60: 348–66

Hellegouarc'h, J. (1972) *Le vocabulaire latin des relations et des partis politiques sous la République*, Paris

Heller, J. (1961) *Catch 22*, New York

Hoffmann, P. and Golitsis, P. (2016) 'Simplicius' *Corollary on Place*: Method of philosophising and doctrines', in R. Sorabji (ed.) *Aristotle Re-interpreted: New Findings on Seven Hundred Years of the Ancient Commentators*, London: 531–40

Hood, P. (2004) *Aristotle on the Category of Relation*, Lanham, MD

Huby, P. M. (1985) 'Theophrastus in the Aristotelian Corpus, with particular reference to biological problems', in A. Gotthelf, (ed.) *Aristotle on Nature and Living Things: Philosophical and Historical Studies Presented to David M. Balme on his 70th Birthday*, Bristol: 313–25

Huffman, C. A. (1993) *Philolaus of Croton: Pythagorean and Presocratic*, Cambridge

    (2005) *Archytas of Tarentum: Pythagorean, Philosopher and Mathematician King*, Cambridge

    (ed.) (2014) *A History of Pythagoreanism*, Cambridge

References

Husik, I. (1904) 'On the *Categories* of Aristotle', *The Philosophical Review* 13: 514–28

Inwood, B. (2012) 'Antiochus on physics', in D. Sedley (ed.) *The Philosophy of Antiochus*, Cambridge: 188–219

Isnardi Parente, M. (1982) *Senocrate-Ermodoro: Frammenti*, Naples

Jaeger, W. (1923) *Aristoteles: Grundlegung einer Geschichte seiner Entwicklung*, Berlin

Jaeger, W., Robinson, R. and Kousnetzoff, N. (1962) *Aristotle: Fundamentals of the History of his Development*, New York

Jansen, L. (2006) 'Aristoteles' Kategorie des Relativen zwischen Dialektik und Ontologie', *Philosophiegeschichte und logische Analyse* 9: 1–33

Johansen, T. (2004) *Plato's Natural Philosophy*, Cambridge

(2015) 'Parmenides' likely story', *Oxford Studies in Ancient Philosophy* 50: 1–29

Jones, H. (1992) *The Epicurean Tradition*, London

Jourdan, F. (2015) 'Materie und Seele in Numenios' Lehre vom Übel und Bösen', in F. Jourdan and R. Hirsch-Luipold (eds.), *Die Wurzel allen Übels: Vorstellungen über die Herkunft des Bösen und Schlechten in der Philosophie und Religion des 1.-4. Jahrhunderts*, Tübingen: 132–210

Journée, G. (2012) 'Lumière et nuit, féminin et masculin chez Parménide d'Elée: quelques remarques', *Phronesis* 57: 289–318

Kahn, C. H. (1960) *Anaximander and the Origins of Greek Cosmology*, New York

(1996) *Plato and the Socratic Dialogue*, Cambridge

(2001) *Pythagoras and the Pythagoreans: A Brief History*, Indianapolis

Kanayama, Y. (2000) 'The methodology of the second voyage and the proof of the soul's indestructibility in Plato's *Phaedo*', *Oxford Studies in Ancient Philosophy* 18: 41–100

Karamanolis, G. E. (2006) *Plato and Aristotle in Agreement? Platonists on Aristotle from Antiochus to Porphyry*, Oxford

Kidd, I. G. (2002) 'Zeno's oral teaching and the stimulating uncertainty of his doctrines', in T. Scaltsas and A. S. Mason (eds.) *The Philosophy of Zeno*, Larnaca: 351–64

King, R. A. H. and Schilling, D. (eds.) (2011) *How Should One Live? Comparing Ethics in Ancient China and Greco-Roman Antiquity*, Berlin

Kirk, G., Raven, J., and Schofield, M. (1983) *The Presocratic Philosophers*, Cambridge

Knox, R. A. (1985) '"So mischievous a beaste"? The Athenian *demos* and its treatment of its politicians', *Greece and Rome* 32: 132–61

König, J. and Woolf, G. (eds.) (2013) *Encyclopaedism from Antiquity to the Renaissance*, Cambridge

Körte, A. (1890) 'Metrodori Epicurei fragmenta', *Jahrbuch für classische Filologie*, Suppl. 17, Leipzig: 529–70

Konstan, D. (2011) 'Epicurus on the gods', in J. Fish and K. R. Saunders (eds.), *Epicurus and the Epicurean Tradition*, Cambridge: 53–71

339

References

Krämer, H. J. (1959) *Arete bei Platon un Aristoteles. Zum Wesen und zur Geschichte der platonischen Ontologie*, Heidelberg
(1964), *Der Ursprung der Geistmetaphysik. Untersuchungen zur Geschichte des Platonismus zwischen Platon und Plotin*, Amsterdam
Lachelier, J. (1877) 'Les dieux d'Épicure d'après le *De natura deorum* de Cicéron', *Revue de Philologie* 1: 264–7
Laks, A. (2007). *Histoire, Doxographie, Vérité. Etudes sur Aristote, Théophraste et la philosophie présocratique*, Louvain-la-Neuve
(2014) 'Diogenes Laertius' *Life of Pythagoras*', in C. A. Huffman (ed.): 360–80
(1993) *Théophraste, Métaphysique, Texte éd., trad. et annoté*, Paris
Lange, F. A. (1866) *Die Geschichte des Materialismus und Kritik seiner Bedeutung in der Gegenwart*, Iserlohn
Lesher, J. H. (1987) 'Socrates' disavowal of knowledge', *Journal of the History of Philosophy* 2: 275–88
Lewis, D. (1969) *Convention: A Philosophical Study*, Oxford
Lewis, F. A. (1979) 'Parmenides on separation and the knowability of the Forms: Plato *Parmenides* 133aff', *Philosophical Studies* 35: 105–27
Lewis, N. (1974) *Papyrus in Classical Antiquity*, Oxford
Lloyd, G. E. R. (2009) *Disciplines in the Making*, Oxford
(2010) 'The techniques of persuasion and the rhetoric of disorder (luan) in late Zhanguo and Western Han texts', in M. Nylan and M. Loewe (eds.): 451–60
(2014a) *The Ideals of Inquiry: An Ancient History*, Oxford
(2014b) 'Pythagoras', in C. A. Huffman (ed.): 24–45
Lloyd, G. E. R. and Sivin, N. (2002) *The Way and the Word*, New Haven
Lloyd, G. E. R. and Zhao, J. (eds.) (2018) *Ancient Greece and China Compared: Interdisciplinary and Cross-Cultural Perspectives*, Cambridge
Loewe, M. A. N. (ed.) (1993) *Early Chinese Texts: A Bibliographical Guide*, Berkeley
Long, A. A. (1996) 'Theophrastus' *De Sensibus* on Plato', in K. A. Algra, P. W. v. d. Horst and D. T. Runia (eds.) *Polyhistor: Studies in the History and Historiography of Ancient Philosophy Presented to Jaap Mansfeld on his Sixtieth Birthday*, Leiden: 345–62
(2006a) 'Arcesilaus in his time and place', in A. A. Long (eds.) *From Epicurus to Epictetus*, Oxford 96–113, rev. repr. of 'Diogenes Laertius, life of Arcesilaus', *Elenchos* 7 (1986): 429–50
(2006b) 'Timon of Phlius: Pyrrhonist and satirist', in A. A. Long (eds.), *From Epicurus to Epictetus*, Oxford: 70–95, rev. repr. from *Proceedings of the Cambridge Philological Society* 204 (1978): 68–91
(2013) 'The eclectic Pythagoreanism of Alexander Polyhistor', in M. Schofield (ed.): 139–59
(2018) 'Aetius, Stoic Physics, and Zeno', in J. Mansfeld and D.T. Runia (eds.) *Aetiana IV*, Leiden: 433–52

340

References

Long, A. A. and Sedley, D. N. (1987) *The Hellenistic Philosophers*, 2 vols., Cambridge

Long, A. G. (2013) *Conversation and Self-Sufficiency in Plato*, Oxford

Lynch, J. (1972) *Aristotle's School. A Study of a Greek Educational Institution*, Berkeley

Mansfeld, J. and Runia, D. T. (1997) *Aëtiana: The Method and Intellectual Context of a Doxographer. Vol. 1: The Sources*, Leiden

Mansfeld, J. (1986) 'Diogenes Laertius on Stoic philosophy', *Elenchos* 7: 295–382, repr. in J. Mansfeld (1990) *Studies in the Historiography of Greek Philosophy*, Assen and Maastricht: 343–428

(1998) 'Aspects of Epicurean theology', *Mnemosyne* 46: 172–210

Markschies, C. (2000) 'Epikureismus bei Origenes und inder orgenistischen Tradition', in M. Erler (ed.) *Epikureismus in der späten Republik und Kaiserzeit. Akten der 2. Tagung der Karl und Gertrud Abel Stiftung vom. 30 September – 3 Oktober 1998 im Würzburg*, Stuttgart: 190–217

Marmadoro, A. and Yates, M. (eds.) (2016), *The Metaphysics of Relations*, Oxford: 1–18

Masson, J. (1907–9), *Lucretius, Epicurean and Poet*, London

Matthen, M. (1982) 'Plato's treatment of relational statements in the *Phaedo*', *Phronesis* 27: 90–100

(1984) 'Relationality in Plato's metaphysics: Reply to McPherran', *Phronesis* 29: 304–12

McDiarmid, J. B. (1953) 'Theophrastus on the Presocratic causes', *Harvard Studies in Classical Philology* 61: 85–156

(1959) 'Plato in Theophrastus' *De Sensibus*', *Phronesis* 4: 59–70

McPherran, M. (1983) 'Plato's Parmenides theory of relations', in F. J. Pelletier and J. King-Farlow (eds.) *Canadian Journal of Philosophy, Supplementary Volume. New Essays on Plato* 9, Guelph, Ontario: 149–64

(1999) 'An argument "Too Strange": *Parmenides* 134c4–e8', *Apeiron: A Journal for Ancient Philosophy and Science* 32: 55–71

Menci, G. (1988) 'Fabbricazione, uso e restauro antico del papiro: tre note in margine a Plinio, *NH* xiii, 74–82', in B. Mandilaras (ed.) *Proceedings of the XVIIIth International Congress of Papyrology*, Athens, vol. 2: 497–504

Menn, S. (1995) 'Metaphysics, dialectic and the *Categories*', *Revue de Métaphysique et de Morale* 100: 311–37

(2010) 'On Socrates' first objections to the physicists (*Phaedo* 95e8–97b7)', *Oxford Studies in Ancient Philosophy* 38: 37–68

Merlan, P. (1954) 'Isocrates, Aristotle, and Alexander the Great', *Historia* 3: 60–81

Mette, H. J. (1986) 'Philon von Larissa und Antiochos von Askalon', *Lustrum* 28: 9–63

Mignucci, M. (1986) 'Aristotle's definitions of relatives in *Cat.* 7', *Phronesis* 31: 101–27

(1988) 'Platone e relativi', *Elenchos* 9: 259–94

References

Moatti, C. (2015) *The Birth of Critical Thinking in Republican Rome*, Cambridge

Mohr, R. and Sattler, B. (eds.) (2010) *One Book – The Whole Universe. Plato's Timaeus Today*, Las Vegas

Morales, F. (1994) 'Relational attributes in Aristotle', *Phronesis* 39: 255–74

Moraux, P. (1973) *Der Aristotelismus bei den Griechen. Von Andronikos bis Alexander von Aphrodisias Bd. I. Die Renaissance des Aristotelismus im 1. Jh. v. Chr.*, Berlin

Mourelatos, A. P. D. (2008) *The Route of Parmenides*, Las Vegas

(2011) 'Parmenides, early Greek astronomy, and modern scientific realism', in N. Cordero (ed.) *Parmenides Venerable and Awesome*, Las Vegas: 81–94

Natali, C. (2013) *Aristotle. His Life and School*, ed. D. S. Hutchinson, Princeton

Nehamas, A. (1999) *Virtues of Authenticity. Essays on Plato and Socrates*, Princeton

(2002) 'Parmenidean being/Heraclitean fire', in V. Caston and D. Graham (eds.) *Presocratic Philosophy*, Burlington VT: 45–64

Nikolsky, B. (2001) 'Epicurus on pleasure', *Phronesis* 46: 440–65

Notomi, N. (2013) 'Socrates in the *Phaedo*', in G. R. Boys-Stones, D. El Murr and C. Gill (eds.), *The Platonic Art of Philosophy*, Cambridge: 51–69

Nutton, V. (2004) *Ancient Medicine*, London

Nylan, M. (2001) *The Five 'Confucian' Classics*, New Haven

(2018) 'On libraries and manuscript culture in Western Han Chang'an and Alexandria', in G. E. R. Lloyd and J. Zhao (eds.): 373–409

Nylan, M. and Loewe, M. (eds.) (2010) *China's Early Empires: A Reappraisal*, Cambridge

Nylan, M. and Sivin, N. (1995) 'The first neo-Confucianism: An introduction to Yang Hsiung's 'Canon of Supreme Mystery' (*T'ai hsuan ching*, ca 4 B.C.)', rev. edn (originally 1987) in N. Sivin: III.1–42

Opsomer, J. (2005) 'Demiurges in early Imperial Platonism', in R. Hirsch-Luipold (ed.), *Gott und die Götter bei Plutarch. Götterbilder, Gottesbilder, Weltbilder*, Berlin and New York 51–99

Owen, G. E. L. (1957) 'A proof in the *Peri Ideon*', *Journal of Hellenic Studies* 87: 106

(1960a) 'Logic and metaphysics in some earlier works of Aristotle', in *Aristotle and Plato in the Mid-Fourth Century*, Göteborg: 163–90

(1960b) 'Eleatic questions', *Classical Quarterly* 10: 84–102

(1965) 'Aristotle on the snares of ontology', in R. Bamburgh and G. E. M. Anscombe (eds.) *New Essays on Plato and Aristotle*, London: 69–75

(1966) 'The Platonism of Aristotle', *Proceedings of the British Academy* 51: 125–50

Palmer, J. (2009) *Parmenides and Presocratic Philosophy*, Oxford

Parisi, A. (2015) 'Citare il Maestro: due menzioni di Epicuro in Diogene Lacone', *Cronache Ercolanesi* 45: 19–31

References

Pease, A. S. (1955) *M. Tulli Ciceroni De Natura Deorum Liber Primus.* Cambridge, MA

Peterson, S. (1981) 'The greatest difficulty for Plato's Theory of Forms: The unknowability argument of *Parmenides* 133c–134c', *Archiv für Geschichte der Philosophie* 63: 1–16

Pfligersdorfer, G. (1957) 'Cicero über Epikurs Lehre vom Wesen der Götter', *Wiener Studien* 70: 235–53

Philippson, R. (1916) 'Zur epikureischen Götterlehre', *Hermes* 51: 568–608

Popper, K. (1998) *The World of Parmenides*, London and New York

Puglia, E. (1988) *Demetrio Lacone: Aporie testuali ed Esegetiche in Epicuro (PHerc. 1012)*, Naples

Purinton, J. (1993) 'Epicurus on the Telos', *Phronesis* 38: 281–320

(2001) 'Epicurus on the nature of the gods', *Oxford Studies in Ancient Philosophy* 21: 181–231

Quinton, A. (1982) 'Authority and autonomy in knowledge', in his *Thoughts & Thinkers*, London: 65–74

Rawls, J. (1971) *A Theory of Justice*, Cambridge, MA

Reding, J.-P. (1985) *Les fondements philosophiques de la rhétorique chez les sophistes grecs et chez les sophistes chinois*, Berne

Reydams-Schils, G. (2007) 'Calcidius on God', in M. Bonazzi and C. Helmig (eds.), *Platonic Stoicism – Stoic Platonism. The Dialogue Between Platonism and Stoicism in Antiquity*, Leuven: 243–58

(2013) 'The Academy, the Stoics and Cicero on Plato's *Timaeus*', in A. G. Long (ed.) *Plato and the Stoics*, Cambridge: 29–38

Rickless, S. C. (2007) *Plato's Forms in Transition: A Reading of the Parmenides*, New York

Riginos, A. (1975) *Platonica – The Anecdotes Concerning the Life and Writings of Plato*, Leiden

Robinson, R. (1953) *Plato's Earlier Dialectic*, 2nd edn, Oxford

Rorty, R. (1967) 'Relations, internal and external', in P. Edwards (ed.), *The Encyclopedia of Philosophy*, New York: 8–125

Ross, W. D. (1924) *Aristotle's Metaphysics. A Revised Text with Introduction and Commentary*, Oxford

(1957) 'The development of Aristotle's thought', *Proceedings of the British Academy* 43: 63–78

Rowe, C. (2007) *Plato and the Art of Philosophical Writing*, Cambridge

(2013) 'Socrates and his gods: from the *Euthyphro* to the *Eudemian Ethics*', in M. Lane and V. Harte (eds.) *Politeia in Greek and Roman Philosophy*, Oxford: 313–28

Rudebusch, G. (1999) *Socrates, Pleasure, and Value*, Oxford

Rudolph, K. C. (2009) 'Reading Theophrastus: A reconstruction of Democritus' physics of perception', PhD dissertation, University of Cambridge

(2018) 'Tastes of reality: epistemology and the senses in ancient philosophy', in her (ed.) *Taste and the Ancient Senses, London*: 45–59

References

Russell, B. (1938) *The Principles of Mathematics*, 2nd edn, New York

Sanders, K. R. (2004) 'Cicero *De natura deorum* 1.48–9: *Quasi Corpus?*', *Mnemosyne* 57: 215–18

Scaltsas, T. (2013) 'Relations as plural-predications in Plato', *Studia Neoaristotelica* 10: 28–49

Schaffer, J. (2010) 'The internal relatedness of all things', *Mind* 119: 341–76

Schofield, M. (1986) 'Cicero for and against divination', *Journal of Roman Studies* 76: 47–65

  (1991) *The Stoic Idea of the City*, Cambridge

  (1996) 'Epilogismos: An appraisal', in M. Frede and G. Striker (eds.) *Rationality in Greek Thought*, Oxford: 221–37

  (ed.) (2013) *Aristotle, Plato and Pythagoreanism in the First Century BC*, Cambridge

  (2014) 'Archytas', in C. A. Huffman (ed.): 69–87

Schwenke, P. (1882) 'Zu Cicero, *De natura deorum* (I 49f.), *NJPhP* 125: 613–33

Scott, D. (1995) *Recollection and Experience: Plato's Theology of Learning and Its Successors*, Cambridge

Scott, W. (1883) 'The physical constitution of the Epicurean Gods', *Journal of Philology* 12: 212–47

Sedley, D. N. (1976) 'Epicurus and his professional rivals', in J. Bollack and A. Laks (eds.) *Études sur l'épicurisme antique (Cahiers de Philologie 1)*, Lille: 119–59

  (1985) 'Three notes on Theophrastus' treatment of tastes and smells', in W. W. Fortenbaugh, P. M. Huby and A. A. Long (eds.) *Theophrastus of Eresus: On His Life and Work*, RUSCH II, New Brunswick, NJ: 205–7

  (1989) 'Philosophical allegiance in the Greco-Roman world', in J. Barnes and M. Griffin (eds.) *Philosophia Togata I*, Oxford: 97–119

  (1992a) 'Empedocles' Theory of Vision and Theophrastus' *De Sensibus*', in W. W. Fortenbaugh and D. Gutas (eds.) *Theophrastus: His Psychological, Doxographical and Scientific Writings*, RUSCH V, New Brunswick, NJ: 20–31

  (1992b) 'Sextus Empiricus and the atomist criteria of truth', *Elenchos* 13: 19–56

  (1995) 'The dramatis personae of Plato's *Phaedo*', in T. J. Smiley (ed.), *Philosophical Dialogues: Plato, Hume and Wittgenstein*, Oxford 1–26

  (1996) 'Three Platonist interpretations of the *Theaetetus*', in C. Gill and M. M. McCabe (eds.), *Form and Argument in Late Plato*, Oxford: 79–103

  (1997) 'Plato's *auctoritas* and the rebirth of the commentary tradition', in J. Barnes and M. Griffin (eds.), *Philosophia Togata II. Plato and Aristotle at Rome*, Oxford: 110–29

  (1998) *Lucretius and the Transformation of Greek Wisdom*. Cambridge

  (1999a) 'Parmenides and Melissus', in A. A. Long (ed.) *The Cambridge Companion to Early Greek Philosophy*, Cambridge: 113–33

References

(1999b) 'The ideal of godlikeness', in G. Fine (ed.) *Plato 2: Ethics, Politics, Religion, and the Soul*, Oxford: 309–28

(2002a) 'Aristotelian relativities', in *Le Style de la Pensée: receuil de textes en hommage à Jacques Brunschwig*, Paris: 324–52

(2002b) 'The origins of Stoic god', in D. Frede and A. Laks (eds.) *Traditions of Theology*, Leiden: 41–83

(2003) 'Philodemus and the decentralisation of philosophy', *Cronache Ercolanesi* 33: 31–41

(2007) *Creationism and Its Critics in Antiquity*, Berkeley

(2011) 'Epicurus' theological innatism', in J. Fish and K. R. Saunders (eds.), *Epicurus and the Epicurean Tradition*, Cambridge: 29–52

(2012a) 'Antiochus as historian of philosophy', in Sedley D. N. (ed.), *The Philosophy of Antiochus*, Cambridge: 80–103

(2012b) 'A guide to the testimonies for Antiochus', in Sedley D. N. (ed.), *The Philosophy of Antiochus*, Cambridge: 334–46

Sharples, R. W. (1985) 'Theophrastus on tastes and smells', in W. W. Fortenbaugh, P. M. Huby and A. A. Long (eds.) *Theophrastus of Eresus: On His Life and Work*, RUSCH II, New Brunswick, NJ: 183–204

(1998) 'Theophrastus as philosopher and Aristotelian', in J. M. van Ophuijsen and M. van Raalte (eds.) *Theophrastus: Reappraising the Sources*, RUSCH VIII, New Brunswick, NJ: 267–80

Shields, C. (2014) *Aristotle*, 2nd edn, Abingdon and New York

Sivin, N. (1987) *Traditional Medicine in Contemporary China*, Ann Arbor

(1995) *Medicine, Philosophy and Religion in Ancient China: Researches and Reflections*, vol. 2, Aldershot

Skeat, T. C. (1982) 'The length of the standard papyrus roll and the cost-advantage of the codex', *Zeitschrift für Papyrologie und Epigraphik* XLV: 169–76

Solmsen, F. (1929) *Die Entwicklung der aristotelischen Logik und Rhetorik, Neue Philologische Untersuchungen* 4, Berlin

(1935) 'The origins and methods of Aristotle's *Poetics*', *The Classical Quarterly* 29: 192–201

Sorabji, R. (1983) *Time, Creation and the Continuum. Theories in Antiquity and the Middle Ages*, London

(1988a) *Matter, Space and Motion. Theories in Antiquity and Their Sequel*, London

(1998b) 'Is Theophrastus a significant philosopher?', in J. M. van Ophuijsen and M. van Raalte (eds.) *Theophrastus: Reappraising the Sources*, RUSCH VIII, New Brunswick, NJ: 203–21

Steel, C. (ed.)(2012a) *Aristotle's Metaphysics Alpha. Symposium Aristotelicum*, Oxford

(2012b) 'Plato as seen by Aristotle. Metaphysics A 6', in C. Steel (ed.) *Aristotle's Metaphysics A*, Oxford: 167–200

Steinmetz, P. (1964) *Die Physik des Theophrastos von Eresos*, Berlin

References

Stratton, G. M. (1917) *Theophrastus and the Greek Physiological Psychology Before Aristotle*, Amsterdam

Summers, K. (1995) 'Lucretius and the Epicurean tradition of piety', *Classical Philology* 90: 32–57

Szlezák, T. A. (1972) *Pseudo-Archytas über die Kategorien*, Berlin

Tarn, W. W. (1951) rev. G.T. Griffith, *Hellenistic Civilization* (1st edn, 1927), London

Tarrant, H. (1985) *Scepticism or Platonism? The Philosophy of the Fourth Academy* (Cambridge Classical Studies), Cambridge

(1993) *Thrasyllan Platonism*, Ithaca

(2004) 'Must commentators know their sources? Proclus *In Timaeum* and Numenius', in P. Adamson, H. Baltussen and M. W. F. Stone (eds.), *Philosophy, Science and Exegesis in Greek, Arabic and Latin Commentaries*, vol. I = *Bulletin of the Institute of Classical Studies Supplement* 83.1, London: 175–90

Taylor, A. E. (1911) *Varia Socratica*, Oxford

Tepedino Guerra, A. (1987) 'PHerc 1232 fr. 6: una testimonanza del libro «Sul fine» di Epicuro?', *Cronache Ercolanesi* 17: 85–8

(1994), 'L'opera filodemea Su Epicuro (PHerc 1232 1289β)',*Cronache Ercolanesi* 24: 5–54

Theiler, W. (1930) *Die Vorbereitung des Neuplatonismus*, Berlin and Zürich

Thesleff, H. (1965) *The Pythagorean Texts of the Hellenistic Period*, Åbo

Tor, S. (2015) 'Parmenides' epistemology and the two parts of his poem' *Phronesis* 60: 3–39

Trabattoni, F. (2010) 'Y a-t-il une onto-théologie dans le Platonisme antérieur à Plotin?', *Études Platoniciennes* 7: 201–15

Trapp, M. (2007) 'Neopythagoreans', in R. W. Sharples and R. Sorabji (eds.) *Greek and Roman Philosophy 100 BC – 200 AD*, London: 347–63

Tsouni, G. (2016) 'Peripatetic ethics in the first century BC: The summary of Didymus', in A. Falcon (ed.) *Brill's Companion to the Reception of Aristotle*, Leiden: 120–37

Turner, J. D. (2006) 'The Gnostic Sethians and Middle Platonism: Interpretations of the *Timaeus* and *Parmenides*', *Vigiliae Christianae* 60: 9–64

Ulacco, Angela (2016) 'The appropriation of Aristotle in the Ps-Pythagorean treatises', in A. Falcon (ed.) *Brill's Companion to the Reception of Aristotle in Antiquity*, Leiden: 202–17

Usener, H. (1887) *Epicurea*, Leipzig

van Ophuijsen, J. M. and van Raalte, M. (eds.) (1998) *Theophrastus: Reappraising the Sources*, RUSCH VIII, New Brunswick, NJ

van Raalte, M. (1993) *Theophrastus: Metaphysics: with an Introduction, Translations and Commentary*, Leiden

Vinel, N. (2014) (ed.), *Jamblique: In Nicomachi Arithmeticam*, Pisa

Vlastos, G. (1956) *Plato's Protagoras*, ed. and trans. M. Ostwald, Indianapolis

(1983) 'The Socratic elenchus', *Oxford Studies in Ancient Philosophy* 1: 27–58

References

(1991) *Socrates: Ironist and Moral Philosopher*, Ithaca

(1994) *Socratic Studies*, Cambridge

Warren, J. I. (2000) 'Epicurean immortality', *Oxford Studies in Ancient Philosophy* 18: 231–61

(2004) *Facing Death. Epicurus and his Critics*, Oxford

(2009) 'Removing fear', in J. I. Warren (ed.), *The Cambridge Companion to Epicureanism*, Cambridge: 234–48

(2011) 'Pleasure, Plutarch's Non Posse, and Plato's Republic', *Classical Quarterly* 61: 278–93

(2014a) 'Diogenes Laërtius, biographer of philosophy', in J. König and T. Whitmarsh (eds.) *Ordering Knowledge in the Roman Empire*, Cambridge: 133–49

(2014b), *The Pleasures of Reason in Plato, Aristotle, and the Hellenistic Hedonists*, Cambridge

West, M. L. (ed.) (1972) *Iambi et Elegi Graeci*, Oxford

Westerink, L. G. (1956) *Olympiodorus: Commentary on the First Alcibiades of Plato. Critical Text and Indices*, Amsterdam

Whitehead, A. N. (1978/1929) *Process and Reality: An Essay in Cosmology*, New York

Wigodsky, M. (2004) 'Emotions and immortality in Philodemus' *On the Gods* and the *Aeneid*', in D. Armstrong et al. (eds.), *Vergil, Philodemus and the Augustans*, Austin: 211–28

(2007) '*Homoiotetes, Stoicheia* and *Homoiomereiai* in Epicurus', *CQ* 57: 521–42

Woodward, G. (1989) 'Star gods in Philodemus, *PHerc.* 152/157', *Cronache Ercolanesi* 19: 29–47

Wynne, J. P. F. (2014) 'Learned and wise: Cotta the sceptic in Cicero's *On the Nature of the Gods*', *Oxford Studies in Ancient Philosophy* 47: 245–73

Zhmud, L. (2012) *Pythagoras and the Early Pythagoreans*, Oxford

(2014) 'Sixth-, fifth- and fourth-century Pythagoreans', in C. A. Huffman (ed.): 88–111

Ziegler, K. (1936) 'Der Tod des Lucretius', *Hermes* 71: 421–40

INDEX LOCORUM

Aelian
VH   *Varia Historia*
3.19   81n6

Aët.   Aëtius
1.7.33   244n8
1.7.34   235
2.7.1   32n38
2.15.7   25n20
2.26.2   25n20
2.28.5   25n20
5.7.2   34n45

Alcinous
Did.   *Didaskalikos*
8–10   276n54
27.1   187, 198
28.1   277n55
28.3   198

Alexander, son of Numenius
On starting points for rhetoric
3.11–12   44

Alexander of Aphrodisias
Mantissa
151.1–13b   277n56

Ammonius
In Cat.   Commentary on
    Aristotle's *Categories*
8.11–19   4n7

Anon. *in Tht.*   Anonymous
    commentary on Plato's
    Theaetetus
col. 54.40   186n4

Antiphon
5.69   48n4

Apuleius
Florida
15.26   186n3

Aquinas
Summa theologiae
Pars prima q1 a8   316n7

Aristophanes
Clouds
206–8   46

Ecclesiazousai
1132   46

Peace
503–5   46

Arist.   Aristotle
APo.   *Posterior Analytics*
72b5–23   131
2.5   86
2.13   86
2.14   86
83a28   274n43
2.19   275

APr.   *Prior Analytics*
1.31   86

Cat.   *Categories*
chs. 1–3   169
1b25–2a4   171n31
1b26   172, 172n34
3b16–21   172
3b36   125n13
5b27   172
6a35   132
6a36   121, 121n7, 123
6a36–7   135

349

Index Locorum

Cat.	*Categories (cont.)*
6a36–b6	124
6a36–b10	127n16, 131
6a36–8b24	120n1
6a38	125
6a39	125
6b1–3	130, 131
6b4	125
6b15–19	121
6b19–27	121
6b28	128
6b28–35	129n20, 130, 131
6b28–7a21	129n20
6b28–7b14	121
6b29–30	129n20
6b34–5	129n20
7a31–b9	128
7b6–7	128
7b15–8a12	121
8a13–28	121
8a28	124n12
8a31–2	121, 135
8a32–5	121n7, 135
8a33–5	135n32
8a35–7	137
8a36–7	135
8a35–b21	121
11a20–3	136
11a20–37	120n1
11a23–36	136

De An.	*De Anima*
404b16–18	140n3
429a9–10	131
429a31–b2	141n6
430a23	127n15

DC	*De Caelo (On the Heavens)*
1.10	93
1.11	93
1.12	93
279a32–280a2	93
280a2–10	94
280a28–32	93
299a30–b14	145n23

EE	*Eudemian Ethics*
1.7	84n15
1217b2–1218b7	117n18

Fragments (Rose)	
673	119n21

GC	*On Generation and Corruption*
318b2–7	27n27
323b1–324a9	140n3
329b17–19	145n25

Metaph.	*Metaphysics*
A.9	84n14, 95
986b27–34	22n8
986b35–6	27n27
987b1–10	90
990a33–991b9	95n36
991b9–993a10	95n36
1031a28ff.	274n43
1031b28–1034a4	95n37
1039a2ff.	95n37
1042b34–6	145n25
1069a20	172n34
1091a8–9	43
1093a26ff.	297n3
M.4–5	84n14

NE	*Nicomachean Ethics*
1.6	84n15
1096a1ff.	274n43
1096a11–17	114
1096a12–13	118
1096a16–17	4n7, 118, 119
1098a20–6	101
1101a6–8	273n41
1101a14–16	273n42
1101b13	136n36
1113a22–b2	111
1116b4–6	92n33
1126b11–12	107
1127a13–b18	107
1127a13	107
1127a33–b5	107
1127b22–6	92n33
1145b23–7	92n33
1145b28–30	92n33
1147b12	110
1155b27–1156a5	88
1159b31	116
1164b6	101n44
1167a22ff.	117

Index Locorum

1168b7–8	116	*SE*	*Sophisti Elenchi (Sophistical Refutations)*
1172a34–6	109		
1172b1–2	109		
1172b3–7	109		
1172b4	106n6	173a1–2	133
1172b15–18	109	173a30–b17	133
1176a15–29	113	173a39–40	130
1177a13–16	113	173b4–5	130
1177a17–26	105	178b36–8	95n37
1178a23–b5	105	181a35–6	131
1178ab7–23	105		
1178a28–b4	105	*Top.*	*Topics*
1178b33–9	105	101b37–102a31	136n35
1179a9–17	105	114a17–18	131
1179a13–15	105	121a1	131
1179a17–22	104, 105, 106, 106n6, 107, 108	142a26–31	136n36
		146a36	136n36
1179a22–3	113	146b2	131
1179a18	106n6	146b3	133
1179a18–19	107n7	146b3–4	136
1179a22–32	104, 107	146b4–15	131
1179a28	109n9	146b12	130, 132

		Aristoxenus
PA	*De Partibus Animalium (On the Parts of Animals)*	*Harm.* — *Harmonics*
		2.39–40 — 97n40
645a15–25	101	*Fragments*
648a25–31	34n44	33–41 Wehrli — 164n6

		Arius Didymus
Phys.	*Physics*	*apud* Stobaeus 46.l.10–13 — 272n35
192b24–7	108	
209a31–b17	94	**Athenaeus**
209b14–15	84n17	59d–f — 86n22
246b8	136n36	187e — 206n7
		220d–e — 65n19
Pol.	*Politics*	507a — 65n19
1253b25–1255b15	131	546e — 218n29
1259b15–1260b25	131	546f — 218n29
1264a11–b6	96	563 — 248n20
1264b26–8	89	
1265a2–4	89	**Atticus**
1265a10–13	89	in Proclus, *On the Timaeus*
1266a1–30	89	i. 392.8–17 — 192n11
Rhet.	*Rhetoric*	in Eusebius *PE*
1358a36–b29	44	11.2.4 — 276n51
1398b30–3	315, 316n6	

Index Locorum

Fragments 1–9 des Places 276n50

Augustine

C. Acad. *Contra Academicos (Against the Academics)*

2.13 245n11

3.38 245n11

De utilitate credendi

11.25 316n7

Ep. *Letters*

118.30 233n45, 234n48

118.30–1 241n71

Aul. Gell. *Aulus Gellius*

Noct. Att. *Attic Nights*

2.9.4 206n7

9.5 204

19.2.5 4n6

In Cat. *Commentary on Aristotle's Categories*

162A Migne 167

Caelius Aurelianus
On Chronic Diseases

4.9 35n50

Cassius Dio
Roman History

55.3 318n11

Cic. *Cicero (Marcus Tullius Cicero)*

Acad. *Academica*

Academic books = *Acad.* 1

1.17 2, 268, 268n19

1.19 270n28

1.30 274n46

1.30–2 274n45

1.32 274n46

1.33 272n37, 274

1.34 3n3

1.34–5 268n22

1.35 245, 269n23, 271n30

1.40–2 244

Lucullus = *Acad.* 2

2.8 281

2.60 264n3, 280

2.62 281

2.63 282

2.64 282

2.118 34n47

Amic. *De Amicitia (On Friendship)*

1–5 290

4–5 288

5 293

6 293

Att. *Letters to Atticus*

13.19.3–5 291

Ad Q. Fr. *Letters to his brother Quintus*

1.3.6 280

2.9.3 232n36

3.5.1 289

Diu. *De Diuinatione (On Divination)*

2.8 284, 285

2.28 285

2.40 230

2.45 284

2.70 285

2.74 284

2.81–7 284

2.84 286

2.137 233n42

2.148 286

2.148–9 285, 286

2.150 280, 285

Fat. *De Fato (On Fate)*

1 292

Fin. *De Finibus (On Ends)*

352

Index Locorum

1.1–12	293	1.46	231
1.14	206n7	1.46–9	240
1.29	266n13	1.48	231
2.7	218n29	1.49	231,
2.20	218n29		235, 237
2.23	218n29	1.71	231n34
2.29	218n29	1.74	231n34
2.30	218n29	1.85	230n31
2.48	218n29	1.105	233n42, 234
2.64	218n29	1.109	235
2.75	229n27	1.111	218n29
2.96	208n9, 217n25	1.114	234n48, 235
3.10	267n16	2.168	283
4.5	269n25, 270n27	3.5–6	283
4.51	269n23	3.95	286
4.61	265, 269n23		
5.9	268n21	*Off.*	*De Officiis* (*On Obligations*)
5.9–11	267, 267n17	1.128	254
5.12	272n37, 273n40	2.31	288
5.14	271n32		
5.59	275	*Or.*	*De Oratore* (*On the Orator*)
5.71	273n38	1.240	268n18
5.87	164	3.68	67
		3.148	266n13
Har.	*De Haruspicum Responso* (*On the Response of the Haruspices*)	*Phil.*	*Philippics*
		1.1	280n1
18–19	287	4.1–2	279
		4.2–4	279
Inu.	*De Inuentione* (*On Invention*)	4.5–6	279
1.101	265n6	*Rep.*	*De Re Publica* (*On the Commonwealth*)
In Pisonem	*Against Piso*	1.12–13	290
69	218n29	1.16	164
		1.34	290
Leg.	*De Legibus* (*On Laws*)	1.34–7	290
2.32–3	287	1.69	279
		2.21–2	293
ND	*De Natura Deorum* (*On the Nature of the Gods*)	2.45	294
		2.51	294
1.10	264, 265n10, 280	2.55–6	279
1.16	270n29	2.57	279
1.18	229n27	2.67	294
1.28	32n38	3.8	290
1.43	225n11		
1.43–9	231, 240	*Sen.*	*De Senectute* (*On Old Age*)
1.43b–44	231		
1.45	231	3	289, 290, 292

353

Index Locorum

Sest.	*Pro Sestio*	Demosthenes	
137	279	60	44
		61.2	44
Tim.	*Timaeus*		
I	164	DL	Diogenes Laertius, *Lives of Eminent Philosophers*
Top.	*Topica*	1.4	318
24	265n9	1.16	10n15
73	265n5	1.19	249n23
		2.109–10	256n32
Tusc.	*Tusculan Disputations*	2.113–20	256n32
		2.120	247
1.26	265n7	3.25	82n9
1.38	265n8	3.35	65n19, 79n2
1.48	225n11	3.37	96n39
1.55	10n16	3.65	3n4
2.17	208n9	3.66	248
3.36	164	4.17	248n19
3.41	218n29	4.22	248n19
3.42	218n29	4.33	245
4.55	164	4.39	255n30
5.33	281	4.40	245
5.34	273n39	5.12	85
5.74	217n25	6.16	65n19
5.88	217n25	6.103–5	253
		6.108–9	123n9
Clement of Alexandria		7.1	249, 251, 256n32
Strom.	*Miscellanies*	7.2	246, 247, 251, 256
2.119	209n11	7.3–5	251, 256
2.131.1	208	7.4	243, 250, 251, 259n33
5.9.59	164n8	7.5	249, 251
		7.6–12	251
Cleomedes		7.7	254
On the Heavens		7.8	254
2.1 410–13	205	7.8–9	251n25
2.1 493–8	206	7.10	254
		7.12	248, 255
Demetrius		7.12–16	251
On Style		7.13	247
296–7	42	7.15	255
		7.15–16	248
Demetrius of Laconia		7.16	246, 254, 257
PHerc. 1012		7.16–24	251
XXIV	211n16	7.24	247
XXXI–XXXII	212	7.25	246, 247n17, 257
XXXIX	211n16	7.25–6	251, 256
		7.26	254
PHerc. 1055		7.27	251
XV	230n31	7.28	249, 251, 255n30

Index Locorum

7.29–30	251	48	229n25, 239
7.30	254	50	215
7.31	251	59.7	236n52
7.31–2	251, 256	62.4	236n52
7.32–4	251	62.7	236n52
7.33–4	250n24		
7.34	247	*Ep. Men.*	*Letter to*
7.36	247		*Menoeceus*
7.38	243	123–4	237
7.39	270n27	133	220n31,
7.40–1	242n3		241
7.62–3	171	135	225
7.127	242n3		
7.134	243n4, 243n6	*Ep. Pyth.*	*Letter to*
7.136	243n4		*Pythocles*
7.139	242n3	89	229n26
7.142	242n3, 243n4		
7.148	243n4	*KD*	*Kyriai Doxai*
7.149	242n3,	1 (scholion)	236
	243n4	20	220n31
7.150	242n3, 243n4	22	220n31
7.160	254		
7.160–7	243	*SV*	*Vatican*
7.162	245, 247n16		*Sayings*
7.163	247	33	203, 215,
7.167	242, 303n13		215n23, 216, 218,
7.174	247		219
7.187–8	250n24		
8.6–7	165n14	Eur.	Euripides
8.14	25n20	*Andromache*	
8.24–35	164	376–7	116
8.34–5	164n6		
10.5	209n13	*Iphigeneia in Aulis*	
10.6	209, 218n29	313	43
10.13	206n7		
10.22	217n25	*Orestes*	
10.24	221n32	735	116
10.122–35	230		
10.123	230	Euseb.	Eusebius
10.123–4	230	*Chronicon*	
10.118–19	223n6	s.a. 94 BC = Oll.171.3	222
10.136	202, 210n14, 216, 218		
		PE	*Praeparatio*
Epictetus			*Euangelica*
3.21.19	242		(*Preparation for*
			the Gospel)
Epicurus		11.2.4	276n51
Ep. Hdt.	*Letter to Herodotus*	14.5.11	245n11
47.1	236n52	14.6.9	245n11

355

Index Locorum

Galen
Placita
3.15   84n17
3.68   84n17

Gorgias
DK B11   44

Hermodorus
Fr 7 Isnardi Parente   134

Heraclitus
DK B40   314n2
DK B50   314n3
DK B101   314n4

Herodotus
1.44.2   237n58

Hesiod
Theogony
727–8   32

Hippolytus
of Rome
Phil. 22.3   230n27

Hom.   Homer
Il. Iliad
2.871–2   213

Od.   *Odyssey*
8.171   51

Horace
Carm.   *Odes*
1.34   223n4

Epistles
1.1.14   318n13

Iambl.   Iamblichus
VP   *Life of Pythagoras*
81–6   164n8
82–6   164n6

*De Communi Mathematica
Scientia*
25, 76.16–78.8   164n8

IG   *Inscriptiones graecae*
II^2 3816   200n16

IK   *Inschriften griechischer Städte
Kleinasiens*
17.2 3901 200n16

Isocrates
Speeches
4.17   44

Antidosis
169–79   81n8

Letter to Alexander
5   81n8

Helen
1   81n8
6   81n8

Lactantius
De ira Dei (*On God's Anger*)
10.17   223n5

De opif. Dei (*On God's Workmanship*)
2.10   223n4
3.21   223n4
6.1   223n4, 223n5
8.13   223n5

Lucr.   Lucretius
DRN   *De rerum natura
(On the Nature
of Things)*
1.1–43   224
1.6   224n7
1.16   224n7
1.40   225n10
1.44–9   226n14
1.54–5   228n23
1.62–79   224, 225
1.66   224
1.72–7   240
1.145   232n36
1.155   227n15
1.304   227n21
1.692   223
1.698   223

Index Locorum

1.704	223	4.1083	223
1.1015	227n15	4.1117	223
2.14	205n4	4.1233	227n15
2.168	227n15	4.1239	227n15
2.434–5	226n15	4.1268	223n6
2.646–51	226	5.1–6	224
2.648	226, 228	5.1–54	225
2.651	227	5.8	225, 225n10, 241
2.985	223	5.13	226
2.1044–7	240n69	5.19	225n8
2.1093–6	227n15	5.10–51	225n8
2.1122–43	229n25	5.51	225
3.1–30	225	5.53	230n29
3.3–8	224	5.122	227n15
3.9	224	5.146–7	228
3.9–10	224n7	5.147	227
3.10	225, 225n10	5.148	227n20, 236n53
3.12	224	5.149	228
3.13	224	5.150–2	227
3.14–15	224	5.151	227
3.16–18	224	5.151–2	227n21
3.18	227n15	5.154	240
3.23–4	229n25	5.155	228
3.322	225, 241	5.309	227n15
3.453	223	5.557	227n20
3.464	223	5.561	227n20
3.821–3	238n60	5.1159	223
3.1042	225, 241	5.1161	227n15
3.1043–4	225	5.1169–71	228
4.43	227n19	5.1173–4	228
4.52	227n19	5.1175–6	228
4.53	227n19	5.1177–8	229
4.59	227n19	5.1179–80	229
4.64	227n19	5.1181–2	229
4.84	227n19	5.1183–7	229
4.123	227n19	5.1194–5	229
4.129–42	239	6.7	226
4.135	239	6.68–78	226, 230n30
4.333	227n19	6.70–1	227
4.130	227n19	6.71–2	227
4.731	227n20	6.73–5	227
4.736	239	6.76–8	227, 238
4.737	227n19	6.86	223
4.738	227n19	6.92–5	224
4.739	227n19	6.522	227n19
4.768–76	228n24	6.1276	227n15
4.800–6	228n24		
4.1032	227n19	Lysias	
4.1069	223	2	44

357

Index Locorum

Metrodorus, fragments as in Körte
  (1890)
fr. 5	207
fr. 6	207
fr. 29	210n14

Numenius, fragments as in des
  Places (1973)
fr. 1a	197
fr. 1.19–23	197n14
fr. 2	190
fr. 11	190
fr. 12	189n7
frs.15–17	189n7
fr. 21	189n7
fr. 22	189
fr. 23	196
fr. 24.22–31	184n2
fr. 24.47–55	195
fr. 24.48–9	196
fr. 24.55–73	197
fr. 24.73–9	195
fr. 25	245n11
fr. 44	193
fr. 52	192, 193n12
fr. 52.44–64	192
fr. 52.64–75	193n13

Olympiodorus
In Platonis Alcibiadem commentarii
  (*Commentary on Plato's* Alcibiades)
2.154 Westerink 83n13

Origen
Contra Celsum	(*Against Celsus*)
3.80	207
3.80.1	207
3.80.26–7	207

Ovid
Met.	*Metamorphoses*
15.1–478	164n10

Parmenides
DK B1.28–32	23
DK B1.30	21, 23n13
DK B6	24n17, 314
DK B6.3–4	24n14
DK B6.7	27n25
DK B7	20n1, 314n5
DK B7.5–6	27n24
DK B8	26, 29, 31, 33, 36
DK B8.15–18	27n24
DK B8.29	28
DK B8.35–41	29n31
DK B8.45–9	31n37
DK B8.53	21, 27n25
DK B8.53–4	24, 26, 27, 29
DK B8.55	27n25
DK B8.53–9	24, 28n27, 30
DK B8.54	24
DK B8.56–9	34n46
DK B8.57–8	28
DK B8.58–9	28
DK B8.60	23, 38n56
DK B8.60–1	24n14
DK B8.61	23
DK B9	28n27, 29, 30, 30n33, 31
DK B9.2	30
DK B10	23n12
DK B12	30, 31, 31n34, 32, 32n38, 34n46, 35
DK B13	31n36
DK B14	25n20, 33
DK B15	25n20, 32n39
DK B15a	32
DK B16	37n52
DK B17	33
DK B18	35

Philod.	*Philodemus*
De dis	*On the gods*

Book 3 (*PHerc.* 152/7)
8.31	229n26
9.41	230

De pietate
col. 12	233n45
112.1 Gomperz	238n63

Index Academicorum (*PHerc.* 1021
  and 164)
VI.41–VII.5	81n5
XVIII 1–8	81n5
Y.1–7	83n11

358

Index Locorum

On Epicurus (*PHerc.* 1232)
XVIII.10–17 219

Plat. Plato
Alcibiades Major (*Alcibiades I*)
109d 54
113b 54
131e 54

Apol. *Apology*
17b–c 47
17d 45
18a 47
21b 41n2, 60
21e 59n2
23b 60
28e 41n2, 59n2
29a 60, 61n7
29a5–6 60n6
29a9–b1 60n6
29a–d 59
29b 61
29b–c 61
29d 59n2
30a 59n2
31c 45
31d 48
34c 47
37b 60n4
37e 59n2
39e 61n9
40a–c 59, 61
40b 61
40c 62
40e 62
41a 61n9
41c 62
41d 61n9
42a 61n9

Charm. *Charmides*
167c 127n18
168b 127n16
168c 127n17

Crito
50a–54e 41n2

Euthyph. *Euthyphro*

4d 144n19
6b 54
14a–c 113

Gorg. *Gorgias*
453b–c 49
454e–455a 45
457e 70, 75n41
461a 70n29, 75n41
462b–463c 85
474a 56
480b 70
482b–c 70
482e 51
486e–488a 42
495d–e 54
499b 52
500b 54
504c–e 47
505d 48
506c 49
506c–507c 48
510a 52
514a 52
515c 48
516b 52
519e 54

Hippias Major
290d–291a 71n33
295a 56
297d–e 56

Hippias Minor
369b–c 43

Lys. *Lysis*
207c 116
212d–e 87n23

Meno
70a 68n25
80a 57

Parm. *Parmenides*
128d6–e1 8n13
130c–d 95
133a–134a 127n18
133b4–6 130

359

Index Locorum

Parm.	*Parmenides (cont.)*		
133c–134e	123, 128	96c1–3	67
133c8	126n14	96c7–d5	68
133c8–d2	129	96d–e	127n16
133d2–5	129	97b	68
133d7–134b1	130	97b4–6	68
134b11–c2	130	97b8–c6	9n14
134d9–e1	131	97b–99d	67
134e5–6	130	99e4–6	69
134e7	130	100a	72
135a–c	95	100a3–7	70, 73
136b1	129n19	100a7	72
142a	127n18	100a7–8	71
158d2	129n19	100d1–2	71
		100d2–3	72
		100d3	72
Phaed.	*Phaedo*	100d9	73
59b10	63n13	100e1–3	71
59b–c	65	101a–d	127n16
60d–61a	41n2	101a1–5	72n34
61d	64	101a5–6	71
62d2–3	131n27	101a8–9	71n32
70a	77	101b2	72n34
70e	64	101b5	72n34
73c–d	274n46	101b8	72n34
75c–d	64	101c2–6	72n34
76d	64	101c8	72n34
77e	77	101d1–2	71, 73
85e3–86d3	74	101d3–4	73
88c1–7	63n14	102a–107a	68, 76
88e–89a	66, 74	102c	127n16
88e5–89a8	63	105a	76
89a	66	105b8–c2	72n35
89a–91c	67	107a8–b3	63, 63n14
89a–107b	66	107b4–5	63n14
89d1–91c6	63n14	107b4–9	64
90b6–7	322n24	107b10	63n14
92c3	74	118a	13, 99
92c6	74	118a16–17	63
93a	75		
93a–94a	75	*Phdr.*	*Phaedrus*
93c10	75	234e	54
94b	75	243e–257b	43
94b1	75	259e–264e	85
96a–100b	67	274b–277a	97
96a8–9	68	276d	98
96a–d	69		
96b	74	*Prot.*	*Protagoras*
96c	68n26	333a–b	70n29

360

Index Locorum

334c–d	42
342a–343c	45
342a–347a	43
360c–d	49

Rep.	*Republic*
424a	116
435c5	132n28
435e1	132n28
436b9–436c2	132
436b9–439c9	132
437b1–c9	132
437c	130
438a7–b2	132
438b	127n16, 127n17
439a2	126n14
439c3–5	132
439d–e	132
439e1	132n28
440e–441a	132
441c6	132n28
442b10	132n28
442c4	132n28
443d3	132n28
449c	116
487b–c	55
517c	117
518b7–8	316n6
520e	117
523–4	127n16
530dff.	324n28
540b–c	117
595c3–4	118
595b9–10	118
600a	163
607c7–8	118
607c7–d2	118
612e–613a	104n4
614b–621d	42

Soph.	*Sophist*
228c4	129n19
253a2	129n19
253b9	129n19
255c	175
255c–d	126n14
255c14	129n19
255d7	126n14

Statesman	
283–5	127n16
283d	127n16
283e	129n19

Symp.	*Symposium*
175e	46
198d–e	45
199d1–e8	126
199e2–4	127
199e3–4	123
200e	126
218a	57

Theaet.	*Theaetetus*
151a	57
155a	127n16
156d3–e7	158n59
160d–e	54
195c8–d1	129n19
204e11	123, 126n14

Tim.	*Timaeus*
28c	187
39e	189
45a–47e	157
45b–d	155, 156, 158
45b–46a2	157n55
45b7	155
45c	148n34, 155
45d5	155
47c–e	153
47d2–3	157n55
47e	157
48e–51b	94
53d	148n34
56a–b	148n34
57d–e	148n34
59e5–60b5	148
60a	148
61c2–d5	143
61d4–62a5	143n16
61e1–4	157n55
62a	148n34
62a6–7	143n17
62b6–c3	145
62c3–8	145
63b–c	146

361

Index Locorum

Tim.	*Timaeus (cont.)*
63c	146
63c–e	146
63c5–e8	145
63e8–64a1	145
64a2–6	147
64b	148n34
64c7–65b3	147
64d	147, 148n34, 156
64d–e	158
64d3	148
64d4	143
64d5	156
64d7	158
64e4–5	148
65a6–c7	147
65b4	143
65b5	143
65c–66a	151
65c1–2	148n33
65c1–3	148
65c1–66c7	148
66d1–67a6	150
66a2–5	157n55
66d	151, 157n55
66e	150, 151
67a	151
67a7–c3	153
67c	156
67c–68d	158
67c4–68b8	155
67c6–7	156, 156n53
67c7–8	156
67e6	155
68a2–3	155
68b6–8	159
68b8–d2	159
80a3–b8	154

Pliny

HN	*Natural History*
13.74–83	157n57
25.3	222n3

Plotinus

Enn.	*Enneads*
5.6.4.1	190n9

6.1.1.28–30 177

Plut.	Plutarch
Adu Col.	*Against Colotes*
1114B	33n43
1114B–C	21n6
1114C	22n10
1114D	22n9
1121F–1122A	186n5
1124E–1127E	210n15
1125B	208, 208n10

Life of Sulla	
26	267n15

Non posse ...	*On the fact that it is impossible to live a pleasant life according to Epicurus*
1089D	202n1, 203, 212, 214, 220n31
1090F	215
1091A	203n2
1098B	209n13
1097A–1098D	210n15

On the E	*On the E at Delphi*
387F	186n3

On the Procreation of the Soul	
1041B–E	192n11

Porphyry	
In Cat.	*Commentary on Aristotle's Categories*
123.35–124.1	135n34

VP	*Life of Pythagoras*
37	164n8
42–5	164n6

Procl.	Proclus
On the Timaeus	
i. 392.8–17	192n11
iii. 103.28–32	189n6

pseudo–Archytas
On the Universal Logos

362

Index Locorum

22.8–14	171
22.11–12	171n29
22.12	171
22.13–14	171
22.14	173
23.17–22	175
23.17–24.5	173
23.17–24.16	174n40
23.21	173n38
23.22–3	176n44
24.4	173
25.1–3	179
25.13–26.15	174n40
29.12	181
30.19–20	176
30.19–31.5	177
30.23–31.3	176
31.1–3	177n47
31.3–5	176
31.32–32.2	183
32.10–14	182

Quintillian

Inst.	*Institutio rhetorica*
7.3.5	229n27

Schol. uet.	
In Hom. *Il.*	Ancient scholia on
	Homer's *Iliad*
2.871a	213n18

Sen.	Seneca the Younger
Ben.	*De beneficiis* (*On Benefits*)
4.4.19	229n27
7.31.3	229n27

De Otio	*On Leisure*
2.1	318n13
3.1	318n13

NQ	*Natural Questions*
7.32.2	201

Ep.	*Moral Letters*
21.9	318n13
22.11	325n30
33.4	325n30
33.11	328n38

66.47	217n25
80.1	328n38
113.23	318n13

VB	*De uita beata* (*On the Blessed Life*)
3.2.3	325n30
25	58n1
26	58n1
27	58n1

Sext. Emp.	Sextus Empiricus
M	*Aduersus mathematicos*
7.16	269
7.141–4	269n24
7.141–260	263n2
8.11–12	172
9.13	230n31
9.43–7	236n55
11.190–91	250n24

PH	*Pyrrōneioi Hypotupōseis* (*Outlines of Pyrrhonism*)
3.245–6	250n24

Simplicius	
In Cat.	*Commentary on Aristotle's Categories*
2.13–14	179
2.14–20	179
7.23–32	4
11.23–12.1	170n27
13.11–15	170
13.16	170
18.27–19.1	170
41.28–32	171
43.29	171
63.21–4	175
63.22	133n29
68.22–3	182
68.24–8	182
73.15–28	177
76.13–17	177
121.13–122.1	175
121.16	173n35
121.17–18	173n38
128.16–129.7	179
159.10–20	121n7

363

Index Locorum

In Cat.	*Commentary on Aristotle's Categories (cont.)*	46.l.10–13+13.36	
		49.8–50.10+13.59	
173.14–16	175		
198.12–199.1	121n7	**Strabo**	
201.34–202.3	135n34	1.15	246
206.10–15	173	13.54	267n15
248.2–18	134	13.614	247
334.15–22	174n39	16.2.4	248
335.4–5	174n40		
340.26	172	*SVF* H. von Arnim, *Stoicorum ueterum*	
340.28–341.2	174n40	*fragmenta* (Stuttgart, 1903–5)	
342.21–5	180	1.10	247
347.13–15	180	1.11–12	245n11
350.10–18	180	1.65	242n2, 275n47
353.19–356.7	181	1.85	243
363.20–9	181	1.94–6	242n2
373.7–32	174	1.124	242n2
378.1–3	177n48	1.142	243
378.1–379.2	176n45	1.153	243
379.8–10	169	1.158	242n2
		1.164	242n2
In Phys.	*Commentary on Aristotle's Physics*	1.176	243n6
		1.247	248n20
9.31–9	32n38	1.250	242n2
230.34–231.5	190n9		
454.18	97n41	**Tertullian**	
601.1–4	5	*De anima*	(*On the Soul*)
601.6	5	3	223n4
604.5–7	5		
793.20–793.23	181	Theoph.	Theophrastus
		CP	*De Causis Plantarum*
SSR	G. Giannantoni, *Socratis et socraticorum reliquiae* (Naples, 1990)		(*On the Causes of Plants*)
		1.1	141n9
		1.21.4	141n9
VI A 53	66n21	3.2.3–5	141n9
VI A 62	65n20	6.1.1	150n43
		6.1.2	149
St Basil		6.1.3	149n35
Humiliae IX *in*	*Nine Homilies on the*	6.2.2	141n6
Hexameron	*Hexameron*	6.3.1	150n43
Scholion XXV	32n39	6.15.1	141n9
Statius		*DS*	*de Sensibus*
Silu.	*Siluae*		(*On Senses*)
2.7.76	223n5	1–58	140
		2	141, 141n6
Stobaeus		4	141, 141n6
1.136.21+13.53		5	157

364

Index Locorum

5.2–7	155, 155n51
5.3–4	155, 158
5.5	156
6	153
6.1	153, 154
6.3	151
6.3–5	151
6.5	151
7	141
9.1	153
15	160n61
19	141n6
22	141
23	141n6
25	152n45
27	141
29	140
31	141, 141n6
32	141n6
35	141, 141n6
36	145n22
39	141n6
40	141, 160n61
41	141n6
43	141
45–7	142
46	141, 141n6
48	141
49	141
51	147n29
52	147n29
53.4	150n44
53.6	150n44
54	141, 145n22, 152n46
55	141
58	141n6
59–91	140
60	140, 154, 158
61	154
61–2	146n28
63	141n6, 146n28
64	141n6, 150n41
65–8	149n37
66	141
69	141
70	141
71	146n28, 160n61
71.7	150n44
72	141, 141n6, 141n8

73.2	150n44
80.1	150n44
80.7	150n44
83	141, 145, 146
83.1	144n18, 150n44
83.2–4	143n17
83.4–5	145n21
83.6–8	146n27
83.8–9	145, 146
83–4	141
84	143n17
84.1–4	147n30
84.4	148, 150n44
84.5–6	148
84.6	149
84.6–11	149
85	154
85.1–6	150n39
85.7–9	153
86.1–8	158
86.6–8	159
86.2	158
87	144
87.2–3	144n18
87.3–7	145
88–9	147
88.1–89.3	146
88.2	146
89	145n22
90.1–8	150n42
90.6	150
91	141, 145n22, 158
91.1–4	154
91.4–10	159
91.5–6	158n60
91.9–10	159

On Weather Signs

59	141n9, 145n22

On Odours

64	141n9
64.9–11	145n25

Thuc.	Thucydides, *History of the Peloponnesian War*
2.35–46	44
5.84–5	43
8.65.2	48n4

Index Locorum

Us.	H. Usener, *Epicurea* (Leipzig, 1887)	*Mem.*	*Memorabilia*
		1.1	91n29
67	209, 218	1.1.2	66n21
68	202	1.1.4	66n21
69	218	1.11	91n29
70	218	1.2	261
		1.16	91n29
Xenocrates		3.11	65n20
fr. 82 Isnardi Parente 269		4.4.1–4	41n2
		4.4.6	70
Xen.	Xenophon	4.6.15	51
Apol.	*Apology*	4.8.5	66n21
4	66n21		
13	66n21	*Symp.*	*Symposium*
		4.56	51
Hellenika	*History of Greece*	5	71n33
1.7.34	48n4	8.5	66n21

GENERAL INDEX

Academic philosophy
  attitude towards *auctoritas*, 2–3, 10,
    17–18, 263–77, 278–95
Academy
  disagreements over interpretation of
    Plato's dialogues, 13, 81–82, 88,
    93–97
  division of *presbyteroi* and
    neaniskoi, 80–81
  founding, 79
  purpose, 79–81
Aeschines, 42, 65, 66n21, 88n24
Aeschylus, 99
Aëtius, 34, 235
Alcinous, 187, 198, 276n54
Alexander Polyhistor, 164
Alexandria, 297, 298, 298n4, 299
Ammonius, 4n7, 200
Anaxagoras, 8, 67, 68n26, 99, 105, 108
Andronicus of Rhodes, 169, 175, 180,
    273n40
Antigonus of Carystus, 248, 251, 259n35
Antiochus, 18, 185n3, 186, 246, 263–64,
    266–75, 275n49, 276, 277, 280
Antisthenes, 65, 65n19, 88n24, 195, 253
Apollonius of Tyre, 248–49, 250, 251,
    252–53, 257, 259, 262
Apuleius, 199
Arcesilaus, 245–46, 247, 248, 255n30,
    264, 271
Archytas of Tarentum, 162, 163, 164n7,
    165, 166, 179, 183
Aristarchus, 213
Aristippus, 65, 88n24, 195, 316, 326
Aristo of Ceos, 290
Aristo of Chios, 243, 245, 247, 253, 254,
    324n27
Aristophanes, 92
Aristotle
  authority in the Peripatos, 100–01

influenced by Plato, 84–101,
    114–19, 120–38
  on Plato's dialogues, 98
  Platonic source, 83–96
Aristoxenus, 97, 164n6, 165
Arius Didymus, 271, 272, 275n47, 277n55
Asclepius of Tralles, 200
ataraxia, 216, 217
Athenodorus, 170
Atticus, 192, 197n14, 276
auctor, 2, 266n13, 269
auctoritas, 2, 2n2, 3, 6, 10, 17–18, 183,
    211n17, 263–77, 278–95, 318,
    325n31
  contrasted with *ratio*, 17, 18, 266,
    278–95
Augustine, 245
Aulus Gellius, 204, 210

bibliography
  of Aristotle, 85
  of Cleanthes, 247
  of Zeno, 243
biography
  of Aristotle, 102, 106
  of Lucretius, 222–23
  of Plato, 78–79
  of Proclus, 200
  of Pythagoras, 163
  of Socrates, 59
  of Zeno, 17, 242–62
Boethius, 199
Boethus, 170–71, 174, 182, 277n56

Caelius Aurelianus, 35
Cai Yong, 306
Carneades, 290
Cassius Dio, 318
Celsus, 207
Chaldean Oracles, 200

367

General Index

Charondas of Catane, 162
Cicero, 2–3, 4, 17–18, 164, 222, 230,
 231, 232n36, 234n46, 235, 236, 239,
 240n68, 244–45, 246, 247, 252, 254,
 257, 259, 263–66, 267, 268, 269n25,
 270n27, 276, 278–95, 325
 Academic scepticism, 3, 17, 245, 265,
 278, 280–82, 285, 288, 292, 325
Chrysippus, 180, 243, 247, 250n24, 251,
 252, 303n13
Cleanthes, 243, 247, 251, 252
Clement of Alexandria, 208–09, 215
Cleomedes, 205–07, 210, 215
Confucius, 300–01, 307, 309
Cornutus, 170, 172n33
correctio, 245, 271
Crantor, 3n3, 266
Critolaus, 271–72
Cynicism
 influence on Zeno, 250, 252–62

Demetrius of Laconia, 16, 206, 210,
 211–21
Demetrius of Magnesia, 251, 258, 260
Democritus, 8, 140, 149, 152, 233n42,
 315
Descartes, 319
dialectic, 12, 21, 41–57, 59, 67, 69, 71,
 73, 86, 95, 108, 189, 196, 246, 251,
 257, 266, 267, 269, 274n45, 316,
 327, 327n35, 327n36, 329n41,
 329n42
Diodorus Cronus, 246, 256n32, 257,
 262, 318
Diogenes Laertius, 17, 85, 164, 209,
 242–62, 270, 270n29, 303n13, 318,
 324n27
Dionysius the Stoic, 243, 247n16,
 303n13, 324n27
Dionysius the Younger, 83
doxography, 242–44, 263n2, 269, 272,
 277n55

Empedocles, 110, 153, 158
Epicrates, 86, 97
Epictetus, 242, 259
Epicureans,
 authority of Epicurus, 184, 185, 195,
 242, 243, 244

Garden, 185, 209
 hedonism, 202–21
Epicurus, 249, 262
 authority in the *De Rerum Natura*,
 8–17, 198, 224–41
 theology, 17, 226–41
Eratosthenes, 246
Euclides, 65, 88n24
Eudorus, 167n18, 170, 173, 175, 177,
 178, 182, 183, 185n3, 186
Eudoxus, 13, 80, 83, 109–13
Euripides, 99, 211
Eusebius, 222

gods
 in Numenius, 189–98
 location in Epicureanism, 226–30
Gongsun Long, 304
Gorgias, 43, 44, 99

Han Wu Di, 301, 309, 310n17
Hanfeizi, 309
Hecataeus, 314
Hecato, 251, 257, 259
Heraclides of Lembos, 247
Heraclides of Pontus, 80, 97, 289
Heraclitus, 8–17, 29n32, 99, 314, 315
Herillus, 243, 303n13, 324n27
Hermodorus of Syracuse, 133, 134
Hesiod, 33, 297
Hestiaios, 97
Hieronymus of Tyre, 271
Hippocratic Corpus, 298
Homer, 43, 51, 99, 115, 118, 211,
 262, 297
Hui Shi, 304, 309
Hume, 319, 323

Iamblichus, 164n6, 170n27, 175, 178
Isocrates, 79, 81n8, 85, 309

Jerome, 222, 223
Jia Kui, 306

Laozi, 301, 302
Leucippus, 8
Li Chunfeng, 307
Li Si, 298n6, 305
Liu An, 304

368

General Index

Liu Hui, 307
Liu Xiang, 298, 299, 300
Liu Xin, 298
Lucretius,
  biography, 222–23
  devotion to Epicurus, 222–41
  theology, 226–241
Lucius, 178
Lucullus, 223n5, 267
Lü Buwei, 304

Melissus, 8
Mencius, 307, 308, 309
Metrodorus, 207, 208, 209–10,
  219, 221
Mo Di, 303, 304
Mozi, 309

Neoplatonists, 3, 84n16, 163, 326n32
New Academy, 186, 264, 265, 266
Nicomachus of Gerasa, 199–200
Nicostratus, 178
Nigidius Figulus, 164
Numenius, 15–16, 184–201, 245
  criticisms of Academy, 195
  interest in Plato's style, 196

Occelus of Lucania, 165
Old Academy, 246, 264, 266, 268,
  268n19, 269, 270n27, 271
Olympiodorus, 83, 119n21
Origen, 207, 209n11, 210, 215
Ovid, 164

Panaetius, 252, 290
Parmenides, 8, 11, 20–40, 92, 99,
  314–15
Peripatetics, 2, 5, 140, 141, 143n15,
  145n25, 147, 150, 158, 166, 167–68,
  170, 266, 268, 269, 270, 271, 272,
  276, 277, 290
Peripatos, 3, 14, 93, 100, 139, 268, 270,
  272
Persaeus, 247, 248, 249, 251
Phaedo, 65, 88n24
Philo of Larissa, 186, 245
Philo of Megara, 246
Philodemus, 219, 229
Philolaus, 64, 163, 164n7

Philoponus, 84n17, 200
philosophia, 296, 312
Plato
  authority for Platonists, 15–16,
    184–201, 276
  authority in the Academy, 3, 12–13,
    78–101
  biography, 78–79
  Forms, 64–65, 69–73, 75, 84n15, 85,
    91, 91n28, 92, 95–96, 99, 114, 118,
    121, 129, 130–31, 188–91, 192–95,
    198, 274–75, 276
  influence on Aristotle, 78–101, 114–
    19, 120–38
  lecture *On the Good*, 97
  purpose of dialogues, 10, 78,
    81–82, 93–98
  Socratic author, 12, 42, 58–77, 79n2,
    86–93
  unwritten doctrine, 81n7, 84,
    91n28, 94
Platonic *dubia* and *spuria*, 88
Platonists, 13, 92, 114–15, 116–19, 167,
  170, 173n37, 176, 177–78, 183, 207,
  245, 269, 275–77, 326
  authority of Plato, 15–16, 184–201, 276
  detachment from the Academy, 16,
    185–87, 201
Platonist commentaries, 185, 199
pleasure, 85, 87, 109–11, 112–13, 147,
  156, 158, 202–21, 255
Plotinus, 178, 186–91, 276n52
Plutarch, 22, 23, 186–92, 202n1, 215,
  267n15, 277
  criticism of Epicureans, 203–4, 208,
    210
Polemo, 3n3, 245, 246–47, 251, 256, 257,
  260, 262, 269
Porphyry, 164, 170n27, 178, 179
Proclus, 200, 326n32
Prodicus, 99
Protagoras, 99
pseudepigrapha, 88n25, 164n10, 168
Pyrrho, 9–10, 262
Pyrrhonism, 200
Pythagoras, 83, 100, 162–83, 164n10,
  195–96, 197, 198, 199, 200, 265,
  314, 324
  writings of, 11, 165

369

General Index

Pythagoreans, 83, 207, 324
  division of *mathematici* and
    acousmati, 164
  writings of, 162–83

Qi Bo, 310
Qin Shi Huang Di, 298, 305
Quinton, Anthony, 319

rhetoric, 11–12, 41–57, 70, 80n4,
    85–86, 91n29, 167n17, 253, 271n30,
    283

Sedley, David, 19, 41n*, 58n*, 64,
    78n*, 102n*, 130n22, 139n*, 156,
    162n1, 184–87, 198, 199, 200–01,
    202n*, 222n*, 226, 239, 240, 242,
    244, 245, 247, 263, 271n30, 281n2,
    329n42
Seneca, 201, 259, 316n7, 318
Sextus Empiricus, 269, 270
Sima Qian, 298, 305n15, 309n17
Sima Tan, 298, 303, 304, 305n15
Simmias, 64
Simplicius, 3, 4–6, 97, 133–34, 168, 170–71,
    175–76, 178–80, 181, 182–83, 276n52,
    326n32
Socrates, 8, 10, 11, 13, 41–57, 79, 87,
    88n24, 89, 90–93, 99–100, 195–96,
    197, 198, 199, 251, 258–62, 302n12,
    303, 315, 326
  as orator, 42–48
  biography, 59
  writings of, 9, 11, 41, 58, 302n12
Socratics, 11, 58–77, 88n24, 91, 197, 253,
    302n12, 316
Sophocles, 99
Speusippus, 3n3, 80, 83, 85, 94, 98
Sthenidas of Locri, 162
Stilpo, 246, 247, 251, 253, 256, 257,
    260, 262
Stobaeus, 165, 275n47

Stoics
  commitment to doctrine, 184, 242,
    243, 303n13, 325
  origins of school, 242–62
Strabo, 247, 248, 267n15

telos, 16, 202–21, 271–72, 276
Theaetetus, 80
Themistius, 167, 181
Theodoret, 243, 247
Theophrastus, 5, 14, 100, 101, 139–61,
    266, 267n15, 268, 271, 272, 277
Thersites, 206
Third Man Argument, 95
Timaeus of Locri, 165
Timocrates of Lampsacus, 209–10
Timon's *Silloi*, 248

Wang Chong, 309
Whitehead, Alfred North, 317, 318

Xenocrates, 85, 94, 133–34, 175, 246,
    251, 256, 257, 260, 269, 270
Xenophanes, 269, 314
Xenophon, 51–52, 65n20, 66n21, 70, 91,
    91n29, 258, 261
Xunzi, 298n6, 307–08, 309

Yang Xiong, 298, 300n8
Yellow Emperor, 301, 310

Zeno of Elea, 8
Zeno of Citium, 180, 185, 197, 267, 269,
    270n27, 270n29, 271n31, 273n39,
    303, 303n13, 318n13, 324n27
  biography, 17, 242–262
  conversion to philosophy, 251, 252, 258
  founder of Stoicism 162, 242, 243, 244
  influence from Cynicism, 250, 252–62
  interest in Socrates, 251, 257–62
  writings, 243, 244, 251, 259n33, 262
Zhuang Zhou, 305n14, 309

370